THE MAGIC OF GOLD

JENIFER MARX

The Magic of Gold

1978

Doubleday & Company, Inc., Garden City, New York

Library of Congress Cataloging in Publication Data

Marx, Jenifer.
  The magic of gold.

  Bibliography: p. 454
  Includes index.
  1. Gold—History.   I. Title.
HG289.M355   332.4′222′09
ISBN: 0-385-11099-5
Library of Congress Catalog Card Number 76–53413

To Marjorie Scribner, my mother

To Marjorie Scribner, my mother

CONTENTS

THE MAGIC OF GOLD

Gold is tried with a touchstone,
Men by gold.

Chilon (*ca.* 560 B.C.)

CHAPTER ONE *The Enchantment of Gold*

Hurtling through the vast silence of interstellar space, attached
to a derelict spacecraft, is a small golden plaque bearing mankind's first message to worlds beyond the solar system. Etched on
the gold surface are the naked figures of a man and a woman
with their return address engraved in scientific symbols, conceiv-
ably understandable to extraterrestrial civilizations.

The plaque was affixed to the antenna support struts of *Pioneer 10* when it was launched in 1972 from Cape Canaveral on a
voyage that has taken it past the planet Jupiter toward a point
on the celestial sphere near the boundary of the constellations
Taurus and Orion.

Oceanic space is vast and empty. It will take 80,000 years for
the golden greeting to travel to the nearest star and more than 10
billion years to enter the closest star planetary system. But because its surface is gold the six-by-nine-inch plaque can be expected to remain eternally shining and smooth, free of tarnish,
scale, or corrosion.

Gold, the most precious of metals, regarded by the ancients as
a divine substance coming from the sun, was a fitting choice of
materials for the space age message. Scientists made the first
human artifact to leave the solar system of gold, not because of
its beauty or mystical associations, but because of the remarkable chemical and physical characteristics which have given it
myriad new applications in twentieth-century industry and technology.

But the very qualities which accounted for gold's magic and

religious connotations are among those which make it useful to the space age. No other metal has played such a consistent and dramatic part in the relatively short history of the frail creatures figured on the *Pioneer 10* plaque. Gold, a light that never dims, has held men in its thrall for thousands of years. No single property predominates in its appeal. The allure is a combination of many factors, each of which may have varying importance for an individual or a society.

Gold is not essential for survival, yet from the dawn of history men have yearned for it, subjugating whole nations, killing entire populations, and expunging civilizations and religions to get the yellow metal. No other substance has aroused such emotions or been invested with such power.

In itself gold is simply a chemical element—a deep yellow, soft, dense element which is classified as a noble and heavy metal. The symbol for gold, Au, is derived from the Latin word for "shining dawn." This symbol was introduced in the eighteenth century replacing the prehistoric symbol which was representative of the sun.

Gold is too soft, heavy, and pliable to be used in tools and weapons. The ancients learned quickly that gold knives take no edge and gold plows make no furrows. Yet priest, ruler, artisan, merchant, adventurer, and citizen have long coveted, sought, and suffered for gold. Men have yet to find a universally acceptable substitute for gold as a store of value. Even in our uncertain times the durability of gold represents a constant, defying both inflation and depression.

The highest attainments of craftsmanship have traditionally been in gold. Despite the ease with which the metal can be worked, it is not responsive to the indifferent artisan. But in the hands of skilled men working down the ages, the precious metal has been transformed into superb objects which mirror the extremes and diversities of history.

"Gold is a child of Zeus," wrote Pindar in the fifth century B.C., "neither moth nor rust devoureth it; but the mind of man is devoured by this supreme possession." Gold is a magic word which conjures a kaleidoscope of images from the myths and legends of every age and culture. More than any other substance, gold, which has been imbued with an inherent duality by man, has the power to inspire and to corrupt both savage and sophisticate.

The dichotomy of behavior gold has provoked is clearly seen by tracing the glittering gold thread through the annals of history and world literature—source of joy and woe from the Golden Apples of the Hesperides to the Klondike poems of Robert Service. The lust for gold which brought men and nations to ruin also spurred exploration, furthered cultural exchange, developed international trade routes, and hastened the development of technology. W. J. Perry, the English historian, wrote that the growth of civilization followed the lines of distribution of the gold fields.

Some of men's most noble and lasting achievements have been fueled by the precious metal or wrought from it. In the first century B.C., Diodorus Siculus made a statement about gold which still holds true. "Nature herself," he wrote, "makes it clear that the production of gold is laborious, the guarding of it difficult, the zest for it very great, and its use balanced between pleasure and pain." Gold has been indispensable as simile and metaphor to writers of all ages. Gold is the image of solar light, symbol of the life-giving principle. In Hindu doctrine it is "the mineral light," representative of the divine intelligence. Goodness, natural loveliness, inner worth, perfection, idealism, and radiant beauty—gold is the material reflection of spiritual quality. Greek writers made such trite and prolific use of the golden adjective that contemporary critics lamented its debasement.

Shakespeare, Milton, Spenser, and Keats employed gold as a favorite simile for things fair and true but also identified gold as the seed of corruption. In much of literature it stands for mammon, greed, lust, and the erosion of humanity and principle.

"How quickly nature falls into revolt / When gold becomes her object," wrote Shakespeare in *Henry IV*, and in *Romeo and Juliet*, "There is thy gold, worse poison to men's souls / Doing more murder in this loathsome world, / Than these poor compounds that thou mayst not sell."

In ancient Greece Anacreon lamented, "In consequence of gold there are no brothers, no parents; but wars and murders arise from it. And what is worse, for it we lovers are bought and sold."

Wisdom and goodness, folly and corruption—opposite sides of the golden coin. The malevolent powers ascribed to gold are patently imaginary but for millennia gold has had an aura of magic which defies the rational. Rich in psychological overtones gold has been identified with the splendors and tribulations of human existence and so we have had ad nauseam golden ages, golden boughs, golden apples, and golden dawns in poems, proverbs, and romances as well as the golden rule, the golden mean, and the golden number.

The lustrous metal, which is itself immune to foulness, has provoked wars, feuds, vendettas, false love, and "dear divorce twixt natural son and sire." "What dost thou not compel the human heart to do, accursed greed for gold," wrote Virgil at a time when already many thousands of slaves had died for it—men, women, children chained together and hacking, sifting, washing gold for Egypt's pharaohs since the fourth millennium.

Throughout the stages of social evolution humans have always loved the gleam of gold. World-wide, religions have employed golden accessories to indicate the sanctity and worthiness of the spiritual ideal and encouraged golden offerings as evidence of people's devotion to it. Divine and secular authority have been bolstered by sumptuous displays of gold embellishing every conceivable surface including ornaments, garments, fabrics, embroideries, cosmetics; façades, walls, floors, ceilings, and other architectural elements; furniture, wood and metal work appointments; ceramics, glass, leather, stone, paper, and shell.

Seldom has the thirst for gold been slaked. With a literal and horrible justice, the King of gold-rich Parthia had molten gold poured down the throat of the defeated Roman general, Marcus Crassus, who had invaded Parthia for its gold in the first century B.C. In medieval Russia counterfeiters were similarly punished with molten gold funneled down their gullets.

Gold is the first element and metal mentioned in the Bible, where it appears in more than four hundred references. "A river flowed out of Eden," says Genesis, "to water the garden and there it divided and became four rivers. The name of the first is Pishon; it is the one which flows around the whole land of Hav-i-lah, where there is gold; and the gold of that land is good."

Throughout history the metal that brought suffering to those who mined or washed it and power and authority to those who held it probably brought the most pleasure to the goldsmiths who lavished their craftsmanship on it. The toolmakers who evolved into the first specialized metalsmiths were regarded with awe. They practiced an art surrounded with an air of mystery and secrecy and could perform feats which amazed their primitive fellows.

The history of gold begins in remote antiquity. But without hard archaeological evidence to pinpoint the time and place of man's first felicitous encounter with the yellow metal we can only conjecture about those men who at various places and various times first came upon native gold. Bits of natural gold were found in Spanish caves used by Paleolithic man about 40,000 B.C.

In a world before memory when Stone Age men wandered in search of roots, berries, and shellfish, gold lay exposed in rain-swollen streams or on ground laid bare by the elements. A man following a watercourse in search of food would have been struck by the gleam of a small tumbled nugget deposited by gravity in the shallows. Picking it up, he would marvel at its glow, the smooth warm feel of it in his palm, and its extraordinary heaviness. He took it home to his shelter. The others in his small group admired it. Perhaps he was content to keep the dazzling stone as it was. But he may have seen the buttery mark it left when rubbed across a rough surface or noted how easily a piece of bone or even his fingernail could score it.

At some point he began to regard it as a kind of talisman, unaware as yet how easily it could be shaped by blows from his stone hammer. Eventually he learned to cold-hammer native nuggets into simple flattened roundels. By that time he may have made an inarticulate association between the sun and the bright lump of stuff that warmed in his hand.

Experts are divided. Was gold the first metal man worked, or was it copper? Gold, copper, and meteoric iron (the only iron known to the ancients) are the only metals found in relatively pure form in the native state and the only metals with significant color in their free state.

Copper, thousands of years before it became the first metal to be smelted from its ore (about 4300 B.C. in western Asia and about 3800 B.C. in Egypt, Mesopotamia, Syria, Persia, and

India), was found as varicolored chunks, thin laminate sheets, and branchlike pieces of pure metal. These broke off from pure copper veins which ran through a matrix of basic stone and copper-bearing ores in much of the Near East.

The oldest metal artifact yet found is a copper pendant made in Iraq some 9,500 years ago. Copper is soft enough to shape by cold hammering yet hard enough to take a fair cutting edge.

Iron, next to aluminum, is earth's most ample metal, but it cannot be worked without extraction from its ore. This did not happen until thousands of years after men had learned, by trial and error, to smelt copper, which melts at a much lower temperature than the 3,650° Fahrenheit needed to smelt iron. Once man accumulated the relatively sophisticated technology to smelt iron it gradually replaced copper and bronze as the basic metal for implements and weapons.

But primitive man knew and cherished nearly pure iron found on the earth's surface in the forms of siderites, metallic meteorites, which ranged in size from pebbles to gigantic masses of several tons. Long before the Sumerians dubbed it "heaven's metal," primitive man recognized its celestial origin. Early smiths managed to chip bits from larger pieces and work them into amulets and ceremonial objects using stone tools.

By 1200 B.C. iron was available to the farmer and soldier in the West, but no one can explain how smiths made the few iron artifacts found at the Royal Cemetery at Ur dating from prior to 2500 B.C. or at the Alaca Huyuk site in Anatolia where archaeologists unearthed a third millennium B.C. iron pin with a gold head and a bit of crescent-shaped plaque. Two six-thousand-year-old sites in Egypt yielded iron beads, an iron knife, and an amulet of silver and meteoric iron.

Gold has never been a utilitarian metal, although ancient and primitive men have made it into bowls, knives, fishhooks, and scrapers. Some archaeologists who contend that copper was worked before gold say that gold was not at all valued by prehistoric man. This seems unlikely. Neither copper nor meteoric iron have a hue or sheen like that of gold nor are they as malleable. Probably where all three metals were found, gold by virtue of its luster was noticed and worked first. The first people who used gold were dust long before the advent of written or oral history, but because gold is imperishable, archaeologists may someday find and date gold artifacts that predate the oldest copper objects. Meanwhile the view prevails that it was only when nomadic hunter-gatherers began the transition to agriculture which required a settled pattern of existence that gold came to be valued.

The Neolithic age was characterized by protofarmers of northern Iraq and Persia, who were leading a farming and stock-raising existence by about 6000 B.C. Over the next thousand years protofarming spread to the Nile Valley, the coastal areas of Palestine, the upper basin of the Euphrates, northern Syria, and central Persia.

People lived in small permanent settlements, made pottery, wove cloth, reared flocks, and cultivated grains such as barley and wheat. Those first farmers became aware of the crucial role the sun played in ripening the grain. They worshiped the sun because it was the source of life-giving light. What could be a more appropriate offering to the sun than gleaming "sun stuff"—gold.

With a settled pattern of existence came specialization. The descendants of the men who had been most skillful at making flint and stone choppers and scrapers became the first metalsmiths. They practiced a craft which required that they devote full time to it. They were unusual men who experimented and tested. Little by little they puzzled out the techniques that yielded the first gold and copper artifacts.

They made tools, weapons, and religious pieces. The metallurgical historian Cyril Stanley Smith writes, "Nearly all the industrially useful properties of matter, and ways of shaping material, had their origins in the decorative arts . . . the first suggestion of anything new seems to be an aesthetic experience."

It was fortunate for the earliest smiths that they had such a superb medium to work in, a metal of such wonderful color and soft rich texture that men through the ages have fashioned their greatest artistic offerings in it, a metal which lends itself to shaping and surface decoration and then remains forever whole and beautiful.

The most obvious appeal of gold is its loveliness; the most significant is what alchemists in the Middle Ages termed its nobility. It is a chemically inert element, and neither air, moisture, nor common acids or alkalis can mar its beauty, which is why gold ornaments fashioned six thousand years ago are as lovely today as when they were made, long after other artifacts have turned to dust. Gold's link with eternity and its perpetual yellow luster led the ancients to think of it literally as sun stuff, and imbue it with an aura of sanctity and magic. Not only Neolithic man but Sumerians, Egyptians, and New World peoples like the Incas and even contemporary primitive groups have regarded gold as the fruit, seed, sweat, tears, or excrement of the sun. Traders took advantage of this hallowed regard for gold to establish an economic role for the metal.

The hoary phrase "withstanding the acid test" referred to gold's stability in most acids and originated before it was widely known that gold, despite its chemical snobbishness, does react with chlorine and other halogens and can be dissolved in a heated mixture of nitric and hydrochloric acid. This mixture was called aqua regia, royal water, by the alchemists because it attacked the royal metal as scale, rust, and time could not.

The primitive metalsmith was delighted by golden lumps which could be hammered without breaking and easily shaped without heating. In relatively pure form gold has unrivaled qualities of malleability and ductility. One troy ounce of gold, for instance, can be drawn into a hairlike thread fifty miles long. The same amount of gold, no larger than a sugar lump, coats more than a thousand miles of silver or copper wire. Before the second millennium B.C. wire was made by rolling out short lengths of gold welded together. In Egypt in the second millennium gold, copper, and bronze wire were drawn through a perforated stone.

Gold can be beaten or rolled into translucent sheets so thin they transmit a greenish light and so delicate they can be moved and straightened with a light breath. One troy ounce can be beaten to a golden film covering 108 square feet. It would be so thin that one thousand sheets would be needed to make up the thickness of this page. A three-inch cube can be made into a sheet covering an acre.

Goldbeating, or the making of gold leaf, was well known in the prebiblical world. It is one of the very earliest of crafts and one of the very few to have resisted mechanization. Early goldbeaters prepared gold leaf in much the same way it is made today, hammering a small amount of gold between sheets of parchment or specially prepared animal membrane and burnishing the gold with gems, semiprecious stones, boar's or dog's teeth. From remote times gold foil was used in Asia and the West to ornament wood, pottery, and textiles.

The Roman historian Pliny wrote that a small quantity of gold could be reduced to 750 leaves each four digits square. Ancient Rome glittered with gold which was applied to the façades and interiors of palaces, temples, and public buildings. The Egyptians made the most spectacular use of it in the overlays of gold leaf on furniture and royal mummy cases.

Five thousand years ago the obelisks raised by sun worshipers as "conductors" to transmit the life-giving, harvest-ripening rays of the divine fire into the earth and fructify it were often sheathed in gold. The Egyptian goldsmiths were not above practicing golden deception. They were the first to coat objects of inferior metal with gold leaf and pass them off as the real thing, a practice which continues even today.

The Greeks, who taught the art of gold leaf to the Romans, not only gilded masonry, sculpture, and wood but also fire-gilded metal by applying gold amalgam to it and then driving off the mercury with heat.

Today gold leaf offered by the devout gleams from thousands of Asian temples such as Rangoon's Shwe Dagon. In the West the dim interiors of countless churches are illuminated by the glow of gold from altars, architecture, and vestments. The gold that shone from Mesopotamian ziggurats now shimmers from gold-plated roofs, the windows and exterior walls of fast-food shops and office buildings.

Gold is an ideal coating material which can be manufactured at relatively low cost to protect against the ravages of weather and time. Gold shines from the spires and domes of public buildings proclaiming their importance. Soluble in oil, gold is used as a film as thin as 5 millionths of an inch on glassware, ceramics, paper, and plastics. It beckons the consumer from decorations on whiskey bottles and shaving-lotion containers. Gold ceramic tiles reflect sunlight on the roofs of motels and restaurants. A sandwich of laminated glass containing a film of gold less than 2 millionths of an inch thick is used for the windows of modern aircraft. The gold prevents icing or misting, reflects glare, and guards against harmful rays of the sun.

Powdered gold in a ground of chalk, marble dust, and an animal glue or size has been used for millennia to gild large and small surfaces, to embellish leather, manuscripts, and miniatures, and for medicinal and cosmetic purposes.

At first gold was worked as it was found. Much later men learned to combine it with other metals to form alloys which increased the element's strength and changed its hue. Gold can be combined with varying amounts of silver, copper, nickel, zinc, palladium, platinum, and iron to produce a wide range of colors including yellow, red, orange, green, blue, white, and purple. In T'ang China an alloy was made with minute traces of iron which turned the gold violet when heated. A rare form of gold appears black because of the addition of bismuth. In nature gold is often alloyed with silver. This natural alloy, called electrum, was used by the tyrant Gyges of Lydia in Asia Minor in the seventh century B.C. to make the world's first coins.

Gold is extremely heavy: one and a half times as heavy as lead and twice as heavy as silver. The lovely sheen and rich texture of a small gold ingot belie its density and weight. The metal is so compact that a cubic foot of gold weighs about half a ton. The heaviness of a gold coin or ornament heightens its sense of value.

Gold melts easily, at 1,063° centigrade, which is well within the range of temperature of ancient cooking fires. When it boils, the metal remains yellow but gives off an unusual purple vapor, which must have added to the goldsmith's reputation as miracle worker.

No one is sure how long before 2500 B.C. gold was worked. What is clear is that by the time the Royal Cemetery at Ur was created, Sumerian goldsmiths had already mastered most technical processes used in goldworking including casting in open molds and lost-wax casting. They had long since discovered how to anneal gold by heating, quenching, and beating over and over.

The first appeal of gold was aesthetic and its first applications were of a magical nature. However, human vanity being what it is, men soon desired gold ornaments for themselves, and goldsmiths fashioned ornaments which attested to the rank of the wearer in life and in death. Much of what we know of preliterate life comes from the way of death. Men and women were buried with comforting gold ornaments and artifacts to smooth the way into the nether world. Many thousands of years later these artifacts are unearthed, casting new light on the past.

In the evolution of barter economy into more sophisticated economic systems gold proved to be the one substance which was universally accepted as payment for goods and services. It could be divided without damage, stored without deterioration, conveniently transported in small amounts which concentrated a great deal of value. It could be easily concealed or ostentatiously displayed as status-enhancing jewelry.

Thus from earliest times gold has moved through history in many guises providing a magnificent medium for the artisan and jeweler; a fitting offering to gods, rulers, and lovely women; a universally prized store of wealth and motive for both heroic and base deeds.

But it is not gold's beauty, mystery, or rarity which recommends it to modern technology. Gold is valued in industry, space, and defense programs because of its resistance to corrosion and change, its high conductivity of electricity, and its superior reflective qualities.

Gold conducts electricity better than any metal save silver and copper. A minuscule amount of liquid gold on a printed circuit can replace miles of wiring in computers. It is found in the minute circuitry of transistors, undersea cables, telephone equipment, radar, televisions, and calculators. A plating as thin as 3 or 4 millionths of an inch is enough to protect a component from deterioration.

Space age applications are not limited to lovely message plaques which may or may not be deciphered in the distant future. Space apparatus and instrumentation have requirements which are met by gold's nobility and capacity to reflect up to 98 per cent of incident infrared radiation. It is such a fine reflector of heat and light that an almost nonexistent film on the heat shield of a rocket engine can protect the fragile instruments within from the searing heat generated by the lift-off thrust and the re-entry into earth's atmosphere.

Edward White, the first American to walk in space, had a gold coating on the umbilical cord which connected him to the

Gemini spacecraft. The visors on astronauts' helmets are gold-coated to filter out both infrared and ultraviolet radiation. The effect of the sun's noxious rays was tempered by gold sheathing on the tiny television camera and other instruments on the moon buggies. Gold-coated nylon was used as a protective shroud for the radio, propulsion, and guidance systems of the *Gemini* craft.

Gold has found widespread application in dentistry and medicine. Because it is malleable, acid-resistant, nonpoisonous, and chemically tasteless, dentists find it ideal for fillings, inlays, and caps. Forty-five hundred years ago an Egyptian had a gold bridge put in his mouth. It was recently found in a tomb near El-Quatta and is the world's oldest known evidence of dentistry. In some areas, like the southern Philippines where a flashy display of gold is considered in good taste, it is not unusual to have all of one's teeth sheathed in gold, or as many as one can afford. The smile of a winsome lass may reveal a small golden heart, flower, or bird inset in the lateral surface of a front tooth.

The medical uses of gold are an ancient heritage. Gold was considered a potent curative force in early medicine. In China gold leaf was considered the most perfect form of matter, and an unguent of gold was the most powerful of Chinese pharmaceuticals. The unalterability of gold linked it with eternity and gave rise to the belief, incorporated in alchemical practice, that gold could give renewed or prolonged life to the body.

In the West *aurum potabile,* elixir of gold, was widely prescribed for a multitude of ills. Ointments, gold salts, and gold pills have been taken through the ages for the treatment of many disorders including tuberculosis and syphilis. Pliny the Elder mentions salves of gold prescribed for ulcers, fistulas, and hemorrhoids. Gold tablets have been touted for their energizing powers even today, and a belief persists among some rural Americans that a sty will disappear if it is rubbed nine times with a wedding band.

Astrological healers claimed that gold medicines ingested under certain signs of the zodiac would cure appendicitis. Several decades ago millions of gullible alcoholics submitted to the costly and painful Keeley cure. The nonsensical treatment involved the injection of gold chloride as a first step.

In recent years injections of radioactive colloidal gold have been used to alleviate the pain of arthritis. Radioactive isotopes of gold have been used to irradiate cancerous tumors. Gold-silver alloy plates have been used in the repair of skull injuries, and gold has been employed in the treatment of certain kinds of ulcers, burns, and some nerve-end operations.

Tongue in cheek, the Italian Vannoccio Biringuccio attested to the therapeutic effects of gold in his sixteenth-century treatise on metallurgy. "Indeed as a medicine it is beneficial to certain illnesses. Nature with her own virtue has endowed gold, as a singular privilege, with power to comfort weakness of the heart and to introduce there joy and happiness, disposing the heart to magnanimity and generosity of works. Many learned men say that this power has been conceded to it by the benign influence of the sun and that for this reason it gives so much pleasure and benefit with its great powers—especially to those who have great sacks and chests full of it."

Indeed, gold has never failed to gladden hearts and fire the imagination. Those who have not had sacks of it have aspired to, and those who have had chests of it have yearned for still more. There has never been enough gold to satisfy the appetite which seems to grow with feeding.

More than 150 substances, animal, vegetable, and mineral, have served as a measure of wealth at various times and in various places. There are cultures where boar tusks or whale baleen purchase a bride that gold could not. But gold has a range of appeal and a host of associations that shells and teeth cannot match.

As a symbol of power both divine and secular and as a measure of value, gold has played a leading role in shaping the human experience. The soft yellow metal has been a catalyst in the ebb and flow of civilizations. Provoking the rise and fall of empires, states, and individual men and women, deathless gold has emerged from the dramas it precipitated unchanged and undiminished.

Because gold endures, it accumulates. A large part of the gold that passed through the hands of the Mesopotamians, Egyptians, Persians, Greeks, Scythians, and Incas, to name but a few of the peoples who had an intimate relationship with the precious metal, is still around. Some estimates run as high as 80 per cent.

The total production of gold throughout history can only be

estimated. Various figures put it at from 80,000 to 110,000 metric tons. Some researchers think these figures too low, particularly in light of new information on gold use prior to the seventeenth century. The South African Government says the production of the last five hundred years, during which the great bulk of gold extraction has occurred, if melted down would form a cube about fifty-one feet square. It seems a small amount in the face of all the human suffering that it stimulated. It is ironic that precious gold, symbol of the pure and good, should almost always have been the fruit of the cheapest human labor and vilest oppression.

Gold, the indestructible, has an Achilles' heel. It is very easily melted. During periods of turmoil, to cover theft, or simply to keep up with the vagaries of fashion gold jewelry, vessels, coins, ingots, and idols were all tossed into the melting pot and emerged in new guise.

Not even royal crowns escaped. In fact, monarchs often had a hard time keeping their regalia out of the pot and out of hock. In England magnificent gold objects that had survived Henry VIII's seizure of ecclesiastical treasure were wantonly melted by Cromwell. In India today women frequently take their gold bangles and rings to the smith to have them brought into line with current fashion.

Gold grave goods, buried with the wealthy, were made to placate the powerful gods and comfort the deceased on his journey into the infinite. But even in ancient Egypt gold consigned to the tomb was often dug up almost immediately by organized teams of robbers. Gold offerings and idols were looted from sanctuaries or seized as war booty. Melted and recast in the taste and temper of the times, gold infinitely beautiful passes through successive ages in a multitude of forms. Gold that bedecked a Mesopotamian princess or graced an Inca palace may now be part of the *Pioneer* plaque soaring far out into the universe where it originated aeons ago when the earth was formed.

The allure of gold has something of the mystical about it; the links with economics and political power were forged long after it achieved pre-eminence as a divine metal. The religious association between the sun and gold contributed to the acceptance of gold as the royal metal and an incorruptible medium of exchange.

Possession of gold enhanced authority, and in the days when rulers were considered actual descendants of the deities or later when they ruled by divine right but were recognized as fully human, gold reinforced a ruler's aura of authority and sanctity. Through the ages temporal rulers have frequently gained power through *sanctissima divitiarum majestas*, the most sacred majesty of wealth.

Many cultures have regarded gold as a mystical element of celestial origin. The Scythians in the seventh century B.C. had a saga of the sacred gold which fell from heaven. A great solar myth underlies virtually all ancient mythologies. Gold, the "seed of heaven," the "excrement of the gods," the Hindu's "mineral light," and the sun with its nourishing heat and light were aspects of the same basic principle.

Sir James George Frazer's *Golden Bough* mentions that until recently central European gypsies believed in a manifestation of the life-giving principle of light-and-gold. They called it the fern seed, and it figures in the myths and ceremonies of many European areas, although today its form has been altered almost beyond recognition. For thousands of years the parasitic mistletoe has been ritually linked with sun and gold, fire and light. Fern seed and mistletoe, vegetable gold emanations of the sun's fire, were thought to reveal earthly treasures of mineral gold if they were gathered at the solstices.

Men believed gold grew as plants and could beget offspring. In A.D. 1540 an essay on "the Generation of Metals" averred that "in some places of Hungarie at certain times of the year, pure gold springeth out of the earth in the likeness of small herbs, wreathed and twined like small stalks of hops, about the bigness of a pack of thread and four fingers in length." Centuries later some Europeans still believed that "the tailings of abandoned mines became so enriched as to be workable at a profit, the amount of gold thus obtained being proportional to the interval of time elapsed."

In fact, although methods of gold refining remained unchanged for thousands of years, men were sometimes able to reprocess old tailings and extract small amounts of gold. In the late nineteenth century several English mining concerns processed ancient tailings piled on the Egyptian desert where they had been left by slave miners five thousand years before. They discovered that the extraction process of the ancients had been such that almost no gold remained. They had somewhat better luck in the mines themselves finding veins and pockets of ore in the twisting, ruined galleries some of which reached six miles inland from the Red Sea shore. The ancient diggings yielded vast numbers of human bones and $3 million in gold before they were abandoned in 1921.

There are areas, particularly in Southeast Asia, where gold mining is surrounded with ritual and the gold itself considered a living thing. The Dyaks of Borneo believe the precious metal has a soul which will avenge itself on those who wrest it from the earth. Miners in parts of Sumatra formerly observed complete silence while gathering gold, the removal of which was considered a theft. If the spirits heard the men, they would punish them. If the miners brought tin or ivory to the mining site, they believed the spirits would make the gold vanish. In neighboring Malaya tin miners regard tin as alive and growing, sometimes in the form of a water buffalo which wanders from place to place.

The men who worked gold were always accorded high status. Among certain West African tribes only a chief may be a smith. And in parts of Sumatra and Borneo goldsmiths were considered neutrals in war and allowed to pass unharmed through hostile territory. The goldsmith of the Karo Batak in Sumatra practiced a sacred craft; before starting work he prayerfully offered his blood, heart, liver, and lungs to the spirits. He considered his tools as animate objects capable of changing their names and function. Thus, he used a "secret" language when working. It was customary for a son to follow his father because if he did not the tools would "ridicule" him. Goldsmiths' tools could not be sold without causing great harm to seller and buyer; they must be inherited.

There is no rational explanation for the lure of gold, but its history, the best documented of any metal, reflects the emotional response it has generally aroused. The pessimist Euripedes noted, "There is a saying that gifts gain over even the gods. Over man, gold has greater power than ten thousand arguments."

The thread of gold is woven into magic, religion, philosophy, poetry, art, politics, economics, science, medicine, and industry. There is scarcely a time or place in which the precious metal has not figured in some way. It has baited the hook of charlatans, con men, and counterfeiters for sixty centuries.

Supplies of gold have never been adequate to meet demand, although there have been moments of unprecedented and disturbing abundance such as when Alexander conquered the golden East and Persian gold flowed into Greece or in the years following the 1849 discovery of gold at Sutter's Mill in California. There have been eras of great scarcity too, particularly following the Fall of Rome when the barbarians didn't know how to work the rich Roman mines.

For thousands of years men strove to manufacture the precious metal. Alchemists have too often been lumped together with the rogues who, in one way or another, have taken advantage of man's greed for gold. Alchemy, practiced in China and the Middle East centuries before Christ, was ostensibly the search for the philosophers' stone, which would transmute base metals into gold and confer eternal life. The alchemists, traditionally regarded with ridicule, did far more than mix dragon's blood and gazelle urine in the smoking retorts of their dank laboratories.

Undoubtedly many of them were swindlers, but the empirical experiments of such men as Geber in eighth-century Baghdad, Robert Boyle in seventeenth-century England, and countless other dedicated scientists laid the foundations for much of modern chemistry, optics, physics, biology, and medicine. Among the fraternity of Hermetic scientists were popes, kings, doctors, and women as well as devotees of arcana and magicians who made a career out of relieving wealthy clients of their gold with the promise of doubling it in their Hermetic laboratories.

In the Middle Ages, the paucity of gold, which kept the alchemists struggling in their reeking dens, propelled men across the seas in search of new sources. King Ferdinand of Spain sent his conquistadores westward to "get gold, humanely if possible, but at all hazards get gold." Before the onslaught of a very few men in chain mail who had fire-belching sticks and rode fleet horses, the Inca, the Maya, the Aztec, and the Carib succumbed. High cultures and low were extinguished.

Indian slaves died like flies, as had the slaves of the Egyptians in the mines of the Kush, where it was more costly to bring in supplies and water for the miners than to bring in replacements. Hundreds of years after Spain's gold-sparked conquest, Russian serfs worked to the death for their imperial masters in the gold fields where twentieth-century slave laborers would dig gold for Stalin.

In the 1890s the hapless Ona Indians of Tierra del Fuego were shot at like rabbits by the rough men who flocked to that desolate, wind-swept tip of South America in a short-lived gold rush.

The world shrank before the exploring traders and intrepid gold seekers who pushed their way beyond the known world's frontiers into harsh lands and across dread seas filled with the chimeras of nightmare and superstition. Greek chroniclers writing in the first millennium B.C. described hostile climate and terrain inhabited by gold-guarding birds of prey and gold-digging ants as large as foxes, but nothing stopped the gold seekers.

There has not been an age without its Eldorado, a fabulous golden land or city shimmering just beyond the ken. The Chinese, Japanese, Indians, the inhabitants of the Near East and the Mediterranean all had tales of legendary kingdoms with inexhaustible golden riches, and often thought to be the abode of the immortals where one could find everlasting peace and joy.

For thousands of years one goal of the quest was Ophir, site of King Solomon's mines. The location of Ophir had been a matter of much speculation in antiquity. The golden land's position shifted from India to Arabia to Africa, and as men explored those zones without finding it the search focused on the Caribbean, Greenland, and South America. Columbus initially felt he had discovered it in the Caribbean. In 1976 United States and Saudi geologists announced they had located Solomon's mine in the Saudi Arabian desert.

Medieval Europe was riveted by the tale of Prester John, a Christian potentate who presided over a mysterious Asian kingdom drenched in gold. The Pope and European kings actually received letters alleged to be from the powerful ruler. His legend persisted through the centuries, and many expeditions were launched to find the man who would be a valuable Asian ally in Christendom's mortal struggle with the infidels.

Eventually Asia was combed and no such golden kingdom found. Men whose dreams of gold could not be quenched then turned to Africa to find Prester John and particularly to Ethiopia, where there was indeed a Christian ruler and a great deal of gold.

Not everyone was satisfied the great John had been found there. Sir Walter Raleigh, not immune to the lure of legend, sought Prester John in the jungles of Guiana, pursuing his golden dream to ultimate ruin.

Before him Spaniards, Portuguese, and even Germans had plunged into trackless jungles, scaled mountains, and braved unknown waters to find Eldorado. The quest took them across North America and throughout Central and South America. Coronado tracked across the lower Midwest in search of Quivira; Balboa looked for Davaive, a Panamanian cacique who reportedly had scores of workers whose only task was to melt gold for his dazzling treasure hoard.

Quivira, Eldorado, the Seven Cities of Cibola, different names, hazy locations, but all equally elusive until Pizarro in 1532 found the golden kingdom of the Inca in Peru which fulfilled, even surpassed, the most glittering dreams.

In the twentieth century, when every bit of land and water has been probed and labeled, the quest still goes on. In the early part of the century the Krupps, the German family of industrialists, mounted a large and costly expedition to penetrate the interior of Brazil in search of a legendary lost city of gold. They organized with characteristic efficiency but were encumbered by too many people and supplies. In the interior they ran out of food, and the animals could find no forage. The Krupps admitted defeat, but there are many who still believe the gold lies waiting in the heart of the Amazon jungles.

The gold seekers throughout the ages have always been unusual men, optimistic, adventurous, and resourceful. Their quest has never flagged, though it shifted from one area to another. One of the first documented prospectors was the Phoenician

Cadmus. In the fourteenth century B.C. he went from Canaan north to mainland Greece, where he found gold and according to Strabo "carried there the alphabet and other germs of civilization."

The Phoenicians were unsurpassed masters of seaborne trade in the ancient world. They sailed through the Pillars of Hercules, out of the familiar Mediterranean. They ventured down the coast of Africa, where they engaged in the famous "silent trade" for gold, and up to the British Isles for tin in the second millennium B.C.

Pursuing the will-o'-the-wisp of gold, men have pioneered new lands, building cities in the wilderness, spreading and blending elements of culture, religion, and technology. Success only served to inflame the desire for more of the stuff. Men have subjected themselves to unbelievable hardships for gold and inflicted incredible suffering on others. To get to the Klondike, men voluntarily undertook the most appalling peacetime advance in history. The lure of gold has drawn men across continents, oceans, deserts, and mountains to lonely deaths and only rarely to a bonanza.

The sea today offers the greatest potential source of gold. Billions of dollars' worth of sunken gold, the accumulation of centuries, lies on the bottom, much of it beyond reach of contemporary diving capability. The greatest amount of ocean gold, however, is in colloidal form and awaits harvesting when and if an economical way is found to extract gold from sea water.

Today when there are so many substances, many of them unknown to antiquity, to catch one's fancy, gold is still aesthetically pleasing and highly valued. Until fairly recently it was undisputed as the preferred way to display wealth, reflect divine grace, and confirm worldly power.

Because of the nature of the metal and the practice, until Christian times in the West, of burying the dead with gold artifacts, we can look today on the work of thousands of nameless artisans who crafted objects of enduring beauty—and in some eras of crashing vulgarity. Sometimes a legacy of gold ornaments, distinctive and lovely, their luster undimmed by the passage of time, is all that remains of a culture. In every age there is an eloquence in the goldsmith's work which reflects his place in history.

Grave gold delights the senses as rusted iron can never do. Gazing, for example, at gleaming Scythian pieces, rich in texture and bold in conception, one feels an empathy for the vigorous nomads who roamed the Eurasian steppes with their horses and cattle two thousand years ago. The magnificent grave goods of the nobles are all we know of the Scythians' material culture, but they bring Herodotus' fifth century B.C. descriptive pages to life.

The ancient practice of furnishing the dead with precious objects and humble but favored possessions has proven a boon to scientists. What we know of the remarkable goldwork of the Egyptians, Sumerians, Mycenaeans, Etruscans, Iberians, Scythians, Celts, Romans, and Greeks comes almost entirely from archaeologists' legitimate excavations of tombs.

Unfortunately for the archaeologist and historian who want to put together a picture of ancient civilizations, grave looting has been going on as long as men have been buried with their gold. Egyptian papyri of about 1100 B.C. tell of official investigations into thefts from royal tombs and other sacred places along the west bank of the Nile at Thebes. The robberies involved political scandal, the involvement of artisans and minor bureaucrats. Eventually it was deemed necessary to transport royal mummies to secret tombs in the Valley of the Kings at Luxor. However, small gangs continued their depredations and managed to despoil virtually every tomb. One of the very few which remained unscathed was that of the minor prince young Tutankhamen, whose splendid tomb was found by Howard Carter in 1922.

In the eighteenth century, when things Etruscan were in vogue, Italian noblemen on whose vast estates Etruscan tombs were located hired peasants to systematically plunder the tombs. Often these men were given strict orders to crush underfoot anything that was not precious, and when a market developed in ceramics the peasants were told to break all pots that were not unique. This inflated the market value of a few ceramics, making fortunes for the landowners, but outraging historians.

There are still countless treasure-laden burials in many parts of the world, and still thousands of grave robbers whose only concern is the clandestine removal of salable items. Despite government efforts to stop them, these men, encouraged by unscrupulous collectors and museums which are not choosy about the provenance of artifacts, probe the ground from Turkey to Central America. In Panama the *guaceros'* illegal trade is so well organized they have even formed a union. Until a few years ago grave gold in Panama was sold under the counter, melted down, and used by local dentists. Now some of the more sophisticated of the characters who once did the melting have turned their hands to forging antique artifacts to supply a growing market.

In most eras the antique object had little of the prestige it enjoys today, although in Greek and Roman times there were discriminating collectors of coins and jewelry. In most cases jewelry, coins, votive pieces, and crowns were recycled endlessly unless they were somehow well hidden or overlooked.

The greatest artistic loss was probably the melting of the incredible masterpieces of goldwork seized by the Spaniards in the New World. They left us detailed accounts of gold-plated buildings, trees, flowers, animals, and birds, all life size, fashioned of gold. With no hesitation they consigned the genius of a dozen cultures to oblivion. The sacred gold was melted down and emerged as the bullion and specie which nudged Europe into an unprecedented inflationary spiral. In the long run the gold of the gods exacted a full measure of revenge on Spain and left Spain weakened and impoverished.

As a monetary metal, gold, after thousands of years of service, is being phased out by economists and politicians who, like J. M. Keynes, view it as a "barbarous relic" and seek to strip it of time-hallowed mystique. Return to a gold standard is no longer possible nor desirable, but monetary gold has its passionate advocates, among them the French and Russians, who argue for some role for the metal, and the debate is not yet over. No currency has ever equaled the record of gold's stability, although a few like British sterling throughout most of the nineteenth century and the post-World War II United States dollar were "as good as gold."

Germans who pushed a baby carriage full of depreciated marks to the store at the end of World War II to buy a loaf of bread or South Vietnamese holding their savings in a currency wiped out after the United States withdrawal in 1975 would have been far better off holding gold. Traditionally in much of Europe and the East, in Asia and Latin America, gold has been the common man's insurance in volatile times. The movement of gold despite restrictions in countries such as India reflects the deep hold it has on security-hungry men.

In times of uncertainty gold keeps its value and represents a form of anonymous wealth which can be transferred without red tape. Gold quietly crosses borders; no questions are asked of it beyond assaying for purity, which is easily done. Gold is still widely used as payment for espionage and intelligence work.

Gold resists being ranked with soybeans and pork bellies on the commodities market. Although it has been dethroned from international monetary supremacy, it still remains the ultimate acceptable form of payment between individuals and nations, whatever their differing philosophies.

While experts continue to debate what part gold should play in global economics, anxious people in Argentina, Indonesia, India, and Brazil continue to trust gold for the preservation of capital. Most countries continue to treat their gold reserves as an asset of last resort despite the fact that as Robert Triffin of Yale pointed out, "Nobody could ever have conceived of a more absurd waste of human resources than to dig gold in the distant corners of the earth for the sole purpose of transporting it and reburying it immediately afterwards in other deep holes, especially excavated to receive it and heavily guarded to protect it."

Some seven thousand years of experience say gold is forever.

CHAPTER TWO *Gift from the Stars*

Gold is almost everywhere: in deer antlers, polar ice, human hair, plants, and the clay underneath Philadelphia. Nature seldom sowed the most coveted of metals as prodigally as along California's Mother Lode. For the most part gold lies universally distributed in invisible and inaccessible form. The estimated gold production of the past six thousand years, roughly 110,000 metric tons, pales beside the 10 billion tons of gold tantalizingly suspended in the oceans of the world and the 50 billion trillion troy ounces present in the sun in the form of hot gas.

The oldest of all the gods, the sun was linked with gold from remote prehistory. The Greek poet Pindar called gold "the child of Zeus," who, like Jehovah, was a sun-god. As late as A.D. 1527 Calbus of Freiberg, a German physician and metallurgist, echoed the current opinion that "every metallic ore receives a special influence from its own particular planet. Thus gold is of the Sun or its influence, silver of the Moon, tin of Jupiter. . . . Thus gold is often called the Sun." It was thought that the metals entered the earth through rays from the celestial bodies.

In a sense the ancients were on the right track. The shining nuggets they cherished are of heavenly origin. Gold is the gift of dying stars, and our sun is a star but not the source of earthly gold. It is the by-product of stellar cyclotrons, produced from suns far older than ours. Geologists have determined from radioactive dating of rocks that the earth was formed about 4½ billion years ago out of a gold-and-silver-enriched interstellar medium which astrophysicists call the solar nebula. The various elements in the sun can be observed by analysis of their spectral lines, and because the relative chemical abundances in the sun are the same as in the earth, scientists were able to determine that the earth, sun, and the entire solar system were formed from the same fiery star dust.

Stars and the stuff between them are composed chiefly of the two simplest atoms—hydrogen and helium, both of which are light. A star is born of dust and interstellar gas. The interstellar core heats up, and nuclear reactions provide energy for the great amounts of visible light and other forms of electromagnetic radiation which pour out of the star and which, in the case of our sun, sustain life on earth.

The nuclear reactions, which are part of a star's life cycle, are much like those in a hydrogen bomb. The abundant hydrogen atoms are burned to form helium. Four hydrogen nuclei are converted into a single helium nucleus, and about 1 per cent of the initial mass of hydrogen is converted into energy according to Einstein's celebrated equation $E=mc^2$.

Eventually a star which is burning hydrogen will consume the fuel in its core. Then it must burn the converted helium. Thus, the star evolves, burning first hydrogen, then helium, and when that is exhausted, carbon. Finally the stellar core turns to pure iron, which is inert and cannot under usual conditions be used as fuel.

Lighter stars then gradually cool off and die. However, massive stars, larger than our sun, undergo more cataclysmic explosions. The unstable stars then generate elements heavier than iron. These red-hot exploding stars, called supernovae, in a last great surge become as brilliant as the whole galaxy, emitting heavy elements like gold, silver, and uranium.

How did the gold created by such incredible detonations get to the gold fields of South Africa, California, the Egyptian desert, or the Klondike? The exploding materials traveling at three thousand miles a second were spewed out into the interstellar medium. They floated about in tenuous gases until an interstellar cloud formed. The cloud then collapsed under local gravitational condensation, and new stars and their accompanying planets were formed.

Our sun and the small rock- and metal-laden planets closest to it—Mercury, Mars, earth, and Venus—were born when the weighty elements solidified out of clouds of cosmic gas. By the time the more distant planets were formed there was little left of the heavy elements which had precipitated earlier on the dense planets closer to the sun.

As the earth cooled, gold, because of its extreme weight, settled beneath the planet's mantle, widely distributed in a thin layer throughout the crust. Today gold is found in a variety of rock matrices. A deposit may be of any geological age and associated with sedimentary or igneous rock.

Toward the end of the Cretaceous period, perhaps 94 million years ago, the molten interior of the planet began to boil and convulse. Mighty movements flexed and snapped the earth's surface thrusting up mountains and volcanoes, twisting and wrinkling the earth's crust. Internal pressure forced molten magma up to form the masses of rock, often granite, which form the base of mountain ranges.

Gold is most often found near granite. The most common matrix for gold is quartz, but veins or lodes are also found in calcite or limestone. The vein material generally includes other metallic compounds. Pyrite, the brassy iron sulphide which resembles gold, is abundant in some veins and has countless times been taken for the real thing—hence its name "fool's gold."

The ore deposits of many metals, including gold, silver, tungsten, and copper, were made during and after this period of igneous activity. Ascending magmas bearing the metals in suspension were forced through the earth's crust into cooler zones of subsurface rock. The metallic elements were deposited in fissures and cracks of faulted rocks in the form of veins or replacements.

If the gold was in an active solution and was deposited in a rock such as limestone, which is unusually prone to chemical action, it could penetrate solid rock and slowly dissolve the rock, replacing it with gold, atom for atom. Such deposits are called replacement deposits.

More often gold was deposited between rock fissures in veins, so called because they appeared, at the surface, to wind through the host rock as veins traverse the human body. Frustrated prospectors discovered, however, that their route is most irregular. Veins vary in pattern, length, thickness, and depth. A vein as thin as a hair ribbon at one point and quite close to the surface can fragment into almost invisible branches, plunge deep, and later emerge as a rich pocket. Veins extend into the earth in tabular form, in sheets or planes at an angle; a vein may be several miles long or terminate abruptly after an inch.

Gold, in veins or replacement deposits, is almost always found together with a gangue, or host material, which keeps it in place. Rock and the gold imprisoned in it make up the ore. The gold does not have to be highly visible to make the ore worth processing. Much of South Africa's gold comes from ore in which the gold is invisible, but modern refining methods have made its extraction profitable. Gold, because of its stubborn refusal to form combinations, is most often found in relatively pure form in nature, almost always alloyed with some silver. It occasionally occurs combined with tellurium as gold tellurides and is a byproduct in the refining of certain copper, lead, and zinc ores. But the bulk of gold is found uncombined, or free, either in primary vein deposits or in secondary alluvial deposits.

The earliest gold mankind found and most of the gold produced before A.D. 1873 when vein mining was introduced to work rich lodes in California, Nevada, and Colorado was alluvial or placer gold, which had been freed by erosion from its subterranean prison, torn away, and washed into streams and rivers. Through the geological ages the earth has been worn down by weathering forces such as rain, wind, freezing, thaw, and plant growth. These agents have mined gold for aeons, removing thousands of feet from mountain ranges like California's Sierra Nevada.

The products of disintegration, ranging in size from massive boulders through rocks and pebbles to even finer particles, were carried into watercourses where they were tumbled and abraded. The farther chunks of ore traveled, the more the precious metal was separated from the gangue or debris. Surface water carried away some of the constituents of metal-bearing minerals which are subject to chemical decomposition during erosion. Silver is not found in alluvial deposits because it decomposes upon contact with chlorides which occur in rain water. But gold retained its identity as it rushed down prehistoric streams.

The high specific gravity of gold, 19.4, assured that the sorting action of the water would carry off lighter sand and gravel debris as bits of gold dropped to the bottom. Gold is about seven times as dense as gravel or sand, and gravity helped concentrate it in sand or gravel bars or in "potholes." Where the stream gradient was reduced or moved slowly around curves, gold particles were trapped in cracks or between stones. Fragments ranging in size from powdery dust to masses of a hundred pounds lay awaiting discovery and collection.

Placer deposits are not always on the surface. In California and Australia there are gold-bearing gravels buried deep beneath thick flows of ancient basaltic lava. The gold in these fossil placers was deposited in prehistoric stream beds and subsequently welded to deep rocks by geologic processes and covered by igneous or sedimentary rock. Sometimes these subterranean placers were exposed aeons later when other streams channeled through the overburden of lava and sediment.

Gold is found as dust, flakes, grains, nuggets, and in curious crystalline branch formations. It was these plantlike structures which supported universal speculation that gold grew as a plant in the rocks. "As fishes die in the water," wrote Thomas Norton, a sixteenth-century chemist, "so metals generated in the earth are subject to rust, corruption and gradual destruction above ground." His tract was devoted to a plea for the closing of gold mines. Miners believed gold deposits should be left alone for certain periods so that nature might replenish them.

In Borneo nuggets were "gods of the soil" and played an important part in propitiatory rituals. Malay miners believed the gold in the earth belonged to a golden deer who chose to give or withhold it. Prayer and fasting preceded gold gathering in various parts of the East Indies where the miners were careful not to remove all the gold they saw lest the "soul" of the gold depart and no more "grow."

Gold can, in fact, be grown as well as mined, but it is hardly profitable. A common plant of the United States and Canada, horsetail weed, has such an affinity for gold that it has been burned for its metallic content. A ton of horsetail grown in low-grade gold fields yields as much as 4½ ounces of gold. Two other plants whose juices trap fine gold are the gogo of the Philippines and the itambamba of Brazil.

Although gold is found virtually everywhere in the world, the major concentrations make a pattern which, especially after the great gold discoveries made by the sixteenth-century Spanish in the New World, began to have great bearing on population distribution.

The greatest sources of gold and the longest-worked deposits are located in the vast continent of Africa. Beginning thousands of years ago men systematically collected gold from the plateau between the Nile and the Red Sea, the sands of the Nile, Nubia in the northern Sudan and Ethiopia as well as in southeastern, central, and western Africa. The incredibly rich gold fields of South Africa, however, had to await exploitation made possible by twentieth-century technology. Today South Africa, which a century ago produced less than 1 per cent of the world's gold, accounts for over 70 per cent of the annual production excluding the Soviet Union, the second largest producer, whose output is a state secret.

Europe's gold is concentrated southeast from the British Isles through France, along the Alps and Balkan mountain ranges, and in rich deposits on the Iberian peninsula. Asiatic Russia has colossal gold concentrations, and considerable amounts of the metal have been produced in Asia Minor, Arabia, the Hindu-Kush, and southern and eastern India. Quantities have been accumulated from the Chinese coast, Korea, Japan, the Philippines, and through the Malay archipelago across the Sumatra, Java, Papua New Guinea, Australia, New Zealand, and Fiji, where gold miners recently struck for a noontime "sex break."

In the Western Hemisphere gold was deposited down the western coastal areas from Alaska, northwest Canada to the Rocky Mountains, down through the Pacific coast of the United States into Mexico, across Central America, and over the northern half of South America.

The known deposits of gold were widespread in antiquity. Gold production in ancient Egypt was so extensive that it almost constituted a monopoly for several thousand years. Gold deposits were worked in India, Africa, Persia, Arabia, Caucasia, Asia Minor, and the Balkans in the millennia before Christ, but production was neither as great nor as continuous as the Nile kingdom's.

The very earliest discoverers of gold limited themselves to picking up random grains or nuggets which lay superficially ex-

posed in watercourses or on the ground. The Greek legends of a
Golden Age may trace their origin to the time when men first
began to systematically look for gold. The gold seekers were few
in number, and the gold of infinite ages lay waiting like ripe
golden fruit for the harvester. The accumulation of millions of
years shone in the limpid shallows of rivers and streams or was
revealed just below the earth's surface when a heavy rain, an av-
alanche, or wind stripped away the topsoil. Ancient writers record instances of gold found when trees or plants were uprooted.
Gold nuggets have been found in the course of digging foundations, wells, and vegetables. In the early nineteenth century
when a great deal of gold was found in the southern Urals, many
nuggets of varying size lay spread under the soil, no deeper than
a crop of potatoes.

Men, always longing for gold, associated it with past ages of
great happiness which were inaccessible to them. They also
ascribed golden attributes in both a physical and a metaphorical
sense to a paradise or abode of the blessed dead which lay somewhere beyond and to which they could aspire. The fifth Mohammedan heaven is of gold. The biblical Jerusalem with streets of
gold typifies the golden dream. The Hindu epic the Rig-Veda
stipulates that he who gives gold will have a life of everlasting
light and glory.

Eight hundred years before Christ the Greek poet Hesiod
wrote of a happier time when the gods created man and lavished
precious gold on him. The sands of the rivers were all of gold
and the great river, Ocean, flowed all around the earth, which
was never troubled by wind or storm. On Ocean's bank was the
blessed abode of the dead, where golden flowers blazed on the
trees. Gold high on the mountains was liquefied by forest fires
and gushed in molten streams over the earth. Whole islands were
made of the precious stuff.

This was the Golden Age. The earth and the flocks were fertile
and man lived in golden plenty and peace. This is how men
chose to recall the lost ages when mankind made the transition
from the harsh existence of hunter-gatherers to the more favorable conditions of settled life and a predictable food supply.

The poet wrote that the gods experimenting with the metals
from the highest to the basest made men first of gold. But when

they disappointed their creators with their behavior, the gods made mortals of less precious silver. However, the silver men were far less intelligent than their ancestors and warred incessantly with their brothers. The gods succeeded them with an inferior race of brass or bronze men who were even more bellicose and violent than the silver. Finally, lamented Hesiod, came the contemporary age of iron filled with toil and sorrow.

In the fifth century B.C. Plato explained the scarcity of gold in his time as a punishment by the great Zeus for man's evil ways. There had been a time when the first men lived in harmony and golden luxury with the gods. The earthly paradise was on the lost continent of Atlantis, which lay due west of the Pillars of Hercules. The golden spires of Atlantis blazed forth to light the whole world and guide Apollo as he drove the chariot of the sun across the heavens each day. The Golden Age came to a halt when men and gods mingled too freely begetting such base beings that Zeus judged them undeserving of such a profusion of gold and blessings. He sank Atlantis beneath the sea, and ever since then, Plato explained, men have had to search and toil painfully for bits of the once abundant gold.

The ancients were unaware of the greatest potential source of gold of all—sea water. Modern man knows but, despite hundreds of theories, patented inventions, and attempts, has thus far been unable to profitably mine the oceans' gold. How did gold get into the oceans? It was washed there atom by atom since earth's superheated halo of steam condensed into the seas. Some gold was deposited beneath the sea bed when the planet was formed and later thrust up in the same kind of movement that shaped terrestrial mountains. Gold wrested from mountains on land and carried in streams and rivers sometimes made its way into the sea too. There are rich concentrations of sea gold in areas that have been fed by gold-bearing rivers in Alaska, Washington, California, Japan, and Australia.

Colloidal gold precipitates to the ocean floor or is stored in natural aquatic miners such as fish, seaweed, and algae. Traces of gold are present in the nodules which cover some 22 million square miles of ocean floor, although their major components are manganese, copper, nickel, and cobalt.

It has been estimated that there is enough gold in the sea

water which covers three fourths of the earth's surface to make every human being a multimillionaire. Men have been trying to get at it ever since 1866, when a French scientist speaking before the American Association of Science said, "Gentlemen, I believe that among other things you will find gold in the ocean."

The first scientific estimate of the amount actually present in sea water was made in 1887 by an English chemist, who figured there were sixty-five milligrams of gold in a metric ton of water. Estimates offered by scientists from Australia to Sweden, varied widely but pointed to several interesting things. There was more gold in solution in polar ice than in the surrounding water. The highest concentrations of all were found in plankton, the minute drifting plants and animals fed on by marine species.

While scientists studied ways to legitimately extract gold from sea water bunco artists were cashing in on various sea gold schemes. In 1897 Prescott Ford Jernigan, a Baptist minister and pillar of the community of Edgartown, Massachusetts, announced that a dream had revealed to him the method to harvest ocean gold. The process involved submerging a zinc-lined wooden box called an accumulator into the water. It was filled with chemically treated mercury, a favorite ingredient in gold-swindling schemes for centuries. An electrical current was passed through the box, and the gold was supposedly absorbed by the quicksilver.

Jernigan convinced two wealthy parishioners to invest in his project. A box was built and a deep-sea diver hired to submerge and connect the device. On a cold February night the box was lowered over the side of a small boat in Narragansett Bay and left for a full running of the tide. When it was hauled up, government assayers found five dollars' worth of pure gold in the box—a promising start.

The parishioners and a few other men put up $20,000 for more extensive tests. In December excited investors formed the Electrolytic Marine Salts Company, in Boston capitalized at $10 million, an enormous sum at the turn of the century. Most of the shareholders were rich eastern Baptists. Within the first year 700,000 shares were sold on the strength of 250 accumulators which allegedly yielded $1,250 each time the tide turned.

The tide finally turned for Jernigan when it was discovered he and his diver had been salting the accumulators with gold. The shenanigans of the swindlers cost investors millions. Many more millions were expended on the quest for sea gold by chemists, engineers, and governments. In 1919 the Germans asked Fritz Haber, the celebrated chemist, to tap the inexhaustible supply of marine gold. Haber was a brilliant man who had helped his country in World War I by synthesizing ammonia so that Germany was well supplied with explosives throughout the war despite England's blockade to keep out Chilean nitrates.

The Germans hoped to extract enough gold to pay their war debt. Haber organized the German South Atlantic Expedition outfitting his ship, the *Meteor*, with a complete laboratory and filtration system. For ten years he plied the oceans, testing water from the mouth of the Rhine to the South Seas. He collected samples from the California coast and the polar icecaps and scrutinized thousands of marine plants and animals.

Initially he was pleased at the amounts of gold his tests revealed. However, he discovered that minute traces of gold in his testing chemicals and apparatus were falsifying the results. When the assay methods were refined, he found very little gold indeed. In 1929 he wrote a letter to a leading German chemistry journal summarizing his decade of travail and commenting, "There is more chance of finding a needle in a haystack than extracting gold from the sea."

The Japanese conducted experiments in the early 1930s, and then the United States, spurred by the rising price of gold and certain promising results, took over. In 1935 Dr. Colin Fink, an internationally respected authority on electrochemistry, announced that after thirty years of research he had developed an electrical method to collect marine gold. Jernigan, the bunco artist, had been on the right track after all with his electric current. Fink's plan involved a simple procedure connecting two metal plates to positive and negative terminals of a battery, inserting them in the sea and letting the gold accumulate at the negative plate.

He said it would be feasible for an ocean liner to "use its propellers as cathodes and plate them with gold during a voyage." Unfortunately Dr. Fink's eureka was a bit premature. It turned out that the negative plate had to revolve at fifteen thousand revolutions per minute before the procedure was effective. At that rate it cost five cents to collect a penny's worth of gold.

Georges Claude, the French inventor who had made a fortune from neon lamps and liquid air, set up an experimental extracting plant in 1936 aboard a steamer that made the Pacific coastal run between North and South America. His extraction plant consisted of a large funnel-shaped apparatus which forced sea water into a long iron tube filled with a compound of iron pyrites. Since finely divided pyrites attract gold, theoretically the gold in the water flowing through the pipe should have remained there. Claude found that there was scarcely one milligram per metric ton in the water. His disheartening results were confirmed by the experiments of others. On the average there are only one to two parts of gold to a million parts of water, although the concentration can be higher. In 1951 water tested from the Sea of Japan showed thirteen milligrams per metric ton. Scientists proposed to extract it by evaporation using sunlight as the source of heat, but nothing came of it.

Filtration and evaporation offer two ways of collecting ocean gold, but both present problems which make their application unlikely. Massive quantities of sea water would have to be processed to yield appreciable amounts of gold. If a totally efficient process were developed, a cubic mile of sea water would have to be screened to produce fifty pounds of gold. In other words, 5 million tons of sea water, more than a billion gallons, are required to yield one ounce of pure gold. In a cubic mile of sea water there is about $370 million worth of gold. But to treat such a volume of water in a year would necessitate filling and emptying two hundred huge tanks of water, each five hundred feet square and five feet deep, two times a day.

Such a feat is not impossible but it is economically out of the question. Human nature being what it is, men will keep on trying to separate gold from water. Nuclear-powered desalinization plants which would produce not only gold but fresh water, power, and salt have been proposed by several researchers who predict they will be in use by the end of the century.

Mining and mineral exploration interests have recently prospected off the east coast of Canada for undersea gold placer deposits. Through the ages sea levels have fluctuated and a portion of offshore areas was once above water. Scientists studied offshore sediment movement, past sea current, and beach wave action as well as geologic formations to determine what areas were most likely to have gold deposits.

Seismic acoustic profiling was employed to examine the ocean bottom. Prospective drill sites were chosen taking into account such past and present features as ancient beach lines and buried stream channels. Test holes were drilled and the cores analyzed to determine the amount of gold present. Enough gold was found in a zone lying off former gold-producing land in Nova Scotia to warrant further exploration. In an area of 36 million cubic yards gold particles worth up to $1.20 were found in a cubic yard. The coarse gold appears to have been left behind when erosion and perhaps glacial action wore away the top of a hill or mountain which had once been above sea level. But the gold-bearing alluvium is covered by fourteen to twenty-one fathoms of water, making it very difficult to process. Mining engineers are designing special suction dredges to suck up the alluvium. On board ship the conglomerate of mud, gravel, sand, and gold would be sluiced. The gold would separate from the lighter tailings, which would then be dumped back in the sea. Before too long gold from the sea may be a reality thanks to new developments in mining technology.

The quality of gold today is measured in terms of carats and in parts per thousand. The word "carat" derives from the Italian *carato,* the Arabic *qirat,* and the Greek *keration,* all of which mean the fruit of the carob tree. This leguminous tree has hornlike pods containing seeds which were once used to balance the scales weighing gold gems and pearls in Oriental bazaars.

The dried seeds were of amazingly uniform weight, about a fifth of a gram, which is the weight now assigned to the metric carat. In the case of gold, the carat is not a measure of weight, but one of purity. Pure gold is 24 carats gold. Because pure gold is so soft, it is usually alloyed with a small amount of copper, nickel, zinc, silver, or other inferior metal to increase its resilience without diluting its beauty. Fine jewelry is seldom made with gold of a purity less than 18 carats—$18\!/\!24$, or $3\!/\!4$ pure gold. Various countries have particular preferences for softer, purer gold. Indians like 22-carat gold and there were riots when the

Indian Government attempted to outlaw possession of it in favor of 18-carat gold in order to decrease gold consumption. Today in the United States because of high gold prices, an increasing amount of mass-produced jewelry is being made with 9-carat gold, which contains only 9 parts gold out of 24, about 37 per cent.

The quality of gold is also measured in parts per thousand. Most of the newly mined gold put on the market by South Africa is 995 gold, meaning that it is 99.5 per cent pure. The Soviet Government refines all its gold production to 999 quality, which is 99.9 per cent pure and can only be produced by subjecting refined gold to a further electrolytic process.

Gold isn't measured on the familiar avoirdupois scale of weights but in troy ounces, a term derived from Troyes, France, where it originated. Both systems are British, although their names are of French origin. The troy system is used to weigh precious metals and gems. The avoirdupois system, used to weigh everything but precious metals, gems, and drugs, takes its name from the French *avoir de pois,* meaning goods of weight.

The two systems of measurement are based on a very ancient unit of measure, the grain, which can be used to convert weight from one system to the other. The troy ounce contains 480 grains, while 437.5 grains constitutes the avoirdupois ounce. Thus, a troy ounce equals 1.097 avoirdupois ounces. A standard 400-troy-ounce gold bar weighs 438.8 avoirdupois ounces, or 27.4 avoirdupois pounds.

Grains were adopted as a unit of weight in ancient Mesopotamia when developing commerce demanded standard units of weight to facilitate transactions. Balances were used to weigh precious metals. Observing that grains of barley or wheat from the middle of an ear tended to be of standard weight despite the size of the ear itself, merchants and traders divided the large major unit, the shekel, into grains. The grain was the hypothetical weight of a grain of wheat. In practice the shekel might vary from 120 grains to more than 200. Multiples of the shekel were introduced—the mina reckoned variously from 25 to 60 shekels and later the talent equal to 60 minas. The mina and the talent were used throughout the Mideast for millennia.

The grain was used in Britain until it adopted the metric system upon joining the Common Market. Almost every country today weighs gold by the gram rather than the grain or pennyweight, although the price of gold is quoted in troy ounces.

CHAPTER THREE *Gold of the Pharaohs*

Gold was plentiful in remote times, but as long as man was consumed by the struggle for survival he had no time for speculation as to how gold came to gleam among the river sands and no energy for concerted search and extraction. When was gold first systematically sought and worked? Certainly many thousands of years after Paleo-man treasured serendipitous bits of it, and long after a Neolithic tribe thoughtfully placed a gold-handled flint knife in the ground with their dead brother.

History focuses on two areas, both in the Near East, where, from earliest times, gold was an important element in religion and politics. Gold was a sacred metal in the two great riverine civilizations of Egypt and Mesopotamia in what is now Iraq. Both valued it highly and used it lavishly, according the metal a place in religion, decoration, and monetary affairs. The Sumerians, their successors the Babylonians and Assyrians as well as the Egyptians worshiped a multitude of deities. Omnipotent sun-gods were revered above all and gold was associated with their worship.

Although Egyptian civilization is not quite as old as that of the Sumerians, who first experienced the larger life in the city-states that evolved from farming communities in the Tigris-Euphrates Valley about 3500 B.C., the Nile people made earlier use of gold. The Egyptians were the first people to extract gold from a quartz reef. Five thousand years ago they had organized large-scale mining operations. Egypt was blessed with seemingly inexhaustible resources of the coveted sun stuff, which were amplified by booty, trade imports, and tribute. Mesopotamia, on the other hand, had no native supply and had to depend upon trade and conquest for gold.

Herodotus called Egypt the gift of the Nile. Without the great river the Egyptians would have struggled in a barren land. The undulating Nile nourished the land and made the Egyptians the most highly favored people of antiquity. Ten thousand years ago farmers and stock raisers who settled along the alluvium-enriched banks of the river recognized the significance of its annual rhythm of flood and flow. They counted on the silted waters to fertilize the crops, which then ripened under the powerful sun.

With security came intellectual curiosity and problem solving. Eight thousand years ago the Nile dwellers had learned how to harness the summer flood. They made observations of seasonal changes in the river and organized communal activities based on what they had learned. They dug canals, protected villages with dikes, dug wells, and made catchment basins to trap receding floodwaters; all very early samples of complex social organization.

The wealth and strength of Egypt from predynastic times depended upon the Nile and also on the sun. By the fifth millennium the Egyptians acknowledged the importance of the river and the sun with rituals and stone-hammered gold offerings. Each day the rebirth of the sun was celebrated and offerings made to the oldest of gods, source of being and father of gold.

A few examples of predynastic goldwork survive. Although not comparable to the magnificent work of later centuries, their beauty and skilled execution indicate that the goldsmiths did not spring full-blown from nowhere but were the inheritors of many generations of familiarity with the soft yellow metal.

In lower Nubia a grave was excavated which contained golden bow tips, thoughtfully placed next to a dead hunter to furnish him with weapons for hunting in the nether world. Necklaces, earrings, and bracelets beaten with flint hammers from alluvial gold were found south of Cairo and may be more than five thousand years old.

The use of gold in ancient Egypt was strictly a royal prerogative. A goldsmith's weight of two hundred grains was found bearing the stamp of Khufu, who reigned in the Fourth Dynasty (2613–2494 B.C.), evidence of the early royal monopoly on gold. Unlike the masses who had no furniture, the royals and aristocrats indulged themselves in gold-sheathed canopied beds, and gold-covered tables, chairs, benches, and coffers were embellished with gold and studded with semiprecious stones and bits of colored glass.

The deities were considered kings and queens with mortal requirements. In the temples their golden statues were surrounded with golden appointments crafted in the great temple workshops. Magnificent utensils and furnishings of gold inlaid with amethyst, turquoise, malachite, lapis lazuli, crystal, and other stones were used for ceremonies of washing (lustration), dressing, and feeding (sacrifice).

The Egyptians had to placate a pantheon of some two thousand deities. Theirs was a propitiatory religion in which men were fearful of the gods and their representatives, the priests, who had the power to interpret the gods' messages, relay human pleas, and perform the rituals essential to good fortune. The priests demanded sacrifices and offerings in the gods' names; increasingly these were exacted in gold.

A good part of life was spent in worship of the gods, and another large part was devoted to preparations for death. One of the most striking features of Egyptian civilization was the emphasis on eternal life. The monumental pyramids, the inscriptions, friezes, bas-reliefs, the elaborate mummification and funerary practices bear witness to this preoccupation of a small percentage of the Egyptian population which was able, through strong central government, to mobilize the rest of the populace as a labor force to prepare for a splendid afterlife.

At first only royal personages were entitled to the afterlife, but by the time of the New Kingdom, about 1550 B.C., everyone who could afford the costly preparations looked forward to it.

The earliest royal burial in which gold has been found was that of a queen buried at Abydos about 3200 B.C. The great Egyptologist Sir Flinders Petrie found four gold bracelets on her linen-swathed arm. They are of gold beads in diverse shapes intermingled with beads of turquoise and lapis lazuli. One has a gold-petaled flower and another is of delicate repoussé beads in the form of temple façades surmounted by a bird, probably the Horus falcon, symbolizing one of the most powerful gods.

In Egypt, as elsewhere, artisans who worked with gold were

an elite class, highly esteemed. The goldsmith's craft was usually hereditary.

In the Twelfth Dynasty, about 1900 B.C., during what historians call the golden age of art and craftsmanship, a master goldsmith named Mertisen vowed no one would succeed in the art "but I alone and the eldest son of my body. God has decreed him to excell in it and I have seen the perfections of his work in . . . every kind of precious stone, of gold and silver, of ivory and ebony." Smiths were often itinerant men who were sure of a warm welcome and full occupation wherever they went. They were among the earliest cultural diffusionists, spreading technique and style from one area to another. Egypt was the first nation to export gold and goldworking techniques. Later smiths, captured from areas such as Mesopotamia, worked in the workshops of pharaohs and temples. In the sixth century B.C. when the Persians, the second greatest gold power in the ancient world, invaded Egypt, they seized native goldsmiths to work in their ceremonial capital at Persepolis.

Egyptian goldsmiths were superb technicians but not innovators. Successive generations of smiths refined and elaborated earlier techniques, but the basic motifs of Egyptian art and craftsmanship remained unchanged for millennia. Jewelry and goldwork relied on stylized floral and leaf patterns, animal and bird forms, the representation of gods and their symbols, and the often used abstract and geometric designs. Symmetry and directness were preferred to imagination. Egyptian goldwork, of which we know so much thanks to dynastic funerary practices and the fantastic durability of gold, has a boldness which appeals to the twentieth century. The range of goldsmithing techniques the Egyptians mastered is awesome.

A 5,300-year-old bracelet in the Cairo Museum shows how very early goldsmiths were able to draw gold wire as thin as a hair. Jewelry in filigree designs was made by soldering spirals of fine gold wire to gold backing. The solder used was an alloy of silver or copper with gold. Egyptian goldsmiths knew how to cast gold and how to beat it into sheets or thick plate to cover wood furniture and film to gild statues. They were masters of chasing and repoussé, the art of forming a raised pattern on thin metal by beating it up from the underside.

In the Twelfth Dynasty the exacting technique of granulation was refined in which minuscule gold globes were sweated onto a gold ground by the hundreds or thousands to form lovely shining patterns. This was a feat practiced for three thousand years, brought to perfection by Etruscan goldsmiths in the eighth century B.C. and lost after Roman times until modern jewelers recently rediscovered it.

The most dazzling Egyptian goldwork is in cloisonné, a technique in which little open-fronted gold cells or compartments with thin gold walls are affixed to a gold ground and filled with small pieces of cut precious and semiprecious stones, enamel, niello, glass, or other material. No one in the ancient East surpassed the Egyptians in the manufacture of this colorful gold openwork. An inlaid gold pectoral jewel belonging to Ramses II has four hundred inlays of turquoise, carnelian, lapis lazuli, and garnet. Nineteenth century B.C. Egyptian goldsmiths discovered how to make enamel inlays as well by heat-fusing a powder of colored glass on gold. A few centuries later they perfected the difficult technique of inlaying a gold design in a different metal. A bronze dagger blade from a tomb at Thebes was inlaid by chiseling out a delicate pattern in the bronze, hammering gold in the grooves and finally making an almost invisible bronze overhang to keep the inlay in place.

The Nile smiths produced goldwork in a wide range of colors. They delighted in the hues of various alloys combining them to achieve polychrome effects. Queen Hatshepsut commented on the greenish cast of the gold from Punt which was due to the presence of small amounts of silver. Some tomb gold with a purple tinge contains so much iron it responds to a magnet. Other pieces have visible flakes of platinum. A lot of native Egyptian gold had a brassy or reddish sheen owing to the presence of copper.

The alluvial gold from the placer deposits of the Upper Nile was purer than the quartz reef gold from Nubia and the Red Sea area which contained more silver. About 2000 B.C. goldsmiths learned the art of separating the silver from gold. Later, when gold, both raw and worked, came to Egypt from Libya, Cyprus, and Asia to supplement native supplies, goldsmiths had a wider range of colors to work with.

The thin dry air of Egypt preserved paintings, flowers, and even cloth. Archaeologists have discovered several tomb paintings and bas-reliefs which show goldsmiths at work including those in the tomb of Asa, a royal official about 2400 B.C. Goldsmiths are weighing ingots of gold, recording the weight, puffing through a blowpipe to increase the temperature of a fire (at just over 1,000° F., gold alloyed with silver or copper melts). Kilted artisans pour molten metal and beat it into sheets just as Cairo smiths in the gold market do today, some 4,400 years later. Hieroglyphics accompany the illustrations explaining that the goldsmiths are overlaying necklaces, shrines, and doors with gold. Other men are shown working in pairs, bending crescentic gold collars and necklaces with falcons at the ends. The first Egyptian hieroglyph for gold, in fact, was a stylized necklace.

Gold and Egypt have been as inexorably linked as Egypt and the Nile. Until the Romans developed hydraulic mining methods to exploit the gold deposits of Spain at the beginning of the Christian era, Egypt was the world's greatest producer of gold. It came from two major zones. One was the area known as Nubia, (from the Egyptian word for gold, *nub*), reaching south into the Sudan and across into the Ethiopian plateau. The other was in Upper Egypt, where a plateau of gold-bearing quartz runs for two hundred miles along the Red Sea coast, sloping sixty miles westward to the Nile.

It was the Nile river sands which provided Egypt with its first great gold supplies. This was gold in Nubia, and in early times there was placer gold on higher alluvial terraces flanking the river. There were rich alluvial deposits in the Sudan and in Ethiopia, from which the gold was washed with relative ease.

The reefs of auriferous rock in Nubia lie between the Nile and the Red Sea. The gold was mined and processed by the slaves and captives who made up Egypt's labor force. It was the Pharaohs' incredible reservoir of manpower that built the pyramids and also made possible Egypt's supremacy in gold. Just as important as the vast gold deposits was the political organization which enabled the government to conscript labor for the service of the state.

At the end of the fourth millennium B.C., a chief of one of the many scattered tribal settlements that had cleared the swamps and farmed beside the Nile for thousands of years succeeded in coalescing the tribes into a kingdom uniting Upper or southern Egypt and the Delta or Lower Egypt. Narmer, or Menes as the Greeks called him, was the first of the divine Pharaohs, founder of the first of thirty-one dynasties. He established his capital at Memphis, near where Africa-oriented Upper Egypt and Western Asia-oriented Lower Egypt met.

During Menes' reign the idea of gold as a reliable standard of value was introduced. Small gold bars were cast, each weighing fourteen grams and stamped with his name. Menes assigned a ratio of 2½ to 1 for silver in relationship to gold. This apparently low valuation of gold is explained by the fact that the Egyptians had no native silver and consequently prized it highly. Kings of the Fourth to Sixth dynasties inaugurated the production of gold rings as currency. They weighed approximately the same as Menes' ingots but had very limited circulation.

One of the oldest maps in the world traces the transport route of a statue through the gold fields in the famous Wadi Hammamat in Egypt's eastern desert. It was drawn on two papyrus sheets in the late second millennium B.C., and shows the roads to the gold mines with hieroglyphs marking wells, trails, mountains, where the gold was dug, and where it was washed. The temporary housing of the government overseers is also marked. The mining operation was so vast that there were two thousand huts built for the mining officials. The slaves received neither housing nor care of any kind. The roads to the mines stretched from the Nile highway in many directions.

The pharaohs, with an increasing appetite for gold, wielded firm control over the royal mines. Gold washed from the Nile in remote times had been less closely supervised because of the nature of placer deposits, but even then a royal tenth was collected when possible. By the end of the fourth millennium gold production and distribution were rigidly controlled.

The gold lay in zones of barren waste. Forced legions of captive men, women, and children were marched to the mines under the whips of government overseers. Sometimes the captives were luckless Nubians who were rounded up and marched long distances to perish in the mines of the Miserable Kush, as the eastern desert was called.

The Kush was a searing zone of desert slopes which could only be reached by trekking painfully over sun-scorched sands and high bleak mountains. The distances were vast but the lure of gold was strong. There was no food, no water, no shade. The soldiers goaded long lines of donkeys and slaves before them. If a child stumbled or fell he was left, his mother driven ahead under the lash. Sometimes as many as half of a slave army perished on its way. Few of the pack animals reached the mines. The Pharaoh Seti in the 14th century B.C. ordered wells drilled along the desert wasteland route. Hole after hole was dry until finally, at Redesieh, water was reached two hundred feet down. To commemorate the improvement of the road to the eastern desert mines, Seti had a temple erected at Redesieh to the mother-goddess Hathor. She was the cow-horned goddess of love and happiness as well as the protectress of the eastern desert. In an inscription Hathor declares, "I have given thee the gold countries." Subsequently the journey to the gold fields was eased somewhat but remained perilous, with whole caravans sometimes becoming hopelessly lost in blinding sand storms.

The tortured creatures who survived to reach the mines were scarcely more fortunate than those who fell on the way. They were condemned to work, naked and without respite, until they died. It was logistically cheaper to work the slaves to death and replace them than to supply food, water, and shelter. One observer wrote that precious water was reserved solely for washing the gold and quenching the fires which were lit to crack the rock matrix in which the gold was found. Thirst-crazed slaves were forbidden even to lick their hands which were damp from washing the ore.

The earliest mines were shallow ditches. To get at the richer veins tunnels were driven into the hillsides. Later inclined shafts were dug. The deepest of these plumbed almost three hundred feet to follow a convoluted vein for fifteen hundred feet. By the fourteenth century B.C. there were many underground mines in Nubia. The remains of at least a hundred mark the ancient workings. At some sites the washing tables and querns or hand mills still stand above galleries which twist and turn for miles under the sands, memorials of an ancient hell.

Before inevitable starvation, thirst, disease, or exposure

claimed the slaves there was always the danger, or perhaps blessing, of being crushed beneath tumbling rock in the narrow galleries lit by the flicker of oil-burning headlamps. In the third century B.C. Theophrastus, the Greek natural scientist, described the manner in which the miners were obliged to work lying on their back or sides in the two-foot-high galleries. Foot by foot they hacked their way along the vein face, lengthening the galleries, some of which were four miles long. Sometimes fires were set and then doused with water to crack the quartz.

Deep in the darkness there was scant air. The fires further depleted the oxygen so that miners died of suffocation or from breathing arsenic fumes released from rock by the fires. The German Georg Bauer, known as Agricola, in his famous sixteenth century A.D. treatise on metallurgy, described what happened to those who inhaled arsenical oxide. The lucky ones "swelled at once and lost all movement and feeling and died without pain." The poison lingered on the floor and walls of the galleries. Hands and feet that came in contact with it puffed up like inflated pig bladders. It rotted skin and blinded eyes. Skin erupted in hideous and excruciating ulcers. Ironically, in Roman times, gold was an ingredient in the salve prescribed for such sores. Mining changed very little through the millennia, and the conditions described by visitors to the Egyptian mines held true for gold diggings in much of the world until modern times.

It is worth quoting, in detail, an account of how the gold of the pharaohs was produced. Diodorus, the Sicilian-born-Greek historian, visited Egypt fifty years before the birth of Christ. He wrote of the mines, incorporating a second-century description by Agatharchides of Cnidus, tutor to one of the Alexandrian Ptolemies who had been to the mines:

> On the confines of Egypt and Ethiopia, is a place which has many great gold mines, where the gold is got together with much suffering and expense. . . . The kings of Egypt collect together and consign to the gold mines those who have been condemned for crime and who have been made captive in war . . . sometimes only themselves but sometimes likewise their families. Those who have been consigned to the mines being

many in number and all bound with fetters, toil at their tasks continuously both by day and all night long getting no rest and jealously kept from all escape. For their guards are foreign soldiers, all speaking different languages so the workers are unable either by speech or friendly entreaty to corrupt those who watch them.

The hardest of the earth which contains the gold they burn with a great deal of fire and make soft and work it with their hands; but the soft rock and that which can easily yield to stone and chisels or iron is broken down by thousands of unfortunate souls. A man who is expert in distinguishing the stone supervises the whole process and gives instruction to the laborers. . . . Those who are especially strong cut the glittering rock with iron pick-axes, not by bringing skill to bear on their tasks but by sheer brute force, and they hew out galleries, not following a straight line but according to the vein of the glittering rock. Living in darkness because of the bends and twists in the galleries, they carry lamps fitted on their foreheads. They contort their bodies this way and that to match the behavior of the rock. What they hew out they throw down on the floor—all this without pause and under the severe lash of the overseer. The boys who have not yet reached manhood go in through the shafts to the rock galleries and laboriously pick up what is hewn down, piece by piece and carry it to the head of the shaft into the light. Men who are more than thirty years old take a fixed weight of the quarried rock and pound it in stone mortars with iron pestles until it is reduced to pieces the size of a vetch.

The women and older men then take these. They have a number of mills in a row and throw the stone on them, standing beside them at the handle in twos and threes, and grinding their fixed weight of stone until it is as fine as wheat flour. . . . There is absolutely no consideration nor relaxation for sick or maimed, for aged men or weak women; all are forced to labor at their tasks until they die, worn out by misery, amid their toil.

A modern analysis of the tailings at one of the Red Sea reef sites worked in ancient times indicated that 1 million tons of ore were removed from that particular mine. It has been calculated that at least 1½ million pounds of gold in toto came from the mines, which were still being worked when Julius Caesar went to Egypt.

When the ore had been reduced to a powder, laborers rubbed it on wide, slightly tilted boards while pouring water on it. This process was repeated a number of times using sponges to aid in removal of the pulverized rock until only the heavier gold dust remained.

The gold dust was weighed and refined in a process called cupellation. The impure gold dust was put into clay vessels called cupels with barley bran, lead, coarse salt in chunks, and sometimes a bit of tin. The salt served as a fluxing agent to fuse the fine grains of gold together. The tin mixed with the gold, hardening it. The bran was a reducing agent which helped remove those impurities which would oxidize, and the lead united with those which wouldn't burn to form a slag.

The cupels were smeared with a coating of mud and baked for five days. When they cooled and were opened, the earthenware body had absorbed the impurities, and a bright button of gold remained. These were melted and cast in the form of rings about five inches in diameter, laden on donkeys, and transported to the capital.

There, the rings were carefully weighed on balance scales, and their value recorded. Once again the gold was melted down and poured into bar molds of several standard sizes. The ingots were stored in the royal treasury and doled out to goldsmiths in palace and temple workshops.

The superintending officials of the Pharaoh often found their fortunes in the gold mines. Men who enriched the King enjoyed particular royal favor. The walls of a tomb belonging to a certain Ameni, who was a superintendent of the official "Expeditions to the Mines" about 200 B.C., are inscribed, "I went to get gold for his Majesty, may he live forever. I went with a company of 400 men of the pick of my soldiers who, by good fortune, arrived without loss of any of their number. I brought the gold I was ordered to bring and the King's son honored me."

The Egyptians consumed an estimated four fifths of the gold production of the ancient world. The Pharaoh was "the good God," physical offspring of the sun-god Re or Ra and the link between the people and the gods. His well-being was essential to the prosperity of Egypt.

The person of the Pharaoh was sacrosanct, his daily routine prescribed by golden ritual. Gold was considered the body of the sun-god, and as the son of Amon-re the Pharaoh was surrounded by the sun's metal. He sat on a golden throne, his arms and bare chest glittering with gold. From head to toe he was covered with jeweled gold. Utensils and accessories were of beaten gold; sedan chairs and ceremonial ships were covered with sheet gold and embellished with jeweled fittings.

The alluvial placers of the Nile yielded an estimated 40,000 pounds of gold. Total Egyptian gold production by the mid-second millennium may have been as high as 1,400,000 pounds.

Gold flowed into the royal treasuries in the form of booty and tribute from defeated states. Thutmose III, the great conqueror, was a lover of beautiful things. The Eighteenth Dynasty King received immense spoils from defeated states. He had a scribe list the booty from his Syrian campaign. Among the objects were flat dishes of costly stone and gold, gold-embellished knives, "a staff of carob wood wrought with gold and all costly stones in the fashion of a scepter, belonging to that foe, the head of which was inlaid with lapis and much clothing of that foe." Thutmose was so impressed by the Levantine craftsmen that he imported goldsmiths to teach the Egyptians. He dedicated his nonbellicose pursuits to rebuilding and adorning temples, and himself designed some of the magnificent gold vessels for the temple of Amon at Thebes.

Some gold came to Egypt from far-distant lands in Africa, Arabia, and the Mediterranean. Thanks to the desire of a woman the famous Egyptologist James Henry Breasted admiringly called "the first great lady of the world" to tell her story, we know of the celebrated expedition to the gold land of Punt. Hatshepsut was the daughter of the empire builder Thutmose I, who was the first pharaoh to be buried in the Valley of the Tombs of the Kings at Thebes. Two women had previously reigned briefly, despite the law of the land which forbade a woman to be pharaoh. But the brilliant, strong-willed Hatshepsut was the first to proclaim herself divine and wear the double crown of sovereignty over Upper and Lower Egypt. She ruled first as regent for Thutmose III, her nephew and stepson. By 1500 B.C. she had seized power and reigned for the next twenty years, cultivating the arts of peace, expanding trade, and building monuments.

Hatshepsut flaunted all the traditional pharaonic trappings including a false ceremonial beard and male attire. She had more than eighty titles, proclaiming her, among other things, Son of the Sun, Mistress of the World, King of the North and South, Giver of the Years, Golden Horus. A woman of such dimensions needed a particularly splended monument to commemorate her life and deeds. Hatshepsut assured her perpetual fame with the completion of a magnificent mortuary temple at Deir al-Bahri, cleverly designed as a graceful complex of terraced, colonnaded shrines which appear to be carved out of the towering rosy cliffs behind. More than 190 statues and biographical reliefs at the temple tell her story. Some of the scenes were calculated to strengthen her tenuous claim to the throne. Thus both her divine birth and her father Thutmose are represented with accompanying inscriptions. Other reliefs commemorate her accomplishments. One series depicts the transport of two obelisks from Aswan to Karnak by water and another the trading expedition to Punt, the land of incense and gold south of the Red Sea.

The Queen fulfilled the prophecy made at her birth that she should be powerful and her reign magnificent. The Eighteenth Dynasty brought Egypt to a brilliant zenith. Hatshepsut conceived grand projects and executed them on a scale that was monumental even by Egyptian standards. As the world's richest and most powerful woman she wanted to make a splendid offering to the chief god of Thebes, Amon Re. She envisioned two gold pillars towering heavenward, flashing over the high walls of the Karnak complex, which was larger in area than the Vatican. Her confidant and chancellor Senmut prevailed upon his mistress to restrain her extravagance. Instead of pillars cast in pure gold, granite obelisks were prepared. The shafts, weighing seven hundred tons apiece, were transported from Aswan to Karnak on a huge gilded barge pulled by thirty boats rowed by nine hundred oarsmen. Hatshepsut planned to sheathe them with electrum. She loved the pale gold and often gilded her face with electrum dust. But the royal treasurer, the Overseer of Gold and Silver, protested. Finally, with duly recorded apology to the god, she ordered that only the peaks of the engraved granite shafts be gilded. Even that required a lavish amount of gold.

The two gold-tipped obelisks rose one hundred feet, flashing in the sun. In her dedication speech Hatshepsut proudly declared that their glow could be seen "on both sides of the river. . . . Their height pierces to heaven. . . . Their rays flood the Two Lands when the sun rises between them. . . . Never was done the like since the beginning."

Reliefs on the tomb of Thuty the treasurer depict him dipping into the royal coffers to present his Queen with twelve bushels of gold for the monuments. She claimed to have done some of the measuring herself. "Hear ye!" she had her scribe record, "I gave for them the finest of electrum which I had measured by the hecket like sacks [of grain]." Her words can still be seen today on the ruined fragments of one of the obelisks which, like many of her other monuments, was defaced and destroyed in a campaign to obliterate all trace of her reign. "You who after long years shall see these monuments," she stated, "will say 'We do not know how they can have made whole mountains of gold.'"

The gold was stripped ages ago. Parts of the fallen obelisk still lie at Karnak; other pieces were carted away for use as millstones turned by camels and donkeys along the timeless river. The other obelisk still stands, the tallest ancient monument in Egypt, a memorial to one of antiquity's most exceptional figures.

Hatshepsut's greatest achievement was reopening, maintaining, and expanding Egyptian trade, which had been strangled during the centuries of domination by the Hyksos, Asian invaders who ruled from about 1720 to about 1567 B.C. From about 2000 onward Egypt mounted one exploratory expedition after another to seek new sources of gold, for the eastern desert yielded less and less. She needed gold, lots of it. During her time, perhaps because of interruption during the Hyksos' occupation, trade, which had once flourished between Palestine, Syria, and even the distant island of Crete, was at a low ebb.

In addition to gold the Queen needed incense, as costly as

gold and as essential, staggering amounts were used in worship, for mummification, and as medicine. By her own account she needed treasure for the completion and lavish appointment of the temple at Deir al-Bahri. The temple was to be her resting place and her father's. The Queen was aghast at continuous desecration of the tombs in the Valley of the Kings at Luxor.

The Queen knew where to look for both gold and incense—Arabia and Africa. The sere Hadramawt Wilderness, which the Romans later called Arabia Felix for its great wealth, had supplied Egypt with incense resins and myrrh from earliest times. The desert incense trees were the preserve of aristocratic families who gathered the precious substance with religious ritual. For thousands of years incense and luxuries from Asia and India received in trade for Arabian incense were exported to Egypt.

Three quarters of a millennium before Hatshepsut the first Egyptian voyage ventured to an even more distant land than Arabia. An Egyptian expedition sent to find an alternative source of Arabian resins, incenses, and aromatic oils which ate up so much of the Egyptian gold supply each year returned from the mysterious land of Punt south of the Red Sea about 2600 with a rich cargo of myrrh and rumors of gold.

A wealthy helmsman named Knemhotep died at a town near the Nile's first cataract about 2300 B.C. His tomb inscriptions indicate the source of his riches. Hieroglyphics explain that with a captain, Khui, he made eleven trading voyages to Punt, bringing back not only incense but gold, ivory, exotic animals, and woods such as ebony, which were particularly prized in treeless Egypt.

The geographical location of Punt has since been lost. It may have been the coast of what is today Somalia or even part of Arabia, but more likely it was on the southeast coast of Africa. In the course of combing the coast of East Africa Egyptian prospectors early in the Fifth Dynasty (circa 2400 B.C.) had seen Africans at the mouth of the Zambezi panning for placer gold. This was not far from the inland area of Mashonaland, where gold had been mined from earliest history. The gold and incense they brought back spurred regular expeditions during the Fifth and Sixth dynasties. A document called the Harris Papyrus, dating from the reign of Ramses III, tells how the Pharaoh about 1180 B.C. established an Egyptian gold-mining colony in a far-off land to the south. This was perhaps the zone around the mouth of the Zambezi, with which the enigmatic fifteenth-century A.D. site of Zimbabwe in Rhodesia is associated. Some scholars contend the East African gold-bearing area is the site of the biblical Ophir, which enriched Semitic kings.

In 1493 B.C. Hatshepsut commissioned a large expedition to seek a source of gold and incense to sail to Punt. She was ever aware that she ruled only by force of personality and cleverness. Her stepson bitterly resented her usurpation of power and waited for one moment of weakness. Hatshepsut conceived of the Punt expedition as a way to reinforce her authority and forge a link with the great pharaohs of earlier dynasties who had established trading relations with the fabled country.

Five great galleys each propelled by thirty rowers sailed under the command of Senmut. The progress of the royal fleet is realistically depicted on the temple walls in graceful, lively bas-reliefs supplemented by lengthy inscriptions. The Egyptian ships emerged from the Gulf of Suez and pushed down the eastern coast of the Red Sea aided by the monsoon winds. The glowing cliffs which give the sea its name are shown rising above the shore.

The explorers arrived in Punt and were greeted by the people. Among them was a princess with the classic protruding derrière of a Hottentot beauty.

Hatshepsut had sent gifts to the people of Punt: a dagger, an ax, tools, leg bangles, bracelets, and necklaces probably of glass, which was new in the Eighteenth Dynasty and widely used for jewelry. The Puntite chiefs are shown receiving beer, vegetables, and wine, "all good things of Egypt, which the queen has commanded." These were consumed at an official feast presided over by an enormous statue of Hatshepsut. Seven of the chiefs are shown paying homage to the Queen's replica. The Egyptians would not have sent gold to a country reputedly overflowing with it.

The Egyptians received gifts far greater in value then those they had given. Porters are depicted bearing load after load of exotic goods to the ships. As they were stowed the galleys rode perceptibly lower in the water. "The ships were laden very heavily," dictated the Queen, "with the costly marvels of the Land of

Punt; all goodly fragrant woods of God's land, with fresh myrrh trees, with quantities of ebony and ivory, with green gold of Amu, sweet smelling resin, ahem incense, holy resin, eye-cosmetic, with apes, monkeys, greyhounds, furthermore skins of the southern leopard and natives of the country with their children. Never was brought the like of this for any god."

Two years after it had set out the royal fleet dropped sail at Kosseir. The Queen was obviously pleased with the exotic treasures. Thirty-one myrrh saplings potted in baskets were a special delight to her. The gold arrived in the form of dust, nuggets, and gold rings such as those shown worn up to the thigh by one of the nobles of Punt.

The spirited bas-reliefs show the royal treasurer presiding over the accounts as the gold is weighed and divided. The omnipresent priests of Amon-re wait their share. With a gold scoop "her majesty acting with her two hands" assisted in the division. Four men scoop gold dust and nuggets from treasure chests as the Queen and her treasurer weigh and record it. Anointed with fragrant oil of myrrh, "she exhaled the odors of the divine dew, her fragrance reached as far as Punt, it mingled with the odors of Punt, her skin was like kneaded gold, and her face shone like stars in a ceremonial hall. . . . Thirty-five hundred years later, the story of Hatshepsut's glorious achievement lives on. Unfortunately none of the dazzling gold ornaments she confessed to loving survived the moltings of the ages.

There were eras when native production was augmented by streams of golden tribute poured into Egypt financing splendid works and furnishing the raw material for glorious artistic achievements. During the reign of the great temple builder Amenhotep III (1417–1379 B.C.) Luxor was built and vast additions made at Karnak. Temples were erected and equipped in Nubia and Thebes. Amenhotep exchanged rich gifts with the rulers of Assyria, Mitanni, Babylon, the King of the Hittites, and even the ruler of Cyprus.

During the Old Kingdom almost all gold had come from the eastern desert. After 2000 B.C. the rulers of the Twelfth Dynasty pushed Egypt's frontiers two hundred miles farther south into Nubia, beyond the Second Cataract, and began to exploit the gold deposits there. The incredible golden fame of Egypt spread far beyond her frontiers. Tushratta, King of Mitanni, the land between the empires of Egypt and the Hittites, whose sister married a pharaoh, wrote his brother-in-law, "Send me much gold, more gold, for in thy land gold is as common as dust."

The gold-hungry rulers of foreign lands envied Egypt's tons of gold. A king of Babylon who had requested gold from a pharaoh was bitter when he received a mere two pounds. "When my fathers and thy fathers established friendly relations they exchanged rich presents," he grumbled, "never refusing each other, the one to the other, whatever beautiful thing they desired. Now my brother has sent me as a gift but two minas. If now gold is abundant with thee, send me as much as thy fathers did, but if it is scarce, send me at least . . . half as much."

After the end of the Old Kingdom, during which the Pharaoh was the focal point of every activity, governmental organization became increasingly complex. The Pharaoh was still regarded as a superhuman ruler, but increasingly authority was delegated to a proliferating group of administrators. Able bureaucrats ran the vast network of civil, military, and temple administrations. The provincial governors or nomarchs gained in stature and power, sometimes ruling as if they were princes.

It was the priests, however, who managed to garner power and gold until by the Eighteenth Dynasty they were the wealthiest and most influential men in Egypt, a potent force the Pharaoh couldn't ignore. The priests were exempt from taxes, and their temples received a share of foreign gold and treasure from every military victory.

The priesthood was normally hereditary. Small temples might have fifty priestly officials, but the large national temples each had many thousands of powerful white-clad priests. Toward the end of the New Kingdom the lands of the Temple of Amon amounted to one twelfth of Egypt's arable land, one of the largest estates in the ancient world.

During the Old Kingdom a noble's heirs were generally responsible for his funeral preparations. Later a man prepared for eternity during his lifetime, setting aside a portion of his estate for a tomb and perpetual funerary rites after his entombment. But these endowments were often looted by the very mortuary priests to whom they had been entrusted. Tombs were abandoned and sacked.

A great deal of the colossal amount of gold consumed by the ancient Egyptians went into the tombs of some ninety pharaohs and countless princes and nobles who had royal permission to prepare tombs. As soon as a pharaoh ascended the throne he chose a site for his tomb and work was begun. Wealthy men spent years preparing their eternal homes. The deceased was believed to continue his earthly life within the tomb. Thus he needed to stock his tomb with every kind of supply. Elaborate tomb equipment, its richness depending on the occupant's possibilities, were entombed with him. Before the Second Dynasty slaves were sacrificed to serve their lord in the afterlife. Later, figurines over which magical life-creating spells could be recited were put in tombs. Statuettes of servants and soldiers were later augmented or substituted by brightly colored paintings.

None of the guardians, modeled or painted, could prevent the looting which was a natural corollary of furnishing the dead with so much gold. Still men commissioned goldworks for their tombs.

Tomb robbing was a recognized profession, generally hereditary and often practiced by the very workmen who had labored on the construction of the tombs. The craftsmen's village of Deir al-Medinah specialized in fine workmanship during the day and first-class pillaging by night. Tomb robbers were not content with easily accessible treasures but tore off the hundreds of feet of linen bandages from mummies, ripping off arms, fingers, and legs to get the gold and jeweled charms placed in the wrappings.

Amenpnufer, a stonemason, made a confession recorded in a papyrus of the Twelfth Dynasty (2000–1700 B.C.) He describes how he and his friends used their copper tools to break into the pyramid of Sekhemra Shedtaui. They stripped the Pharaoh and his consort of their gold, tore the gold sheathing from the coffins, and divided the loot. Amenpnufer was arrested and imprisoned in the mayor's office. However, following a pattern that was to be repeated ad infinitum for the next 3,500 years, he bribed his way out and returned to a life of crime.

Architects devised ingenious methods to foil break-ins, but the tombs which remained unscathed were rare indeed. By the beginning of the Twenty-first Dynasty, ca. 1050 B.C., almost every royal tomb in the valley at Luxor had been disturbed.

The gold looted from tombs found a ready market. The metal was often melted down and divided. Gold was officially a royal monopoly. However, illicit tomb gold was available to whoever could barter for it. Gold was not regular currency but was used commercially as a unit of value weighed against goods and services. Some looted gold found its way through trade to foreign lands.

When times were hard, gold from the tombs was bartered for land, grain, or slaves. The men who worked on the necropoli were not peasants. They had no crops to sustain them in lean times and went hungry when their pay was short. Government officials could sometimes be persuaded to look the other way as tombs were broken into by desperate men.

The latter part of the New Kingdom was marked by a period of increasing poverty and lawlessness. A royal inquest was held in the Twentieth Dynasty to probe the proliferating thefts from the tombs and sanctuaries on the Nile's west bank at Thebes. A confession of one of the robbers is preserved in the Abbott Papyrus. "We opened their sarcophagi and their coffins in which they were. We found the august mummy of the king with his divine axe beside him, and many amulets and ornaments of gold about his neck. His head was overlaid with gold, and the august body of the king was wholly covered with gold, his coffins were burnished with gold and silver, within and without and inlaid with all kinds of stones." The witness describes how he and his associates stripped all treasures from the King and Queen's tomb and then set fire to their coffins.

Accused thieves were tortured before the court if they had not immediately confessed. If after torture they confessed but not to the expected degree, they were tortured further. There is no record of what happened to the confessed robbers in the verbatim records of the examinations. However, at the beginning of a trial the accused swore to tell the truth on pain of banishment to Nubia—and the desert gold mines.

In spite of the royal commission's efforts the dead were not safe in the monumental pyramids. Finally, around 1050 B.C., all the royal mummies at Luxor were relieved of their gold furnishings, put in plain wood coffins, and transported first to a secret burial near Hatshepsut's temple at Deir al-Bahri and then to tombs in the hidden Valley of the Kings at Thebes. Even in that valley, to which access was restricted, the royal dead could not rest. Gangs of robbers, often fighting pitched battles with armed guardian-priests, ferreted out the concealed chambers carved into the limestone cliffs.

Long after the dynastic Egyptians had disappeared Napoleon's conquest of the mysterious and romantic country sparked a craze for Egyptian antiques that swept Europe. Tomb robbing had a renaissance. Not only the Egyptian descendants of pharaonic thieves raped Egypt's ancient heritage but also foreigners, some professing to be archaeologists. "With every step I took I crushed a mummy in some part or other," wrote an unconcerned Italian treasure hunter who smashed his way into tombs with the aid of a battering ram.

In the course of the nineteenth century reputable archaeologists with scholarly intent, under French and British leadership, undertook disciplined excavations in Egypt. All too often they would spend months painstakingly preparing to enter a tomb or chamber only to find that they had been beaten to it centuries before. Sometimes the archaeologists chanced upon a tomb containing artifacts. What frequently happened in such a case was that during the night local thieves, who had been shadowing their steps, would recklessly rip into the record of the past, hauling away mummies, statues, furniture, papyri— anything that greedy antique merchants would buy for European clients.

The Cairo Museum has splendid artifacts from the mass graves at Deir al-Bahri. For once the thieves led the scientists to the treasure. In the second half of the nineteenth century archaeologists fruitlessly sought traces of the treasures long missing from the graves but could find none. When a few artifacts of the period were clandestinely offered for sale in Luxor, an Egyptologist from the museum began to be suspicious. He moved into a Luxor hotel and spread the word that he would pay handsomely in gold coins for antiquities. Before long he was brought artifacts that were obviously from the Deir al-Bahri burials.

It turned out they had been discovered by men from a nearby

village whose ancestors had been tomb robbers for centuries. The villagers, who also were experts at counterfeiting antiquities, treated the treasure as a communal bank, taking out only as much as they needed and keeping the rest in reserve. Through the museum official's detective work the state was able to claim the cache.

In the Valley of the Kings more than twenty-seven Pharaohs were entombed. One, an unimportant young king, was miraculously overlooked by 3,200 years of looters. In spite of his political insignificance, Tutankhamen is perhaps the best known of all the Pharaohs because of his incredible gold-filled tomb.

Its discovery by British archaeologists Howard Carter and Lord Carnarvon is one of the most dramatic chapters in the annals of archaeology. The contents of the tomb have provided the world with the largest single collection of Egyptian goldwork. The furniture, implements, weapons, and toys in Tutankhamen's tomb are the fullest material evidence of the quality of ancient Egyptian existence, breathing life into a testament in stone and papyrus.

Over two thousand articles were buried with the nineteen-year-old King. It took Carter over eight years to catalogue the multitude of grave goods which included ceremonial regalia, domestic articles, and even linen underclothing. The works in gold included rings, collars, and pectorals of absolute technical perfection and great beauty. Some were of cloisonné work, inlaid with polychromed glass. One pectoral was formed of over 170 inlaid gold plaques. There were countless bracelets, bangles, rings, circlets, all of gold and many set with gems.

There were golden statuettes of the King performing rituals, sacred animal heads in solid gold, scale models of the gilded royal ships and canoes some complete with a miniature golden throne set on deck. Familiar and favored possessions were included to comfort the young Pharaoh. A collection of mechanical toys and a simple slingshot with pebbles were found amid all the golden paraphernalia, a touch which makes the Son of the Sun seem far more human than all the ostentatious treasures.

Not very much is known of Tutankhamen, who died about 1350 B.C. He succeeded the heretic Pharaoh Ikhnaton, husband of the beautiful Nefertiti. Ikhnaton introduced the first monotheistic religion in history. He was a religious fanatic who attempted to replace the crowded pantheon of Egyptian religion with the worship of a single deity, Aton, a form of the ancient sun-god. His reforms were unpopular with the many priests whose treasures were confiscated. Worship of the sun weakened at his death. Tutankhamen returned to the more orthodox worship but evidently didn't abandon the sun cult altogether. Perhaps because the taint of heresy clung to his short reign, later, more rabidly orthodox rulers attempted to expunge his name from all records. Until the twentieth century Tutankhamen was forgotten.

Carter and Carnarvon believed, in the face of almost universal skepticism, that they could find an unrifled tomb. For six tedious and disappointing years they directed Egyptian laborers who cleared tons and tons of rubble and dug trench after trench in the valley. They based their faith on a few shreds of evidence including a faïence cup bearing Tutankhamen's name. The cup and gold foil fragments bearing the King's figure and that of his Queen had been found earlier by an American archaeologist, Theodore Davis.

The Britishers found nothing and in November of 1922 were about to admit defeat when the reward came. Carnarvon was in England, and Carter's laborers were digging through sand drifts and fallen rock at the base of a bluff. They came upon an opening. Carter found a passageway barred by rubble and stone. The men worked their way through the dark, twisting, and very narrow corridor. A sealed barrier confronted Carter. As it was broken through he knew he was on the verge of a discovery but had no idea of its magnitude. He recalled, "Slowly, desperately slowly, it seemed to us as we watched, the remains of the doorway were removed, until at last we had the whole door clear before us. The decisive moment had arrived. With trembling hands I made a tiny breach in the upper left hand corner. Darkness and blank space as far as an iron testing rod could reach, showing that whatever lay beyond was empty. Widening the hole a little, I inserted a candle, and peered in. At first I could see nothing, the hot air escaping from the chamber causing the candle to flicker. But presently, as my eyes grew accustomed to the lights, details of the room within emerged slowly from the mist: strange animals, statues and gold—everywhere the glint of gold."

In one of the smallest of tombs Howard Carter had found a resplendent treasure unparalleled in the history of archaeology. At first he thought he had found an inviolate tomb. But he discovered that seals from various reigns following Tutankhamen's death had been applied to the outer door, the last in the Twentieth Dynasty. Evidently thieves broke in soon after the entombment and were stripping a small annex when guards surprised them. Carter found their footprints in the three-thousand-year-old dust. The necropolis guards had made no attempt to reorder the chamber's contents. Elaborate gilded chairs, ivory gaming boards, gloves, cups, weapons, and funerary models lay jumbled about in a state of confusion.

Tutankhamen's tomb was unusually small, more the size of a noble's tomb than a king's. The chamber barely able to contain the huge nest of golden shrines which hid the three coffins. Many scholars think the boy-king was buried in haste, perhaps in a tomb prepared for the powerful courtier-priest Ay, who ruled briefly after he forcibly married Ankhesenamun, Tutankhamen's widow. This view is supported by the volume of funerary objects jammed into the small chambers with apparent disregard for order.

In the antechamber Carter's flashlight revealed three large golden couches with elongated bodies and strange heads of sacred mythological beasts. One had a rhinoceros-headed lion at one end and a cow in panther skins at the other. Against the far wall were two life-size carved sentinels clad in gold skirts, gold headdresses, and gold sandals. Gold amulets, jewelry, and charms, many set with semiprecious stones, lay everywhere. There was an inlaid gold throne, chairs, tables, and storage chests covered with gold, all beautifully executed. And there was food and drink for the young man-god who had left the bright world of the Nile but lived on.

The awesome amount of royal gold means little in itself. Tutankhamen was a minor figure, and his tomb, although packed with gold, certainly contained far less than those of more powerful pharaohs. What is astonishing is the superb craftsmanship.

The gold was worked in a profusion of styles and techniques, with an unfailing sense of proportion and design.

Tutankhamen's marvelous throne is an example of Egyptian goldwork at its most beautiful. The entire throne is covered with gold and encrusted with semiprecious stones, brilliant blue faïence, and colored glass. The effect is incredibly rich. Great winged serpents wearing crowns form the arms. The legs are those of a lion; the two in front support golden lion's heads. But it is the back panel which is most beautiful and most unusual. Egyptian art was ruled by severe convention. Through the centuries artists limited themselves to portraying the human figure in certain stereotyped poses in time-honored proportions. Egyptians were depicted in paintings and bas-reliefs in profile. Only slaves, foreigners, and peasants were exempt from such formalized representation.

Yet the sculptors and goldsmiths at Ikhnaton's court enjoyed a breath of freedom, from convention. For the first time royal personages were shown in informal poses. Ikhnaton's short-lived religious revolution stimulated an impulse toward freedom in aesthetic expression which lasted a bit longer and carried over to Tutankhamen's court. Some of his tomb furnishings reflect the new naturalism. A gifted goldsmith worked a scene of incredible charm on the twenty-inch-square sheet of gold which forms his throne's back panel. The colorful composition is in gold and silver, inlaid with calcite, carnelian, faïence, and colored glass. Tutankhamen is shown in profile sitting comfortably with one arm resting easily on the back of his throne. He gazes with obvious affection at his lovely Queen, whose slender curving form is delicately accentuated. She tenderly smooths scented unguent on his shoulder from a small pot held in her other hand. The two figures are brilliantly portrayed; their flesh, dress, ornaments, high wigs, and headdresses are elaborated in richly hued colors. Their robes fall in liquid gold and silver pleats. Such an intimate and naturalistic scene worked in glowing precious metals, glass, and stones is a remarkable work of art for any age and was all the more so in ancient Egypt.

One wall of the chamber which contained the throne had a sealed door of thick stone flanked by two more golden guards. The archaeologists admirably curbed their mounting curiosity about what lay beyond as they worked with scientific deliberation on what they had already discovered. The door was not opened until February of 1923. Stone after stone was removed to reveal one wall of a golden shrine with inlaid panels of blue glaze and magic symbols ensuring strength and safety. The shrine measured seventeen feet long by eleven feet wide and nine feet high.

A gold cornice representing the sacred royal cobras ran around the top. Inside was what Carter called "the most beautiful monument that I have ever seen." It was made up of a second shrine, a third, and a fourth, each of decreasing size and sheathed in heavy gold plate. In the interstices were myriad funerary objects of a richness and ostentation characteristic of the period.

The fourth shrine had within it a slab of rose granite which weighed 1¼ tons. Two years after the tomb had been discovered Carter rigged the monolith with a block and tackle. Sadly, Lord Carnarvon, his partner and sponsor, had died of pneumonia and missed the most dramatic moment of all. The lid of the sarcophagus was slowly raised as a select group of international Egyptologists and Egyptian officials crowded into the tomb. The slab was removed to reveal nothing but white linen shrouds. Sighs of disappointment from the assembly changed to expressions of astonishment as Carter pulled back the ancient cloth and twentieth-century eyes looked on the seven-foot-long gold effigy of the boy-king whose wife had ministered to him, whose people had worshiped him, and who had lain 3,274 years in a darkness which had spent the light of all his gold.

The golden youth was represented in the round, his arms across his breast, his full mouth vulnerable, his handsome nose finely modeled. The eyes were of argonite and obsidian, the lids and brows of lapis lazuli inlaid in the sensitively sculpted gold. The coffin rested on a lion-shaped bier. Two golden goddesses set with gems kept watch over the effigy. The King's face and hands were wrought in solid gold of a slightly different color than that of the gold-plated body, enhancing the quality of naturalism. A small wreath of perfectly preserved flowers which still retained their color eloquently evoked his Queen's last farewell.

Work on the tomb excavation proceeded in fits and starts. Bureaucratic tangles, court cases, and disagreements within the group sometimes brought the project to a halt. It was 1925 before Carter began work on the second gold-sheathed coffin which had been found within the golden effigy. It was almost seven feet long. The wooden cover was carved in relief and represented the King as the god Osiris. The sheet gold covering it was paved with glass carved to look like turquoise, lapiz lazuli, and red jasper. Yet a third coffin lay snugly inside the second, covered as the others had been with linen shrouds.

The innermost coffin was completely wrought of beaten gold two and a half to three millimeters thick. It was almost six feet two inches long and terribly heavy. Eight men could barely lift it. Within lay the mummified Tutankhamen, a portrait mask and hands of beaten gold resting on the bandaged body. The mask was a magnificent object covering his entire head, upper chest, and shoulders. On his feet were gold sandals, the surface etched to resemble wickerwork. His fingers and toes were sheathed in gold. Gold bracelets encircled his forearms.

The mummy itself was badly deteriorated. An excess of funerary oils which had been poured over the body formed a black pitchlike substance which fastened the mask to the bandages. Tucked into the hundreds of feet of linen bands wrapped around the body were personal ornaments and magical charms—golden amulets to guide the mummy through the nether world and guard him from evil spirits. From the neck to the stomach alone there were thirty-five objects in seventeen groups, nestled in thirteen layers of linen. These included a large collar in chased gold. In all there were one hundred forty-three gold charms and pieces of jewelry. A splendidly burnished gold diadem encircled Tutankhamen's head. Gold bands over his forehead held a linen headdress, and underneath it was a linen skullcap embroidered with a delicate design of minuscule gold and faïence beads.

Examination of the Pharaoh's features showed that the goldsmiths who had modeled the death mask and the coffins had been faithful to his likeness. Embalmers had replaced the King's heart before wrapping him in linen bands. His other vital organs including the brain, which had been removed by inserting forceps through the nostrils, were housed in miniature gold coffins.

The world was awed by the magnitude of Carter's discovery, by the sheer amount of the gold immobilized in Tutankhamen's tomb. The variety, beauty, and magnificence of the artifacts reflected the sophisticated world of a people who administered a far-flung empire and developed a culture which produced magnificent works of art and the technology and social organization to carry out remarkable projects.

The first pyramid was erected about 2800 B.C. for King Zoser, fourteen centuries before Tutankhamen. Fourteen centuries after Tutankhamen, the ancient golden civilization had all but died and the language of the Pharaohs had been forgotten. Gold had enriched Egypt for thousands of years. Gold from the Egyptian earth and water, the mines of conquered territories, and gold in tribute and trade had fueled Egyptian supremacy. The final result of all this golden wealth was to tempt Egypt into over-reaching herself. The empire expanded until there was too much territory to defend from nations which were gaining strength that rivaled her own. Gradually at first and then precipitously Egypt lost her prestige and power. The empire fragmented and foundered.

The twentieth-century sensation-loving public was not content with the greatest archaeological and artistic treasure ever found. Following Carter's discovery, rumors of a "Curse of the Pharaohs" sent pleasant shivers down the spines of tabloid readers in a dozen countries. The "Curse" has been done to death in books and articles but continues to fascinate. It has probably made certain segments of the public more aware of ancient Egypt than even the treasures of Tutankhamen.

The first of an alleged three dozen archaeologists, scientists, and scholars to die mysteriously was Lord Carnarvon. He succumbed to a relatively mild case of pneumonia, weakened by high fever induced by a badly infected insect bite. A bizarre sidelight: His beloved fox terrier, who was in England at the time, howled and keeled over dead at the precise moment his master expired in Cairo. One other peculiar note: At the very instant life went out of Carnarvon, the lights went out all over Cairo. No technical explanation for the power failure was ever found.

Carter was mistakenly believed to have found a simple clay

tablet among the artifacts in the antechamber. The hieroglyphics, according to press reports, were decoded to read
"Death will slay with his wings whoever disturbs the peace of
the Pharaoh." The curse was unusual, for the Egyptians, unlike
other Eastern people, such as Semitic cultures, used them spar-
ingly. Only the Pharaoh might utter a curse.

The British archaeologists were not in the least put off by the
warning message but feared their superstitious laborers might
be. Thus, according to the "Curse" literature, no written mention
was made of the tablet, and it somehow disappeared from the inventory; it was never even photographed.

A second curse was supposedly inscribed on the back of a
statue in the tomb's main chamber. Through the years strange
circumstances surrounded the deaths of those who disturbed the
sleep of ancient Egypt's kings and queens. Newspapers, movie
makers, and sensation-seeking writers had a field day. Explana-
tions for the mysterious deaths have been legion and include
poisons with undiminished potency which had been left in the
tomb and breathed in by modern men. Radioactive materials and
ultraradiant cosmic energy harnessed by the ancients have been
credited with long-range revenge by some "Curse" buffs.

In 1972 the "Curse" was reportedly still operating. Tutankhamen's gorgeous mummy mask was removed from its case
in the Cairo Museum and packed with other gold from the tomb
to be flown to London. Two RAF bombers carried the treasures,
insured at about $55 million, to England for a display commemo-
rating the fiftieth anniversary of Carter's discovery. The day the
golden pieces were taken from the museum, Gamal Mehrez,
director-general of the Museum's Antiquities Department, collapsed and died—a fifty-two-year-old man with no previous record of ill health and "confessed believer in the 'Pharaoh's
Curse.'" However, the recent traveling display to Tutankhamen's
gold which enthralled millions of museum goers in the United
States seems not to have produced any sign of revenge from beyond the grave.

The masses of Egyptian peasants and laborers today have
never heard of the curse or even of Tutankhamen, but they, like
their ancestors, covet the precious yellow metal of the sun. Although gold was a royal monopoly in ancient times, by about

1300 B.C. even commoners often had a few ounces hidden away, a nest egg called *sankh,* meaning "to cause to live."

In Cairo's gold market the tradition of holding a bit of gold is carried on. The gold merchant sits by his scales and displays gold bangles, lockets, amulets, and rings. They are crudely fashioned, a poor shadow of the superb artistry of dynastic Egypt. But this is gold for everyone, not the exclusive property of the noble rich. In Egypt as in so many other parts of the world there remains a strong peasant feeling for something that will not shrink with inflation, that cannot be traced or taxed, and that can be either tucked away in a safe, dark place or proudly displayed on a wife or daughter. The people of the Nile carry on today an affair with the precious metal that has lasted for more than six thousand years.

CHAPTER FOUR *Mesopotamian Gold*

Among the foreign sovereigns eager for handouts of Egyptian gold was a fourteenth century B.C. king of Babylon. Amenhotep IV answered his request with a present of bullion weighing twenty minas, about twenty-two pounds. Instead of thanks the Pharaoh received two complaints, inscribed on clay tablets. The Babylonian wrote that after his goldsmiths put the bullion in the refining furnace three quarters of it disappeared leaving less than five minas of pure gold. He diplomatically pretended that the gold must have been debased without the Pharaoh's knowledge, but his disappointment was clear.

The King of Babylon badly needed gold to enhance his temporal power and adorn his brilliant and sophisticated court. His gods through their insatiable priests demanded great quantities of the gleaming metal. His people, the world's first city dwellers, craved gold for jewelry, for the famous Mesopotamian embroidered textiles, and for the gold ingots which, along with silver and lead, had begun to replace barley as a medium of exchange in the third millennium. At her marriage a woman was given a "special present" of gold, silver, or lead by her husband which remained her property even if divorced by her spouse.

From its early beginnings Mesopotamian civilization had valued and coveted gold. But in sharp contrast to Egypt, Mesopotamia had no native gold or silver. Nor did the bleak plateau embraced by the Tigris and Euphrates have much copper or lead with which to make tools and weapons. The Sumerians who developed the first true cities some five thousand years ago in what is modern Iraq had very little stone and even less wood.

The sere wind-swept "Land Between the Two Rivers" seems a

most unlikely setting for the world's first civilized society. Yet it was in that river valley, tortured by nature with alternate drought and ravaging flood, that men first burst forth with a series of dazzling inventions and developments. Mesopotamians developed the first practical system of writing, wrote the first epic poetry, compiled the first code of laws, made the earliest astronomical calculations and laid the foundations for mathematics. They were also the first to use the arch and wheeled vehicles.

In the region known as Sumer and later Babylonia, what today lies from Baghdad to the Persian Gulf, the earliest merchant class and systems of international trade evolved. Historical motives have changed little since antiquity. Then, as in modern times, the desire for raw materials motivated territorial expansion and trade. Although Mesopotamia had no gold whatsoever of its own, it became the second greatest focus of gold use in the third millennium.

The civilization of Mesopotamia was born at least five thousand years ago with the cities of Sumer which were the fruit of millennia of cultural development in small settlements dotted over the river valley. The climate was largely hot and dry, save for the reed-covered marshlands of the southern Euphrates. It was the accumulation of silt in gently sloping levees there which first attracted early farmers who came from the north. They were joined by other groups. The resulting ethnic mix produced a people who attained, through co-operative efforts at irrigation, a security of life based on the arts of agriculture and stock raising.

For the first time in history man was able to give full rein to his ingenuity, to plan and dream and join in community effort beyond that necessary for subsistence or defense. A man contributed to communal efforts and was guaranteed certain benefits. The barley, wool, leather, and textiles the Sumerians, Babylonians, and Assyrians produced in abundance were the wellsprings of prosperity and the basis of long-distance trade which brought them coveted gold.

For some twenty-seven centuries, from about 3000 B.C. until the invasion by Alexander the Great, Mesopotamian culture flourished. The earliest farmers ten thousand years ago lived in mud-plastered reed huts and later in mud brick houses of several rooms very like those of Iraqi peasants today. Elaborate palace and temple complexes were also built of mud brick.

Unlike stone, adobe does not endure but crumbles under wind and rain. Over the centuries shifting sands took their toll on the palaces and gilded temples which had once reared heavenward over the plain. "The dwellings of Agade are filled with gold, its bright-shining houses with silver . . . its walls reach skyward like a mountain," exulted a Mesopotamian poet. But only shapeless mounds remained when thirteenth-century travelers returned to Europe with tales of ruined cities buried in the Eastern sands. Mesopotamian civilization was unknown save for numerous Old Testament references to Ur of the Chaldees, home of the patriarch Abraham, to Babylonia and Assyria, and some rather vague passages in the works of Greek and Roman historians. Until nineteenth-century archaeologists started probing the low rubble-strewn mounds silted over in the Iraqi desert, no one even knew that the Sumerians had existed.

The first diggers on the desert mounds were primarily French and Englishmen who dug unmethodically in the mid-nineteenth century with an eye for any object that might be of value in a Europe suddenly mad for Eastern antiquities. A few were genuinely concerned with the mute story told by bricks, bones, and pottery shards, but the majority were treasure hunters.

The early years of the twentieth century saw the advent of Near Eastern archaeology as a scientific discipline, and by 1920 systematic excavations of ancient Iraqi sites were under way.

The greatest stroke of good fortune was probably the discovery of many thousands of inscribed clay tablets. From about 3000 B.C. a privileged class of scribes wrote in infinite detail about every aspect of Mesopotamian life from regal proclamations to conjugal disagreements.

The work of archaeologists and classical scholars in the past hundred years has confirmed the most extravagant literary references to the golden wealth of the Mesopotamian cultures. The most spectacular find was Sir Leonard Woolley's discovery of the cemetery at Ur.

If it were not for the excavations at Ur where a number of royal tombs have yielded a bounty of precious objects made of gold, silver, semiprecious stones, rare woods, and ivory, we would know little of Mesopotamian material culture. The amount of gold, although less than would be buried with an Egyptian prince, is amazing. It indicates that even though the Sumerians had no gold at hand they made every effort to acquire the deathless metal—which they prized as highly as the Egyptians.

The Ur culture established itself in the third millennium along the fertile levees of the lower Euphrates. It was heir to earlier agricultural communities which settled where the marshes provided fish and waterfowl and forage for the flocks of sheep and goats.

A number of scattered towns lay along the riverbanks on land high enough to be safe from flooding. Most of them were haphazard expansions of prehistoric settlements. A city like Ur may have had as many as 300,000 inhabitants. But the average ancient city was very small by modern standards, generally covering no more than fifteen acres. Homer's Troy, for example, encompassed about five acres.

Within the early cities was a segment of the population which did not fish or farm. It was composed of the rulers, officials, merchants, and artisans; the first full-time nonagricultural specialists. The rulers were dynastic kings who claimed divine right to rule. They were regarded as deities and surrounded themselves with great pomp and a great deal of gold.

According to Sumerian legend, prosperity blessed Mesopotamia when the gods "made the ewe give birth to the lamb . . . [and] the grain increase in the furrows." It was wealth from the flocks and fields which made civilization possible. A new and venturesome group of specialists, the merchants and traders, evolved to handle the agricultural surplus and provide a wide range of requisites and luxuries. The commercial entrepreneurs embodied the characteristics which made Mesopotamia, despite great natural obstacles, first in so many innovations and inventions.

Practical, daring, and opportunistic, the merchants made history as they carried the overabundance of Mesopotamian produce to distant lands. The Land Between the Rivers was always less insulated than Egypt and more open to outside currents. The traders organized donkey caravans to cross the desert wastes of

Syria to the Mediterranean coast, where they traded for gold, silver, wood, shells, and incense. Their cargo trains wound painfully up the Zagros Mountains of Iran as far north as Armenia's Lake Van. They braved the territories beyond the Taurus Mountains to bring back gold, silver, and the metals of necessity—copper, lead, and iron. Amber came from the far north of Europe via the prehistoric amber road and was worth its weight in gold.

A sophisticated urban populace demanded luxuries. The bazaars offered a tempting variety of exotic imported goods. To satisfy discriminating consumers and make a fat profit, the traders plied the Persian Gulf as far as India—the treasure house of antiquity. They crossed the Arabian Sea to trade with Ethiopia and Somalia. They brought back foreign goods and foreign ideas from Egypt, Africa, the Levant, India, and Asia. Tales of exotic lands and customs which fertilized the imaginations of the Mesopotamians and expanded their horizons were as much a part of traders' stock as gold, lapis lazuli, amber, timber, and stone.

Archaeological excavations of goldsmiths' shops have furnished a remarkable amount of information about early metalworking. The Mesopotamians were from the beginning skilled metalworkers. Some scholars believe they developed independently of the Egyptians. Others feel that along with imports of raw gold from the Nile kingdom came goldworking techniques which were adapted by Mesopotamian smiths.

Archaic Mesopotamian goldworkers learned the art of refining gold by cupellation and applied chemical principles in compounding unusual alloys far in advance of many others. Clay tablets give formulae for refining which show that gold of a very high degree of purity could be dependably produced. This reliability was a vital step in making gold a primary standard of exchange.

The formula inscription read approximately as follows: "x minas of gold put in the furnace and after heating y minas of gold remained. x minas minus y minas equals the loss through heating."

As early as the fifth millennium B.C. metallurgists knew how to extract copper from its ores. Within a thousand years smiths mastered the simple metallurgy of gold, silver, copper, lead, and the alloy bronze. Initially bronze was made of copper and arsenic. Then it was produced by smelting ore which contained both copper and tin, and finally a more accurate method was evolved in which copper ore and tin ore were smelted separately and then alloyed together. A bit after 3000 B.C. the Sumerians of southern Mesopotamia were importing copper ores from Asia Minor and tin ore from the southern Caucasus.

The metalsmiths came into their own in the cities. They produced objects of great beauty and utility. Jewelry, ornaments, tools, and weapons made in those days when religion, daily life, and art were closely intermingled bear the personal style of their maker as well as the larger imprint of the culture. The goldsmith worked for gods and rulers he believed in totally. His work integrated technical skill and creative confidence. He could cast gold either in flat open molds or in three-dimensional closed molds. He even used the exacting lost-wax process to produce elaborately detailed castings. Individually cast pieces were soldered or riveted together to form large objects. Goldworkers made minuscule gold beads and enormous embossed gold sheets with equal assurance.

Sheet gold, formed by much beating, burnishing, and annealing, was used to form figurines often made in several pieces. The crafting of hollow ware is difficult. It requires renewing gold's elasticity through alternating heating and quenching. Hammering makes gold brittle and hard, and annealing is the only way to thin and stretch the metal into hollow shapes. The gold was not immediately modeled over a wooden core, since it would have had to be removed for every annealing. A calf's head which was part of a harp, in gold and lapis from Ur, is one of many gold figurines from the cemetery which shows the skill of the Mesopotamian smiths.

To work such a figure in high relief, a piece of sheet gold was hammered into a rough bowl shape for the lower jaw, forehead, and nose. The goldsmith then formed separate pieces for the ears and neck. He worked at shaping the muzzle and chin, hammering inside and out. Finally he annealed the whole and filled it with bitumen and maybe a wooden core. The delicate details of the nostrils, mouth, and eyes were chased on the gold. When the gold hardened, he warmed it to get the sticky bitumen out. Then it was annealed once again, refilled with bitumen, chased, and so on until it had been satisfactorily completed.

Parchment-thin sheets of gold were also used to adorn sculptural elements such as doors, walls, or furniture. The gold was often stamped with an over-all design and bejeweled with semi-precious stones.

Embroidery is a very ancient art. Egyptian carvings and paintings show richly embroidered sails on ceremonial barges, embroidered vestments, and clothing. Some of these were Mesopotamian imports. The sumptuous embroidery of Mesopotamia was internationally famous. Gold and silver threads drawn to gossamer fineness were used lavishly with dyed linen threads and stones to create rich pictorial detail and colorful naturalistic motifs on fine linen textiles.

The focal point of most cities was the temple complex, dominated by a lofty ziggurat rising toward heaven, a shining ladder for the gods to descend to earth. The paramount authority in Sumeria was religious. The irrigated land belonged to the temples, which organized the population as a labor force. Thousands of clay tablets recorded the operations of the temples. The priests spoke for the gods demanding services and offerings. The scribes kept careful track of who owed and who paid.

Encouraged by the priests, the Mesopotamians believed man existed to serve the deities. The life of each city revolved around the temple dedicated to its guardian. The principal temple at Ur was dedicated to the moon-god Nanna by King Ur-Nammu, whose law code, portions of which have been found on cuneiform tablets, preceded that of Babylon's Hammurabi by more than three centuries and is over a thousand years older than the laws of Moses.

The temple at Ur had a ziggurat which rose seventy feet above the city walls. Sixty ruined feet of it mark the site today. The ziggurat was a stepped brick tower often faced with brightly glazed ceramic tiles and having a small shrine at the summit. The ziggurats, some of which were 290 feet high, were built on a broad man-made mound. An external staircase ran or spiraled up the side from base to summit. It is related to the pyramid, but the gleaming ziggurat dedicated to life and the connection between earth and heaven is the antithesis of the sunless, sealed Egyptian tomb. The remains of more than thirty ziggurats and their temple complexes have been discovered by archaeologists.

The fabled Tower of Babel, mentioned in Genesis and long a symbol of human vanity, was actually the ziggurat of Babylon's chief temple. Today little remains of the wondrous metropolis but a confused mass of rubble mounds extending along the Euphrates about seventy miles south of Baghdad. The finest surviving Babylonian monument is the thirty-six-foot-high Ishtar Gate decorated with lions, bulls, and dragons in colored relief on blue-glazed tiles.

The cities of the Tigris-Euphrates plain, sharing a common language and culture, vied for supremacy. By the eighteenth century B.C. Hammurabi had established Babylonian hegemony. Centuries of battling, particularly with the Assyrians to the north, preceded the Neo-Babylonian dynasty, which gave Babylon its golden age. The eleventh and last dynasty (626–539 B.C.) destroyed Assyria and ruled over an empire from the Mediterranean to the Persian Gulf before being overthrown in 539 B.C. by Cyrus the Great, who annexed the Cradle of Civilization to his burgeoning Persian Empire.

Babylon was one of history's most ambitious and most successful urban developments. It was carried out under the celebrated King Nebuchadnezzar, who razed Jerusalem in 586 B.C., burning the Temple and exiling the Jews to Babylonia. The city was built on both banks of the river and encircled by vast walls. As many as a hundred gates, all of them of stout bronze, pierced the walls. Atop the walls were turrets with a space wide enough for a four-horsed chariot to pass. Historical chronicles describe buildings and roofs covered with gold and glistening in the sun. Archaeologists have found fragments of bricks and tiles covered with a clear, bright yellow glaze, which may account for such descriptions, since they must have glittered like gold in the strong Eastern sun. The most famous of all Babylon's constructions were the Hanging Gardens, the Temple of Marduk, and the Tower, which was called Etemenanki—"House of the Foundation of Heaven and Earth."

The Temple, called "Esagila" or "House of the Lofty Head," dated back to Babylon's first dynasty in the nineteenth century

B.C. It was sacked by Hittite invaders who made off with the sacred golden statues of Marduk and Sarpanit, which were recovered years later, stripped of their encrustation of gems and much of the gold. The idols were redecorated, and throughout the years of strife between the Babylonians and Assyrians, the Temple was alternately ravaged and elaborately restored.

Under the Neo-Babylonian dynasty the temple reached a peak of splendor. The city during that epoch was filled with shrines and altars built alongside houses and shops or at street crossings. A contemporary inscription lists altogether at Babylon 53 temples to the great gods, 55 shrines dedicated to Marduk, 300 shrines belonging to the earth divinities, 600 shrines for celestial divinities, 180 altars to the goddess Ishtar, 180 to the gods Nergal and Adad, and 12 other altars to various divinities. Imagine the golden offerings!

Herodotus visited Babylon in the fifth century B.C. Although he must have seen a good deal of the splendor he describes, some of it he had secondhand, since by that time the city had largely been destroyed at Xerxes' orders (479 B.C.). Deciphered inscriptions have confirmed most of Herodotus' observations.

Following the ancient Eastern tradition, the exterior of the large temple was plain. The 470-foot-long edifice was located in a huddle of smaller shrines and courts across the street from the Tower. From the outside the only thing that caught the eye was the monumental shining doors. They were of bronze, a marvel of technical skill decorated with gilded and chased panels and leaves.

The interior was paneled with marble above which were paintings in vivid reds, blues, and blacks. Statues of the gods were dressed in gold-embroidered garments. Gold gleamed from the canopies and hangings. The "golden sky" of the Esagila was known far beyond Babylon's frontiers.

Herodotus relates that gold gleamed everywhere. He describes the Esagila's chief inhabitant as a seated figure of Zeus (Marduk) with a throne, footstool, and table near him. They were all made of solid gold and weighed a total of eight hundred talents. A talent was about sixty pounds. This would have been twenty-four tons of gold, an impossibly high figure. But even allowing for hyperbole on the historian's part, there was certainly an extraordinary amount of gold in the temple.

Outside in the great courtyard were enormous altars for various types of sacrifices. One of these was also made of gold, and close by it stood a figure of Marduk in solid gold some twenty feet high.

The temples and sanctuaries had treasuries where the accumulated offerings, vestments, ritual furnishings, and gold-embroidered clothing and canopies of the gods were kept. Despite precautions thefts were frequent. A scribe recorded, "The gold tablet which is missing from the temple of Ashur has been seen in the possession of the sculptor X . . . the king should take steps to have him sent for and questioned. . . ."

A goldsmith in the service of the same temple complains of the difficulty of gaining access to the treasury. "I have made the crown of Anu. . . . I have received 12 minas of gold by way of an offering to Bal, and I have used them for the jewels of the goddess Sarpanit. . . . Everything has been deposited in the treasury of the Temple of Ashur, and no one can open it except in the presence of the priest of X. . . ." He petitions the ruler: "Will the king be graciously pleased to send someone duly authorized to open the treasury so that I can finish the work and send it to the king?"

When Cyrus led his conquering Persians into Babylon, he ordered them to respect the sanctity of the Esagila and the Tower. They continued to function until Darius' gold-greedy son, Xerxes, who had no such scruples, slew the high priest, stripped the sacred treasures, and allowed the complex to fall into a state of disrepair. Alexander the Great in 331 B.C. occupied what was left of Babylon and envisioned restoring the great Tower as a monument to his victory. He planned to favor Babylon by making it his principal capital. To this end he set a large force of men to work clearing the debris. However, when Alexander saw how slow progress was in the face of such vast ruin, he reckoned that it would take ten thousand men more than two months just to clear the rubble and abandoned his grand scheme.

The ziggurat or temple Tower was even more magnificent than the Temple. It towered almost three hundred feet above the ground from a huge platform three hundred feet on a side and was truly one of the greatest architectural marvels of the ancient world. The original tower dated back to a much earlier dynasty, but Nebuchadnezzar had told his architects to "raise the top of the tower that it might rival heaven." It lay within an enormous walled courtyard, which Herodotus said was a quarter of a mile square.

The Babylonian ziggurat was composed of seven imposing platforms of diminishing size, each faced with a different color of glazed brick. At Khorsabad archaeologists have excavated a temple complex with a ziggurat which once stood about 135 feet high. It still stands as high as the fourth story, and from the multicolored bricks lying on the site it has been figured that starting from the base the terraces were successively white, black, red, white, red-orange, silver, and finally gold—the metal of heaven.

Excavations have confirmed Herodotus' description of access to the magnificent Etemenanki by means of a spiral ramp, of brightly enameled blue bricks which wound up to the Temple. Within the shrine was a gold table, a chair, and a splendid couch which were always ready for Marduk whenever he chose to descend to visit the priestess-wife who lived there waiting for him. The rite of sacred marriage between the two was considered the source of Babylonian prosperity.

It was fortunate for the survival of the greatest trove of Mesopotamian treasure that the burials at Ur were discovered when archaeology was out of its infancy and less oriented to accumulation of artifacts at the expense of careful study and recording.

In 1854 while the European rage for antiquities was in full swing the British consul at Basra was attracted to a sixty-foot-high mound which dominated a desolate part of the southern Mesopotamian plain. He dug about in the mound and found inscriptions at the base of the ruined ziggurat which led to identification of the site as Ur of the Chaldees, of biblical renown. Sixty-eight years later the University of Pennsylvania and the British Museum joined forces for a large-scale systematic excavation under the direction of Sir Leonard Woolley. Woolley worked at Ur from 1922 to 1934 making spectacular finds spanning twenty-five centuries of civilization from prehistoric hut dwellers to the houses and temples of the Sumerians at the top of the mound.

Soundings down to sterile soil revealed that the earliest occupation of the site had been by prehistoric people of the Ubaid period, about 4300 B.C., dwelling in mud-daubed reed huts and carrying on some trade with distant areas. The first stratum was covered over by eight feet of river silt. When occupation began again, it was by people who used similar artifacts. Woolley believed, and many scholars concur, that the flood which destroyed Ur covered all of low-lying Iraq and was the Great Flood of the Sumerian Epic of Gilgamesh and the Bible. Woolley found that by 3000 B.C. there were already the beginnings of a ziggurat.

He was clearing an area southwest of the traces of the ziggurat platform in 1922 when he came upon the tombs of the rulers of Ur. Proceeding with scientific detachment, he did not begin to excavate the golden treasures until 1927 and did not finish until 1930. The graves, some of which date to about 2800 B.C. and others to 2500 B.C., were not intact. Many had been looted ages before. But some had escaped violation and contained an array of grave goods that amazed the world with their abundance, richness, and high degree of creative workmanship.

Eventually more than 1,800 burials were excavated from different levels in a pit sixty yards wide and almost eighty yards long not far from the temple site. Woolley, aided by his wife and 140 workmen, uncovered 450 graves in the 1928–29 season, among them the burials of the kings and the extraordinary death pit which contained 74 skeletons of a king's retainers who appear to have voluntarily accompanied him to the tomb. There were to be 15 other such macabre burials.

The dynasts of the Ur culture, which stretched along the Lower Euphrates Valley, ruled over small, densely populated cities. Their authority was probably limited to a small geographical area and yet they acquired indisputable wealth.

Woolley describes the burial of one of these rich princes, Meskalam-dug:

> The body lay in normal fashion on its right side; round
> the waist was a broad belt of silver . . . from which

hung a gold dagger and a whetstone of lapis lazuli and gold beads, hundreds in all; between the hands was placed a bowl of heavy gold. A larger oval gold bowl lay close by, and near the elbow a gold lamp in the form of a shell, while yet another gold bowl stood behind the head. Against the right shoulder was a double axe-head of electrum and an electrum axe-head of normal type was by the right shoulder; behind the body there were jumbled together in a heap a gold headdress, bracelets, beads and amulets, lunate earrings, and spiral rings of gold wire. . . . The prevailing note was struck . . . by the gold, clean as when it was put into the grave; and most of all by the helmet which still covered the rotten fragments of the skull. It was a helmet of beaten gold made to fit low over the head with cheek pieces to protect the face, and it was in the form of a wig, the locks of hair hammered up in relief, the individual hairs shown by delicate engraved lines.

Woolley called the helmet, which was beaten from a single nugget of fifteen-carat gold, the most beautiful artifact found in the cemetery and claimed, with ample justification, that if the art of the Sumerians 4,600 years ago were to be judged on the strength of the helmet alone, they would be accorded high rank among the civilized races.

Most of the shaft graves at Ur had been dug over several generations to receive the bodies of simple people who were buried with the bare essentials for eternal life. The royal graves were in great contrast. They were characterized by a long sloping ramp which led down to a tomb of brick or stone constructed deep within the pit.

The richest and most grisly of the royal graves was that of Queen Pu-Abi (Shubad) and her husband, Abargi. The King's tomb had been dug previously and it appears that robbers broke into it while her tomb was being readied. It was probably looted by the very men who were laboring on the Queen's tomb, which lay adjacent. Whoever broke in resealed the roof to conceal the theft and apparently no one at the time was aware of what had happened.

Abargi's tomb contained few funerary goods but did yield the remains of sixty-three servants—courtiers, soldiers, and musicians—as well as an ox-drawn chariot. Other burials contained as few as six servants or as many as eighty. The practice of accompanying a dead sovereign with servants later ceased in Sumeria as it did in Egypt. However, classical authors and excavations in parts of central Asia prove such rites continued there for more than another two thousand years. The Mongoloid Ahoms of Assam continued to equip their aristocratic dead with gold and slaves until the seventeenth century A.D.

In the case of the Ur burials a royal funeral was conducted with great ceremony. The open pit was covered with reed mats on both walls and floor. The body of Queen Pu-Abi had been borne by sledge into the pit and placed in the crypt.

Then, as musicians played their golden harps and lyres, a procession of retainers, soldiers, courtiers, musicians, and women evidently filed down the ramp followed by chariots pulled by oxen or donkeys and their grooms and drivers.

The women wore brightly dyed garments embroidered with gold and silver and headdresses of gold, lapis, and carnelian. By the maidens' skulls Woolley found gold and silver hair ribbons, the silver barely a streak of purplish dust after so many thousands of years. On one female skull there were no ribbons. Instead a rolled-up silver ribbon was found where her pocket would have been. She must have been late for the ceremony and didn't have time to put it on—a very human note amid the debris of bones and finery.

In the chamber and outside in the pit everyone evidently took up his place, and as musicians at the top played, each of the faithful retainers drank from a little cup of metal, clay, or stone that she or he had brought. In the cups was a powerful narcotic or poison which had been brought along or dipped, in some cases, from a cauldron waiting at the bottom. Then they all calmly lay down and waited for death, which hopefully came before the tons of earth were thrown in to fill the pit.

Woolley describes what he found in Pu-Abi's tomb: Against the end wall of the stone chamber lay the bodies of 9 women wearing the gala head-dress of lapiz and carnelian beads from which hung golden pendants. . . . A little way inside the entrance to the pit stood a wooden sledge chariot. . . . In front of the chariot lay the crushed skeletons of two asses with the bodies of grooms by their heads . . ." "We came to another group of bodies, those of ten women, carefully arranged in two rows. . . . At the end of the row lay the remains of a wonderful harp . . . ; across the ruins of the harp lay the bones of the gold-crowned harpist. . . ."

The variety and richness of the goldworks found in Pu-Abi's grave illustrate the versatility and superb assurance of the goldsmiths of Ur. In the inner chamber where she lay surrounded by her intimates were many treasures including a gold feeding cup shaped like a boat and a similarly shaped gold bowl. The bowl has a handle of twisted wires threaded through tubes and soldered to the body, which was soldered from two halves. The feeding cup has a fluted body the surface of which is chased with a delicate band of chevrons echoing a motif of bolder chevrons around the rim.

A small gold cosmetic bowl was found with traces of green eye make-up in it. A gold tumbler raised out of a flat gold disk shows how competent the Ur smiths were at the difficult art of beating gold into hollow ware.

The Queen was provided with a golden dagger fourteen inches long with a lovely hilt carved of a single piece of lapis lazuli studded with gold. The blade and sheath are gold. One side of the sheath is almost plain, relying on the natural sheen of the gold for its beauty. The other is decorated with open filigreelike fretwork.

Pu-Abi's smiths made her a little cast-gold toilet set she probably used while she was alive. It contained an ear scoop, a head scratcher, and a tweezers. Hundreds of gold beads were in the chamber along with cast-gold amulets in the form of birds and a bull with a chased design. There were many ornaments in repoussé and granulation, all lovely and distinguished by a sensibility for the natural beauty of the metal itself coupled with astounding technical virtuosity.

Although the contents of the tomb had not been plundered, the overlying earth had crushed everything including the Queen's complex and delicate headdress. Like those of her attendants, but far more elaborate, it was made of paper-thin sheet gold especially for the burials as the Greeks later made funerary wreaths. The Queen wore a bulky ceremonial wig upon which the headdress was set. The ornament was formed by an intricate series of linked chains and pendant leaves with etched veins. Above them was a tier of gold willow leaves and flowers inset with white calcite and blue lapis. Beneath the leaves, over the Queen's forehead, was a row of overlapping gold rings. The three wreathed tiers were strung on chains of red carnelian and lapis beads, and springing from the very top of the headdress was an arrangement of raised golden blossoms with lapis centers. The effect of the magnificent headdress was balanced by enormous double-crescent-shaped earrings and other gold ornaments.

Perhaps the most beguiling of all the gold pieces found at Ur is a small polychrome statue of a ceremonial goat. He stands almost twenty inches high and is sculpted of wood with face and legs sheathed in gold foil, the belly in silver. The fleece is fashioned of small inset bits of engraved white shell. His horns, shoulders, and beard are of lapis lazuli, and is reared against a golden tree which bears gold leaves and blossoms.

A surprising amount of third-millennium gold was found at Ur, and history records that the Mesopotamians who succeeded the Ur culture made great use of the precious metal. Where, since they had none, did their supplies come from?

The Sumerians and their successors had valuable items to trade for gold. The evidence from tombs indicates that their gold came from Arabia, Egypt, and perhaps to a lesser degree from India and central Asia.

There was plentiful gold in the Ural-Altai region of central Asia. Alluvial gold deposits had been worked there since prehistory and became a primary source for the Near East in later times. There were also concentrations of gold in southern India's Kolar region and both gold and lapis lazuli in the Hindu Kush at the head of the Oxus Valley. However, these regions were very far away. Although some gold from them reached Mesopotamia it is probable that most of the gold received in trade and tribute for at least 2,200 years came primarily from the three gold-bearing areas of Arabia and from Egypt.

Gold came from central Arabia, from west of Bahrain, which was not an impossible distance for overland caravans to traverse.

Along the Red Sea there were two auriferous areas. The Upper Yemen area above Aden, which is associated with the biblical Sheba, was known to the ancients for its gold, as was the region of Midian below the Gulf of 'Aqaba in the north. Gold from these coastal zones may have been carried to Mesopotamia by ships, like those models found in the Ur tombs, which sailed along the coast of Arabia and into the lower Euphrates.

The ancient world is brought into clearer focus as scholars and archaeologists turn up fresh evidence illustrating the extent of communication between cultures and across great distances in remote times. The powerful motive behind such communication and the development of trade was to find sources of gold and other luxuries which became necessities with the refinement of civilization. The driving force behind territorial expansion can also be linked to gold as men strove to control the sources of supply of such a powerful metal.

The Egyptians and Mesopotamians were not the only people who loved gold and had talented smiths to work it into glorious forms thousands of years ago. Until forty years ago archaeologists thought the people who lived in central Anatolia in the early Bronze Age were rather primitive agriculturists. However, in 1935 archaeologists began excavating a tell, or mound, at Alaca Huyuk about one hundred miles east of Ankara in north-central Turkey and made a startling discovery which not only revised former estimates of archaic Anatolian development but also added a new chapter to the history of goldworking.

The diggers brought to light a massive treasure of dazzling goldworks and precious objects from a royal necropolis of thirteen tombs dating about 2500 B.C. The variety and profusion of rich objects revealed that the aristocrats of the early Anatolian Bronze Age, whose culture overlapped in time with that of Ur and of Troy II, enjoyed a life of wealth and luxury, based partly on trade.

The site is at the junction of three of the world's earliest trade routes—to Mesopotamia, to the Black Sea, and to the Aegean—and was continuously occupied from about 4000 B.C. The first settlement was a simple community of farmers and a few traders. It evolved into a more complex city in which there was a group of sophisticated people of means and accomplishment.

The small cemetery was used for several generations. The tombs are of uncertain date—between 2600 and 2300 B.C.—and are located in the midst of the city among buildings. They are shallow rectangular shafts lined with stones. The bodies, individually or in male-female pairs, were placed on their sides in a flexed position in one corner, usually facing south, with religious and personal objects placed before them. The burials of single women were furnished with an especially great amount of gold and silver objects indicating some women enjoyed high social position. The dead were given splendid burials with many personal ornaments of every sort. In one chieftain's tomb were a massive chased bracelet, a spirally wound hair ornament, a pair of rings, and a pair of loop-headed pins as well as the weapons which were invariably placed with every male. The blade of one dagger was of iron, the rarest metal known at that time and still relatively rare a thousand years later.

Women were buried with rings, pins, bracelets, diadems, anklets, and buckles all of gold and silver. Everyone was given household goods and toilet articles including gold and silver goblets, chalices, jugs, and bowls. These were not crudely executed but fine pieces, many of which were elaborately decorated with repoussé designs. A wooden chest with an inlaid pattern of gold and silver bands, which somehow miraculously survived, was excavated from one of the stone-lined pits.

Religious objects unearthed at Alaca Huyuk indicate that the religion of the people was based on a mother-goddess fertility cult. Figurines of females with pronounced sexual characteristics, some suckling a child, and animal statuettes of oxen, stags, and lions were found along with an abundance of the solar disks used in sun worship.

The Alaca Huyuk treasures furnish ample evidence of the sophisticated level of metallurgical technique these people had developed. The style of the gold, silver, and bronze pieces is almost purely Anatolian with little Aegean or Mesopotamian influence. However, some of the pieces, particularly some of the animal figures, are suggestive of the steppes. Some strange copper horns foreshadow similar ones made many centuries later in Etruria and several styles of gold pins are almost identical to pins found at Troy II. A few other burial sites in Anatolia have yielded grave goods of this same period in gold, silver, copper, and bronze but none have been as splendid.

Most of the gold and silver objects found at Alaca Huyuk appear to have been made in the northern part of Anatolia and must have come in trade. The Anatolian goldsmiths made eloquent use of sheet gold, gold wire for filigree, repoussé, and they decorated their work with semiprecious stones including jade. They showed a preference for pale electrum. It is interesting that the pottery from the Alaca Huyuk tell is quite primitive in style compared to the refined metalwork.

The Anatolian Plateau slopes gently down to the Black Sea. Across the sea in the trans-Caucasus area were contemporary burials equally lavishly endowed which have only recently been discovered. The Kuban Valley of the northern Caucasus attracted Indo-European-speaking peoples who flowed south in a series of great waves. The Kuban River fertilized the rich black alluvial soil by thrice yearly flooding. In the latter part of the third millennium there were widespread aristocratic burials in the region.

There, 350 miles across the sea from Alaca Huyuk, is the great royal cemetery of Maikop. Archaeologists excavated a kurgan burial covered with huge vertical limestone slabs. Underneath the mound was a wooden mortuary house divided in three chambers. A man, sprinkled with ocher, lay in the central one under a canopy with gold and silver supports. He was surrounded by many gold ornaments, gold vessels, and silver vases chased with animal decorations. Many of the gold objects show a strong link with Southwest Asia and Mesopotamia.

During the third millennium the accumulation and use of gold was spreading in the eastern Mediterranean. The Minoans of Crete were becoming increasingly powerful and the focus of the first great gold culture outside the East.

1. Egyptian tomb painting showing Isis kneeling on a stylized gold necklace, the first hieroglyph for gold. Eighteenth Dynasty.

2. Painting depicting goldsmiths at work in upper registers. From the Eighteenth Dynasty tomb of Vizier Rekhmara.

3. Back panel of throne of Tutankhamen found at Thebes. Fourteenth century B.C. Photo by Harry Burton. Griffith Institute, Ashmolean Museum, Oxford.

4. Anubis on a gilt pylon guarding the entrance to innermost treasury of Tutankhamen's tomb. Photo by Harry Burton. Griffith Institute, Ashmolean Museum, Oxford.

5. Lid of gold sarcophagus of Tutankhamen. Photo by Harry Burton.

6. Tutankhamen's gold funerary mask. Beaten gold, yellow and red, inlaid with glass and faïence.

7. Amulet of Sakhmet, Memphis, Egypt. Twenty-sixth Dynasty, ca. 660 B.C. University Museum, Philadelphia.

8. Headdress of Queen Shub-ad, shown on reconstructed head and wig. Ur, Mesopotamia. Ca. 2700 B.C.

9. Magnificent gold helmet found by Woolley at Ur, raised from sheet gold and decorated with repoussé and chasing. Ca. 2700 B.C. British Museum.

10. Gold vessels from the Royal Graves at Ur. Ca. 2600 B.C. British Museum.

11. Lyre from Ur in shape of bull's head. Gold and lapis-lazuli., Ca. 2600 B.C. University Museum, Philadelphia.

12. Detail of head of ram in the thicket statuette from Ur. Ca. 2600 B.C. University Museum, Philadelphia.

13. Gold pitcher with relief decoration in repoussé found near Amasya, Turkey. Ca. 2400–2300 B.C. Museum of Archaeology, Ankara.

14. Gold brooch; pin with six-lobed head passes through the figure-8-shaped plaque. From Alaca Huyuk Royal Tombs. 2400–2300 B.C. Museum of Archaeology, Ankara.

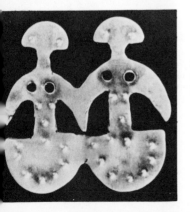

15. Gold twin idols from Alaca Huyuk cut from sheet gold decorated with pierced holes and repoussé dots. Museum of Archaeology, Ankara.

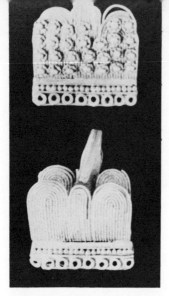

16. Basket-shaped gold earrings of gold wire with appliqué rosettes, granulated borders, and appliqué loops of gold wire. From Troy. Ca. 2300 B.C. Archaeological Museum, Istanbul.

17. Death mask from the Royal Necropolis at Mycenae; found by Schliemann. Greek National Museum of Archaeology, Athens.

18. Mycenaean engraved gold seal ring. Sixteenth century B.C.

19. Phoenician fenestrated ceremonial ax; detail decorated with filigree. Byblos, nineteenth-eighteenth century B.C. National Museum, Beirut.

20. Phoenician necklace with pendant head of a Gorgon; repousse and filigree. Sidon. Fifth–fourth century B.C. National Museum, Beirut.

21. Etruscan bowl hammered out of sheet gold and covered with a bloom of very fine granulation. From Praeneste. Late seventh century B.C. Victoria and Albert Museum, London.

22. Gold pectoral ornaments from Rhodes. Greek. Seventh century B.C. British Museum.

23. Scene from a Greek terra-cotta vase showing miners underground. Corinthian. Sixth century B.C.

24. Hellenistic victory wreath, gold from time of Alexander.

25. Hellenistic diadem with popular Heracles knot, thought to aid healing of wounds. Twenty inches long. Thessaly. Third century B.C. Benaki Museum, Athens.

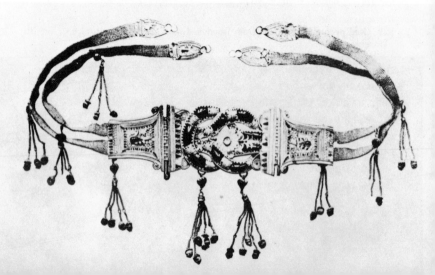

CHAPTER FIVE *Mythmakers' Gold*

There is a story as old as Western civilization which tells of a band of lovely maidens wandering in the flowering summer meadows along the Mediterranean shore. Loveliest of them all, her flowing hair tossed by a gentle shore breeze, was Europa, daughter of the King of Sidon. She gathered fragrant narcissus, hyacinths, and roses and placed them in an exquisitely engraved gold basket made by Hephestos, lame goldsmith of the gods. Zeus, looking down from Olympus, was smitten with love for the graceful princess. Changing himself into a splendid bull, he lay at her feet. Europa was completely captivated by the gentleness of so mighty a creature. Despite the warnings of her handmaidens she climbed on his broad sleek back, whereupon he plunged into the sea. He swam with her to Crete, his own island, where she lived happily and bore him glorious sons. One of them was Minos.

Minos, so another myth relates, was the powerful King of Crete, which was the steppingstone between all the eastern Mediterranean lands. His invincible fleet controlled the seas and sailed far for gold. Minos conquered Athens in retaliation for the treacherous murder of his only son by the jealous King of Athens, and threatened to annihilate the city unless the terrible tribute he demanded were not paid. He exacted that every ninth year seven of Athens' finest youths and seven of the most beautiful virgins be sent to the palace of Knossos on Crete to be sacrificed to the monster Minotaur who dwelt in the dark subterranean labyrinth there.

The Minotaur was, as everyone knows, half man and half bull. He was the offspring of Minos' wife and a sacred bull, which had been given the King by Poseidon, god of the sea. Daedalus, the celebrated architect and inventor, was commissioned by Minos to build a sunless "palace of confinement" in which to imprison the monster. The royal mansion above trembled with the anguished roars of the mad beast and the screams of his victims until Theseus, greatest of Athenian heroes, slew the Minotaur and escaped from the labyrinth by following a thread provided by Ariadne, Minos' tenderhearted daughter.

These are familiar stories which have been told to countless generations. Until less than a century ago they were beloved as the fanciful imaginings of ancient bards; no one dreamed they were based on ancient events.

But in 1899 a near-sighted Englishman began digging on Crete and made a discovery which revolutionized history and gave new life to the classical myths. Sir Arthur Evans, wealthy scholar and curator of the Ashmolean Museum at Oxford, went to the island tracking the source of some ancient signet seals he had seen in an Athens antique shop. He stayed on to dig a bit and on the second day struck the Bronze Age palace at Knossos.

It was Evans, dedicated, testy, and patient, who gave the name Minoan to the dazzling civilization which flourished on Bronze Age Crete some thirteen hundred years before Periclean Athens. For the next thirty years he devoted his considerable fortune and his unflagging energy to the life and times of Europe's first civilization. The Minoans practiced the arts of living far in advance of other Europeans. He brought these vivacious, multifaceted people from the tenebrous shadows of myth into the sun-drenched light of Mediterranean history.

His excavations uncovered a palace of staggering size, a labyrinthine complex, decorated with hundreds of brightly colored frescoes of Minoan life. They included scenes of lithe young men and women leaping over the horns of charging bulls in ritual games. This was the first tenuous bit of evidence linking the Greek legend of the Minotaur with historical fact.

All myths grow out of human experience and have a nucleus of truth around which centuries of retelling form accretions and changes. The story of Minos was that of a powerful sea king who actually did hold sway over the eastern Mediterranean. The myth of the Minotaur echoes the widespread worship of the bull as symbol of procreative power and strength. Paleolithic man had invoked such powers in cave paintings tens of thousands of years ago, and both the Egyptians and the Assyrians had cults of bull worship. Frescoes, pottery, and goldwork all reflect the importance of such a cult to the Minoans.

The story of Europa is, in mythic guise, the history of how civilization spread from the eastern and southern shores of the Mediterranean to Europe. The bold, bright Minoan civilization sparkled among the people descended from farmers and herders who came to the island in successive waves from Anatolia in central Asia Minor and perhaps were later joined by immigrants from Egypt and Libya.

The first settlers brought their culture with them. They lived in caves, worshiped a powerful mother goddess, and cultivated the olive, grape, and corn. It was stock raising and the surplus of grain, wine, and especially olive oil which formed the mainstay of Minoan prosperity before the advent of Cretan metallurgy. The island Odysseus called "hospitable, handsome and fertile" was fortuitously located at the crossroads of Aegean maritime traffic and yet was isolated enough in the early centuries of development so that the inhabitants could devote themselves to agriculture without fear of invasion.

Starting around 2500 B.C., the Minoans became master smiths. Their ships sought and brought back raw gold, copper, tin, and silver. Cretan smiths worked them into the highly prized manufactured goods exported throughout the known world. No other nation could surpass the bronze weapons and tools of the Minoan armorers or the quality of their delicate goldwork.

Crete was also famed for her "oxheads," the dollars of the Bronze Age. These were gold or silver ingots in the shape of oxheads. They bore the imprinted device of the Cretan mint and were accepted everywhere as units of value while simultaneously serving as weights. Larger ingots of copper or bronze were cast in the form of outspread ox hides and weighed as much as sixty-four pounds. In the second millennium B.C. the stamped oxheads and oxhides were honored as an international medium backed by Cretan power.

The Minoans celebrated the familiar world of sun, and fertile nature in their life and art. They became great seafarers and brilliant long-range traders, expanding their trading activities in a network of commercial stations and establishing spheres of influence throughout much of the eastern Mediterranean.

Increasing affluence accompanied their rise to power at the hub of the Mediterranean. The Minoans enjoyed a gay and cultivated life, which must have been the most pleasant existence in antiquity. They lived in comfortable stone houses, constructed with timber frameworks to withstand earthquake tremors. They dressed elegantly and indulged a taste for opulence, surrounding themselves with the luxurious accouterments of the Bronze Age good-life. The first large engineering works of Europe were the Minoan viaducts, harbors, irrigation channels, aqueducts, and paved roads. The first ornamental European gardens were the extensive royal gardens in the palace complexes.

Many of the men were often away on long sea voyages, leaving the women in almost total freedom. Minoan Crete is one of the few places in the world where women were coequal with men. They participated in games, ruled at home, and made significant contributions to the minor arts. Men and women even shared jewelry styles four thousand years before the vogue for unisex.

At first the inhabitants of Crete were not sea-oriented, having descended from pastoral Anatolians. For a long time Egyptian captains sailed for them under the Cretan flag. But when the barbarian Hyksos invaded Egypt and her power declined for a century or so, Cretan mariners gained control of the seas. The three hundred years between 1800 and 1500 B.C. marked the apex of Minoan maritime and commercial dominance in the Mediterranean.

They anticipated the Phoenicians as great navigators and traders. Minoan ships traded with other Aegean islands, with groups on the Greek mainland, particularly the Mycenaeans, whose culture and goldwork they profoundly influenced. They had commercial contacts with parts of Asia Minor, Syria, and Cyprus. Cretan adventurers founded bases on Rhodes and Cyprus and perhaps on the mainland as well.

In exchange for agricultural produce and the pottery and metalwork which were their chief source of wealth, the Minoans imported raw materials essential to their base metal industries as well as great amounts of gold, some silver, Syrian dyes, Eastern incense, ivory, rare woods, semiprecious stones, and amber.

They traded with Egypt for Nubian gold. In the tomb of an Egyptian official at Thebes is a fresco of slim dark men in foreign dress bearing on their shoulders weapons, ingots in the shape of oxhides, and a golden bull's head. These gifts are for the Pharaoh and the men are labeled "Keftiu," from "the Isles of the Great Sea." Archaeologists were puzzled about the provenance of the Keftiu until Evans' discoveries at Knossos revealed them as Minoan traders.

An indication of the artistic riches of the Cretans comes from an inscription listing tribute sent to a pharaoh about the middle of the second millennium B.C. when Minoan civilization was already eroding. Among the treasures were "bars of gold and silver, silver rings, baskets filled with lapis lazuli, ornamental vessels, some shaped like heads of bulls, lions, dogs, griffins and goats which were made of gold, silver, copper and silvergilt. . . ."

For much of the Minoan era Crete was spared the violent upheavals which marred the early development of so many cultures. Their mighty fleet of warships and merchant vessels acted as a powerful deterrent to would-be invaders. The palace of Knossos, standing high above the sparkling Aegean, needed no fortifications nor forbidding walls encircling it. Minos and his successors flaunted their power safe in the conviction that no one would assault the magnificent sea-girded palace.

Minoan cultural life centered on the palace complexes at Knossos, Mallia, and Phaistos. They were built on the sites of previous simpler palaces, also unfortified. The palace of Knossos is a maze of over twelve hundred chambers, galleries, courtyards, corridors, bathrooms, and storerooms brightly decorated with the marvelous frescoes which illustrate Minoan life.

The palace had a huge central courtyard where as many as five thousand spectators could watch ritual games. Many of the chambers were apartments for the royal family and their courtiers. But Knossos was far more than the most elaborate building of prehistoric Greece. Many areas of the vast complex were designed as administrative offices, council chambers, religious shrines, audience rooms, and offices where clerks and scribes kept clay tablet records in Minoan script.

Other large rooms were for the warehousing of grain, oil, and wine. There were storerooms too for pottery and metalwork. The goldsmiths, armorers, and potters had their workshops and quarters attached to the palace.

Unlike Egypt where all riches accrued to the Pharaoh and his fellow divinities and where the architecture was on a monumental scale intended to honor the gods and awe the commoner, Minoan Crete was a place where man felt very much at home. There is a singular absence of preoccupation with death, the hallmark of so many prehistoric cultures.

Egyptian artists subscribed to a realism almost photographic in its static quality. The work of the Minoan artist and goldsmith is realistic, even conventional in a sense, but because he looked at the world with an impressionistic eye the familiar forms are infused with his own *joie de vivre*. A strong decorative quality with a lavish progression of rhythmic motifs such as whorls, spiral coils, or plant and animal forms is characteristic of Minoan work. The goldwork of Crete is poles apart from the solemn golden regalia of the Mesopotamians or the showy ornaments of the Nile kings.

The art of the metalworker was surrounded by a body of magical lore, and the Cretan smiths strove to keep their skills secret as they worked in the well-equipped workshops of the Minoan kings. They were thought to owe their abilities to supernatural beings which the classical Greeks also recognized, among them the Dactyls, who were the creatures credited with the discovery of iron and its uses. The Dactyls inhabited Crete's Mount Ida and aided bronze workers. Other beings called the Curetes and Corybantes were armorers, and the Cabiri were the magical guardians of all smiths. According to tradition the Telchines were gifted workers in gold, silver, and bronze who made the first statues.

By the time of Homer, long after the cataclysmic end of the Minoan culture, a goldsmith gained Olympian stature. Hephaestus, Vulcan to the Romans, was the only ugly immortal. He was lame as well and created female robots out of solid gold to

aid him in his workshop. He produced all the immortal's weapons, ornaments, and furnishings. He was also the god of fire, and
the Greeks often attributed volcanic eruptions to his working at
a subterranean forge. Hephaestus was popular with the Athe-
nians who honored mortal goldsmiths. With Athena he was patron of the crafts and presided over the ceremony in which a
youth was admitted to the city organization.

Hephaestus was most famous for his work in gold, ivory, and
gems. To classical Greeks' chryselephantine statues, carved of
ivory and adorned with gold, represented the pinnacle of artistic
achievement. The Minoans were the first to use such a combination of materials. Much later classical Greek sculptors such as
Phidias and Polyclitus were celebrated among their fifth century
B.C. contemporaries not for their work in marble that has survived, but for chryselephantine statues.

Several Minoan chryselephantine pieces made about 1500 B.C.
exist to show how very different in feeling Minoan art was from
the more stereotyped art of Egypt, Mesopotamia, or Anatolia.
The graceful figurines of the snake goddess now in Boston, the
girl bull leaper in Toronto, and a gold and ivory boy at the
Ashmolean are early evidence of the emergence of a distinctly
European aesthetic. They are modeled with a tenderness and in-
dividuality new to art; made for the pleasure of man, not the
gods. The amount of gold is small but effectively used to enhance the ivory carvings. Gold jewelry, nipples, and snakes
adorn the figures but do not detract from their intense facial expressions.

Early Minoan goldwork bore the imprint of the islanders' origins. Examples found in rock tombs are simple and unelaborated
pieces of jewelry hammered out of sheet gold. The early smith in
those bucolic days employed a limited range of techniques. But
within five hundred years as Crete began her rise to prominence
the goldsmiths honed their technical skills. As gold became more
plentiful smiths evolved an inventive Minoan style.

During the Middle Minoan period (circa 2100–1550 B.C.) the
inspirational motifs remained the animal and foliage forms of
earlier times and emphasized purely geometrical patterns as
well. The goldsmith, like the painter, was ruled by convention
limiting him to a number of themes and patterns. Yet he man-

aged, within this framework, to achieve a dynamic and harmonious feeling. Imported gold, for example, was fashioned into necklaces with beads representing daisies in relief, double conventionalized argonauts, octopus, papyrus and lily blossoms, and even cereal grains all fashioned with a characteristic freshness. Gold cups were decorated with flying fish, dolphins, birds, and beasts.

The Minoan goldsmith was a technical virtuoso. He knew not only how to work with filigree, soldering, inlay, and granulation but how to damascene daggers by inlaying scenes in gold, electrum, silver and black niello (a mixture of lead, silver, sulphur, and copper).

The Cretans made much use of gold foil which was often inlaid with amber, crystal, and gems. Steatite (soapstone) vessels with designs carved in relief were covered with foil and it was applied to bronze as well since they had learned the technique of gilding bronze. They knew too how to gold-plate cups and vessels by bonding sheet gold to silver.

One such piece is a cup from a royal Helladic tomb at Dendra. The cup, made in the sixteenth century B.C., has an outer embossed and chased side of silver with galloping bulls. The inside is of smooth gold sheet.

From the same tomb comes the famous gold Octopus Cup, a magnificent example of the chasing and embossing which were the forte of the Minoan goldsmith. A man with obvious empathy for marine life has worked a repoussé scene with sporting dolphins and four great octopuses lying among undulating seaweed and rocks.

The Minoans favored intaglio scenes on gold ring bezels, necklaces, and gold plaques. Motifs including cocks, blossoms, gods, and fish were made by first cutting the design into a matrix of bronze or stone such as granite or basalt with chisels, borers, and punches. Then a sheet of gold foil was fastened over the matrix with a thong, and a punch or horn employed to force the gold into all the crevices of the intaglio mold. The more refined pieces were further decorated by chasing on the surface after they had been embossed.

Celature, the art of chasing-engraving-carving-embossing, was much loved by the later Greeks. A Greek word, *toreutike*, covered all the techniques. Homer attributes skill in toreutike to Odysseus, who made his own marriage bed "fair with inlay work of gold and of silver and of ivory." The Romans called the art *caelatura* and thus it passed into English as celature and was greatly admired through the seventeenth century A.D.

The centuries from 1700 to 1400 B.C. were brilliant ones during which Minoan goldwork reached a pinnacle. Fortune smiled on the island as gold flowed from all the world into the palace workshops. Elegant ladies, whose costumes of colorful flounced skirts, aprons, and breast-baring bodices are represented on so many walls and pieces of pottery, ordered little gold plaques in myriad forms to attach to their skirts.

They purchased earrings and pendants, necklaces and rings decorated with stylized bull's heads, deer, aquatic birds, conch shells, and other natural forms. One lovely pendant has two human heads modeled in repoussé with elaborate coiffures sweeping back and curling about the tiny ears. Another shows a human figure clasping a duck by the neck.

Two beautiful treasures from Knossos embody the Minoan love of spirited luxury. One is a royal sword in which the underside of the pommel forms a golden acrobat arching his body back in a dynamic circle, effortlessly touching toes to head. The other is a game board from the palace of gold, silver, lapis lazuli, rock-crystal, and ivory inlays for a game in which the object was to capture the four bastions of the "citadel" by moves regulated by dice.

Two specialties of Cretan goldsmithing are particularly interesting. One is the exquisite work in miniature of which only a very few pieces have been found. The Royal Treasury at Knossos contained several including a minuscule lion, a duck, a fish, and a heart, all equally tiny and perfect, marvels of granulation and gold-soldering.

The other distinctively Minoan type of goldwork was the gold double ax. The great Mother Goddess assumed many guises including the double ax and the horns of the bull. She was the most potent force controlling Minoan life. The double ax, *labrys*, origin of the word "labyrinth," was the most sacred symbol of the Minoan religion. Countless of these ritual axes in gold, stone, bronze, marble, ivory, and silver were made as votive objects. Sacred caves have been discovered where thousands were concealed.

Crete produced almost no gold of her own. Yet outside of Egypt the island was the greatest consumer of gold in the ancient Mediterranean judging from the growing body of textual and artifactual evidence.

Most of the gold came from Egypt, with which Crete had a strong trading relationship from the third millennium B.C. During the periods when Egypt was riven by internal strife or under foreign domination more of her colossal accumulation of gold became available to nations who could afford to trade for it.

Nubian gold from Egypt was, in time, supplanted by imports from other sources in the Aegean and southwestern Europe. It is likely that a fair amount of gold came from the island of Siphnos, not far from Crete, which exported gold and silver through classical Greek times. Some probably came from Cyprus, which came under Cretan domination and was the chief supplier of copper. Cypriote gold deposits were still productive when the island came under Venetian rule in the fifteenth century A.D.

A rich source of raw gold must have been the auriferous area of southwestern Europe running north from the island of Thasos at the northern end of the Aegean, through Thrace and Macedonia, the Balkans, and thence across the Danube stretching to the Carpathians in the east and westward to the zone where the Alps reach the Adriatic.

Varying amounts of gold were extracted from this vast area from time immemorial. Copper picks found in association with many shallow pits indicate that there was a great deal of mining activity in the second millennium B.C., which is the period of greatest Cretan absorption of gold.

Minoan mariners made regular voyages to the northernmost ports of the Aegean to trade for the Balkan and Carpathian gold. It is unlikely, however, as some have suggested, that the Cretans themselves organized gold mining in the area.

It is not inconceivable that such a venturesome maritime people as the Minoans sailed to even more distant areas for precious and essential metals. Ships flying Minoan colors quite likely reached Tartessus in southern Spain which was a treasure house of gold, silver, and tin. They may even have sailed through the Pillars of Hercules, out of the known world into the Atlantic and through the tempestuous Bay of Biscay to Britain. Cornish tin and Irish gold, traded on England's southern coast, were the goal of the dauntless Phoenicians, who braved the seas somewhat later. Thus far the only real indication of such long-distance Minoan trade is semiprecious red stones of Cornish origin which have been unearthed from Knossos.

The second millennium B.C. was a time of growth in the Mediterranean area. Not only the Minoans but the bellicose Mycenaeans on the Greek mainland and the Trojans on the Asian shore of the Aegean prospered.

Sometime after 1400 B.C. the proud palace centers of Crete, which had been tumbled in the past by earthquakes, were destroyed by fire, and the bright light of the peaceful Minoan civilization dimmed. Not all of the Minoans perished in the cataclysm, which may have been caused by earthquake or submarine volcanic eruption. Life continued on a diminished scale but soon Achaean invaders, including Mycenaeans, from continental Greece established themselves on the island, dwelling among the ruins. Trade passed to other hands, the artistic Minoan genius withered, and the last vestige of the first European civilization was extinguished after 1200 B.C., by the barbarous northern Dorians.

After 1400 B.C. when Crete no longer absorbed so much gold the Mycenaeans and Trojans took up the slack. Familiar ancient tales evoke the golden splendor of Agamemnon's Mycenae and the golden wealth of Priam's Troy.

The Troy of which Homer sang was one of many settlements on a rocky outcrop overlooking the narrow strait of the Dardanelles (Hellespont) on the Asian shore of the eastern Mediterranean. Excavations have shown that although the Trojans of successive settlements loved gold, the availability of the yellow metal fluctuated widely. Troy I had almost none, but Troy II, Schliemann's golden city, about 2000 B.C., was rich in the precious metal, and Troy VI, which lasted from about 1500 to about 1200 B.C. when it was sacked and burned, had renewed stocks following centuries of scarcity. The period of abundant gold parallels the rising sea power of the Mycenae, the fall of

Knossos, and the consequent availability of Minoan gold which had been looted by the continental Greeks from Crete.

Troy had its origins about 3000 B.C. as a very small rock fort only fifty-four yards in diameter, dominating the fertile plain and overlooking the sea four miles away. Later a series of fortresses gave way to the monumental gates of larger towns such as Homeric Troy. These economically viable cities supported talented goldsmiths and armorers who excelled at making bronze weapons which were exported as far as central Europe.

The Trojans raised and exported horses, which were much in demand in the violent world of the later second millennium B.C. Archaeologists have found thousands of spindle whorls and infinite sheep and goat bones pointing to the export of textiles. But the secret of Trojan wealth and power was not agriculture but a highly favored geographical position. From four miles inland Troy controlled the strategic Dardanelles which divided the Mediterranean from the Sea of Marmara and the Black Sea just beyond it. The Trojans exacted tolls from ships they piloted through the narrows. The hilltop citadel also controlled an important land route on the Asian seaboard, and the Trojans collected fees for transporting cargoes overland to a point where they could be re-embarked to cross the strait.

The Trojans maintained commercial links with the metal- and timber-rich regions around the Black Sea and with Greek cities such as Mycenae. Through trade their cultural influence spread as far away as the Balkans.

The gold of Troy came from several sources. Gold from concentrations worked in the Caucasus in the third millennium B.C. had been crafted into jewelry and vessels for people such as those buried at Maikop in the Kuban Valley. During the second millennium it is likely Troy received gold from the Caucasus and some washed from alluvial deposits on the Phasis River south of the Caucasus on the Black Sea. Some gold in the form of manufactured objects came from Crete, and some raw gold must have come from the gold mines at Abydos, less than thirty miles away, which the Roman geographer Strabo visited around the time of Christ.

The Troy of the *Iliad* was a city that flourished five hundred years before Homer's day. The poet wrote in the ninth century

B.C. just as Greece was emerging from long barbaric centuries of privation and chaos when the golden civilizations of the ancients were but a misty race memory. His epic of sea adventure, of love, and of battles won and lost was woven out of surviving fragments of oral tradition and the verses of earlier poets which he sparked with vivid details of his own time.

People, then as now, were hungry for grand stories of adventure and daring, of people whose passions and courage loomed larger than life. They listened avidly to the tales of Helen's incomparable beauty, of how she was stolen from her husband, King Menelaus of Sparta, by the Trojan prince, Paris. For more than 2,500 years the story has been told how the forces led by Agamemnon, King of golden Mycenae and brother of the cuckold Spartan, left their women and their lands for ten long years to wage war against Priam's Troy. The world loved the ancient epic which described the golden luxury of Troy, whose palace smiths forged golden armor for King Priam and exquisite ornaments for the fair Helen.

One man from childhood was fervently convinced of the truth underlying the myth. A romantic nineteenth-century German named Heinrich Schliemann sought Priam's Troy with the *Iliad* under his arm and the ridiculing laughter of Europe's historians ringing in his ears. Scholars never considered for a moment that Homer recounted actual events of real people and places.

Schliemann was born in 1822, the son of a wayward clergyman and a mother who died when he was small. His dour childhood was colored by the romantic tales of Troy his father told him. Before he was eight he was given a copy of Jerrer's *Universal History* containing illustrations of the sack of Troy. As a young grocer's apprentice working from 5 A.M. until 11 P.M. he encountered a miller who, when in his cups, could recite endless passages in the original from the *Iliad* and the *Odyssey*. Although he couldn't yet understand a word of it, Schliemann's imagination was fired by the sonorous ancient poetry. Despite his father's avowal to the contrary he was convinced that somewhere the ruins of Troy lay waiting.

For forty years he doggedly pursued his dream and eventually gave the modern world two priceless gifts—ancient Troy and golden Mycenae.

He ran away from home, worked in Amsterdam, and then embarked for America but was shipwrecked in the North Sea and
almost died of exposure. When he was sufficiently recovered, he
became a clerk with a firm of Amsterdam indigo merchants. He
proved so adept at business that the firm sent him as their representative to St. Petersburg, where he set up on his own and
made close to a million dollars.

Before he was thirty he had taught himself seven languages,
four of which he became proficient in after a mere six weeks of
study each.

He journeyed to the newly discovered California gold fields to
trace his brother. Ever alert to a commercial opportunity Schliemann set up in banking and after nine months of buying and
selling the gold dust and nuggets brought to him by forty-niners
departed an even richer man and an American citizen by virtue
of having been in California when it was admitted to the Union.

The small intense German added immeasurably to his fortune
with shrewd profiteering during the Crimean War. He traveled
extensively, making millions dealing in cotton and tea, mastered
nine more languages, and at the age of forty-one retired from all
business activity to devote himself to finding the Homeric cities.

In 1871 he went to the mound at Hissarlik on the Turkish
shore of the Aegean near the Dardanelles where he believed
Priam's Troy lay. With him was his eighteen-year-old wife,
Sophia. She had been found for him by the Archbishop of
Athens, a friend of Schliemann's, in response to a written request
for a beautiful, well-educated but poor young woman. He stipu-
lated his bride must be enthusiastic about Homer and classical
Greece.

Sophia became his devoted assistant. In four excavation campaigns in the years up to 1890, Schliemann and his "Helen" dug
at Hissarlik with a crew averaging 150 laborers. They found not
one Troy but nine. In between excavations in Turkey the inde-
fatigable archaeologist dug in Greece at Orchomenos, where he
discovered the Treasury of Minyas, and at Mycenae, where he
unearthed shaft graves brimming with golden treasures of a style
never seen before.

Schliemann mistakenly assigned Priam's sacked capital to the
second-level city up from sterile ground, Troy II, which was in

fact a thousand years older than Homeric Troy, dating from the second half of the third millennium B.C. He trenched ruthlessly through seven strata of occupation, including the level now considered the city of the *Iliad,* in his all-consuming quest for the fabled city. He acknowledged, ". . . I was forced to demolish many interesting ruins."

Schliemann has suffered at the hands of historians and popular writers who have cast him in the role of a gold-greedy, self-aggrandizing character.

His literal acceptance of classical sources and his unbridled enthusiasm caused him to make gross errors in chronology and interpretation, but these do not detract from the brilliant contributions he made to history and archaeology. He was a humorless character driven by a sense of mission, certainly not a sympathetic type. But neither was he the dilettante treasure hunter he has been made out to be. He not only found cities thought nonexistent by classicists but was the first to document stratigraphy in a Near Eastern mound. After initially destroying much of what he was trying to preserve, Schliemann set high standards of detailed observation, notation, and publication.

On a torrid June morning in 1873 just one day before the scheduled end of that season's excavation, Schliemann's faith in Homer and his amazing energy were rewarded by the electrifying discovery of an incredible golden treasure hoard hidden in the charred rubble of the second stratum. To get to that point 230,000 cubic meters of earth had been removed from the mound.

He had not expected anything unusual that still summer day. He and Sophia, working at some distance from the others, were digging under some dangerously overhanging rubble. Suddenly Schliemann froze. The unmistakable shimmer of gold caught his eye. He looked around to make sure no one was looking in his direction. Quickly, urgently he whispered instructions to his wife. She was to proclaim a holiday, telling the laborers that it was his birthday and they might have the rest of the day off to celebrate. The crew was delighted at the respite and left with dispatch lest Schliemann change his mind.

The archaeologist spread Sophia's red shawl on the earth of the pit. Heedless of massive stones which threatened to topple on them at any moment the couple feverishly dug out the gold. He never doubted that the 8,763 pieces of gold jewelry and ornaments had belonged to Priam.

He explained how he thought the trove came to be there. "Apparently someone in Priam's family had hastily packed away the treasure in boxes and carried them out without even taking time to remove the keys from the locks. Then, on the walls, this person met his death either directly at enemy hands or when struck down by a flying missile. The treasure lay where it fell, and presently was buried under five or six feet of ashes and stones from the adjacent royal house."

That night, in their nearby wooden cabin, Sophia and Schliemann sat dazed before the rescued hoard of shimmering diadems, brooches, pendants, rings, bracelets, chains, plates, earrings, buttons, and even gold wire and gold thread. By lantern light he took a pair of four-thousand-year-old earrings and an elaborate golden headdress composed of 16,353 individual pieces, and reverently adorned his Greek wife with them; now she was truly his Helen of Troy.

The goldwork of Troy was on a magnificent scale. Much of it is very similar technically and stylistically to other Anatolian finds of approximately the same period such as the burials at Alaca Huyuk and the trove found at Dorak in western Turkey which mysteriously vanished soon after it was excavated. Some of the ornaments showed strong Minoan or Mycenaean influence. But whether Asiatic in feeling or Mediterranean, the Trojan gold had a pleasing delicacy and lightness.

The gold brought Schliemann universal fame. The crackpot was vindicated beyond his dreams. It also brought, as treasure invariably does, a lot of trouble. He had been digging without a permit. The Turkish authorities got wind of the find and immediately had his house searched. Not a trace of gold was found. With the help of his wife's family the whole shining hoard had been spirited out of the country to Athens.

Years of battle with government authorities followed. Schliemann was determined to hang on to the unique treasure so that it might be preserved intact. He had hoped for support from the academic community. But the exclusive little world of scholars had no fondness for the outsider who directed his copious reports not to them, but to the tremendously curious nineteenth-century public. Caught in the crossfire, Schliemann was sniped at by the intellectual establishment on the one hand and the Turkish Government on the other.

Eventually the Turks demanded he turn over half of what he had found. He refused, was sued, lost, and in 1875 was fined ten thousand francs. The shrewd millionaire didn't pay the fine but made the Turkish Government a gift of fifty thousand francs and subsequently was issued a permit to continue digging.

The treasure, easily worth a million francs, was his. It was displayed throughout Europe, and every nation submitted bids to house it in a permanent display. Schliemann chose to give it to Germany, where it was displayed in the Berlin Prehistorical Museum until World War II. During the war much of it was hidden in an air-raid shelter at the Berlin Zoo. At war's end the Russians seized Priam's treasure, unique in all the world, and it disappeared behind the Iron Curtain. Nothing has been heard of it since. Schliemann would weep to know that the glorious Trojan legacy has probably been melted down into anonymous bars. The Museum at Troy, set up by the University of Cincinnati doesn't have even one piece of Trojan gold.

Homer hailed the Greek mainland city of Mycenae as "Golden Mycenae," richer and mightier than Troy. Having found Homer's Troy, Schliemann next worked at Mycenae using archaeological techniques he had refined over the years. This time he carried as his guide not Homer, but the writings of Pausanias, the illustrious Greek traveler who visited Mycenae about A.D. 170 and described it in detail. Schliemann found the site with far greater ease than Troy. The great Lion Gate, surmounted by a cyclopean stone slab, still stood where it had guarded the entrance to Agamemnon's palace.

The great Bronze Age palace-fortress, its massive stones gilded by the southern sun, commanded a vital pass between Argos and Corinth about eighty miles southwest of Athens. From it the hills sloped down to a fertile plain and the Aegean. Others had dug there before Schliemann. Antiquities-hunting shepherds who sold their finds to Athenian dealers for a few drachmas rooted around the monumental ruins. But no one had ever made a proper excavation of the golden city of ill-fated Agamemnon, his wife, Clytemnestra, and their children, Orestes and Electra, the tragic family caught in a sinister chain of events which moved and inspired writers from Homer and Aeschylus to Eugene O'Neill and Jean-Paul Sartre.

In five shaft graves cut deep in the stony soil, over which sheep had grazed for thousands of years, Schliemann found fifteen skeletons and an unsurpassed treasure of Mycenaean gold. He took them to be the corpses of war-weary Agamemnon and his men who had been slain at the banquet given for them by his deceitful wife and her lover, Aegisthus, when they returned from the long siege of Troy. Actually they were not the bodies of prehistoric Greece's richest king, but of Mycenaean princes and their families of the sixteenth and fifteenth centuries B.C. who lived some four hundred years earlier than the Trojan War. Despite his error of identification the German showed the world that there had indeed been a great Mycenaean civilization which anticipated classical Greek developments in the fine arts and architecture by a thousand years.

The bodies in the graves were literally covered with gold and jewels. An infant was wrapped for eternity in a snug bunting of gold foil. The adult corpses had been laid out in magnificent raiment and covered with gold, gems, and semiprecious stones, weapons, and ornaments. Schliemann looked at the skulls to which atrophied bits of flesh still clung and saw the Homeric heroes. The bones crumbled to dust within minutes of exposure to the nineteenth-century air. But the blazing golden death masks, the portraits of the dead, showed no sign of corrosion. "I have gazed on the face of Agamemnon!' Schliemann rhapsodized as the first mask of a bearded warrior came to light.

There were six of the masks which were traditionally placed on the corpses of chieftains and kings along with elaborate breastplates of the same precious stuff to keep them safe from evil forces. Five of them were roughly made, two of them representative of a distinctly different physical type with great moon-faces.

The mask which Schliemann took to be Agamemnon's is the only artifact to give a feeling for what the warlike yet civilized Mycenaeans looked like. It is the severe portrait of a face with a strong narrow nose beneath straight brows, a virile man with thin lips framed by a curling mustache and a luxuriant beard. It reveals a warrior who had much more in common with the hunter-warriors of the Caucasus and Persia than with the graceful, beardless Cretans.

Like the Minoans the Mycenaeans took their inspiration from nature and had a penchant for geometric patterns, but their vision of the world was even more abstract. Barbaric themes predominate in their goldwork—the hunt and the battle. The pieces are technically perfect; the effect is splendid but a bit savage, lacking in the Minoan sense of charm and exhibiting a diminished sensitivity to rhythmic proportion. Not surprisingly, the epitome of the goldsmith's art is seen in the weaponry. The greatest skill was lavished on bronze dagger blades into which were set remarkable foliage patterns or scenes of the chase in gold. Mycenaean smiths had learned the sophisticated technique of using various alloys of gold to achieve a rich polychrome effect.

Diadems, bracelets, necklaces formed of embossed pendants, plain shallow bowls, fluted beakers and footed cups, golden masks and pectorals, all attested to the great wealth of the dead. Artifacts of international origin were abundant too, evidence of Mycenaean trading activity. Long ropes of Baltic amber lay with ostrich eggs from Nubia and silver stags from the mountains of Asia Minor.

In one grave where three women had been interred, Schliemann gathered over seven hundred thick gold leaves. In the same grave were lovely sheet-gold roundels about two inches in diameter incised with squids, octopuses, butterflies, whirls, spirals, and flowers. They were pierced with tiny holes for attachment to clothing and lay with heavy gold pins and gold belts among shreds of rotted fabric.

In another shaft were three skeletons arrayed with macabre elegance; five ornate gold diadems crowned each skull. A rock crystal duck and a collection of beautifully modeled gold figurines in the form of lions, deer, and griffins had been placed in one grave. Forty-six swords had been furnished a group of five males. It seemed a lot but another shaft which held only three warrior princes yielded ninety swords and daggers. Gold and arms were indisputably the most prized possessions of the Mycenaeans.

Even today it is not certain who those fierce, gold-rich warriors were whose civilization was a blend of the barbaric and the refined and whose achievements were echoed in the classical Greek legends. Very few Mycenaeans of course, enjoyed as rich a life as the buried aristocrats. Slaves, taken in battle, and subject peasants did most of the work. Deciphered records list more than a hundred occupational specialties among the Mycenaeans including goldsmith, baker, saddler, potter, shipwright, forester, and unguent boiler. Their treasure, at least, fared better than the Trojans'. It was kept together, and much of it can be seen on display at the National Museum in Athens.

The great age of the Mycenaeans lasted through the fourteenth century B.C. down to about 1200 B.C. when the internicene warfare which broke out after Agamemnon's murder and was intensified by Orestes' revenge culminated in destruction by fire of the palace.

Sporadic attacks by the northern Dorians prevented the Mycenaeans from recovering their prosperity and position of leadership. Finally, about 1120 B.C. it is thought that Mycenae fell to the Dorians who overwhelmed the Aegean world, plunging it into a maelstrom of chaos and uncertainty which lasted until the advent of the Classical Age about 750 B.C.

The Mycenaeans had established themselves on the Greek mainland about 2000 B.C. and from their agricultural beginnings were an enterprising and accomplished people. By 1700 B.C. they produced many varieties of olive oil, some of which was shipped to Egypt along with hides, timber, wine, and dye. In return they received gold, linen, papyrus, and rope.

The horse-drawn chariot, which they introduced into European warfare, was a potent weapon in their skilled hands. Much of their treasure was amassed through battle, looting, and piracy, which were regarded as legitimate pursuits throughout most of antiquity.

But it was a diffused network of trading connections which sustained the Mycenaeans. The original Mycenaeans had been land-oriented farmers, but over the centuries living in proximity to the Aegean they became proficient mariners, and as Minoan power was eclipsed Golden Mycenae reached her zenith. The Mycenaeans were the commercial middlemen between Europe and Asia. The prosperous eastern Mediterranean's growing demand for gold, copper, tin, and amber stimulated the hitherto lagging development of much of Europe. Trading bronze arms, armor, the magical double axes they had incorporated into their own culture, faïence, and pottery, Mycenaean ships called on ports where they could find essential raw materials, gold, and the other luxuries which are the concomitants of thriving industry.

After they sacked Knossos, the Mycenaeans took over the profitable Cypriote copper industry. They dispatched mainland settlers to Cyprus to dig new mines, and Cyprus replaced Asia Minor as the chief source of copper. Little tin was found in Greece so the Mycenaeans opened up the western end of the Mediterranean to trade as they sought the metal which was needed for bronze production. They traded with southeastern Spain and settled traders in Sicily and perhaps southern Italy.

They dealt with central Europe as far north as the Baltic. The Mycenaeans' copper ingots were exchanged as barter currency throughout the Mediterranean and have been found by archaeologists as far away as Sardinia, Malta, Romania, and France. It seems possible that the Aegean mariners, urged on by the desire for metals and the exotic imports that sophisticated consumers craved, traded on the south coast of Great Britain as the Minoans may have before them. Mycenaean artifacts of gold, bronze, and pottery have been found in England and Ireland. However, they may very well have been carried there by Phoenician ships.

Many Mycenaean artifacts have been found at Amarna on the Nile's east bank, where Ikhnaton established the capital of his brief monotheistic reign. The early Greeks imported a lot of raw gold from Egypt and during the period of Mycenaean dominance exported wrought-gold objects to Egypt as the famous Tell el-Amarna letters have revealed.

Enterprising Mycenaean traders settled in the ports of Syria, Lebanon, and Israel where they exchanged Greek goods for ivory, spices, and purple dye. Their presence was felt all over Europe and the Near East and had an important influence on late Bronze Age technology and economics.

Some gold reached the Aegean smiths from the Caucasus. The nucleus of the classical legend of Jason and his Argonauts probably dates from the Mycenaean period and is a recollection of a prehistoric Greek gold trading venture. West of Tiflis in the U.S.S.R., where so much Scythian gold came from, archaeologists have found gold and bronze artifacts of Mycenaean type dating back to the sixteenth and fifteenth centuries B.C. Jason and the Argonauts allegedly descended from Cadmus, the Phoenician prospector King. According to Strabo, Cadmus in the fourteenth century B.C. went to Greece and settled in Thessaly, where he found gold.

The legend recounts how Jason and his courageous band voyaged to the distant kingdom of Colchis beyond the eastern shore of the stormy Black Sea to reclaim a magical golden fleece which was guarded by a dragon in the sacred grove of Ares.

Jason captured the fleece with the help of the princess Medea, who fell in love with him after she had been struck with one of Cupid's arrows. Aphrodite, Cupid's mother, promised him a reward for smiting Medea—a shining gold ball embellished with deep blue enamel made by Hephaestus. The immortals, like lesser beings, were not above the lure of gold.

One who did resist was Medea. Jason took her back to Greece with him. She bore him two sons. Her sorcery helped him in every undertaking and even gave him the secret of eternal youth. Jason, however, was an ambitious man. He refused to marry her, preferring an advantageous match with the daughter of the mighty King of Corinth. He displayed neither love nor gratitude for the Colchian sorceress and tried to force her and the children into exile. Medea spurned the fortune in gold he tried to buy her compliance with.

To avenge the terrible wrong done her, she sent a magnificent robe of cloth-of-gold enriched with gems and anointed with deadly poison to Jason's bride. According to the story, as the princess donned the robe, her flesh began to melt from her bones and she suffered a ghastly death. In anticipation of Jason's rage, Medea killed her two sons, rather than have them slain by less merciful hands, and as Jason approached her house in fury, she rose into the air in a dragon-drawn chariot and soared out of sight. Thus ends the story of Jason and his gold. Like most myths it contains a germ of fact.

The Golden Fleece itself was just that: sheepskin staked to the bottom of gold-bearing streams to trap alluvial gold. They were used throughout much of the ancient world. As late as the nineteenth century prospectors in the United States and Australia used sheepskins or rough wool blankets. Gold has an affinity for oil, and the tangled, lanolin-sticky wool attracts the heavier particles of gold while sand and other detritus is carried away by the current.

The Persians maintained a vast force of slave laborers to work sheepskin sluice boxes night and day when the spring floods washed gold down the Tigris and Euphrates rivers toward the Persian Gulf. King Darius in the sixth century B.C., who prospected for gold as well as looted it, had the operation well organized. Slaves tended the fleece-lined river beds and caught any light bits of float gold which had escaped in skins held taut against the current. Camel caravans supplied the washers with fresh skins and carried away gleaming loads of golden fleece.

CHAPTER SIX *Gold in Biblical Times*

The Bible is a rich source of information on the role gold played in the turbulent millennium before the Christian era. The pages of the Old Testament resound with the clash of arms, the fury of battles which raged in the Near East during the centuries before Christ. It was a time of perpetual upheaval as powerful gold-hungry states vied for supremacy and little nations struggled to survive. The Semitic peoples of Palestine, Syria, and Lebanon were in a terribly vulnerable position. They lay between the pincers of the great powers. Egypt flanked them to the west, Babylonia and Assyria to the east. But most menacing of all was the vast Hittite Empire. During the era when first Crete and then Achaean Mycenae became master of the Aegean and the world's chief user of gold outside Egypt, the expansionist Hittites were subjugating weaker states. Leaders often responded to Hittite overtures with alacrity, not wishing to see their cities destroyed and their people enslaved. In the mid-fourteenth century B.C. the brilliant Hittite King Suppiluliumas brought his empire to its peak through a consummate blend of diplomacy and military strategy. He had treaties drawn up setting the terms of the relationship with vassal states inscribed on tablets of solid gold. Clay copies of the treaties were stored in the chief temple treasuries of both the Hittite capital and the capital city of the newly won vassal state.

Under Suppiluliumas the Hittite Empire rivaled that of Egypt, stretching inland from the Mediterranean coast as far as northern Iraq and from the western part of Asia Minor along the Aegean to the mountains of Lebanon in the south. Suddenly in the late second millennium, the empire crumbled as hordes of sea-raiders swept down on the Hittites and then moved south toward Egypt wreaking havoc along the Mediterranean littoral.

In the chaos following the depredations of the Sea Peoples, there was a great deal more gold available to the Israelites and the Canaanites, or Phoenicians as the Greeks called them. Gold was still a rare and precious commodity. But the collapse of Mycenaean dominion of the Aegean halted the flow of gold north from Egypt. Once again in the history of gold the focus was on the Near East. The protagonists this time were the Phoenicians, supported by the Israelite kingdom of David and his son, Solomon.

The story of gold is the story of trade, and the Phoenicians were the greatest seafaring and mercantile people of antiquity, surpassing all in skill and daring. They sailed farther than anyone before. No one after them ventured as far as they had into the perilous unknown for well over two thousand years. Shipbuilders, middlemen, manufacturers, miners, and metalworkers, the Phoenicians and their descendants, the Carthaginians, figure prominently in the history of gold, discovering completely new sources of the precious metal.

The origins of the Phoenicians in the Bronze Age are hazy. By the second millennium B.C. Semitic-speaking people calling themselves Canaanites or "merchants" had evolved from a mixture of indigenous tribes and Semitic immigrants who filtered to the coast from the hinterland. Later, this ethnic mix was leavened by the addition of sea-wise Aegeans who fled the barbarian invasions; gradually these people became the Phoenicians Homer referred to as a "race of mariners."

From the outset the Phoenicians were a pragmatic people of exceptional boldness, looking for profit rather than conquest. Hemmed in on the east by high forested mountains which rose close to the rocky coast and unable to develop large-scale overland trade to the southeast because of Arab monopoly of the caravan routes, the Phoenicians turned to the sea.

They learned astronomy from the Babylonians and plied the trackless seas setting a course by the stars. Confident and brave, the men of Tyre, Byblos, Sidon, and the lesser cities ventured where no one else dared. Beyond the familiar waters of the eastern Mediterranean, where ships were seldom out of sight of land, they sailed past Sicily, the Balearic Islands, and Iberia. Through the Pillars of Hercules into the forbidding Atlantic with its strange winds, currents, and monster-haunted deeps. The east Phoenician entrepreneurs ranged far afield establishing commercial outposts wherever they could drive an advantageous bargain, exchanging trinkets for far more valuable goods.

For centuries the Phoenicians stood at the commercial center of the ancient world. The gold trade from east and west, north and south, passed through their shrewd hands. Political flexibility and a canny instinct for survival enabled them to survive, despite Assyrian and Babylonian buffets which greatly weakened their economic power, until in 332 B.C. Alexander the Great sacked the island city of Tyre after a nine-month siege.

But for centuries the Phoenicians, who shared a common culture, remained a group of city-states with divided loyalties. The Phoenician cities led by Tyre and Sidon, explored, colonized, and traded. By the time the Phoenicians reached their apogee in the twelfth century B.C. they had been trading for a millennium. [Egyptian tomb reliefs of the mid-third millennium depict a stubby merchant ship from Byblos on the Nile. By the sixteenth century B.C. Byblos carried on a lively trade with Egypt. Byblos' early trade was nourished by Egyptian and Mesopotamian demand for the pines and cedars of Lebanon.]

The Canaanites of Byblos also dealt in the perfumes of Arabia, which were consumed in enormous quantities. But as the empires of the Nile and the Tigris and Euphrates burgeoned there was an intensified demand for metals, and Byblos and then the other Canaanite cities became a vital connection in the metal trade.

The Phoenician galleys exported eclectic ideas and technology along with trade goods. Their craftsmen and metallurgists were adept at working gold and ivory, carving wood, and smelting iron. They knew how to produce transparent glass and exported a great deal of linen, wool, and silk cloth. Some of it was embroidered and dyed with Tyrian purple, the most highly prized dye of antiquity, which was extracted from the murex shellfish.

They built and furnished ships, temples, and even cities for other states. Rich gifts were frequently presented to foreign rulers to entice them into future trade, and also to assuage potential invaders who could so easily crush their small cities. The kings of eight of the sea cities made common cause in 877 B.C. and took an offering to the Assyrian King as he crouched with his armies on the northern frontier of Lebanon. A court scribe recorded what they brought: "gold, silver, tin, copper, copper vessels, linen robes with many colored borders, big and little apes, ebony boxwood, ivory and walrus tusks—this even a product of the sea—and they kissed my feet."

The Assyrian was well pleased. He gave the sea kings a contract to provide cedar wood and other materials for a vast palace he was building. Several years later when it was finished he invited delegations from the Phoenician cities to a lavish housewarming that lasted ten days. Thus, for a while, the Phoenicians, who could not permit themselves enemies, remained on good terms with the mighty Assyrians.

Copperware, votive figurines by the score, beads, glassware, jewelry—the mariner traders supplied everyone's heart's desire. The metal trade was the lifeblood of the adroit trading cities which were independent of each other but occasionally subservient to a common overlord. In their search for gold, they traded with their enemies the Greeks, with Africa, Iberia, and Britain. They often bartered the gold and silver from one place for the utilitarian metals from another. Central European gold, no longer absorbed by the Mycenaeans, was added to the world's growing supply by Phoenicians trading overland with Transylvania and Bohemia.

More and more people who were neither priests nor kings aspired to have a gold ornament or two. Gold rings which had been used in early Egypt, in the early Irish gold culture, and to some extent in Troy and Mycenae began to figure in Levantine life. "Thy cheeks are comely with rows of jewels, thy neck with chains of gold." The Song of Solomon mentions the gold chains which, like rings, served as adornment and a particularly attractive form of portable currency. Rebekah at the well was presented by Abraham's servant with a gold nose ring of half a shekel's weight and bracelets weighing ten shekels.

The Bible is an excellent mine of gold lore of the Phoenician period. There are more than 500 references to gold in the Old

Testament alone. Iron, brass, and copper together are mentioned in less than 250 places.

The earliest mention of *aurum potabile,* the solution of gold still used as a cure-all, occurs in Exodus.

Gold tempted the Hebrews to turn from their one God while Moses left them to confer with the Lord on the mountain. The fickle people, anxious for something tangible to worship, turned over their gold jewelry to Aaron, who had it all melted and cast into a Golden Calf.

When the patriarch returned and saw what had happened, he ground the idol to powder. He mixed the powdered gold with water and made the Israelites drink it—the *aurum potabile* so beloved of medicine men through the ages.

Yahweh ordered his people to make no idols of gold or worship any precious metal. Job recalled the antecedent sun worship and the gold-sun association when he declared, "If I have put my faith in gold and my trust in the gold of Nubia . . . If I ever looked on the sun in splendor or the moon moving in her glory, and raised my hand in homage, this would have been an offense before the law, for I should have been unfaithful to God on high."

Biblical references mirror the ambivalent human responses to gold. There are admonitions against coveting gold and prohibitions against using it on the one hand but, on the other, gold is deemed most excellent for the embellishment of the Temple and all manner of ceremonial objects. The New Testament Book of Revelation promised a heavenly Jerusalem, a city which "was pure gold, like unto clear glass." Gold is the offering favored by God, who ordered the Philistines to pay a trespass offering of five golden emerods (charms) and five golden mice when they returned the Stolen Ark.

The strong lure of gold for fallen man is evoked in the Genesis account of how soon after expulsion from the Garden mankind "began to gather gold, silver, gems and pearls from all parts of the earth, and made idols thereof a thousand parasangs high."

The Tabernacle, the portable sanctuary constructed by Moses in the wilderness period, is described as resplendent in gold elements. It was financed by contributions of gold and materials.

The value of the ceremonial gold exceeds several million dollars, far more than the wandering Hebrews could have brought out of Egypt. Most likely, the elaborate description postdates the construction of the Temple and is an effort on the part of biblical authors to attribute the splendor that marked Solomon's court to the early austere days of the Hebrew tribes.

The two goldsmiths of the Exodus, Bezaleel and Aholiab, who was in addition "an engraver, a seamster and an embroider," made the priest's robe or ephod "of gold, with violet, purple and scarlet yarn and finely woven linen. The gold was beaten into thin plates, cut and twisted into braid to be worked by a seamster. . . . The waistband was of the same workmanship and material as the ephod" and made according to the detailed instructions the Lord had dictated to Moses.

The breast piece was worked in gold and yarn and set with rows of gems, all set in gold rosettes. Tinkling bells of pure gold hung all around the hem of the magnificent garment, and the skirts were embroidered with pomegranates.

Bezaleel and Aholiab crafted scores of gold objects for the Tabernacle: an altar, two guardian angels, a table, and architectural elements as well as flagons, vessels, plates, dishes, and bowls made of beaten gold. The Lord had a keen interest in how His gold was to be worked. "See to it," He instructed Moses, "that you work the design you were shown on the mountain." Following His commandment, the goldsmiths wrought the famous Menorah in fine gold in the form of a flowering seven-branched almond tree. Fire pans and tongs also of pure gold were made for the huge candelabrum.

The Menorah turned up again as part of the treasure in Solomon's Temple and figured in even later chapters of history. When Nebuchadnezzar conquered Jerusalem and took part of the population in bondage to help renew his magnificent capital, the Menorah was looted along with other Temple treasure. When Cyrus I, founder of the Persian Empire, marched into Babylon in the sixth century B.C., he released the enslaved Jews. He also returned to them what was left of the gold including the Menorah, which had somehow escaped melting, and encouraged them to go home and rebuild their capital. This act of apparent generosity was prompted less by humanity than by the pragmatic awareness that economic slaves can furnish more golden tribute than shackled slaves.

In A.D. 70 when the Romans razed the Jerusalem Temple, they stripped it and looted the treasuries. Among the spoils carried to Rome and exhibited in triumph was the Menorah. A reproduction of it can be seen today sculpted on the triumphal arch erected in honor of the conquering general Titus, who later became Emperor.

During the siege of the Temple many of the starving Jews who had taken refuge in the sanctuary attempted to flee under cover of darkness. Almost every one fell into the hands of Roman soldiers. Believing the Jews had swallowed gold and jewels, the soldiers slit open their bodies in search of treasure. Josephus recorded that in one night alone two thousand were slain. Titus was appalled. He ordered an auxiliary legion decimated as punishment and warning but the butchery of the Jews continued. The victorious general also tried to spare the world-famous Temple, ordering that his men were not to touch it. However, the chambers filled with gold bewitched the troops, and they could not be restrained from an orgy of looting and burning that left the sanctuary in ruins.

The eighteenth-century historian Edward Gibbon wrote that somehow the Menorah became the property of the Carthaginians and subsequently of the Byzantine general Belisarius when he added North Africa to his burgeoning empire in the sixth century A.D. According to this account, it remained in a Christian church in Jerusalem until the Persians sacked the city some two hundred years later when it disappeared forever.

An even more intriguing story suggests that the Emperor Maxentius took the golden Menorah and other treasure with him in the fourth century A.D. as he fled Rome, which had turned against him. Unable to progress or battle, he cast all the cumbersome gold into the Tiber. Perhaps it is still there deep in the dark mud with the moldered bones of murdered Emperors.

Throughout history gold has been the basis for many an unlikely partnership. Five hundred years after Queen Hatshepsut's expedition to Punt, Solomon, King of the Israelites, and Hiram,

King of Phoenician Tyre, organized a joint fleet to seek the fabled golden bounty of Ophir. This was the start of a mutually profitable trading alliance.

Solomon's father, the warrior-king David, had united the Kingdom of Israel. He accepted gifts of materials and skilled Phoenician craftsmen from Hiram whose offshore trading city of Tyre was so rich "silver there was heaped up as dust and fine gold as the mire of the streets." The war over, David had prepared to build a temple to the one God that would transcend all previous sanctuaries. He pledged his personal fortune of about three thousand talents of gold to finance the project and levied a tax on his people which raised an additional five thousand talents. The total of gold from David's treasury and the people's "contributions" indicates that owing to geopolitical changes there was far more gold in circulation than in preceding times when possession had been stringently limited to kings and priests.

David died leaving detailed instructions with his son for the Temple around which the political and religious life of the Jews was to revolve for so many generations. The pages of the Old Testament record every fascinating detail of its planning, construction, furnishing, and dedication.

The Israelites had ample funds but needed timber, dressed stone, rare woods, precious metals, and embroidered cloths. They also lacked the skilled craftsmen to execute such a grandiose project. So Solomon responded to the overtures Hiram, astute man of commerce, had made to King David. He arranged for the loan of Phoenician architects, masons, carpenters, and smiths gifted in crafting gold and bronze. Hiram, eager to set the hook in such a promising customer as the flourishing young Hebrew nation, also provided the raw materials.

The Jerusalem Temple was on a scale unmatched since the pyramids. Solomon drafted conscript armies of laborers. Some worked at home, others were sent to Lebanon. Thirty thousand woodcutters went in relay teams of ten thousand a month to fell the towering fir and cedar trees from the mountain slopes which had long provided timber for foreign palaces, temples, and ships. Seventy thousand porters brought back the timber and the stone quarried by eighty thousand masons. In return, during the seven years the Temple was under construction, Hiram received a huge annual payment in wheat and olive oil to sustain the growing population of his little island city-state.

The Temple, a monument to the Hebrew god, was built on the model of a Phoenician temple. A flight of ten steps led up to the entrance of the long narrow building with ten-foot-thick walls. The interior was approximately 135 feet long, 35 feet wide, and 50 feet from floor to ceiling and was divided into three chambers ablaze with sanctified gold. The wooden walls were hung with sheet gold, embossed with patterns of lotus blossoms, palm trees, and chains. "He covered the whole house with gold, its rafters and frames, its walls and doors."

The most holy place, the inner sanctuary, was covered with six hundred talents' worth of fine gold, and the nails were made of fifty shekels of gold. The altar was of gold and so were the ten lamp stands and ten tables. Within the golden ark lay the stone tablets of the Commandments. Two sphinxes, called cherubim in the Bible, carved of olive wood and covered with gold, stood guard over the ark with outspread wings. Solomon ordered saucers, tossing bowls, snuffers, fire pans, and ceremonial vessels made of red gold for the Lord's House. When all the furnishings had been completed, he brought the gold and silver treasures of his father and stored them in the Temple treasury.

Then Solomon prevailed upon Hiram to lay out 120 talents of gold for the construction of the sumptuous House of the Forest of Lebanon. This was to be a palace for his family. The Israelite King was "a great lover of women" and had a reported seven hundred wives and three hundred concubines to house. The palace took thirteen years to complete and was appointed with gold from the enormous throne carved of ivory overlaid with gold to the plates and cups. No silver was used "for it was reckoned of no value in the days of Solomon." He had two hundred shields of beaten gold and three hundred bucklers of beaten gold, each weighing three minas. Millions of dollars' worth of rare gold, even allowing for biblical exaggeration, went into Solomon's Temple and palace proclaiming the prestige and growing luxury of the people whose forefathers had fled from Egypt and wandered in the desert.

The Queen of Sheba made a state visit to Solomon and

brought him "an hundred and twenty talents of gold," perhaps as much as 6,500 pounds. The African Queen knew his reputation for wealth; a small present would have been an insult. Conquest and trade filled Solomon's coffers with gold. "Now the weight of gold which Solomon received yearly was 666 talents, in addition to the tolls levied by the customs officers and profits on foreign trade, and the tribute of the kings of Arabia and the regional governors." That would total some 40,000 pounds of gold annually. Obviously the authors have taken a bit of license in this Old Testament chronicle, but there is no doubt that Solomon was very well supplied with gold.

How did the Hebrew kingdom acquire so much gold? Under David and Solomon ancient Palestine made a remarkable transition from a totally agrarian culture to an economically viable nation involved in international trade.

Iron and copper deposits in Israel were worked with the aid of Phoenician technicians. The Book of Job, Chapter 28, includes an exceptional passage on early mining. The account, which emphasizes the great length of the galleries cut into the rock, is taken chiefly from Phoenician sources. The following translation is from the New English Bible.

> There are mines for silver and places where men refine gold; where iron is won from the earth and copper smelted from the ore; the end of the seam lies in darkness, and it is followed to its farthest limit. Strangers cut the galleries; they are forgotten as they drive forward far from men. While corn is springing from the earth above, what lies beneath is raked over like a fire, and out of its rocks comes lapis lazuli, dusted with flecks of gold. . . . Man sets his hand to the granite rock and lays bare the roots of the mountains; he cuts galleries in the rocks, and gems of every kind meet his eye; he dams up the sources of the streams and brings the hidden riches of the earth to light.

About 1000 B.C. camel transport was introduced ro replace the slow donkey caravans whose routes had been limited by requirements for frequent water. The export of the treasures of Arabia

Felix—gold perfumes and incenses—was no longer forced to follow the ancient twelve-hundred-mile-long incense route which wound through sandy wastes from oasis to oasis. Some of the new camel trails had their terminus in Israel. Solomon's customs agents determined whether caravans laden with exotic goods might continue on to Egypt or Phoenicia and levied duties which were an important part of the national income.

The joint Arab-Israeli gold venture came about because both Solomon and Hiram wanted to go right to the source of Ophir's fabled wealth. If, as seems possible, the biblical Ophir was the Punt of the Egyptians where Ramses III had established organized gold mining a couple of centuries before, it was on the coast of southeastern Africa. However, there are some who speculate that it was not in the Zambezi area but in southern Arabia.

In the spring of 1976 a Saudi-American geological team explored the Mahd adh Dhahab, a sere mountainous area which lies midway between Mecca and Medina on the north-south trade route which has led to the port of 'Aqaba for over four thousand years. Their findings support the speculation made in 1931 by K. S. Twitchell, an American mining engineer, that the mines of the Mahd adh Dhahab, or Cradle of Gold, were the site of Solomon's legendary mines and the source of some thirty-four tons of gold in ancient times.

It has long been known that gold was mined here from about A.D. 660 to circa 900. Worked again from 1939 until 1954, the old mines produced silver and some sixty tons of gold. The recent expedition, however, found ample evidence of biblical mining. It is likely that abundant gold in the form of nuggets, crystals, and wires lay near the surface and could be mined with crude copper and stone tools. Thousands of stone hammers and grindstones for crushing ore litter the deep mine shafts and rocky slopes. Not only were the mines found rich enough to pinpoint the Madh adh Dhahab as the most likely site of Ophir but, just as important, the area would have been easily accessible. The gold diggings are only 370 miles south of 'Aqaba, Solomon's port at the head of the Gulf of 'Aqaba, and 150 miles inland from the Arabian coast.

Solomon had married a pharaoh's daughter and it is possible that he learned through the Egyptians where Punt/Ophir lay.

He had two assets to bring to a partnership: his knowledge of Punt/Ophir and of a Red Sea port which was a perfect staging point for a naval expedition into the Red Sea or the Indian Ocean. Israel was still without the materials to build ships, shipwrights, or mariners. The Tyrians could supply these better than anyone else. Ezion-Geber, near modern Eilat, was selected as the site for construction of the fleet.

A Phoenician source quoting a priest supports the several biblical references to the venture. "Although," wrote the priest, "there were great palm forests in the neighborhood of this place, there was no timber suitable for building purposes, so Joram [Hiram] had to transport the timber there on eight thousand camels. A fleet of 10 ships was built from it."

Hiram sent timbers and sails, men to build the ships, and experienced seamen and officers to sail them. "And these, in company with Solomon's servants, went to Ophir and brought back 420 talents of gold to King Solomon," of which Hiram got his share. Another telling recounts that Solomon had "a fleet of merchantmen at sea with Hiram's fleet and once every 3 years this fleet of merchantmen came home bringing gold and silver, ivory, apes and monkeys." Some renderings say "apes and peacocks," others "apes and slaves," which is possible since the Phoenicians were, in fact, renowned slavers.

The secretive Phoenicians modus operandi was to make every effort to discourage commercial competition by concealing raw material sources and trading routes. They formed a partnership with the Hebrews only because they needed access to a Red Sea port and because initially they didn't know how to reach Ophir. Business was business with the Phoenician merchants, and it is to be presumed that once they had been shown the way, they no longer needed a partner. The Hebrews evidently never made the voyage again. In fact, a century later the Israelites, under Jehoshaphat, tried to reach Ophir, but the ships they built without Phoenician aid sank as soon as they were launched.

The Phoenicians were so secretive that they made no maps and never committed any of their vast lore of geography and navigation to writing. What they did offer were spine-chilling tales of ghastly demons, treacherous tides, and entangling seaweeds that lay in wait for any who ventured out into the Mare

Altum, the high seas. More than once a Greek or Roman ship shadowing a Tyrian or Sidonian galley was lured onto rocks or led on a wild-goose chase. Heedless of danger, the Phoenicians sailed north, past Brittany to England, and 1,000 miles into the Atlantic, 3,300 miles from Tyre and Sidon. Phoenician coins have been found as far west as the Azores. They also frequented the Canary Islands, from which they collected a vegetable dye, superior to the murex purple, but after Roman times the Azores and the Canaries were lost for many centuries.

Some time before 1100 B.C. the Phoenicians sailed westward 2,300 miles to found a colony in the myterious land of Tartessus, in southern Spain. One of the greatest sources of mineral wealth in the ancient world was the Iberian Peninsula. For many centuries Tartessus was the distributing center for prodigious amounts of Iberian gold, silver, copper, iron, lead and quicksilver. Tartessus, the Tarshish of the Bible, was a mysterious city of veiled origins somewhere near the mouth of the Guadalquivir River. Its highly cultivated people were very active in the early bronze trade. They appear to have sailed as far as Ireland and Britain. They became independent allies of the Carthaginians after 800 B.C. and were destroyed about 500 B.C., perhaps by Carthage. These enigmatic people left no remains of their civilization save a few stone carvings and a number of gold treasures which may or may not be theirs.

A handwritten document regarding Tartessus, which is fascinating even if it was most likely influenced by the discovery of Aztec and Inca gold, recently came to light among uncatalogued papers in the Archives of the Indies in Seville. The manuscript, dated A.D. 1580, tells how in ancient times men of Tyre had landed near Gibraltar where they "mined a vast amount of gold and silver" from the mountains. They sailed away and returned later to found the colony of Gades (Cádiz). "At that place they discovered a great temple which, once in the past, had belonged to the Tartessans." The faded writing describes how the walls of the abandoned temple were hung with thick sheets of gold. Closer to the shore the settlers found two great columns of gold and silver which shone far out at sea.

The Tyrians stripped all the gold from the sanctuary as well as the "gold, silver and gems in extreme abundance" which they found in ruined dwellings which appeared to have been precipitously abandoned. In one house they found a replica of an olive tree of solid gold hung with emerald fruit. Unloading the ships they had come on of everything but anchors, water, and food, Phoenicans set sail for Tyre with their fabulous treasures. "Why," asks the author in archaic Spanish, "did the people whose things these were go? Why had they left such wealth behind?" "Andalusia," the document concludes, "was a most important source of both gold and silver for the Phoenicians."

He was right about Andalusia and Gades, although much of the rest of his tale is equivocal. The Tyrian settlement at Gades, which had access to the gold mines of southern Spain, came under Carthaginian occupation around 600 B.C. Carthage was founded on the fertile North African coast near modern Tunis in the ninth century B.C. by a band of Tyrians who fled an Assyrian siege of their city. Greek legend held that Carthage was founded in 814 B.C. as the outcome of contention over the throne of Tyre between the King, Pygmalion, and his sister, Elissa (Virgil's Dido), who was the great-niece of the notorious Phoenician princess Jezabel. The colony grew into a powerful and wealthy city in its own right, though tainted with a gruesome tradition of infant sacrifice which persisted long after it had ceased elsewhere.

The settlers of Carthage took over many of the eastern Phoenician colonies and founded new ones at various strategic points. Carthage gave birth to Hamilcar Barca and his son, Hannibal, who in the third century B.C. crossed the Alps with his armies and elephants and nearly toppled Rome. He also subdued the last remnants of opposition in southern Spain thus securing a monopoly on Iberian gold deposits.

Most amazing of all, the Carthaginians were able to bar Greek exit from the Mediterranean, which came to be called the Internal Sea, and they carved out for themselves an African empire second in size only to Egypt's. They brought new supplies of Africa's gold, ivory, wild beasts, and human slaves to the Mediterranean world.

"The Carthaginians," wrote Plutarch, the Greek friend of Roman emperors, "are a hard and sinister people, cowardly in times of danger, terrible when they are victorious. . . . They have no feelings for the pleasures of life." Both Romans and Greeks shared this view of their common enemy. Greece hated and fought Carthage: Rome succeeded in wiping it from the face of the earth.

The Carthaginians trading for gold along the west coast of Africa practiced a form of silent barter described by Herodotus. The "dumb commerce" they developed was used in African trade almost to the end of the nineteenth century A.D. in places where the natives feared slave raids.

> There is a country in Libya [wrote Herodotus], and a nation, beyond the Pillars of Hercules, which the Carthaginians are wont to visit, where they no sooner arrive but forthwith they unload their wares, and having disposed them after an orderly fashion along the beach, leave them, and returning aboard their ships, raise a great smoke. The natives, when they see this smoke, come down to the shore, and, laying out to view so much gold as they think the worth of the wares, withdraw to a distance. The Carthaginians come ashore and look. If they think the gold enough, they take it and go their way; but if it does not seem to them sufficient, they go aboard ship once more and wait patiently. Then the others approach and add to their gold, till the Carthaginians are content. Neither party deals unfairly by the other; for they themselves never touch the gold till it comes up to the worth of their goods, nor do the natives ever carry off the goods till the gold is taken away.

The Carthaginians dealt in West African gold and North African placer gold well into the second century B.C., maintaining complete silence about their activities. Their chief commercial rivals, the Greeks, continued to believe that beyond the Strait of Gibraltar the world came to an end. After the fall of Carthage, Africa became again the Dark Continent awaiting discovery by explorers yet unborn.

Because of the emphasis on barter, Carthage did not mint coins until the fourth century B.C., three hundred years after the

Greeks. From acting as middlemen in the trade of manufactured goods, the Phoenicians and Carthaginians expanded to make similar products themselves as a way to increase their profits.

Carthage pioneered trade in cheap goods. Her forte was pawning off baubles for the metals that were her mainstay. Plautus, the Roman playwright, in his satire *Poenulus* (The Little Carthaginian), pokes fun at the Carthaginians with a comic character who sells shoelaces, whistles, nuts, and panthers. Roman audiences laughed uproariously at the portrayal of the Punic merchant as huckster and charlatan.

Much has been written of the mongrel style and lack of creative imagination that afflicted Phoenician crafts. It is true that the Carthaginians were more interested in volume than quality and that the Phoenicians turned out staggering quantities of copper and bronze bijouterie on the world's first assembly lines. The east Phoenicians, however, especially the people of Tyre and Sidon, were highly skilled artisans and goldsmiths technically without peer.

The Greeks grudgingly granted the east Phoenicians first place in the working of precious metals. Homer in several places describes magnificently wrought Sidonian gold bowls with scenes in repoussé. Between 800 and 600 B.C. Phoenician goldsmiths established workshops in Greek cities where Greek apprentices studied. Greek jewelry of that period reflects the orientalizing style of the Phoenicians.

They had learned many techniques including repoussé, enameling, and granulation from the Egyptians and had picked up some stylistic flourishes from the Minoans and Mycenaeans. The Phoenician smiths were quick to borrow a motif from here, a touch from there, successfully incorporating divergent elements into a golden bowl or ornament. Early Phoenician goldwork was Oriental in feeling, reflecting Egyptian, Canaanite, Mesopotamian, and Cypriote influences. Later design was more attuned to the Hellenistic world. The emphasis in Phoenician workshops was on meeting current market trends rather than on expressing a personal or national aesthetic.

Nevertheless, there were distinctive Phoenician products such as elaborately carved furniture which was often gilded, bejeweled, and embellished with gold-covered ivory panels. Assyrians collected Phoenician furniture and it is frequently mentioned in the Old Testament. The Phoenicians were great carvers of ivory. The ivory for the panels and for gilded figurines, combs, spools, and ornamental plaques came from the tusks of walrus or the elephants which still roamed the area. The Carthaginians actually raised elephants on commercial ivory farms.

One sculpted ivory panel from a throne or chair has survived. It shows a jeweled ivory lion at the throat of a gilded slave. The background is an intricate and lovely pattern of flowers in relief in gold and blue enamel with three large blooms of red carnelian. The small but beautiful array of gold objects which has been found in burials discovered in Lebanon in recent years is evidence that a certain promiscuity of style did not diminish the flair of the Phoenician goldsmiths.

The Phoenician and the Carthaginian have not come down through history as sympathetic characters. Apart from their genius at international trade, their undisputed mastery of the seas, and bold explorations, the Phoenicians are remembered as their adversaries represented them, a brutal and venal people. The dark odor of sacrifice clings to the Carthaginians, whose libraries were obliterated when the Romans razed the city and sowed salt in the furrows. They cannot speak for themselves. There is no literature or artistic testament of their daily lives to arouse our sympathy.

There is another Mediterranean people whose origins, like those of the Phoenicians, are obscured by time. The Etruscans, like their occasional allies, the Carthaginians, cannot speak directly to the biased charges of their enemies. The enigmatic Etruscans of central Italy, however, left a vibrant legacy in gold, clay, and paint. Their funerary art and golden artifacts evoke our compassion and clearly show their vitality and uncomplicated love of pleasure.

The language of the Etruscans, written in Greek characters and as yet undeciphered, survives in only a few fragmentary inscriptions and texts. But many statues and frescoes celebrate the domestic and ceremonial rounds of these paradoxical people who combined a depressing Eastern attitude toward fate with unrestrained zest for life, love, and luxury.

Archaeological excavations have brought to light artifacts in gold, clay, and paint of wealthy Etruscans, who were reviled by their Greek and Roman contemporaries as pirates and unbridled sensualists at the same time. They were envied as skilled metallurgists, warriors, and traders. Modern man responds to the Etruscan self-portrayal. Atop a sarcophagus a fond couple reclines, the husband's arm protectively encircling his wife. United, they face eternity with gentle smiles. For almost two thousand years painted banqueters lolled in the dark on tomb walls until the world learned of their existence. Wine-flushed matrons served by nude slave boys watched with their husbands as dancers and musicians performed. Men, women, children, and slaves are frozen in time in bright processions, dancing, feasting, battling, and playing at the games that were such an important part of Etruscan life.

The Etruscans' pictorial legacy enhances our appreciation of their incredibly fine goldwork. Etruscan goldsmiths crafted gold with a fantasy and originality that has never been surpassed. They made unusually large pieces of fantastic elaboration. They were at ease with filigree and repoussé. The Etruscans were the practitioners par excellence of granulation in which minuscule spheres of gold, as small as 1/1000 of an inch in diameter, were juxtaposed in typical geometric patterns or in clusters, lines, or cones and affixed to the gold surfaces of vessels and jewelry. One exquisite small bowl in London's Victoria and Albert Museum has a design worked in more than 137,000 globules. The effect has been likened to that of light caught on early morning dew. Etruscan goldsmiths achieved astonishing effects without the use of polychrome stone or enamel inlays, relying on the intrinsic beauty of the gold itself.

Unlike the royal graves of previous gold-using cultures, Etruscan tombs contained no ceremonial weapons. What they did yield were lavish amounts of opulent jewelry. In the seventh century B.C. Phoenician and Greek wares imported into Etruria in volume stimulated the incorporation of Oriental motifs by Etruscan artisans. Symbols such as sun and moons, sphinxes, palmettes, sirens, and the fantastic animals of the East had a magical significance and appeared in profusion on the golden bracelets, earrings, necklaces, and fibulae the Etruscans adored.

The virtuosity of the goldsmith shone best perhaps in the

fibulae, or safety pins, which fastened Etruscan garments. Through the years they changed in style, being larger or smaller and more or less lavishly decorated with granulation, the most ethereal filigree or repoussé. Sometimes the fibulae were so exaggerated in size and so overloaded with ornament as to be decidedly vulgar. One extraordinary fibula is a massive piece, a foot high. It was found in the tomb of a noblewoman, part of a spectacular treasure in gold, ivory, and amber which included ornate gold ear pendants composed of several pieces fastened together and elaborately covered with repoussé patterns. Lying among the crumbling bones were rings, bracelets, a sixteen-inch-high breastplate, and pierced gold plaques which may once have covered an entire garment. The breastplate is completely covered with small abstract motifs of characteristic Etruscan design intermingled with flowers and foliage.

The fibulae were frequently dazzling creations creating processions of animals in the round. Three-dimensional horses, lions, and sphinxes embellished with granulation parade up the bar of one pin. The end of another, also covered with animals, terminates in a curved fastening surmounted by five fierce repoussé lions who are held in check by two ornate gold bands.

The wives of rich nobles and merchants were terribly flashy by Hellenistic standards. They flaunted their wealth, decking themselves out in flamboyant displays of gold jewelry. Wealthy Etruscan women enjoyed status and influence greater than those of other cultures. They were buried with gold ornaments, furnishings, and appointments after a pleasant life. They banqueted with their men, proposed toasts, and drank in public, all of which led the more austere Greeks and the severe Romans to brand the Etruscans as debauched, lascivious, and materialistic. In Rome a man tried for murdering his wife who had merely tasted wine was acquitted, and in Greece women were kept in virtual seclusion. The free intermingling of the sexes in Etruria gave rise to prurient tales that young women financed their doweries through prostitution, and the Romans wrote that the shameless Etruscans made love in public.

Etruscan love of music, considered excessive by the Romans and Greeks, is illustrated in hundreds of friezes where feasting, hunting, and games are all accompanied by music. The horn and trumpet were said to be Etruscan inventions. According to Aristotle they were so musically oriented that they "fought, kneaded dough and beat their slaves to the sound of a flute."

These colorful people were entrenched in Tuscany by the eighth century B.C. and by the fifth century B.C. ruled widely throughout central and northern Italy from Lombardy in the north to Rome in the south. Various theories ascribe their origins to Tyre, Troy, Asia Minor, or the indigenous Villanovans who migrated from northern Italy about 1000 B.C. The most persuasive theory postulates an Asia Minor homeland.

Herodotus, writing when the Etruscans were still prominent, claimed they came from Lydia in western Turkey. Chronic famine forced the Lydians to divide. Half remained with their King. The others marched overland with the King's son, Tyrrenhus, to Smyrna. There they built a fleet of ships and sailed with their worldly goods to seek a new home. Herodotus says they settled in Umbria on Italy's west coast, subduing the native Villanovans, in the eighth century B.C. Such migrations were not uncommon in the unsettled first millennium B.C. when southern Italy was colonized by Greeks, and North Africa and other parts of the western Mediterranean by the Carthaginians. Supporters of the Lydian theory of provenance point to the marked similarity of Lydian and Etruscan funerary practices and the Oriental mentality of the Etruscans, so unlike that of the Italic peoples.

There is not yet enough conclusive evidence to solve the puzzle. In any case, a highly developed culture of warriors and traders came to fruition in a short span of time. Etruria boasted large well-appointed urban centers at the same period the Greeks established trading colonies in southern Italy and on Sicily and paralleled the traditional founding of Rome in 753 B.C. by Romulus, who in his infancy was saved and suckled by a wolf.

Etruria was never a unified nation but, like Phoenicia, a loose confederacy. At least twelve major city-states shared a common language and culture. Etruscan wealth was founded on farming, piracy, and, above all, international trade in base metals. Their land was blessed with rich deposits of iron, copper, lead, and tin.

Gold was regarded as the index of wealth but central Italy had no native gold and the Etruscans relied primarily on trade to get the precious metal.

A great deal of iron came from the island of Elba, where the ore lay near the surface and was so abundant that the Etruscans could be excused for thinking it magically replenished itself. At first the ore was smelted on the island, but later a processing plant was put into operation at Populonium on the mainland coast. Huge mountains of slag accumulated. After World War I when Europe was starved for iron, those towering slag piles were profitably worked for the iron the Etruscan process had left behind.

The Etruscans traded raw copper and pig iron, fine bronze articles, and the shiny black pottery called bucchero ware with the Greeks, Greek colonies, cities in the eastern Mediterranean, and with Carthaginian ports in North Africa, Cyprus, and Spain.

The nature of the imports is reflected in the overwhelming amounts of Greek artifacts found in such tombs as Praeneste, Caere, and Tarquinia. They were so enamored of anything Greek that Etruscan tombs of the wealthiest era (600 to 400 B.C.) have proven a more fertile source of Hellenic jewelry, statuary, ceramics, and ornaments than Greece itself.

Etruscan gold came from several sources. Trade with Carthage brought both Spanish gold and gold dust from Africa. The Etruscans got a good supply of raw alluvial gold from the upper reaches of the Po, whose tributaries descend from the western Alps. It appears they also acquired a certain amount through commerce with central France, where there were extensive supplies of placer or alluvial gold. Some gold reached Etruria in the form of finished Greek gold wares and jewelry.

Etruria's domination of the western Mediterranean trading lanes, so vital in the Iron Age, eventually crumbled before the superior Punic Navy, but the two powers had previously maintained amicable relations. Carthaginian vessels carried Etruscan merchandise and brought gold and luxury items back to Italy.

Both peoples regarded with alarm the Greek spread to the west and joined forces to fight the creation of a Greek enclave on Corsica. They succeeded and Etruria took Corsica and the

Carthaginians got adjacent Sardinia. This effectively kept the Greeks from reaching Spain and maintained the Punic monopoly on Iberia's mineral treasures.

Proof of Punic-Etruscan relations came to light with recent archaeological discoveries made at Pyrgi, the port used by inland Etruscan cities including Caere, famed for its goldwork and reputed to be one of the richest cities in the entire world. Classical authors made frequent reference to a temple on the shore at Pyrgi which was bedecked with gold and had a great treasury filled with gold and silver.

In 1964 archaeologists discovered the remains of the temple. Among the artifacts they excavated three folded gold sheets. Written about 500 B.C., two of the beaten gold plaques bore Etruscan inscriptions and the third was in Punic. Parallel texts record the dedication of the temple by the ruler of Caere to a goddess worshiped by both peoples. She was Uni to the Etruscans and Astarte to the Carthaginians, the goddess of fertility and sexual love. The golden texts indicate that there were some Carthaginians living at Pyrgi. Twenty-nine tiny nail holes pierced the gold sheets which may have been removed from the sanctuary during an attack and buried for safekeeping. Whoever took them down carefully placed twenty-nine diminutive gold nails in the folds of the gold sheets.

Rome's first historical character was an Etruscan, Tarquin the Proud. For a century following Tarquin, Etruscan kings ruled the nascent city. Around the beginning of the sixth century B.C. they were driven out but left a strong imprint that colored Roman life for centuries. Etruria bequeathed to Rome her dress, religious practices, engineering projects of sewer system, roads, and flood control. Etruscans created the Forum, where the courts, markets, Senate, and citizens' assembly governed the life of the rude city that grew to empire.

Unfortunately, in spite of the wealth, power, and natural advantages the Etruscan cities had in common, they were unable to suppress internecine squabbling long enough to confront together the growing might of Rome. By 280 B.C. the Roman Republic had crushed every one. For several centuries the Etruscan language survived as a rustic dialect in the Tuscan hills. But eventually every trace of the culture that gave Italy its first taste of grandeur vanished save the neglected stone tombs dotting the rustic landscape.

Then, in the European Dark Ages, bands of hungry outlaws found and plundered thousands of Etruscan tombs making off with gold and jewelry, smashing pots and other artifacts deemed of no value. In the Renaissance there was a flurry of interest in the shadowy Etruscans. But it was the fantastic discoveries of the nineteenth century, coming from long-lost burials in the malarial Tuscan swamps, that really brought the Etruscans to the attention of the world.

In the 1820s a peasant who was plowing a field about forty miles north of Rome at Vulci crashed through the roof of a buried necropolis with his team of oxen and landed in Etruscan gold.

The property the necropolis was on had been sold by the Pope to Napoleon Bonaparte's brother, Lucien, Prince of Canino. With absolutely no regard for art or history the prince, in a manner which set a precedent for other landowners, began to ruthlessly cannibalize the Vulci necropolis. He worked it as thoroughly as if it were a gold mine. Indeed, it was a gold mine. In four months of indiscriminate looting his laborers recovered more than two thousand relics of gold and silver, more than any other ancient site in the world had ever produced.

Soon, anyone with a plot of ground in the heart of Italy was scrabbling in search of buried gold. It was easy work; finding the telltale clues which signaled the presence of a tomb, breaking in, and then carrying out the loot which dealers in Rome and Florence fell over each other to buy. The antiquarians bought cheap and sold dear to avid collectors from all over Europe and the United States.

Two men stand out from the greedy throng. George Dennis, the founder of British Etruscology, was consul in Italy in the 1840s and one of the few men interested in the Etruscans as a people. He devoted his life to piecing together their history as it was revealed through the art and artifacts from the tombs.

The other savant was an immensely wealthy English numismatist Richard Payne Knight, who died in 1824. His collection of gold, jewels, coins, and ancient bronzes forms the core of the British Museum's Etruscan collection, the world's greatest.

Dennis was present at the opening of a burial at Vulci in 1843. He watched the prince's workmen as they labored under the vigilant eye of an armed superintendent. The men found dozens of whole bucchero vessels, with their lovely metallic sheen intact. These, and all other pottery, were smashed underfoot on orders from the prince, who wanted only gold and silver artifacts removed. The overseer made sure that everything but objects of precious metal was destroyed—ceramics, furniture, musical instruments, and statuary. Dennis couldn't persuade him to spare even one vessel as a souvenir. This ghastly act of desecration was repeated at each site. In spite of the hundreds of thousands of artifacts that were smashed, thousands somehow survived. The six thousand Vulci tombs were worked for 150 years and yielded an estimated 85 per cent of the Etruscan vases in the museums of Florence and Rome.

Nineteenth-century ladies had a passion for the lovely, showy gold jewelry that once adorned Etruscan matrons. Lucien Bonaparte's wife inaugurated the vogue by wearing an incredibly beautiful assemblage of pendants, jeweled earrings, and armlets which made her the envy of society women. The work of the foremost goldsmiths of Paris or Vienna paled next to ornaments which had bedecked warm-blooded Etruscan beauties in life and solaced them as they lay tranquilly through the ages, forgotten under the Italian earth.

The rage for things Etruscan spawned an industry in turning out counterfeit gold jewelry and ceramics. Today there is a black market in genuine Etruscan objets d'art and an even brisker trade in artifacts made and aged by talented Tuscan forgers, descended perhaps from the distinguished craftsmen of Etruria.

CHAPTER SEVEN *Persian and Greek Gold*

During the seven hundred years preceding the birth of Christ the emphasis on gold as a sacred metal gave way before its increasing importance as a potent factor in economics. The arena of greatest gold use shifted in those centuries from Asia to Europe, where it was to remain until the disintegration of the Roman Empire. Even as the peoples of the Levant and the enigmatic Etruscans enjoyed the availability of more gold than they had previously known, the real golden focus was elsewhere. The chief protagonists, gold-rich Persia and gold-poor Greece, struggled for supremacy until the towering figure of Alexander the Great brought the mighty Persian Empire to its knees, releasing the world's largest store of gold, the accumulation of generations of Persian kings, and changing the course of history.

Many of the essential features of Western civilization as we know it are the fruit of the relatively short but profuse flowering of human thought and activity in the Greco-Roman world. The Greeks and, in a different way, the Romans anticipated the full range of human potential and lit up the world with a many-faceted brilliance which still shines today, as do the surviving objects wrought in gold by their distinguished craftsmen.

With the historical period came the penchant for detailing in written form man's progress in the physical and spiritual world. Whereas tracing the thread of gold woven through prehistoric human experience is almost exclusively limited to sorting archaeological evidence, it now becomes possible to follow the story through multiplying literary references.

Emerging in the eighth century B.C. from centuries of material and intellectual poverty, Greece throbbed with energy. Hellenic

Fifteenth-century German illustration showing the legendary giant ants believed to mine gold.

27. One-third stater of electrum struck by Alyattes, King of Lydia (610–561 B.C.), bearing head of a lion, the royal symbol.

28. Gold daric issued by Darius the Great, King of Persia (521–486 B.C.). Obverse shows the King with spear, bow, and quiver. A Persian soldier received 1½ darics a month in pay. One military expedition was so large that 4 million darics were paid out to its participants.

29. Stater of Alexander the Great (336–23 B.C.) portraying the head of Athena modeled after Phidias' famed statue at Athens.

30. Reverse of Alexander's stater showing the goddess Nike, the Winged Victory, and bearing the Macedonian's name.

31. Pentadrachm of Ptolemy I of Egypt (323–285 B.C.). The first coin to bear the portrait of a living person.

32. Stater of Philip of Macedon—reverse. The philippus of 23-carat gold depicts a two-horse chariot, or biga, used by the Macedonians in battle. This is the coin which served as a model for barbarian issues such as the Bellovaci staters.

33. Gallo-Belgic stater struck by the Bellovaci barbarians in imitation of the first gold coins they had encountered as they migrated westward through the Danube Valley—the staters of Philip of Macedon. Ca. 125–100 B.C.

34. Gold bowl with three lions; repousse and engraved with lions' heads in full round. Marlik culture, ca. 1200–1000 B.C. Archaeological Museum, Tehran.

35. Large gold bowl decorated with repoussé and engraved scenes. Hasanlu, Ca. 1000 B.C. Archaeological Museum, Tehran.

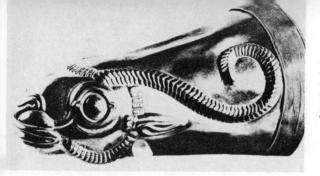

36. Achaemenid gold situla or cup with gazelle's head, rim decorated with threadlike gold wire. Hamadan. Fifth century B.C. Archaeological Museum, Tehran.

37. Achaemenid gold bracelet from Oxus Treasure. Originally inlaid with enamel or stones. Amu Darya Basin. Fifth century B.C. British Museum.

38. Gold plaque from Ziwiye Treasure, Iran. Seventh century B.C. University Museum, Philadelphia.

39. Gold plaque from Ziwiye Treasure with horned animals and catlike masks in relief. Iran. Seventh century B.C. University Museum, Philadelphia.

40. Scythian gold pectoral of Greek workmanship with forty-eight individually cast figures soldered onto frame of twisted gold wire. Fourth century B.C. Kiev Historical Museum.

41. Detail of Scythian pectoral showing lion and panther attacking a boar. Fourth century B.C. Kiev Historical Museum.

42. Detail of Scythian pectoral showing a nomad milking a ewe. Fourth century B.C. Kiev Historical Museum.

43. Scytho-Siberian gold plaque from collection of Peter the Great depicting a monster and tiger in combat. The State Hermitage Museum, Leningrad.

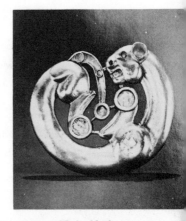

45. Scytho-Sarmatian gold shield plaque from Peter the Great's Collection in the form of a coiled panther. 11 cm (4 5/16 in.) in diameter. Late seventh or early sixth century B.C. Hermitage.

44. Gold bottle of Greek workmanship depicting scenes from Scythian life or mythology. Fourth century B.C. Hermitage.

46. Incised gold sheet sandwiched in glass depicting Jonah and the whale from a catacomb in Rome. Third or fourth century A.D. Louvre, Paris.

47. Roman opus interrasile gold cup; octagonal with panther handles, originally set with gems. One of two from the Pietroasa Treasure, Romania. Fourth century A.D. National Museum of Antiquities, Bucharest.

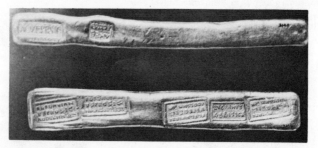

48. Roman gold bars from the Sirmium mint (Balkans) officially stamped. Of the type used to pacify the barbarian chief. Fourth century A.D. British Museum.

49. Wall painting from Christian catacombs outside Rome showing an early Christian miner.

50. Roman gold stater of Flaminus, 196 B.C. British Museum.

43. Scytho-Siberian gold plaque from collection of Peter the Great depicting a monster and tiger in combat. The State Hermitage Museum, Leningrad.

45. Scytho-Sarmatian gold shield plaque from Peter the Great's Collection in the form of a coiled panther. 11 cm (4 5/16 in.) in diameter. Late seventh or early sixth century B.C. Hermitage.

44. Gold bottle of Greek workmanship depicting scenes from Scythian life or mythology. Fourth century B.C. Hermitage.

46. Incised gold sheet sandwiched in glass depicting Jonah and the whale from a catacomb in Rome. Third or fourth century A.D. Louvre, Paris.

47. Roman opus interrasile gold cup; octagonal with panther handles, originally set with gems. One of two from the Pietroasa Treasure, Romania. Fourth century A.D. National Museum of Antiquities, Bucharest.

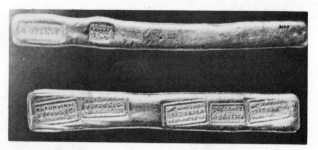

48. Roman gold bars from the Sirmium mint (Balkans) officially stamped. Of the type used to pacify the barbarian chief. Fourth century A.D. British Museum.

49. Wall painting from Christian catacombs outside Rome showing an early Christian miner.

50. Roman gold stater of Flaminus, 196 B.C. British Museum.

51. Byzantine gold coin.

52. Byzantine coin (reverse).

53. Aureus of Emperor Nero (A.D. 54–68) Nero reduced the weight of the aureus but not its purity.

54. Rare gold ring money of first century B.C. Britain. Such rings were introduced from Ireland after 1600 B.C.

55. Fragment of the Mold cape, an elaborate repoussé gold garment from first millennium B.C. Found in Flintshire, Wales. British Museum.

56. Irish gold collar with cupped terminals and repoussé decoration. Seventh century B.C. Victoria and Albert Museum, London.

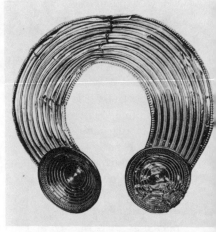

civilization was fertile ground for the elaboration and transformation of previous social, economic, religious, and philosophical values. In parallel revolutions man gained a new dignity, his life new meaning, although running close to the surface was the ages-old current of superstitious barbarism.

The Aegean had been in economic and cultural contact with the Near East before the curtain of the Dark Ages fell, severing the exchange of goods and ideas which had nurtured Minoan Crete and Mycenae. The grim years of invasion and upheaval in Greece were matched by a similar period in Asia Minor and the Levant during which Solomon's Israel and the Phoenician cities had made the most of short-lived intervals of relative independence.

The history of Greece is interwoven with that of the Near East: Hellenic Greece most intimately with that of the Persian Empire forged by Cyrus the Great and his successors. Convulsions wracked the Near East as first one group and then another vied for power during the first millennium B.C.

In the ninth century B.C. Assyria, one of the most aggressive states, embarked on a series of uninterrupted raids and then full-scale wars which expanded her empire from the middle Tigris area to Syria, Turkey, and lower Mesopotamia. For a brief period Assyria held sway over Egypt, and Sargon II boasted in his annals that seven Greek kings of Cyprus paid him gold in tribute. Under Ashurbanipal in the seventh century B.C. the Assyrian Empire was the most extensive state the world had seen, spreading from the Nile to near the Caspian and from Cilicia in southern Eastern Asia Minor to the Persian Gulf.

The royal annals list exultantly the great amounts of gold, silver, female slaves, furniture inlaid with gold and gems, and other booty that flowed into the Assyrian treasuries and temples to the omnipotent sun-god Ashur. They describe too, most matter-of-factly, ghastly tortures, wholesale slaughter, the razing of cities and enslavement of whole populations. The Bible brands the Assyrians as brutal warriors, armed with deadly iron weapons. Their own artists confirmed that assessment in bas-reliefs glorifying carnage and cruelty. Realistic scenes from reliefs at the great palace at Nineveh show the heads of enemy kings displayed as grisly blossoms on trees in the royal gardens.

Internal dissension and continual flare-ups in the subject territories, whose chief duty was to maintain payment of tribute, severely strained the cohesion of the empire. Assyrian records mention tribal peoples of the northern Iranian hills including the Medes, who eventually shook off the Assyrian yoke and about 670 B.C. succeeded in subjecting the Persians to the south. Late in the seventh century B.C. the King of the Medes joined with the ruler of newly independent Babylon to bring down the once invincible Assyrian Empire, which was riddled with rot and exhausted by centuries of warfare.

Details of the siege of Nineveh, the Assyrian capital, and the suicide of the last Assyrian monarch, Sardanapalus, were given by Diodorus. He was indebted for his information to another Greek, Ctesias, historian and doctor at the Persian court of Artaxerxes II (404–358 B.C.) in Babylon. His book, the *Persica*, of which only a few fragments survive, drew upon the Babylonian national archives.

Sardanapalus in this account may be the composite of two Assyrian rulers. He has the name and position of Ashurbanipal, Assyria's last major king, who was a man of learning and a patron of the arts. Archaeologists discovered some twenty thousand clay tablets in the ruins of his library at Nineveh which constituted the most extensive historical works composed up to that time.

The figure of Sardanapalus has been assigned the character and sad end of Ashurbanipal's effete brother, Shamash-shumukin, King of Babylon. Classical authors described how rebel forces besieged the great city of Nineveh, which was surrounded by double walls and a deep moat, eight miles in circumference.

For almost three years the Assyrian capital held out as the last of thirty Assyrian monarchs alternately harangued his people to resist and gave himself over to the debauchery that had marked his sybaritic reign. When he saw the cause was without hope, he gave each of his two sons and three daughters three thousand talents of gold and sent them away to fend for themselves.

Inside the palace precincts he had slaves build a pyre four hundred feet high, topped by a fragrant cedarwood chamber one hundred feet long. Inside were placed his treasures, the fruit of generations of conquest—gold vessels, gems and gold jewelry, gilded furniture and golden ornaments of many styles from the many countries who had paid homage to Assyria. He had, according to the historians, 150 gold tables and an equal number of gold couches piled in the chamber. On top of the tables were 10 million talents of gold and ten times as many of silver. The luxuries of all the world were crammed into the chamber—purple robes, embroidered with gold, precious incense and perfumed oils, resins and ointments, rich garments and carved ivory.

When all was ready the King, followed by his concubines, mounted a wooden stairway to the treasure-filled room and gave the order to light the pyre. It is said the blaze darkened the sky with smoke for fifteen days, during which the people of Nineveh, unaware of their King's fate, believed him to be offering sacrifices for the sun-god's intervention.

In the early nineteenth century the romantic Eugène Delacroix painted a magnificent canvas commemorating the death of Sardanapalus, filling the scene with lush images evoking the Oriental excess of the last of the Assyrians. Nineveh was razed. Assyria was obliterated. The Medes and Babylonians divided up her territories and her gold. The world rejoiced at the collapse of the mighty and looked with mounting alarm at the Medes. They ruled in Iran, upper Mesopotamia, and in Syria, where they touched the frontiers of Lydia, another new power in Asia Minor.

Babylon, which held lower Mesopotamia, blazed bright under Nebuchadnezzar, but religious conservatism and cultural exhaustion fostered the decay which soon brought the glittering city to its doom.

While the Babylonian King, Belshazzar, dined from the gold plates his father had looted from the Temple of Jerusalem, heedless of impending ruin, the Medes and Persians, under the leadership of Cyrus, a dynamic young man of the Persian Achaemenid family, swooped down on the vulnerable metropolis, which gave itself up in 539 B.C. By the time Cyrus died fighting in central Asia, nine years later, he had launched the Persians on the way to empire. From that time on the fates of Persia and Greece were intertwined.

In a meteoric rise the Persians threw their snare over nation after nation until their empire stretched from the Black Sea to the eastern Mediterranean and across into the northern fringes of

India. One by one they subjugated all the world's known gold-bearing regions, save Carthaginian Spain and a few restricted zones of Greek production. The world had never seen such golden majesty as in those years when rivers of precious tribute poured into the treasuries of "the Great King, King of Kings, King of the Countries Possessing many Kinds of People, King of this Great Earth Far and Wide." When Darius the Great sat enthroned in his splendid new palace at Persepolis, representatives of some thirty vassal states knelt in homage as they proffered golden tribute.

Even before the gates of Babylon swung open before Cyrus, two kingdoms, Phrygia and Lydia, both rich in native gold, were absorbed by the fledgling Persian Empire. Phrygia, in west-central Asia Minor, was a prosperous country noted for the fertility of its land and cattle but especially for its gold. Gordium, the capital, was the seat of King Midas of legendary fame. Until recently he, like so many others, was thought to be a purely mythical figure, but archaeological excavations at Gordium have revealed royal tombs and the existence of a dynasty of kings named alternately Gordios and Midas.

According to tradition, the first Phyrgian ruler was poor King Gordius, whose assets were limited to a pair of oxen. His son, Midas, was a simple but generous soul who once offered hospitality to a stranger. His guest turned out to be the foster father of the god Bacchus. To thank him Bacchus granted the King one wish. Without reflecting on the possible consequences Midas requested the Golden Touch and it was granted.

Ordering an extravagant banquet to celebrate his good fortune, Midas was amazed to find his food turn to inedible gold lumps as it touched his lips. His cherished daughter became a golden statue under his loving caress. The blessing was a curse and he begged Bacchus to remove it. "Go and wash yourself," commanded the god, "in the waters of the Pactolus." Midas did so and the Golden Touch passed from the King to the river. From then on, says the Greek legend, the sands and water were laden with gold. The story reflects the awe with which the gold-poor Greeks regarded the Pactolus, which was the source of a great deal of Asia Minor's gold.

The actual location of the river is unknown to modern geography, but its riches were real enough in Greek and Roman times. Modern historians think alluvial gold dust washed down from Mount Tmolus in the Anatolian highlands gilded the Pactolus. But by the Imperial Roman era all the gold-bearing quartz matrix had been eroded by the force of water rushing down the steep mountain stream and the river ceased to yield. Phrygia was enriched not only by the Pactolus but by gold from mines near Troy and at Lampsacus on the Dardanelles. Additional gold most likely come from distant sources via trade.

Their kingdom lay two hundred miles inland, but the Phrygians had trade ties with the Ionian Greeks. The historical Midas, married to a Greek princess, was the first foreigner to make an offering to the Oracle at Delphi who subsequently attracted an international following and a lot of foreign gold.

The Phrygians shared the abundant gold of the Pactolus with Lydia, a gold-rich state to the south, until early in the seventh century B.C. when an invasion of nomadic Cimmerians overthrew Midas. The King committed suicide by poison as the barbarians, flushed out of southern Russia by the Scythians, stormed his palace ramparts.

Midas' chariot remained at Gordium according to ancient authors. It was in the main temple, the shaft tied with a knot of great intricacy. Whoever could untie the knot, said an oracle, would become Lord of Asia. In the fourth century B.C. a Macedonian general, scarcely more than a boy, took one look at the complex knot which had resisted the effort of myriad ambitious warriors, and, as his army looked, slashed through it with a single stroke of his gleaming sword. Alexander fulfilled the oracle and went on to become Lord of the world.

Once the wild Cimmerians had devastated Gordium, the Phrygians never regained strength and yielded their position to Lydia. The capital, Sardis, was only forty miles from the Aegean and had long been in touch with the east Greek world. Under such kings as Gyges and Croesus, Sardis became a cosmopolitan capital, the financial center of the Near East, and a magnet for traders, bankers, goldsmiths, and political exiles.

The Lydians were talented manufacturers and merchants. Their capital was fortuitously situated on the Royal Road, the great east-west highway joining Assyria to the eastern Mediterranean. The caravan route ran 1,677 miles, from the Lydian-controlled Greek colony at Ephesus on the Aegean to Susa, and was heavily traveled. The Lydians were middlemen between East and West, absorbing and transmitting goods and ideas. Herodotus, ever informative, writes that they were the first *kapeloi*, or retailers with permanent shops.

The Lydians were culturally influenced by the Greeks, whose prosperous coastal trading cities they came to control. Lydia offered Greece ornaments and jewelry of gold and electrum, purple rugs, patterned and embroidered textiles, perfume, and other goods. However, one Lydian offering to Greece stands above all others. The Lydians developed the world's first true coinage and profoundly influenced the course of economic affairs.

Trade stimulated the development of mathematics and the evolution of systems of weights and measures. The need to expedite commercial exchanges led men very early to supplement simple barter with objects such as cowries, cattle, rings and ingots of copper, bronze, or gold. Cowrie shells, for example, had many of the desirable qualities of a medium of exchange. They were portable, durable, could not be counterfeited, and in many areas were enhanced by mystical associations. Cowries formed out of gold were among the earliest examples of the goldsmith's art. The shells circulated as currency throughout much of the ancient world, and Marco Polo found them still very much in use in remote mountain areas of thirteenth-century Asia.

The division of human labor into specialities complicated simple barter. A farmer who wished to acquire a bronze sword had a problem if the smith didn't want the ox he offered in exchange. He faced a dilemma too if he wanted some wine or something of far less value than the item he had to bargain with. Prehistoric man may have invented a medium of exchange when he bartered a surplus fleece for something he didn't need for subsistence. He traded his fleece for a copper tool which he planned to keep until he needed to use it in trade for something essential.

The economic system of Egypt, although it made use of gold as a standard of value, was based on barter in which sacks of grain and linen cloth were units of exchange. In ancient times cattle formed an important standard of exchange. *Pecunia*, the

Latin for "money," derives from the word *pecus,* meaning "cattle." Cattle, however, have serious drawbacks—they are not easily portable or divisible and they require constant care, food, and water.

Men soon learned that pieces of metal of certain uniform weights were superior to livestock for trade. Rounded bits of gold weighing roughly 8.34 grams each and called shekels were used in Babylonia. In Palestine the gold shekel weighed approximately 16.4 grams. And of course there were the gold ingots of Menes in the fourth millennium B.C. and his successors' rings; however, they were too valuable for routine transactions. But bars and rings such as those of the Egyptians and Irish were among the earliest metal currencies. The bar was particularly convenient because a *taleis,* meaning "something cut off," could be hacked off to equal the value of any purchase, making them almost infinitely divisible. This advantage was also a drawback inasmuch as sharpers often shaved a bit off every bar that passed through their hands, thus accumulating enough to cast their own bars and decreasing the value of the original bar.

Early in the second millennium B.C. priests of the Temple of Moon God at Ur traveled with letters of credit written on clay tablets. They procured supplies en route leaving a tablet to be redeemed at the Temple for a specified amount of gold or silver. Temples were the world's first banks. Babylonian tablets record loans from the temple treasuries as early as 2000 B.C. Gold stored in the sacred buildings was thought to have divine protection from theft so that private and royal treasures were often left there on deposit.

The lumps of gold, rings, ingots, shekels, and talents which had been introduced to ease otherwise awkward transactions and to free commerce from the stringent limitations of unadulterated barter had themselves a serious deficiency. The weight and purity of each piece of gold were subject to fluctuation so that each exchange was accompanied by tedious and time-consuming weighing and assaying. The process used most often to test the quality of gold used the touchstone, or Lydian stone as it was called. This was a black stone like jasper which the goldsmith rubbed with the gold object to be tested. Theophrastus wrote that these smooth stones were only found in the river Tmolus. The mark left on the stone was then compared to a mark made by a touch needle.

A complete set of touch needles was made up of three sets of twenty-four needles each. The needles of the first set contained varying proportions of gold and silver; those of the second set gold and copper; and the third set combined the three metals. The needles of each set were usually arranged on a ring. The first needle was of one part gold and twenty-three parts of the inferior metal. The proportion of gold increased with each needle until the twenty-fourth needle was of pure gold. It was from this ancient system that the division of gold into twenty-four carats derives. "This method is so accurate," wrote Pliny, "that they do not mistake it to a scruple."

Ancient Egyptian texts describe a process for gold plating copper which could fool the touchstone but not hold up to an even older method which did more than test the surface of the gold in question. A sample of the gold was removed, weighed, and then heated to drive off impurities. The quality was figured by determining how much weight the sample lost in the fire.

In the eighth century B.C. natural lumps of electrum from Lydian river beds were used in commerce. Tests have shown their gold content varied from 36 to 55 per cent. Since lumps of higher purity were being imitated, Lydian merchants began to mark those which had already been tested so that they could be recognized and the time-consuming testing avoided. These were in effect the first private issues of coins.

The next step was to begin making electrum coins of uniform weight and size. King Allyates seems to have minted the first cast electrum coin in the seventh century B.C. and marked it with a lion's head.

The earliest examples of such coins come from the foundations of the famous Temple of Artemis at Ephesus, on the west coast of Lydia, the Ionian city established by the Greeks where St. Paul founded a church under Timothy and John. Archaeologists excavated thick, bean-shaped coins from under the foundation where they seem to have been placed in the same way coins in later times were set under a cornerstone or under the step of a ship's mast.

The coins circulating in Lydia and the Greek cities of Asia Minor had a device stamped in relief on one side and bore anvil marks on the other. Their intrinsic value fluctuated according to the percentage of silver, but their weight was always close to eight grams, unless they had been filed. They became popular because of the way they speeded transactions, and it is thought that prosperous private merchants struck their own issues. The types stamped on the coins were symbolic of the man or city which issued them. Ephesus' coins were punched with a bee, Miletus' with a lion, for example. Originally these were not so much intended for trade as for official payments, but they did find their way into the market place. Greek mercenaries in Lydian employ were paid in electrum coins, which they quickly parted with in the Lydian and Ionian markets, which offered a wide array of attractive goods.

It was the last Lydian dynast, Croesus, whose name still stands for boundless wealth, who is credited with taking the gamble out of coin exchange. In the mid-sixth century B.C. he established a bimetallic system, issuing coins of both gold and silver of guaranteed quality. In 1968 archaeologists working at Sardis uncovered Croesus' mint refinery and more than three hundred ceramic vessels in which electrum was separated into gold and silver.

Croesus refined electrum for purely economic reasons. The ancients found the pale gold aesthetically pleasing and valued it highly for making into goblets. Pliny wrote that kings drank only from goblets of the white gold because they had the power of detecting poison. Historians have sometimes called the Roman credulous for believing that an electrum goblet warned the imbiber of the presence of poison by hissing and displaying a rainbow in the bowl.

In fact, however, Pliny was right. When arsenic, a very common poison, was poured into a goblet of electrum, the metal did indeed hiss and flash a colorful film. The cause of this seeming magic was chemical. Traces of iron in the gold, which had not been volatilized in the refining process, reacted with the arsenic to form the film, which was iron oxide. The hissing noise came from escaping gases caused by the reaction of arsenic with the sulphides and arsenates trapped in the metal bowl. The iron-oxide film could be removed, leaving the electrum unchanged to the naked eye. However, microscopic examination would have revealed a minutely beaded surface.

The famous lozenge-shaped stater issued by Croesus and stamped with his device of the facing heads of a lion and a bull was the world's first universally accepted coin. A far cry from the elaborate and beautiful issues of Greece and Rome, they nevertheless were acceptable to nomadic barbarian and sophisticated urbanite alike because they had the backing of the powerful Lydian state, the fame of which was known to all.

The introduction of dependable currency had a far-reaching effect. The Greeks quickly adopted coinage, primarily in silver, while the Greek colonies, the Persians, and most of southwestern Asia based their currencies on gold. Mainland Greece, with so little native gold, used the plentiful silver of the Laurium mines near Athens for coins until Philip II of Macedon, father of Alexander, issued huge quantities of gold staters bearing his likeness.

The twenty-three-karat gold for Philip's staters, which were Europe's first gold currency, came primarily from the mines of Thrace in northern Greece, which Cadmus had worked. Later great quantities of these found their way to Rome, where they served as the first gold currency following the Roman conquest of Macedon in the second century B.C. They were widely circulated and have been found all over Europe and Asia. "Philippus" became a synonym for any type of fine gold coin.

Coins played a vital part in the spread of Greek civilization and streamlined commerce in the western Mediterranean, coastal France, Spain, Sicily, and in southern Italy. In the Greek colonies of Syracuse and Tarentum gold was mined for coins as early as the fourth century B.C.

Croesus' innovation had another far-reaching effect. It democratized gold. The statesman Solon, who framed Athen's democratic laws, noted that the richest men "have twice the eagerness that others have." Ambition rewarded the merchant, soldier, even the farmer with gold coins that could be collected and held without losing their quality or value.

New areas of specialization were the natural outgrowth of coinage. The counterfeiter was making copies as early as the sixth century B.C. There is a story, which Herodotus called silly

but may well be true, that Polycrates, the tyrant of the Greek island of Samos, had a large number of gold-sheathed lead coins
struck to bribe the besieging Lacedaemonians in 525 or 524 B.C.
Counterfeit coins were distributed as pay to soldiers on more
than one occasion.

There was a need for money-changers and for bankers. As
more gold came into the hands of individuals outside the palaces
and temples, the goldsmiths found themselves not only melting
coins to fashion into ornaments and offerings but also acting as
bankers. Frequently it was the goldsmith, who was already familiar with the precious metal and traditionally regarded as possessed of special powers, verging on the magical, who stored
coin or bullion for clients.

Little by little goldsmiths came to perform such functions as
drawing up contracts and acting as loan bankers. They were the
first usurers, loaning out at interest part of the gold which had
been entrusted to them by men chary of keeping it in their
homes or carrying it on robber-infested caravan routes. The
goldsmith gave the depositor a receipt for his gold, and this
evolved into a system of bills of exchange.

The gold backing the receipts and bills paid up in the goldsmith's vaults. He lent some of it out, sometimes all of it, and was
then unable to make good on the paper presented for exchange.
To counteract this and other abuses laws were passed governing
the lending of money. In many places it was a crime to charge
interest, but the moneylender never lacked customers despite the
regulations. Goldsmiths continued to act as bankers throughout
much of history, and in European cities goldsmith's districts became the banking centers. Lombard Street, the financial heart of
London, was once goldsmiths' row. The founder of the Bank of
England and many other early bankers started business as
"goldsmiths who keep running cashes." International bankers,
whole dynasties of Italians and Germans, became indispensable
members of society, sometimes more powerful than the kings
they served.

Croesus, who started it all, was himself an internationalist and
a man of great power. He held sway over all of western Asia
Minor, but his hand rested lightly on the Ionian Greek colonies
over which he had control. He gained favor with many Greek

states by his tolerant policies and generous gifts. Sparta asked him to send gold in exchange for a statue of Apollo and he chose to give the gold as an outright gift.

The formidable Persians, led by the military genius of Cyrus, were growing stronger with each day and casting covetous eyes on the Lydian Empire. Croesus remembered the aid the Delphic Oracle had given King Gyges a century before in gaining the Lydian throne (in exchange for more than eighteen hundred pounds of worked gold) and the golden throne that Midas had dedicated to the Oracle. He sent to Delphi to find out if he ought to go to war with the Persians. The Oracle replied by prophesying that if the Lydian King attacked the Persians, he would destroy a mighty empire. Overjoyed, Croesus sent rich gifts of thanksgiving to the Shrine of Apollo at Delphi, which outshone the magnificent offerings of his predecessors and must have stunned the Greeks, who seldom saw gold in any quantity.

To the international center the Hellenophile ruler sent two gold staters to each Delphian, couches plated with gold and silver, gold vessels, arms, electrum, jewels, spears, shields, and statues of women, lions and bulls, and an immense treasure in gold ingots. Herodotus states that "he melted down a great quantity of gold and made it into ingots, six palms [close to eighteen inches] in length and three in breadth, and one palm high; and their number was 117. Four of these were of pure gold, each weighing 2½ talents [about 550 pounds total]; the others were of electrum, weighing two talents and two mixing bowls of great size . . . of which the golden one . . . weighed over 8½ talents. . . . He also sent a golden figure of a woman 3 cubits high . . . and dedicated his wife's necklaces and girdles."

The total of the King's generosity amounted to some 7,500 pounds of gold! Alas, he had been too credulous. The answer of the Oracle proved double-edged. Croesus made war on Persia and a mighty empire was indeed destroyed—his own. Herodotus wrote that the Persian victory was due not to their superior strength but because the smell of their camels panicked the horses of the Lydian cavalry. As Persian troops sacked burning Sardis Croesus asked Cyrus what his troops were doing. Cyrus responded they were plundering Croesus' city and carrying off his riches. "Not my city," said Croesus, "nor my riches. They are no longer mine. It is your wealth they are pillaging." The sack of Sardis marked the end of Lydia and another step in Persia's ascent to mastery of the ancient world.

When Lydia fell to Cyrus, the Persians were introduced to coinage. Within fifty years the bimetallic system had spread throughout Asia Minor, and under the Persians it became a vital force in commerce, taxation, and everyday life. The Lydians had invented true coinage, but the Persians were the first to base government economy on money rather than on barter.

Darius, who ruled from 552 to 486 B.C., issued the first coins with a portrait. These darics were enhanced by the likeness of the King of Kings, whose name was recognized throughout the ancient world. His coins have been found in tombs from the amber shores of the Baltic to Africa and throughout central Asia, an indication of the extensive role they played in trade. The coinage of gold was a royal privilege, but the Persians allowed subject cities and states to mint silver. In all, vast numbers of coins were issued. The Persian emperors maintained the integrity of their coinage unlike some of the Greek city-states, which began early to water their gold coinage with copper or silver alloys in a vain attempt to stretch their resources. Shrewd merchants spotted debased coins and raised their prices accordingly, creating inflation, which has plagued mankind ever since.

Kings and merchant princes played on the deeply embedded religious regard men had for gold when they turned it into a powerful economic asset. Presented with the opportunity to acquire the precious yellow metal, men have seldom turned aside. Few chapters in history have been shaped by gold, both glorified and bloodied by the sun stuff, to the degree the Persian Empire and Alexander's Greece were.

Gold brought Persia power and glory. It bought her friends and sowed dissension among her enemies keeping them from uniting against her. Ultimately the golden empire fell to the young genius from Macedon who marched east liberating colossal amounts of golden treasure to tip the balance of history and change the course of European civilization. Save for the deluge of New World gold which flooded sixteenth-century Europe, the world had never seen such golden treasure as blazed in ancient Persia and Hellenistic Greece.

Persian conquest, like that of the Spaniards in Mexico and Peru, was fueled by gold lust. After Lydia fell, Cyrus, his son Cambyses, Darius, and Xerxes systematically brought to heel the states of Asia Minor and the Near East. The Achaemenid dynasty, begun by Cyrus and extinguished by Alexander, was marked by efficient administration, military superiority, and a great infatuation with gold. The Achaemenids were liberal rulers who divided their vast empire into provinces or satrapies which were allowed to maintain their own customs, religions, and languages as long as they anted up the requisite golden tribute.

The Persians were great lovers of gold, not for its shimmering beauty or its magic associations, but because they recognized its economic and political power and made it work for them. Herodotus said that Darius discovered the greater part of Asia. By the time he died the Persian Empire spread from the Nile to beyond the Caspian Sea, from northern Greece across Asia Minor, down past the Persian Gulf and across the Near East, thrusting into the golden fringes of northern India. All of the world's known gold deposits were under Achaemenid domination save those in Spain controlled by the Carthaginians. And even some of the Punic gold came to Persepolis, Darius' magnificent capital, via the conquered Levantine cities which served as depots for Carthaginian gold.

Gold, raw and worked, poured into the royal treasuries at Ecbatana, Susa, and Persepolis. The Royal Road, which had been much improved since Croesus' time, streamed with caravans bearing tribute, booty, and the glittering harvest of far-flung gold mines and alluvial deposits. Royal inspectors, the "King's eyes and ears," traveled its length checking and reporting. The Persian monarch's omnipotence rested on the gold heaped in the treasuries. Year by year it accumulated. The Persians used much gold for ornament and ceremony. Their craftsmen were highly skilled but the beauty of gold was always subordinate to the economic power of the metal. Most of the gold that came to the state was melted down into featureless ingots which were stored and used as needed for coinage to run the complex and costly bureaucratic machinery of empire and to finance the constant military operations of conquest and suppression of restless vassals.

The craving for gold was insatiable. When several Persian galleys laden with gold sank in a battle with the Greek Navy, King Xerxes had two divers salvage the treasure. According to Herodotus, whose account is the first of divers recovering sunken treasure, the two, a Greek named Scyllias and his daughter, Cyane, successfully brought up the gold but were refused the reward Xerxes had promised them. They were detained aboard the royal galley, presumably for other salvage jobs. They jumped overboard during a nocturnal storm and revenged themselves on the treacherous King by cutting the anchor cables of the Persian ships, causing many collisions. Scyllias and Cyane eluded their captors by swimming underwater nine miles to shore perhaps using hollow reeds to breathe through.

The colossal stock piles which eventually came into Alexander's hands came from many sources, some long known to Europe and the Mediterranean, others revealed for the first time. The earliest sources were Asia Minor itself and the most ancient supplier of all, Egypt, which had capitulated to Cambyses, the unstable son of Cyrus the Great, in 524 B.C.

At that time Egypt was still producing great amounts of gold. Even four hundred years later, just before the Roman conquest, the Ptolemies were harvesting forty thousand pounds or more a year of Egyptian gold.

In addition to the traditional workings Cambyses was attacted to the great gold deposits of the Ethiopian deserts and the Sudan island of Meroe in the Upper Nile. Ethiopia was a land of mystery from which distorted tales filtered back of monstrous men with dog faces and others with no nostrils. The Egyptians believed the Ethiopians, handsome and slender, lived incredibly long because they ate only meat and milk. They entombed their dead in great crystal pillars and had endless amounts of gold at their disposition, according to contemporary Egyptian reports.

Cambyses found no monsters, no crystal pillars, but he did find the gold and it exacted a terrible toll. He led a gold-seeking expedition into the trackless wastes where the men became hopelessly disoriented. His troops were crazed with heat, hunger, and thirst. They ate all the pack animals and then drew lots. Every tenth man was slaughtered to feed the survivors. Most of the Persians perished, but Cambyses managed to find his way back to Persia and golden luxury. His mental instability deteriorated into insanity and four years later he killed himself.

The Persians for quite some time had access to the abundant gold on the Greek island of Thasos and on the northern mainland. The Thracian mines were producing as much as four thousand pounds of gold a year in the fifth century B.C. Herodotus visited Thasos, which yielded a bit less, and described the workings as "a great mountain which has been all turned up in the search for metal."

Gold was found in quantity in Greek Sicily. Mines were dug, but the seepage of underground water flooded many of them, so they were abandoned. In the third century B.C. Archimedes, the genius mathematician and inventor born in Syracuse, helped solve the problem of flooding. He invented, or perhaps perfected, what he had seen in Egypt, where he had studied at Alexandria, a screw pump for lifting water from the mines. Called the Archimedian screw, it is still used in Egypt and other areas in irrigation and mining.

Vitruvius, the Roman engineer and architect, credited Archimedes with the discovery of the general principle of hydrostatics. According to one story King Hiero of Syracuse showed him a crown allegedly of pure gold and asked if it might not contain an admixture of silver. Archimedes was thinking about this as he stepped into a bath and observed the water overflowing. It suddenly struck him that by putting the crown and equal weights of gold and silver separately into a full vessel of water and noting the variation in overflow the additional mass introduced by the presence of an alloy could be measured. He was so excited, says the story, that without dressing he ran home to his laboratory shouting "Eureka, eureka"—"I have found it, I have found it."

Gold came from the Red Sea islands and from Arabia Felix. During the Emperor Tiberius' reign the Roman Strabo wrote about the camel-herding nomads of the area, where "there is a river which carries down gold dust, though they have not the skill to work it . . . gold is dug from their land, not as dust but in nuggets which need little refining. . . . They pierce these and string them on flax, with transparent stones alternating and make chains and put them on their necks and wrists . . . and they market their gold cheaply to their neighbors . . . for they lack the skill to work it, and the metals they get in exchange, silver and copper, are rare in their country." Diodorus, writing even earlier, marveled that the river "brings down so much shining gold dust that the mud at its mouth positively glitters!"

Insects, animals, and birds were credited by the ancients with digging for gold or guarding it in many areas including Tibet, Siberia, Arabia, and India. Enormous and ferocious ants were said to be particularly industrious miners. One of the places where they reputedly labored was on the Red Sea islands. The Ethiopians, wrote the ancient authors, had devised an ingenious method for wresting the gold from the insects. Every morning the nomads fastened large saddle baskets on female camels which had recently borne young. They had them swim to the islands, leaving their babies behind. The ants dug gold and looking around for a good place to store it, saw the baskets and filled them. When they were full, the Ethiopians led the hungry camel babies to the water's edge, where they cried for mother's milk. The camels, hearing the plaintive cries, plunged into the sea and swam to their offspring bringing with them the fruit of the ants' labors. In another version of this tale, which enjoyed wide circulation in antiquity, the camels were replaced with brood mares.

From the Armenian area at the eastern end of the Black Sea came gold from the source Jason had sought. The waters of the Phasis River, rising in the Caucasus, must have been almost as golden as those of the Pactolus. In early Roman times when the Pactolus was depleted, Strabo wrote that the mountain torrents brought down gold which was collected by a nomadic people, red-haired and blue-eyed, called the "Lice Eaters." "These barbarians," he wrote, "catch it [the gold] in troughs perforated with holes and in fleecy skins."

One of the richest gold areas under Persian control was that of Bactria and Sogidana. This vast district lay between the Punjab and the Aral Sea on either side of the Oxus River, and included much of modern Kafiristan, Kashmir, Bukhara, Afghanistan, and Dardistan north of the Himalayas. The Persians exacted more than twenty thousand pounds of gold annually from the area. Much of the gold was collected from the waters of the great Oxus, which rises south of Samarkand and rushes west toward the Aral and Caspian seas. A great deal came too from the Indus River, which rises in Tibet and flows through West Pakistan into the Arabian Sea.

It was Bactrian gold that Herodotus reported was paid in tribute by the "Indians," who collected it from prospecting ants. "Where they live," he noted, repeating the Indian tale, "it is desert, on account of the sand; and in this sandy tract of desert are ants, smaller than dogs but larger than foxes. . . . These dwell under the ground and turn up the sand; and the sand which is brought up contains gold. . . . The Indians come to the place with bags and fill these with sand, riding away as fast as they can; for the ants, as the Persians say, detect them by smell and give them chase . . . so that, unless the Indians got away with a start while the ants are still gathering not one of them would escape."

There are accounts of these giant insects being captured and brought live to the Persian court for all to marvel at. However, Strabo reports that rather than take them alive, poison bait was spread about on the ground. Through classical times up to the mid-sixteenth century stories circulated of alleged specimens of these monster ants. "Genuine" bits of their skins and feelers, like pieces of the True Cross, were always turning up.

Pliny the Elder wrote of ants the size of wolves who sound like something from a Japanese science-fiction film. They had soft, sleek pelts like panthers and dug gold on the islands in the mouth of the Indus River. "Such is the speed and savagery the love of gold awakens in them," he noted, that if the camel-mounted men who stole their gold were not extremely swift in escaping they were torn apart by the giant ants.

Modern scholarship has suggested a number of possible sources for these ancient horror stories. The Greek Megasthenes wrote that Indian gold came from a plateau in the mountains on the frontiers of Kafiristan and Tibet. It is conceivable that the furry burrowing ants were a distortion of the dogs of ancient Tibetan gold miners. Ants, particularly the harvester ants (*Pogonomyrmex occidentalis*) of the southwestern United States, surround their mounds with a fortress of pebbles and show a preference for gold when it is available. In Australia, the southwestern United States, and other regions, burrowing animals have made more than one prospector unexpectedly richer by a nugget or two. It is possible that the ants of the ancients were small beasts like marmots, which tunnel under the topsoil as moles do and could easily turn up gold in an area of auriferous earth. The size, speed, and ferocity of these gold-digging creatures were totally without foundation. Most likely these fables were concocted by traders who wanted to scare competition off.

It was near the Oxus, known today as the Amu Darya, in Turkestan that the greatest cache of Persian treasure was found. In 1877 a large number of varied gold objects were offered for sale, one by one, by local peasants. None of the villagers would tell the Moslem traders who purchased the gold where the pieces came from. Eventually through the untiring effort of Captain F. C. Burton, the English traveler, the Oxus hoard was assembled and is now in the British Museum. It appears to have been a temple treasure which was buried in the fifth or fourth century B.C. for protection from invaders.

Included in the Oxus Treasure are a number of open bracelets with finials in the form of real or mythical animal heads, armlets, necklaces, a sword scabbard, hair ornaments, a variety of cast-gold heads, and many other objects which betray by style and execution their provincial origin. A gold chariot drawn by four horses formed of sheet gold was modeled with the typical wheels of vehicles which traversed the Royal Road, whose rutted stones are still visible in places today. There were many interesting rectangular plaques etched with scenes from Persian life and the figures of warriors, servants, and tribute bearers.

In 480 B.C. Xerxes launched the greatest invasion the world had seen, invading Greece by land and by sea with hundreds of thousands of troops. Pythias of Lydia entertained the King of Kings and his men at Sardis before they bridged the Hellespont. The Lydian was so wealthy that he was able to curry Persian favor by making an incredibly generous contribution to Xerxes' campaign. "As soon as I heard you were coming down to the Sea of Hellas I wished to give you money for the war, and I found on calculation that I had of silver 2,000 talents and of gold 4 million darics all but 7,000. And this I give you." This added about 10,000 pounds of silver and 7,000 pounds of gold to Xerxes' war chest.

Xerxes rode forth in a golden chariot, in resplendest battle dress at the head of his endless army. A sea of men flowed across the Hellespont. They marched from Asia to Europe on a causeway constructed of boats held together by massive Egyptian rope cables. Sod-covered planks were laid across the one-mile span, and parallel screens were raised so that the horses, camels, and donkeys would not shy. A canal had been dug at Xerxes' orders across the Mount Athos peninsula to accommodate the Persian fleet of one thousand ships. A modern find of some three hundred gold darics in the vicinity is evidence of the use of Persian gold in wartime.

Xerxes led one of history's most exotic armies. Behind him marched a thousand select Persian spearmen bearing lances decorated with golden pomegranates, nine thousand spearmen with silver pomegranates, ten thousand Persians in fish-scale armor carrying spears with golden apples. Many thousands of cavalrymen were followed by streams of skin-clad Ethiopians wielding stone weapons, mustachioed nomads of the Eurasian steppes, Phrygians, Mysians with pointed stakes, Iranians with bronze weapons, an Arabian camel corps, and bringing up the rear was a great confused multitude.

Before crossing into Europe Xerxes made offerings to the rising sun, casting a golden bowl and a golden libation cup into the Hellespont. At the Archaeological Museum in Tehran there is an exquisite golden bowl such as the one he must have thrown into the sea. The bowl is a sensitive goldsmith's translation of petals and stems into curving golden planes. As the light plays on the rhythmically placed, softly swelling forms, the bowl glows with shimmering golden life. Running around the exterior rim of the eight-inch vessel is an inscription in three languages—Old Persian, Elamite, and Babylonian—identifying the bowl's owner as Xerxes.

At the mountain pass at Thermopylae the Spartans made a heroic but suicidal stand against the Persian invaders. From Mount Aegaleos Xerxes, enthroned under a golden canopy, watched in mounting horror as the small Greek Navy, paid for by the citizens of Athens, who were all shareholders in the silver mines at Laurium, turned a foregone Persian victory into one of history's greatest routs in the Battle of Salamis. Aeschylus, veteran of the

battle, recalled the carnage in his play *The Persians*. As the bra-
zen prowed Greek triremes, outnumbered three to one, rammed
the floundering enemy galleys, "hulls rolled over, and the sea itself was hidden, strewn with their wreckage, dyed with the
blood of men. The dead lay thick on all the reefs and beaches and
flight broke out."

Despite their resounding victory at Salamis, the Greeks were
unable to check the terrible onslaught. For seven months Xerxes'
armies cut a swath of terror and destruction across the country.
When they reached the gates of Athens, they found the city
deserted save for a skeleton force, the keepers of the temple
treasuries and those too poor or dispirited to have fled. Athens
was put to the torch, the temples plundered and the gods toppled. The bitter Greeks nursed their loathing for the Persians
until a century and a half later Alexander exacted a full measure
of revenge.

Greece had been gold poor during the years that first the
Medes and then the Persians were amassing the precious metal.
While countless slaves panned the rivers of Mesopotamia, Asia
Minor, and southern Russia and others labored to wrest the stuff
from mines in broiling Egyptian deserts and the frozen mountains of Siberia, the Greeks struggled to get control of relatively
small amounts of gold. Greek coinage was based on silver from
the great Laurium mines at the tip of Attica not far from Athens.
The Mycenaeans had first worked the mines in the second millennium B.C. In classical times they were worked by slaves on
two-hour shifts who were forced to crawl on their bellies in the
yard-high tunnels, some of which are as deep as 350 feet. Archaeologists have found rings where the slaves were chained to
the mine walls.

Gold was so scarce in seventh century B.C. Greece that the
gold-silver ratio was 1:13. Persian gold proffered as bribes to
keep the small, autonomous city-states divided won more victories for Persia in Greece than did her armies. The Persians
shrewdly dispensed gold darics to fortify weak frontiers and buy
tenuous alliances. The Achaemenid Army many times entered
cities through gates which swung open after gold had changed
hands. Herodotus coined a word, *medizing*, to describe how Persian (Median) gold could buy Greek friendship.

The sentiment of a sixth century B.C. Greek poet survives as a fragment. "There's nothing else that matters—only money." Money and gold did matter, a great deal. Although gold was scarce in relation to the incredible wealth of it held by other peoples, it was available to the Greek upper classes. Rich women coveted gold ornaments and flaunted their wealth in showy displays of jewelry and gold-embroidered clothes. Corinthian love of luxury and sensual pleasure were famous in the seventh century B.C. and influenced the fashions of other Greek cities.

There is a story of Periander, dictator of Corinth, who needed gold to stave off political enemies. He announced a great festival to which all the women of the city were invited. According to the tale, when all were assembled the tyrant gave a word to his soldiers who fell upon the matrons stripping them not only of rings, necklaces, pendants, and earrings but of gold-embellished robes as well. He reaped enough from these involuntary contributions to shore up his position and remained in power for another forty years.

The squabbling city-states overcame, at least temporarily, the jealousies which divided them, and in 479 B.C. combined Greek forces won two important victories against invading Persian armies. These successes precipitated a series of revolts in the Greek cities of Asia Minor. After the Battle of Plataea the Spartan general, showing his men the gold vessels and plate from the royal baggage train, said, "Look at the foolishness of the Medes. With such provision for life as you see, they came here to take away from us ours which is so humble." Every dead and wounded Persian was relieved of his gold ornaments, and for many years the battleground was searched for treasure. The Delphic Oracle, once asked how to find treasure, responded with characteristic advice, "Leave no stone unturned."

Taking heart from these few triumphs, the Greeks formed the Delian League to drive back the Persian forces and regain the gold mines of Thrace and Macedonia. The league formed under the leadership of Athens and was named for the sacred isle of Delos, where the league treasury was located in the Temple of Apollo. It grew from a voluntary coequal confederacy into the Athenian Empire, which forced members into submission. The treasury was moved to Athens, and eventually the annual assessments were wrung from reluctant members by Athenian enforcers.

From time out of mind what gold the Greeks had was stored in temples. After the Battle of Plataea a part of the gold spoils was made into a golden tripod and dedicated to the shrine of Apollo at Delphi. This important sanctuary was the depository for a percentage of the gold reserves of almost every Greek state as well as an internationally venerated shrine.

Gold held in temples was legally the government's and could be removed at will. It was in the form of ingots, sacred objects, or occasionally coins such as the beautiful Lampascene staters coined by the Greek city in Asia Minor because they were more acceptable than silver in zones of Persian influence. The Greek city-states also occasionaly issued gold coins in times of national emergency, when silver could not purchase allies or vital imports.

At the end of the fifth century B.C., after twenty-five years of war with Sparta, Athens' silver reserves were exhausted, so a decision was made to melt down a part of the accumulated golden offerings made to Athena in the Parthenon for coinage. Many years later the sacred debt was repaid with interest in the form of "a wooden rack in which are the punch dies and anvil dies with which the gold coins were struck."

In the fifth century B.C. the Athenian general and statesman Pericles used the proceeds of Athenian extortion from league members to rebuild a ruined city and to finance Athens' Golden Age, the most glorious of epochs, unsurpassed in intellectual, architectural, and artistic achievements. With the money looted from the Delian League's defense funds Pericles honored the gods and made the city of Athens something, as Plutarch later wrote, "in a short time for all time, with a bloom of perpetual newness."

The Parthenon, designed as a monument to Athenian imperialism and homage to the city's patroness, was one of his greatest projects. For fifteen years the country's foremost engineers, architects, craftsmen, and artists labored on the most perfect example of the temple form which dominated the great rock of the Acropolis rising above the crowded city.

The resources of the Athenian Empire were devoted to the elaboration of the capital. The Parthenon was financed by the annual tribute to Athena, to which was added an additional two hundred talents yearly. Pericles' friend the sculptor Phidias supervised the construction of the Parthenon, and a band of citizen inspectors kept the accounts. Phidias was not only a sculptor but a goldworker without peer. For the Parthenon he created a truly remarkable chryselephantine statue of Athena which was a wonder of the ancient world. Contemporary descriptions of the work, which was carried off to Constantinople in the fifth century A.D. and lost sometime thereafter, acclaim it as the finest, most noble work of art ever made.

The figure of the goddess of wisdom and chastity towered thirty-eight feet above the marble floor of the temple and was situated so that the rays of the sun caressed her ivory face and blazed from her golden robes and crown. She was of ivory and gold—more than two thousand pounds of gold. Under the artist's magic touch raw gold became fluid vestments and majestic ornaments fashioned in such a way that the precious metal could be quickly stripped from the wooden core in case of emergency. It so happened that not long after the statue was unveiled, the gold was removed but not because of war.

Charges were made that Pericles and Phidias had conspired to steal a part of the gold that had been apportioned for the Athena. One version of the story states that when the gold was weighed some was wanting and Phidias was fined forty talents of gold and convicted of theft.

The citizens of Olympia, however, didn't believe in his guilt and offered to pay the fine if he would create a chryselephantine statue of Zeus for their city. He complied and created a sixty-foot-high seated Zeus, which outdid the Athena and was one of the Seven Wonders of the World. It was housed in a shrine which was the focal point of the Olympic games, the most significant religious and athletic celebration in Greece, held every fourth year.

For nearly a millennium the Olympian Zeus remained seated on a great throne of gold, ivory, and ebony, encrusted with precious stones. His robes were gold-chased with an elaborate pattern of blossoms and leaves. His ivory feet were shod in gold, and a crown of golden olive branches rested on his massive ivory head. In one hand he held a gold scepter inlaid with gems and in the other a gold and ivory statue of Victory. The statue was so awesome and magnificent that the great god himself was said to have shown his approval by hurling a bolt of lightning before it.

Neither of Phidias' monuments survived, but archaeologists have discovered his workshop at Olympia and the terra-cotta molds and tools used in making the Zeus. They were led to the site by a literary source—Pausanias, the same second century A.D. traveler who guided Schliemann to Mycenae's treasure.

The two statues were perhaps the most splendid of their kind, but there were many, many others. Remains of a life-sized bull of gilded silver have been found at Delphi. It appears to have been made in Ionia and sent as an offering to the shrine. Artistic expression in fifth-century Greece was most often worked in less expensive materials such as marble, clay, and stone, but the inspiration for much of it came from the gold and ivory work of the Minoans. Marble statues echoed smaller ivory carvings, and even very large statues were brightly painted, gilded, and embellished with ivory.

Gold figured prominently in classical Greek literature. Golden dawns, sunsets, smiles, blooms, and virgins were favorite conceits of the poets and so overused that simile was dulled by repetition.

There were so many golden images of the gods that men came to believe the divinities were themselves created of gold. Mortals sometimes claimed to have golden parts. Pythagoras, who claimed superhuman origin, had a golden thigh which he once, so Aristotle said, flashed for all to see at the theater. This was not a new concept. In Egyptian literature the pharaohs of the fifth dynasty were described as issuing from their mother's wombs with their royal titles inlaid in gold on their limbs.

A seventh-century hymn lauding Aphrodite brings to mind the colorful Greek statues which were powdered with gold dust while damp. "She was clad in a robe outshining the brightness of fire, a fine robe of gold enriched with many colors shimmering like the moon over her tender breasts, a marvel to see. And she had twisted brooches and shining earrings, flower shaped, and round her soft throat were lovely necklaces."

Goldsmith fathers passed their skills to their sons, and family firms were established which gained widespread fame and grew enormously wealthy. A family on the island of Samos had an association which lasted more than four generations. One on Chios was called upon to execute works in many distant places.

Greek jewelry styles in the eighth century B.C. were strongly influenced by the introduction of Egyptian and Babylonian motifs: the geometric patterns, animal and human figures beloved of Phoenician smiths who opened ateliers in continental Greece and on Rhodes. Persian elements also began to appear in Greek work in gold and silver particularly in the rhyton and deep bowls such as the Achaemenids had. The international shrine at Delphi attracted offerings from many distant areas, and it was probably there that Greek goldsmiths were introduced to foreign styles. Then, too, there were the Ionian smiths, the Greeks of Asia Minor who were in close contact with the Scythians, for whom they executed much goldwork. Some of their production reached Attica and added to the expanding repertoire of the goldsmiths there.

Sumptuary laws have been issued throughout history limiting or prohibiting the use of gold for personal adornment. In ancient Greece women were long denied the right to wear gold jewelry —a measure advocated by Plato in his *Laws*.

In the sixth century B.C. goldsmiths were commissioned primarily to execute religious pieces and ornaments for autocrats and noblemen, but seldom for women. In his excellent book *Approach to Greek Art*, Charles Seltman writes that in the fifth century B.C. women were the recipients of a small but increased number of jewels and goldsmiths continued to turn out orders for religious offerings, for the Greco-barbarian chieftains of Asia Minor, for noblemen and civic governments. However, the fourth century B.C. initiated an era of magnificent jewelry for women. Persian gold supplemented Macedonian stocks and production from a few Greek islands such as Syphnos and from the Greek colony of Sicily. Nouvelles riches matrons indulged themselves in lavish displays of golden ornaments that would have shocked the austere Greeks of an earlier age when sumptuary laws forbade the use of gold in an effort to conserve the rare precious metal for state use.

Pathetically little of the goldwork of classical Greece remains. The long years of economic and political crises fated most of it to the melting pot, but what escaped are some of the most breath-takingly lovely examples of the goldsmith's art. From the fourth century B.C. on, Greece prospered as the relatively large number of extant goldworks indicate. The treasures of Asia channeled west by Alexander changed the complexion of the Greek world. Powerful states languished and once-struggling cities gained vigor, their citizens enjoying unprecedented luxury. In Philip of Macedon's time Phocian Greeks warring with central Greece raided the treasury at Delphi looting the shrine's great treasures. "Then it was," wrote Athanaeus, "that gold blazed up among the Greeks, and silver came romping in."

Typical examples of Greek goldwork are a pair of gold earrings with bright glass beads on a hoop below the perfectly modeled miniature head of a dolphin who holds a gold pebble in his mouth. Jewelry was colorful, and gold bracelets with animal head terminals often incorporated rare materials such as blue glass or rock crystal. The Greek smiths turned out lavish jewelry: rings with cabochon gems, elaborate necklaces with flat mesh chains, earrings and diadems in repoussé or cast and embellished with enamel or granulation or set with gems. They also executed orders from wealthy Greeks for tableware of all kinds and religious ware, almost none of which has survived.

The Metropolitan Museum of Art in New York has a very rare golden phiale, one of the cups used for pouring liquid offerings which were most often of silver and bronze. The shallow bowl is 9¼ inches in diameter and decorated with a row of beechnuts and three rows of acorns in repoussé. The acorns of the outer row alternate with bees, and in the center of the bowl is a golden boss surrounded by a delicate floral motif. A miniature Eros of Athenian workmanship is characteristic of the precision and delicacy of late fourth-century goldsmithery. With feathered wings upraised the tiny figure rests one hand jauntily on a pillar and holds up an apple in the other. It is a perfectly executed diminutive sculpture and loses nothing by magnification.

It was inevitable that with so much more gold and so many more people able to afford jewelry there would be a decline in the quality of the goldsmith's art. The number of goldworkers burgeoned, but many of them lacked the skill of the established smiths as numbers of somewhat pedestrian pieces show.

Rivalry with Sparta sparked the long Peloponnesian War. That and Pericles' death in 429 B.C., followed by a dreadful plague, ended the Golden Age of Athens. The Athena of the Parthenon was divested of her golden raiment to finance the fighting. Privately owned gold went into hiding. The Persians took advantage of the civil strife to extend control over the northern Greek gold mines.

It was the Machiavellian King Philip, ruler of Macedon, the extensive tribal kingdom north of Greece, who launched the mission his son would accomplish—the defeat of the Persian Empire. Exploiting the disabling rivalries of most of the Greek states, Philip conquered much of the country spawning new cities and stimulating trade in the process. He opened huge new gold mines at Mount Pangaeus, from which came the gold for his famous coins. Like the Persians he made the most of the power of gold to persuade. He boasted that he could take any citadel to which he could take a donkey load of gold.

Philip became master of all Greece and formed a new league to invade the Achaemenid realm. As he camped on the shores of the Hellespont prior to crossing into Persia, he was slain at a banquet by a treacherous Macedonian noble, reported to have been bought with Persian gold. It fell to Alexander, King at twenty, to complete his father's plan.

"My son, thou art invincible," intoned the Delphic Oracle. Armed with these words, the beardless youth led forty thousand troops, five thousand horses, and a professional gold prospector into Asia in 334 B.C. In the ensuing eleven years of campaign Alexander won an empire that spread over more than 1½ million square miles and all but monopolized the world's gold sources. He covered 22,000 miles, never losing a battle, mapping unknown territory, and establishing scores of new cities which he colonized with old or wounded veterans to whom he gave land grants.

Alexander terminated Persian control of the profitable trade routes to the west and shipped the Achaemenid gold to Greece along with myriad exotic luxuries and novel ideas, all of which stimulated the Greek world and then the Roman. "Then rose the sum of wealth with far flung might," wrote Pindar commemorating the Macedonian's glorious deeds. The ratio of gold to silver fell from 1:13 to 1:11½ in Philip's time and to an unheard-of

1:10 when the Hellenistic Empire was swamped with Persian treasure.

Alexander, whose ideal hero was Cyrus, founder of the Persian Empire, was himself a man of heroic proportions, outshining even the Homeric heroes. In the brief span before his untimely death at thirty-three, the charismatic warrior-king flashed like a golden sword through the world. His epic empire did not long survive him, but he achieved mythic status passing into the legends of three continents and coming down to modern times as one of history's most fascinating figures. Early Christians portrayed Jesus in his likeness, and even today nomadic chieftains in Turkestan proudly claim descent from the Great Iskandar.

Alexander the Great—genius general, epileptic, bisexual, brilliant statesman—was lavish with friends and capable of generosity toward conquered foe. He was avid not only for riches but the love of all the world. Even after he had broken the back of the supine Persian Empire and assumed for himself the titles and powers of the King of Kings, he could not rest. A consuming ambition drove him on until he pushed his devoted men beyond their endurance and reigned from Egypt to India.

It was at Issus, near the modern Syrian border, that the blond young general first came face to face with the imposing six-and-a-half-foot-tall Persian King. The King of Kings took to the field of battle supremely confident, buoyed by the presence of his vast baggage trains of gold, his Queen, who was also his sister, his children, and the Queen Mother, Sisygambis.

Riding a golden chariot, in gorgeous array, he towered above his armies—a sea of men of every tongue and complexion. Alexander met him with a tightly compressed, mobile army superbly disciplined, which turned Persian triumph to Persian rout. Darius fled in the heat of battle, abandoning his women, children, and much of his gold.

After the encounter, Alexander surveyed the Persian monarch's palatial tent with its appointments of gem-encrusted gold—tableware and toilet articles of Oriental magnificence, furniture inlaid with ivory and covered with sheet gold, a gold throne, and a sumptuous bath. "So this is what it means to be a king," he is said to have exclaimed. Damascus, Sidon, and Tyre yielded their treasures to him. From Damascus he took the Persian King's war chest. At Sidon tradition avers that he found so much gold he ordered much of it buried and never went back for it.

During the siege of Tyre, Darius, whose family had been captured at Issus, sent an embassy wth a ransom offer. He would pay Alexander the huge sum of ten thousand gold talents and cede him all lands west of the Euphrates. "I would accept," Parmenio, one of Alexander's generals reportedly said, "were I Alexander." "I too," was the celebrated retort, "if I were Parmenio. But I am Alexander." He refused the offer, declined to make peace, and stormed Tyre ending the seven-month siege of the island city, slaughtering all the men and selling the women and children as slaves.

He pressed on. In Egypt he was hailed as Pharaoh and Deliverer. At Babylon, where he entered in a gold-plated chariot, he was hailed as King by the inhabitants. He delved into the colossal treasury there to dispense several months' pay to his mercenaries, showering gold on his favorites and even giving the Babylonian priests gold to finance the reconstruction of the ziggurat which Xerxes had knocked down. He continued to make extravagant gifts, presenting his men with golden victory wreaths, coins, and jewelry. It amused him to be asked for a sum and then be able to give an amount in excess of the request. He freed the gold that had lain in the treasuries of the Persian world and it began to flow through his armies, quickening the pulse of the local economies and ultimately of Europe.

Alexander became King of Kings . . . King of All the Earth, Far and Near. As he marched into the wilds of central Asia, "a moving world was his camp." Countless troops, grooms, craftsmen, armorers, secretaries, merchants, doctors, engineers, speculators, women, and children were swept along with him. Indulging his flair for the theatrical and to merge Persian and Macedonian into one race, he married Darius' daughter, the princess Barsine, and at the same time wed eighty of his favorites to aristocratic Persian maidens and regularized the unions of some ten thousand common soldiers with their Persian mistresses.

The court chamberlain, Chares, described the nuptial festivities. A huge pavilion, eight hundred yards in circumference, was erected, supported by thirty-feet-high gilded columns set with jewels. Golden draperies and carpets of gold, purple, and scarlet decorated the pavilion. The conqueror furnished bridal chambers for each of the couples with silver-plated couches, his alone covered with gold. The celebration lasted five days, during which he received embassies from the vassal states which once paid tribute to Darius. They sent him presents of jeweled gold crowns worth fifteen thousand gold talents.

Alexander had provided doweries in gold to the newlyweds, and this money was soon pumped into the market place and taverns of Susa. When the Greek soldiers incurred debts and the merchants and innkeepers of the city complained, Alexander offered to settle all accounts. It cost him ten thousand talents but endeared him even more to his men, who held him in awe. Alexander took on many of the trappings and attitudes of Oriental despots much to the discomfiture of his Greek troops, who felt that the golden luxury of Persia was going to their leader's head. He even attempted to impose Persian court ritual which involved prostration in the presence of the King, but the Greeks and Macedonians refused to abase themselves and made snide comments until Alexander astutely abandoned his efforts. His magnetism and his genuine concern for his troops, thousands of which he knew by name, were such that in spite of a volatile temper and his affinity for Eastern absolutism, his men stayed by him.

The gold of Persia was responsible for one of scholarship's great losses. One of the officers married at Susa was Eumenes, a learned Greek who had been Philip's private secretary before serving his son. At a time when Alexander was short of cash he had asked his most intimate associates for a loan. All had given at once and freely, knowing that they would be repaid with great interest. However, Eumenes gave little and grudgingly. His stinginess piqued Alexander, who arranged for the seemingly accidental burning of his tent. In the charred rubble lay not only a fortune in gold, some one thousand talents in coin, but tragically, the royal archives and all of Alexander's Persian correspondence.

The greatest haul of gold came from Persepolis. When Alexander left the city in flames to avenge Xerxes' firing of Athens a century and a half before, he took with him the treasure of generations of opulent Achaemenid kings. It was enough, said Alexander, to burden five thousand camels and twenty thousand mules. Beasts and wagons groaned under lustrous cargoes of gold bullion and coins, gold tableware, jewelry, and gems. There were exquisite robes and tapestries, furniture of exotic woods overlaid with gold and ivory, and golden luxuries which beggared description from every land on earth.

The magnificent ceremonial complex at Persepolis originated with Darius the Great, who constructed a great terrace against a mountainside on a majestic mile-high plateau at the heart of the empire. His successors erected a series of palaces, treasuries, vast colonnaded audience and banquet halls, armories, and barracks. Persepolis was twice the size of the Acropolis at Athens, and in contrast to the Greek complex, which honored the gods of a free people, Persepolis celebrated the divine majesty of the Achaemenid King of Kings.

His likeness and titles were everywhere—on façades, parapets, doorjambs, and window sills. Craftsmen, sculptors, and smiths from every corner of the empire labored years to create the dazzling capital which was designed to awe the god of light, Ahura-Mazda, and the men of all the earth. The thousands of bas-reliefs, today stripped of all color, show a fascinating diversity of types, hair styles, and costumes. Solemn figures of foreign emissaries which once glowed with rich glazes of blue, crimson, yellow, purple, and green today march in silent stone procession amid the columned ruins bearing tribute to the Oriental King.

Powdered gold dust once shone in the beards of frieze figures as it did in the beards of Persian courtiers whose elegant robes of state were richly woven or embroidered with gold thread. The carved figures of King and crown prince were once adorned with gold, silver, and jewels. The robes of some of the Persians are traced with designs which represent golden bracteates or clothing ornaments. These were often appliqués one and two inches across depicting vegetable motifs and animals both real and fantastic and sewed on garments in quantity. One stunning piece found by archaeologists is a roundel in the form of a snarling lion with a great sweeping openwork mane. Another is a rounded openwork plaque of two rearing lions in profile sharing a single high relief head presented full face.

Achaemenid art with its harmony of design and delicacy of

technique reflects the many currents that moved through the empire and converged in the cosmopolitan centers. Craftsmen came from afar bringing their native styles. Archaeological evidence indicates that most of the goldsmiths at the Persian court were Egyptian or Median. The northern Medes introduced the animal style seen in the bracteates and best shown in the drinking vessels called rhyta, which combine a bowl with a stylized animal figure in the round. Both elements were raised from a sheet of gold and joined with an almost invisible seam. A seven-inch-tall rhyton in the Metropolitan has a bowl decorated with ribbed bands. At the rim is a band of forty-four double-twisted wires, each $\frac{7}{1000}$ of an inch thick, totaling 136½ feet in length! The head is that of a winged lion-monster with a richly textured mane. The legs, teeth, tongue, and palate were added separately and the whole is a masterpiece of Achaemenid art. At Persepolis a number of rhyta have been found of gold, of silver, and of electrum, which may well have been the special poison-detecting vessels cherished by ancient royalty.

Alexander had been able to hold his armies in check when other cities were taken, but at Persepolis he gave them one day free during which they ran amok, looting, raping, and slaughtering. Many Persians were killed for sport by soldiers already so laden with gold they didn't bother with ransom. The Persian treasurer, a bureaucrat par excellence, managed to keep the palace vaults intact. He turned them over to the invaders and was made governor by Alexander.

Alexander figured the haul from Persepolis at three times what he had taken from the Persian's administrative capital at Susa. The treasury there yielded 2 million pounds of gold and silver, chiefly stored in ingot form. He found another 500,000 pounds of gold darics at Susa and such a wealth of jewels that they were never reckoned. It is said that of all the palace treasures the only thing that the great Alexander chose for himself was an exquisite gem-encrusted gold box. He took it to house his most precious possession, the copy of the *Iliad* which his childhood tutor, Aristotle, had edited for him.

Just as it was not greed for ancient gold that motivated Schliemann in his search for Troy and Mycenae, it was far more than gold lust which drove Alexander across the world on an eleven-year odyssey that ended in Babylon, where his battle-worn, drink-weakened body succumbed to a fever. The man of unlimited ambition who shared with his men the crippling ice of mountain passes and the searing heat of the Indian deserts embodied the Greek spirit with its belief in what a man can do when he exercises his full powers. Alexander believed in himself and his mission. He addressed his assembled troops: "It is a lovely thing to live with courage," he said, "and leave behind an everlasting renown."

When he died on a hot June day in 323 B.C. his generals, the Diadochi, embarked on a bitter power struggle that tore apart the empire in far less time than it had taken to build. Three dominant powers emerged—the Egypt of the Ptolemies, which was to maintain Hellenistic rule until Cleopatra's death in 30 B.C.; the Selucid Empire in Syria; and the Macedonia of Antigonus.

At Alexander's death a workshop was set up where the leading goldsmiths of the world labored on a sarcophagus and funeral equipment worthy of the "World-Seeker." "It was," said an eye-witness, "more magnificent when seen than when described," the most splendid funeral display in history.

Sixty-four mules with gilded crowns and trappings, gold bells, and collars studded with gems pulled the huge gold shrine. Within it was a coffin of beaten gold enclosing the body of Alexander preserved with spices. Week after week, month after month, the catafalque progressed, crossing a thousand miles, reverenced in every village and city. Ptolemy managed to divert it to Egypt, where it came to rest at Alexandria, the crown jewel of Alexander's seventy cities. There the golden coffin stayed, the object of adoration and sacrifices until the degenerate Ptolemy IX melted the sarcophagus to mint coins for the army payroll three centuries later. When the coffin was opened, Alexander's face, three hundred years old, was reportedly as clear and handsome as in life.

There is a persistent legend, one of thousands that grew up about Alexander, which has to do with buried gold. It was said that when Darius III fled toward Ecbatana he took with him huge amounts of gold. When he was murdered it could not be found and was presumed to have been buried somewhere around Ecbatana at the King's command. He had ordered the soldiers who concealed it silenced by death, and there was no one left to reveal the treasure's location.

Persians, Greeks, Parthians, and Romans all searched for Darius' gold. The Romans were particularly tantalized by the Ecbatana treasure. When the Triumvirate of Pompey, Caesar, and Crassus divided the world in three parts in the century before Christ's birth, Crassus, already the richest man in Rome, headed east into Asia. Ignoring the advice of the contemporary poet Horace, who admonished "Be wise—ignore the hoard of gold once hid," Crassus hoped to find the treasure that had eluded Alexander.

According to Plutarch the treasure hunter got off to a most unpropitious start. As he set out from Rome one of his political opponents placed a burning brazier at the city gate casting incense on the flames and invoking curses of so dreadful a nature as Crassus passed through that no one believed he could avoid disaster.

At Brindisi, where he was to sail from, an old fig seller warned him not to embark. But the gold-hungry Roman was not to be deterred. He overruled the galley captain, who urged a southerly route because of bad weather. Crassus insisted they go by way of Carrhae, on the direct route for Ecbatana.

At Carrhae Nemesis caught up with Crassus in the form of a large Parthian army. He was captured, and his enemies, aware of his gold lust, amused themselves by pouring molten gold down his throat. His gold-filled head was sent as a trophy to the Parthian monarch while he was at a performance of Euripides' *Bacchae*. One of the play's props was a "head" of Pentheus. The King tossed the players Crassus' head to use saying they might keep the gold if the performance was good.

Other Romans looked for gold at Ecbatana without success. One of the most notable attempts was allegedly made by the Emperor Trajan. He reportedly believed so vast a treasure must be in a particular river bed, so he sent out a great number of workers to dig a new channel for the river so the river bed could be examined. However, this imaginative effort revealed no glint of gold, and for all we know it still lies hidden.

CHAPTER EIGHT *Nomads' Gold*

The fabled Ecbatana treasure, if there is one, has never been found, but a gold hoard from an outlying part of the Persian Empire was unearthed in 1946. It was discovered by chance and almost lost through the gold greed of Iranian villagers. A shepherd boy, walking near the town of Ziwiye in northwestern Iran, stopped to investigate something shining among the rain-washed ruins of an ancient citadel. As he was grubbing in the earth, extracting what proved to be several pieces of worked gold, a merchant passed by and saw him. The man convinced the ingenuous shepherd to part with his gold for a few coins. The man buried the gold in his yard while planning what to do with it. However, the lad had told his parents of his discovery and the subsequent transaction. They went to the village chief with the story. He led a group of men to the merchant's house, where they beat him and dug up the gold. The villagers went to the citadel site and unearthed many more pieces of worked gold. By the time the authorities got wind of the treasure the peasants, ignorant of the archaeological and artistic value of the gold, had broken up the pieces and divided them. With great difficulty most of the fragments were assembled and given to experts, who spent many months trying to restore them. Eventually, the collection was put on display.

The Ziwiye treasure is provincial, marked by a lack of sophistication and a degree of mediocre craftsmanship. Nevertheless, it is fascinating and contains many beautiful pieces. Unfortunately, examples of the goldwork of metropolitan Persia are extremely rare since most pieces were melted or lost through the long march of history. So, until the day when a buried cache of Achaemenid masterpieces may come to light, the Ziwiye and

Oxus treasures and the occasional find will have to represent the magnificence of the Achaemenid Empire.

The Ziwiye trove appears to have been buried in a trough in the late eighth or seventh century B.C. The variety of gold and ivory objects represents a blending of many West Asian styles. Some scholars suggest that part of the treasure formed part of the royal dowry of King Esharhaddon's daughter, who married the Scythian King, Partatua. Others assign the treasure to the Medes or believe it may have belonged to a high Assyrian officer.

The goldwork includes a funnel with a curved handle, many heavy gold bracelets ending in animal heads, gold furniture terminals in the form of beasts and birds, and a gold hand net with two finger rings. It reflects influences of the Assyrians, Scythians, Mannians, Urartaeans, and even Phoenicians. A number of repoussé and chased-gold pectorals were found, including a large ceremonial breastplate with two rows of monsters and animals flanking the Tree of Life. The monsters are a blend of Assyrian and Phoenician styles, whereas some of the animals are distinctly Scythian in feeling.

The villagers damaged a gold plaque almost a foot long and over six inches high which weighed nearly a pound. It is now reduced to twenty-three framed fragments decorated with reclining mountain goats and stags in repoussé. What was once a magnificent 4½-pound silver bowl covered with gold appliqués of Scythian inspiration was also split among the treasure hunters. All that remains is a fragment with gold flower petals, lynxlike creatures, birds of prey, and geometric forms.

Many of the Ziwiye pieces were of Scythian origin. The Scythians were nomadic horsemen of the Eurasian steppes. They ranged north and east of the Black Sea in southern Russia and Greece, and even Egypt. They were one of a number of nomadic groups who roamed from the Danube to China and swirled down out of the Asian heart land in the first millennium B.C. to make devastating incursions into Asia Minor and the Near East.

More is known of the Scythians than of the other steppe peoples thanks to Herodotus' lengthy ethnographic notes on them in his *History of the Persian Wars*. The modern world knows them best through their legacy of golden ornaments found in Scythian burials. The Scythians prized gold as the heavenly metal. They had a lot of gold and used it in myriad ways. The warrior tribesmen adorned themselves and their beloved mounts with gold trappings and ornaments, using the richly gleaming metal for covering arms, shields, helmets, belts, and girdles. Death was softened for a royal Scythian by the inclusion of a rich inventory of gold objects in his tomb as well as the presence of his favorite mounts and concubines.

No one had any idea of the profusion of the nomads' gold or its rare beauty until 1715 when Peter the Great and his Empress at the christening of the Russian heir were given a gift of nomads' gold. They received twenty ancient gold repoussé and cast plaques which had been found in kurgans—the burial mounds of Siberia. The Emperor was fascinated by the plaques, which may have been shield ornaments. Shaped into emblematic animals, they radiated great vitality and unusual beauty. Peter had them put in a museum along with later gifts of gold in the animal style and established guidelines forbidding tomb robbery and the melting down of historical gold artifacts. Since the eighteenth century southern Russia has yielded thousands more superb gold masterpieces, from kurgans deep in Siberia and in the gold-rich Altai Mountains near the Sino-Soviet border. Americans had an opportunity to see the gold from the lands of the Scythians when selected items from U.S.S.R. museums were displayed in New York and Los Angeles. Even the most jaded critics were overwhelmed by the stunning beauty and virtuosity of the barbarian gold.

Herodotus' notes on the bizarre customs of the Scyths and other steppe nomads were long regarded as fictional. But recent archaeological discoveries substantiated even the most exotic of his accounts. In the fifth century B.C. he visited the bustling Greek trading city of Olbia on the Black Sea and the Dnieper River to gather material about the Scythians. A great deal of his information must have come from the Ionian Greek merchants who traded with the nomads.

The historian devoted Book Four of his work to the Scythians because they had denied Darius the Great a crucial victory in his bid for mastery of Greece.

About 513 B.C. Darius determined to starve Greece into submission. To do so he had to contend with the Scythians, who supplied Greece the bulk of her wheat, cattle, and fish. The Scythians had migrated to the rich steppelands from central Asia in the eighth century B.C. and founded an empire based on a confederation of separate tribes which shared a common culture. They displaced the Cimmerians, who had long been masters of the Caucasus. For thirty years during the seventh century B.C. the Scythians were masters of Asia Minor. They invaded Syria and Judea and only a colossal bribe of gold restrained them from swooping down on Egypt. They pillaged, burned, and exacted tribute without mercy. "Their insolence and oppression spread ruin on every side," wrote Herodotus. "They scoured the country and plundered every one of what they could."

The Scythian pieces in the Ziwiye treasure belong to this period of hegemony. However, when the Medes became lords of Persia, they managed to push most of the nomads back until they were concentrated in southern Russia, where they entrenched themselves and grew wealthy. They continued to raid caravans and loot what they could, but they also developed into the chief suppliers of agricultural products for food-poor Greece, exchanging their products at the Greek cities on the Black Sea for weapons, gold ornaments of Greek manufacture, and sweet Olbian wine.

As part of his master plan to take Greece Darius crossed the Danube with a large army to drive the Scythians from the steppe and strangle the supply line to the Greeks. He boasted that he would return victorious within sixty days. But while the days and weeks wore on, the fleet nomads evaded him. Always a day ahead of the Persians, the quicksilver tribesmen in Greek chain mail and bright felt costumes burned everything in their path and poisoned all wells. Darius realized the futility of trying to reap the wind and withdrew, frustrated and weakened by lack of supplies and vicious enemy attacks on his army's vulnerable flanks. After Darius' retreat the Scythians maintained their foothold in southern Russia until they were gradually thrust out of the steppes into the Crimea by the Sarmatians, whose women fought alongside their men. By a hundred years before Christ the last trace of one of history's most interesting peoples vanished.

Herodotus mistakenly wrote that the Scythians "use neither iron nor silver, having none in their country; but they have

bronze and gold in abundance." In fact, they did make limited
use of iron and silver, but gold seems always to have been not
only abundant but of particular importance. "The Royal Scythians," wrote the historian, "guard their sacred gold with most es-
pecial care, and year by year offer sacrifices in its honor." By the
nomads' own account they descended from the son of Zeus and a
creature, half snake and half woman, who was the daughter of
the Dnieper River. This ancestor had three sons who together
ruled the land. During their reign four gold implements fell from
the sky—a plough, a yoke, a battle ax, and a drinking cup. Each
brother in turn tried to pick up the implements, but at the approach of the elder two the gold blazed up. The youngest
brother was able to pick them up without flames breaking out so
he became the paramount ruler and forefather of the Scythians.

The gold of western Asia is even today concentrated in the
area of the Ural and Altai mountains and the gold of eastern
Asia in the Kolar region of Siberia. Both of these zones were
worked in remote antiquity. An eighteenth-century traveler in
Siberia wrote of visiting ancient gold mines. He found copper
and stone tools belonging to early miners who wriggled through
twisting tunnels to get at the quartz from which the filaments of
gold were extracted with sharpened boar fangs.

Herodotus' copious notes on the Scythians are in strong contrast to the paucity of information about other contemporary
nomadic people. Fantastic stories circulated of bald men, canni-
bals, one-eyed men, and other monsters in the unexplored
Siberian area.

Tales of the one-eyed Arimaspi and the gold-guarding griffins
mentioned in Hesiod and Herodotus probably grew from a grain
of truth. The one eye may well have been the forehead lamp of
ancient miners in the Ural-Altai area. There is a theory that the
griffin myth originated with the Mycenaeans, although the ferocious creatures may have merely been created to keep competition away. The Greek word *grypos* means "hook-nosed" and even
before the Mycenaeans came to power, their prospectors may
have ranged far from home searching for metalliferous areas. To
the northern nomads they would have appeared quite "beaky."
In *Apes, Ivory and Jade,* Kirk Meadowcroft suggests that the
Mycenaeans, before they had developed technical skills, could

have hired out as guards at Phoenician-controlled gold mines and along the Phoenician trade routes and been paid in gold.

Herodotus, without quite believing it himself, describes the Arimaspians, a legendary race of one-eyed folk who dwelled above the Issedones in the far north where feathers (snow) filled the air eight months out of twelve. These horsemen lived near a river filled with gold which was guarded by ferocious griffins. The griffins, favorite subjects of Persian artists and goldsmiths, were often depicted as having the body of a lion, two pairs of powerful wings, and the head and shoulders of a giant bird of prey. Aeschylus called them "the hounds of Zeus, who never bark, with beaks like birds." They attacked whoever tried to steal their gold, shredding the hapless victims with razor-sharp beaks. They could pick a man up in their massive claws and drop him to a terrible death on jagged mountain peaks.

Herodotus also describes the curious burial practices of the Issedonians. When a man's father died, his body was chopped into pieces and mixed with the flesh of sacrificial sheep and partaken of by all of the deceased's relations at a great banquet. His head was "stripped bare, cleaned and set in gold," turning into a prized relic which was brought out for an annual celebration.

Horses and cattle were at the very core of nomadic life. The nobles had vast herds of horses or ponies, but every Scyth had at least one fine mount on which he lavished much attention. Saddles, covered with brightly dyed felt, were often embellished with gold plaques. Cheek plates and bridle frontlets were fashioned of gold in openwork animal shapes, and reins, bridles, and other trappings were covered with embossed gold. The horses buried with a warrior of high rank were richly caparisoned in gold. In the grave of one Scythian chieftain, who was buried with masses of gold objects for the afterlife, the remains of 360 horses were found.

For over two thousand years men discredited Herodotus' tales of the passionate riders who drank from the gold-lined skulls of their enemies, made cloaks of human skin, and inhaled the narcotic fumes of burning hemp seeds which made them "shout for joy." Archaeological evidence from the steppe kurgans now corroborate Herodotus' arresting accounts which would otherwise seem quite incredible.

What remains incredible is the remarkable manner in which the gold of the so-called barbarians was crafted. It was worked into objects of such beauty and intensity that they have the power to evoke in the twentieth-century viewer a strong feeling for a lost age of heroic ferocity.

Scythian gold falls into two general categories: the indigenous style known as animal art of the migratory peoples and extraordinary Hellenic pieces reflecting nomadic themes executed by Greek goldsmiths in Asia Minor for Scythian patrons. The Asiatic horsemen had a keen appreciation of the subtlety of Greek art and commissioned pieces from goldsmiths of the Black Sea settlements.

The animal style evolved from the prehistoric wood and bone carvings made by nomads from China to Persia. The Scythian goldsmiths seldom depicted human figures or even the cattle and horses upon which their free-wheeling life style hinged. They preferred images of stags, griffins, goats, and other real or imaginary creatures. A strong element of sympathetic magic may have accounted for this; perhaps they felt that a gold image of a swift, strong, or fierce creature imparted invincible qualities.

Violence was an important element in the life of the Scythians and dominates their art. Whoever gave quarter on the harsh steppelands was lost. Gold animals are characteristically shown locked in mortal combat. Themes such as griffins attacking mountain goats emphasizing the helplessness and vulnerability of the attacked and the power of the attacker are common in the art of many Near Eastern civilizations. The Scythians may have been stylistically influenced by Achaemenid Persia, which lay on the western border of their grazing lands.

Scythian goldwork with its beveled edges and blunt powerful lines manages to compress a remarkable rhythm and energy into small, contained spaces. Free-flowing forms and repetitive designs are hallmarks of the animal style. Typically, an animal's outstanding feature is dramatized by repetition or exaggeration; we see eyes, ears, lips, or horns are dramatized by adapting geometric forms such as heart-shaped ears, spiral horns, or markedly curved lips. In order to accommodate the elaborate animal figures in a restricted space, the bodies are sometimes distorted or twisted creating a sense of barely restrained energy. Recumbent or battling stags and felines were a favorite with the Scythian goldsmiths, particularly for decorating weapons. Most often they were depicted with the legs contracted, perhaps to indicate that the creature was dead or passive.

Another Scythian convention was the incorporation of smaller creatures within the silhouette of a larger animal. A 6½-inch gold plaque from Peter the Great's collection shows a tiger locked in a deadly tangle with a horned predatory beast whose mane and tail tip are formed of five miniature stylized griffin's heads. A remarkable early example of Scythian animal style at its purest is a panther totem of the late seventh or early sixth century B.C. It is a large gold plaque which may have adorned an armor breastplate. The panther's legs are drawn up under a body formed of strongly articulated masses. The sinewy neck is thickened and lengthened and terminates in a head decorated with colorful inlays of glass, paste, and stones. The sweep of the tail and the creature's paws are made up of miniature wildcats.

A later example is a somewhat abstracted recumbent stag, 12⅜ inches long, which may have been a shield emblem. The contour of the rear haunch is elaborated into a griffin's head. A lean greyhound stretches along the beveled planes of the stag's unnaturally long throat and a dog, a lion, and a hare are worked in repoussé within the body outline. The antlers have nine tines, a magical number, forming a serrated pattern. Behind the last antler is a ram's head with downcurving horns. This piece, commissioned from a fourth century B.C. Greek smith, was found in a tomb in the Crimea.

The Greeks along the Black Sea for the most part enjoyed a peaceful coexistence with the Scythians. The nomads, with whom they had little in common save a love of gold, admired their skill at goldworking. The Greek goldsmiths lavished great care on sumptuous pieces they made for Scythian iconography, which also reflected Hellenic, Persian, and Armenian (Urartaean) influences. The Scythians didn't abandon the animal style with its visceral, magic appeal and the refined Hellenistic work. The two coexisted, and animal totems and exquisite Greek pieces of breath-taking delicacy were often buried in the same kurgan.

A 1971 find, a twelve-inch-wide gold pectoral, is far and away the single most stunning piece of Scythian gold. It is of fourth

century B.C. Greek workmanship and is a masterpiece in miniature. The pectoral is perfectly proportioned, blending the balance
and refinement of Hellenism with the stark, elemental life of the
steppes. In forty-eight individually cast figures ranging from humans to grasshoppers, the artist has created a virtuoso contrast
of Scythian domestic life with the wilderness outside the en-
campments. The exquisite figures are soldered onto the top and
bottom of three registers separated by four rope coils of diminishing diameter, tapering to the curved ends of the pectoral,
which are hinged and elaborately worked with gold mesh,
repoussé, and chasing. The middle register is filled with sheet
gold and richly decorated with flowers, buds, leaves, and ten-
drils, on which four sculpted birds perch.

In the upper register mares and cows suckle their young. Two
nomads with quivers lying by sew a fleecy sheepskin tunic. A
third figure intently milks a ewe with tightly curled fleece while
a fourth figure, sculpted, like the others, in the round, seals an
amphora. This scene of domestic life is flanked on each side by a
pig, a goat, a kid, and a bird.

The lower zone of figures deals with the themes central to the
precarious existence of the steppes. Three pair of griffins with
great feathered wings tear into the backs and necks of three
powerless horses. This poignant scene leads into sculpted lions
and tigers sinking their fangs into a deer on one side and a boar
on the other. At the tapering ends of this band sleek hounds
chase hares, and pairs of grasshoppers confront each other.

A gold comb from the Ukranian Solokha kurgan called the
Witch's Mound is a beautiful example of Greek fourth century
B.C. workmanship. The perfectly modeled teeth of the comb,
which is five inches high and five inches wide, are topped by a
frieze of five minuscule recumbent lions. Above the lions is a
miniature battle group in relief which creates the illusion of
three-dimensional sculpture. The Greek artist has treated barbarian subject matter with perfect classical mastery of the material.
Three warriors in the Scythian dress of baggy pants and Greek
armor, one mounted on a rearing horse, engage in furious combat above a horse lying on its back as blood streams from a fatal
wound.

Since the Scythians rarely depicted themselves, much of what
is known of their appearance comes from such Hellenic pieces as

the comb and a gold vessel which depicts the nomads convers-
ing, stringing a bow, treating a mouth ailment, and bandaging a
comrade's wounded leg. On this and other pieces the Scythians
are shown with full, luxuriant beards and mustaches and almost
never without their characteristic shield, bow, and the gorytus,
which was a combination quiver and bow case. Herodotus noted
that often it was made from the tanned skin of a slain enemy.
"The skin of a man," remarked the historian whose eye missed
not a detail, "is thick and glossy and whiter than most other
hides."

Human figures were rare in the Scythians' indigenous art, but
one gold plaque about 6½ inches long is of exceptional interest
because it not only shows how the Scythians saw themselves but
has a subject of great literary interest. A warrior lies under a
leafy tree resting his head in a woman's lap while a seated companion holds the reins of their two horses. The motif of the warrior lying with his head in a maiden's lap reflects a legend which
has survived. It is found today in a folk song of the Hungarians,
who are linguistically and ethnically descended from the nomads
who swept into central Europe in the early Middle Ages.

Motifs and themes prominent in nomadic art spread across
Europe with the migrations westward and surfaced not only in
ballads and epics but in early medieval art, appearing in Carolingian illuminations and gold jewelry, and in Celtic, Gothic, and
Viking goldwork and art.

An interesting postscript links the Scythians with modern
times. In the late nineteenth century the Louvre purchased with
great excitement and fanfare a "Greek marvel," a golden tiara
said to have been found in a kurgan burial in the land of the
Scythians. The lovely diadem bore a Greek inscription dedicating
it to a certain Saitaphernes. The acquisition attracted a great
deal of publicity, and even after it was learned that the piece was
a forgery by Rouchomowsky, the master goldsmith of Odessa,
who proudly claimed the tiara as his handiwork, the museum
authorities were loath to admit their mistake. He had taken the
inscription from a genuine dedication dating to the third century
B.C. which commemorated the erection of a fortification around
the city of Olbia as a protection against a Scythian chieftain
named Saitaphernes and his hordes, whom the Greeks had fruitlessly attempted to mollify with offerings of gold.

CHAPTER NINE *Rome*

Imperial Rome dazzled the landless rustics who were drawn to the glittering capital by handouts of cheap corn, spectacles designed to keep them docile, and, above all, the smell of gold. Never has wealth been as extravagantly displayed as in ancient Rome, the golden heart of a vast empire through which the treasures of the world flowed. Those who flocked to the great teeming city were awed by the gleaming luster of gold-leaved or fire-gilded wood, masonry, and marble. Roofs, façades, temple doors, statuary, and mosaics all shone with gold.

Gold, the tangible symbol of *sanctissima divitiarum majestas,* the most sacred majesty of wealth so dear to the empire, was flaunted by those who had it to an unprecedented degree. It was used without restraint to satisfy ambition and appetite. The Romans did not share the superstitious regard for gold which enhanced its value for the Oriental. Nor did they have the Greek appreciation for the metal's intrinsic beauty. The pragmatic Romans adored gold, craved gold for its tangible value. With gold, power and prestige could be purchased and maintained. Roman avarice was notorious. "*Salve Lucrum*," "Hurrah for Profit!" exclaimed a mosaic inscription in the shop of a cloth merchant excavated at Pompeii. Another retailer had the motto "Gain Is Joy" set in his floor.

Gold was the metal of ostentation and universally acceptable in exchange for other symbols of wealth. Beginning with the territorial conquests of the republic in the third century B.C. women and even men weighed themselves down with gold. Ovid described the fashion for incredibly ornate, overworked bracelets. One he saw was fashioned into a serpent weighing ten pounds.

"Why are you so anxious to carry your wealth on your person?" he asked a matron decked in pendant earrings reaching almost to her shoulders, bracelets, brooches, and rings on every finger. Propertius, seeing a similarly attired woman, remarked, "Here comes a matron dressed in her descendants' inheritance."

More often than not, good taste ran a poor second to lavish display, and quality was subordinate to quantity not only in jewelry but in other applications of gold as well. In Greece homes had been simple; grandeur and magnificence were reserved for the homes of the deities. In Rome, however, secular architecture was more daring than sacred building, stimulated by the excessive Oriental tastes of Egypt's Hellenistic kings, which came to Rome along with Cleopatra's gold. Augustus and his successors constructed palace complexes filled with rare and costly luxuries. Gold, the ornamental metal par excellence, was put to a thousand uses. The epitome of Roman grandeur, eclecticism, and vulgarity was Nero's famous Golden House, the Domus Aurea. There he presided at extravagant banquets at which the flowers alone cost as much as 4 million sesterces, or approximately $400,000. "Only a miser counts what he spends," sniffed the sybaritic Emperor.

Opulence became the byword in buildings, furnishings, and dress. The emperors were aped, albeit on a lesser scale, by the upper classes, who vied with each other in ostentation. Some of the great private houses boasted as many as four hundred domestic slaves. Later, when it was no longer a distinction to be filthy rich, taste became more selective and refined.

Although Roman taste was not as refined as the classical Greek, there was a keen appreciation of Hellenic antiques. The Romans were mad for antiques and like the nouveaux riches of other ages were often deceived by clever forgers. There were busy workshops in the capital where expert goldsmiths turned out jewelry and gold coins of hoary pedigree. One could buy a gold object of almost any alleged age and origin. Pasiteles, a Greek from southern Italy, spent sixty years in Rome working in gold, silver, and ivory. He was renowned for the fidelity of his copies of classical Greek pieces and is remembered as the Vasari of ancient Rome for writing a five-volume history of art.

The poet Horace, who lamented that gold greed was endemic

to Rome, satirized the myriad legacy hunters who ingratiated themselves with the wealthy. He cautioned the gold-hungry Romans not to laugh at the story of Tantalus, whose parched lips yearn toward water always just out of reach. "*Mutato nomine, de te fabula narratur,*" he said. "Change the name and the story is about you."

Poets and artists not immune to the lure of gold addressed flattering works to rich men in hopes of receiving golden thanks. The relatively temperate Augustus himself gave liberal golden tokens to poets and writers.

Gold was never more blatantly the "bloody fruit of oppression" than during the Roman era. Greed knew no bounds. Pliny wrote of the death of Gaius Gracchus, the idealistic reformer whose legislation to unite the classes aroused the ire of the aristocrats. The Senate, jealous of the popular young tribune, offered the weight of his severed head in gold to whoever would murder him and end his democratic reforms.

Gaius fled across the Tiber and then ordered his faithful servant to kill him. The slave plunged a dagger first into his master's heart and then into his own. A "friend" of the reformer's cut off the head and brought it triumphantly before the Senate—but not before filling it with molten lead to increase his golden reward.

Gold fueled Roman politics and economics. The object of almost every territorial conquest was either a land that produced gold or one that had centuries' worth of accumulated treasure. Egyptian, Gallic, Balkan, and, above all, Spanish gold were the backbone of the Roman economy. From about 150 B.C. to the establishment of the empire in 31 B.C. the influx of gold from Spain mounted. In the first century before Christ it was the single most important factor in the transition from a rather modest standard of living to a mode of prodigious opulence. Gold coinage made it possible for plebians as well as patricians to acquire a personal stock of the precious metal. Even slaves were occasionally able to save enough to buy their freedom.

At the peak of empire, Rome controlled every gold-bearing area known to the West. Gold was essential for buying power at home and luxury imports from abroad. Over the centuries a sophisticated system of finances evolved which included checks,

57. Electrum torc of the early Iron Age, first century
B.C., from the Snettisham Treasure. British Museum.

58. Sarmatian fibula in gold over bronze depicting a man holding enemy's head at
arm's length. Maikop, Kuban region, Russia. First century A.D. University
Museum, Philadelphia.

59. Early medieval costume adornments. Gold and bronze-gilt with inlaid glass and semiprecious stones. From Merovingian graves. Metropolitan Museum of Art, New York.

60. One of the pair of gold shoulder clasps with garnet and cloisonné enamel decoration from the Sutton-Hoo ship burial. Seventh century A.D. British Museum.

61. Byzantine nomisma showing Basil (A.D. 976–1025) with his brother, Constantine VIII. Basil, famed "Slayer of the Bulgarians," ruled forty-nine years and had a reputed personal reserve of 200,000 pounds of gold.

62. Methods of ventilating gold mines. Agricola's *De Re Metallica*. New York Public Library, Rare Book Division.

63. German Imperial Crown, also known as the Nuremberg Crown or the Crown of Charlemagne. Probably made at the monastery of Reichenau for the coronation of Otto I in A.D. 960. Byzantine style with eight panels of 21-carat gold decorated in champlevé enamel with scenes from the Old Testament, gems and pearls. Hofburg, Vienna.

64. The Towneley Brooch of enameled gold. German. Late eleventh century. British Museum.

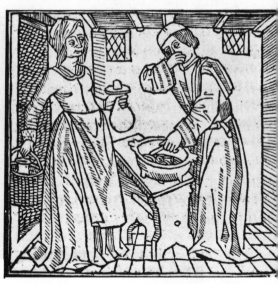

65. The crown of St. Stephen of Hungary, early twelfth century, in Byzantine style with champlevé-enameled plaques depicting religious and secular figures. Decorated with filigree, cabochon gems, pearls, and cloisonné enamel.

66. Alchemist performing an odiferous experiment. French, 1491, by Jean Du Pré. Spencer Collection, New York Public Library.

67. "The Alchymist." Etching by W. Baillie after painting by Teniers the Younger. Library of Congress.

68. "The Young Chemist." Engraving by Jorma after painting by Teniers. Library of Congress.

69. Henry VIII by Holbein, 1450.

70. English milled half pound; first British machine-made coins. Struck by London mint under direction of Eloye Mestrel at direction of Elizabeth I in 1561.

71. English gold coins from the British Museum. 1. Henry III, gold penny. 2. Edward III, noble. 3. Henry VI, angel. 4. Henry VII, sovereign. 5. Charles II, guinea.

72. Armada Jewel, gold with enamel and gems. Back lifts to reveal miniature of Queen Elizabeth I painted by goldsmith and painter Nicholas Hilliard. Presented by the Queen to Sir Thomas Heneage in recognition of his efforts as Treasurer at War. Victoria and Albert Museum, London.

73. Head of a crosier with a crowned angel in copper gilt, champlevé enamel and glass paste. French, Limoges, from mid-thirteenth century A.D. Private collection.

74. Royal Gold Cup. French. Ca. A.D. 1380. Made for Duc de Berry. British Museum.

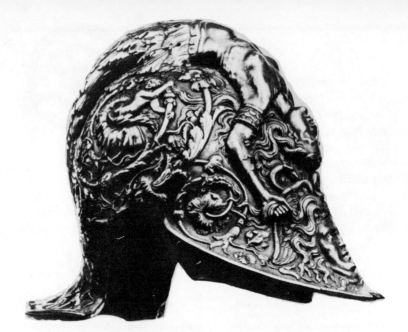

75. Renaissance parade burgeonet in steel and gold inlay with mermaid crest. Signed by Philippo de Negroli of Milan in 1543. Thought to have been made for Francis I, King of France, 1515-47. Metropolitan Museum of Art, New York.

76. Triptych tabernacle of silver parcel-gilt, enamel, and mother-of-pearl. Made by master goldsmith Perchtold for Abbot Rupert of the Benedictine Monastery of St. Peter in Salzburg. 1494. Salzburg. Private collection.

mortgages, and joint-stock companies, but gold continued to be the best hedge against inflation and the most trusted unit of value. As the empire slid into a morass of bankruptcy and bloodshed, gold was often the only acceptable medium of exchange. This was particularly so after the third century A.D. when watered currency precipitated crippling inflation, stripping men of their savings and tumbling property values.

The history of Rome is a story of continuing struggle—the defeated against the conqueror, the slave against the master, and Roman against Roman. It is a tangled saga glittering with gold; yet Rome herself had no gold when she embarked on the career that was to propel her to world dominance and eventual downfall. The precious metal, which was so scarce in the early republic that it played no role in the monetary system and accounted for a minuscule percentage of the treasury reserves, became Rome's chief export.

In the eighth century B.C. few would have guessed that tiny Rome, a settlement crowded on the hills above the Tiber River, would become Mistress of the World commanding the greatest empire in history. From humble origins in farming villages scattered along the Tiber, Rome grew into a rigidly organized city-state ruled by kings. By the sixth century B.C. Rome turned her attention to bringing the Italian peninsula to heel. The patricians rose and, according to tradition, expelled their last Tarquin King, an Etruscan, at a time when Etruscan power was fading on land and sea.

One by one youthful Rome annexed territories and subjugated the Italic tribes. Rome was increasingly involved in a system of alliances which drew her into the external affairs of other groups. Within Rome there was a strong drive for territorial expansion. The population of Rome expanded rapidly, and when a new territory was taken, it was first looted and then settled by colonies of farmers.

Rome began her meteoric rise only after Alexander, when the center of the world's wealth, measured in terms of gold, shifted from Persia to the central Mediterranean. During the centuries of Etruscan hegemony a very small amount of gold had trickled into the embryo city. With the decline of the Etruscans even that small supply dried up. It is interesting that the first compilation of Roman law, the Twelve Tables, about 450 B.C., forbade the burying of gold with the dead, an unusual prohibition, motivated by a critical deficiency. Pliny wrote that the city could raise no more than one thousand pounds of gold to buy peace from the invading Gauls in 390 B.C. That was after a century of republican development and amounted to less than half the gold Phidias had used for his Athena fifty years before and less than one seventh of the gold that Croesus had bestowed on Apollo's shrine at Delphi a century and a half earlier.

Gradually Rome extended her influence to northern Italy and began to tap the Etruscan source of alluvial gold at the head of the Po in the eastern Alps. By the third century B.C. she was well launched on a policy of aggrandizement. The machinery which assured the perpetuation of a wartime economy and continual territorial expansion for the next six hundred years was in motion and gold was the fuel.

After the mid-third century B.C. Rome began to look further afield for new lands to conquer, and gold started to flow into the capital as subject states were looted and then organized for the exploitation of natural resources and the extraction of tribute and taxes. The conquering armies brought back bullion, coins, provincial taxes, and treasure in gold which financed the growing opulence of Roman life and exacted a terrible toll in human suffering. Little of the gold that came to Rome stayed. Most went out in payment of the furs, spices, amber, eunuchs, jewels, carpets, silks, and brocades that the Romans, who had once prided themselves on thrift and plain living, craved with ever-increasing appetite. While patricians dined on camel's heels and flamingo tongues served on golden platters, slaves labored and died by the thousands in the gold mines. What had been a tight-knit community of free farmers became a complex state which depended increasingly on internal slavery and the brutal and ultimately unprofitable exploitation of the conquered.

Rome conquered southern Italy. She gained gold in booty and indemnities from the rich Greek commercial settlements and began to reach out across the Adriatic to the gold-producing areas of the Balkans. However, the most dramatic increase in Roman gold supplies came with the subjugation of Spain, which had been to the Carthaginians what Mexico and Peru were to become to the sixteenth-century Spanish—an apparently inexhaustible storehouse of gold.

In the period from 264 to 133 B.C. Rome became an international power. In three Punic Wars gold-poor Rome, relying at first on armies of conscripted peasants, pitted herself against the mighty maritime empire of the Carthaginians and won control of the Mediterranean. To win the First Punic War, Rome, a nation with no prowess at sea, built a fleet and trained troops to maneuver in naval battles. At first they were quite successful but soon began to suffer one shipwreck after another until about sixteen hundred ships and countless men had been lost in tempestuous seas.

The Carthaginians were confident of victory. They knew the meager resources of the Romans. At the beginning of the first war in 264 B.C., Carthaginian emissaries returning from a diplomatic mission to Rome had regaled the North African city with tales of how one silver table service was shared by the entire Roman aristocracy and passed from house to house.

When the treasury was almost empty, the Senate assessed itself to build a last fleet. This gesture tipped the balance. Carthage surrendered much of the treasure house of Spain and the islands of Sicily, Sardinia, and Corsica. She also paid an indemnity of 4,400 gold talents—a talent was worth about $13,000. The newly won islands became the first provinces, and the Romans continued the Greek and Carthaginian practice of exacting tribute in precious metals and grain rather than in troop levies as they did in Italy.

Many of the Roman campaigns seemed to be little more than great gold- and slave-hunting expeditions. Whole cities and nations had been enslaved before in antiquity and Rome continued this policy on a grand scale. The 30,000 inhabitants of Tarentum were sold, as were the entire populations of Capua and Syracuse; 140,000 Corinthians and the entire aristocracy of Macedonia— the Greek intellectuals, doctors, and bankers—all went on the block at Rome's central slave market on the island of Delos.

In the wake of the Roman armies came the *magnari*, the wholesalers who bought up the slaves and spoils. The lion's share of booty went to the generals, but the soldiers did very well. Men fought not for the glory of the nation, but for profit.

The wholesalers were among those who advanced colossal sums for campaigns. They made bids to generals on the eve of battle and often became wealthy overnight. Looted gold and slaves made many millionaires and fostered discontent in the common soldiers who were loath to return to their farms and pay accumulated taxes, having tasted the spoils of war.

The Italian earth, which had been fruitfully worked for centuries by small farmers, fell gradually into the hands of a relatively few magnates who carved out vast latifundia manned by platoons of slaves. The moneyed aristocrats bought land cheaply from veterans and oppressively taxed farmers. Later estates were acquired through the proscription lists which condemned an emperor's enemies and made his lands available to the ruler's friends for a fraction of their value.

Between the First and Second Punic Wars wealth in gold mounted in Rome, concentrated in a few hands. Livy wrote that before the Second War began in 218 B.C. Rome had 4,000 Roman pounds of gold (the Roman pound was 5,040 grains, quite a bit lighter than the English pound of 7,000 grains) in the treasury. This was a niggling amount compared to what Alexander had seen, but represented a fourfold increase since 390 B.C. Luxury began to creep into the life of Stoic Rome in this interval, as evidenced by the repeated promulgation of sumptuary laws. These forbade ornate jewelry, fancy dress, and elaborate meals and were universally ignored, particularly by the senators who issued them. Hannibal, the daring Punic general, collected a large number of illegally worn gold rings from the hands of dead Romans after one Italian battle in 216 B.C.

The Second Punic War, which ended disastrously for Carthage in spite of Hannibal's audacious march of men and elephants across the icy Alps, brought stupendous amounts of gold to Rome. The most costly of all ancient wars yielded the golden seeds of both the rise and fall of Rome. The greatest prize was Spain with its gold and silver mines. In addition, she heaped up the royal treasure of Syracuse, 2,070 pounds of gold from Capua, over 270 pounds from New Carthage in Spain, and some 5,000 pounds from Tarentum. In 210 B.C. a tax was levied for the first time on the privately owned gold of Roman citizens, another indication that gold ownership was increasing.

There were probably at least 10,000 pounds of gold at Rome before Flaminius conquered Greece in 194 B.C. He added some 5,000 pounds of gold in the form of bullion, coin, and objects, such as 114 crowns and a huge gold shield to the treasury. The gold of Spain paid for the Greek campaign and laid the groundwork for the pernicious rot that weakened the republic. In the half century after 200 B.C. Romans whose family wealth had long been reckoned in agricultural terms became incredibly rich, living in Oriental splendor. The influx of gold and Eastern taste stimulated excesses of conspicuous consumption, corruption, and venality. The riches and hedonism of the East hastened the disintegration of the old virtues: *pietas, gravitas,* and *simplicitas.* The gap between the haves and have-nots widened until it was a yawning chasm into which the republic toppled in a series of ghastly civil disorders.

Carthage, Macedon, Syria, Gaul—all enriched Rome as indemnities, tribute, slaves, and booty poured into the capital. Gold primed the business class at the expense of agriculture. The equestrian order, the business class, grew rich with incredible ease participating in tax-farming ventures and growing fat on lucrative state contracts for public works. They were aided by the exclusion of senators from direct participation in business and became extremely wealthy and influential, always pushing for ruthless exploitation of subject territories. The senators, however, managed to acquire huge fortunes in commerce through the talents of loyal freedmen. They also derived income from vast land holdings in scattered parts of the empire, the management of which they left to skilled slaves.

Industry was very slow to develop but bankers and moneychangers flourished. The bankers managed investments, cashed checks, lent and borrowed money. They even paid interest on deposits. Huge sums were lent to tributaries to meet payments to the state at such exorbitant rates of interest that they could never be paid back. Usury was so brutal that the same word, "sector," applied to both moneylender and cutthroat.

Upper-class women had an unusual degree of autonomy as wealth and corruption loosened the old moral code. They brazenly indulged in extramarital affairs. No longer content to adorn themselves with virtue, they dressed seductively in the diaph-

anous silks of the East and overloaded themselves with gold
and jewels from their wigs of blond northern hair to their moroc-
con leather shoes. Lollia Paulina, once wed to Caligula, flaunted
jewelry worth as much as 40 million sesterces when she went out
in society. Pliny quipped that she carried the receipts with her to
prove its worth.

"Pure women," gibed Ovid, "are those who have not been
asked and a man who is angry at his wife's amours is a mere rustic." The majority of affluent women were, of course, neither
wildly lascivious nor exhibitionistic, but they too made gold ornaments an important part of their costume, and both men and
women shared a passion for rings.

Under Tiberius rings were a badge of rank worn only by men
who descended from at least three generations of freemen. Later,
as the number of well-to-do freemen greatly increased, the restriction was relaxed although only a freeborn Roman was officially entitled to wear them. Eventually men and women wore
multiple rings on every finger. A satire of Martial describes a
man who wore six on each finger day and night and Elagabalus, who had thousands, never wore the same ring twice.

Roman goldsmiths drew from four inspirational sources: Etruscan, Hellenistic, Eastern, and barbarian. Early jewelry reflected
the Etruscan influence. Subsequently Greek models were copied
by Italian goldsmiths who seldom equaled either Etruscan or
Greek workmanship. Greek goldsmiths came to Rome to work
and were recognized masters at gem-cutting. The Romans
adored stones—emeralds, sapphires, rubies, pearls. Pliny lists over
a hundred varieties. Those who couldn't afford the real thing
made do with excellent imitations. Roman forgers were particularly good with emeralds. Superb counterfeits were sold by
shady jewelers well into the nineteenth century A.D.

Contact with the luxury of the Greek cities of southern Italy
and the East inspired derivative jewelry, a fashion for gold
brocades on walls, covering couches and beds, and gold-
threaded tapestries on marble floors.

In the centuries just before the Fall of Rome goldwork
reflected the heavy taste of the northern barbarians. Celtic
and Germanic styles emphasizing massive goldwork paved with

garnets and other stones was in vogue. Repeatedly as Rome tee-
tered on the brink of bankruptcy, emperors issued sumptuary
decrees but women always managed to circumvent the restrictions on luxuries. Tiberius was forced to admit defeat, commenting, "Without luxury how could Rome, how could the provinces
live?" and allowed the goldsmiths to continue their work.

Relatively little Roman jewelry survived antiquity and almost
none of what must have been a tremendous amount of gold
plate. Although Roman goldwork tends to be somewhat heavy, a
bit coarse, and lacking in imagination, there were many outstanding exceptions. The acme of Roman goldwork is displayed
in the magnificent coinage issued in such abundance from the
time of Augustus onward.

Rome's contribution to the goldsmith's repertoire was limited
to the development of two previously invented decorative techniques. One was perfection of the opus interrasile, the pierced
goldwork so common in Byzantine jewelry, and the other was
niello work, a type of champlevé enameling in which a fusible
alloy made of various combinations is used to fill cavities in the
gold with black linear patterns instead of polychrome.

A first century A.D. goldsmith's shop is depicted in a charming
fresco at Pompeii. It illustrates technically sophisticated cherub
goldsmiths turning out pieces with filigree, repoussé, chasing,
granulation, and burnishing. Apprentices are shown making
chains, riveting, and casting.

The Romans perfected the fire-gilding process the Greeks had
used to apply gold to masonry and sculpture from the mid-first
millennium B.C. in which powdered gold was combined with
mercury. The mixture was spread on the object to be coated and
then heated. The quicksilver vaporized leaving a thin, uniform
layer of gold. This process, called amalgamation, is today outlawed in many countries. The reason is described in a 1745 English treatise, The Book of Trades.

It is "dangerous to the constitution: few gilders live long: the
Fumes of the Quicksilver affecting their nerves and rendering
their Lives a Burthen to them. The Trade is in a few Hands
most of them Women." Even in ancient times the connection was
known between the loss of teeth, falling hair, tremors, mental

disorientation, and death that afflicted goldsmiths and mercury poisoning, but the practice continued and Rome shimmered with gilded surfaces, inside and out.

Gold leaf was used for architectural applications, furniture, and also in the production of glass, at which the Romans excelled. Gold-leaf medallions sandwiched in glass have been excavated from the Catacombs near Rome, where they were embedded in the mortar sealing Christian tombs in the fourth century. A layer of gold was etched with Christian motifs or biblical scenes and put between two thin layers of glass in the form of a bowl or vessel. The whole piece was fused to seal the gold, and presumably at the death of the owner, the section bearing the design was ground down into a roundel for decorative application on the tomb. This gold-glass technique had a renaissance in eighteenth- and nineteenth-century Bohemia. Inserts of gold elaborately etched with hunting scenes, armorial devices, or devotional subjects were slipped between two thin plates of glass to form beautiful vases and bowls, which were avidly collected.

The Romans had hordes of deities who governed every aspect of life and were the object of endless rites. There were simple shrines to the homely gods of prerepublican Rome and huge glittering temples to the more powerful deities. As the city grew, new gods were introduced through conquest. They were welcomed by the Romans who gave new names to the divinities of Greece, Egypt, and Asia Minor, making room for them in a city crowded with golden temples. Their numbers increased as the emperors added temples for worship of themselves and their relatives.

Within the temples were bevies of priests and priestesses ready to intercede with the gods upon payment of gold. The more gold, the better the performance. Ceremonies had to be carried out perfectly to be effectual. Not infrequently something flawed a ritual, and it had to be paid for and repeated as many as twenty times before the priests pronounced the gods pleased.

The greatest of the gods was Jupiter, who had many temples. The holiest was that on the Capitoline Hill, which he shared with Juno and Minerva. It had been rebuilt several times since the founding of Rome and featured a three-storied colonnade around a spectacular gold and ivory colossus of the god. Domi-

tian in the first century A.D. spent $22 million to gild the doors
and roof. In the fifth century A.D. a Roman general stole the
gold-plated doors to pay his troops, and the Vandals stripped the
roof of its golden tiles.

Roman life was punctuated by great public entertainments—
bread and circuses—to keep the plebians happy. Among the
most splendid were the triumphs offered at the return of conquering heroes. The first was given in 168 B.C. when the general
Paulus Aemilius returned victorious from Greece with unprecedented spoils and having won the Macedonian mines for Rome.

Plutarch, writing of his conquest of Epirus, described how
Aemilius assembled the mountains of treasure that overwhelmed
Rome when it was paraded through the streets. "He sent for ten
of the principal inhabitants of each city and fixed a day for them
to bring whatever silver and gold could be found in their houses
and temples. With each of these he sent a centurion and a guard
of soldiers under the pretense of searching for and receiving the
precious metals, and as if for this purpose only. But when the
day came they rushed upon all the inhabitants (who had
previously been disarmed) and began to seize and plunder them.
Thus in one hour 150,000 persons were made slaves and 70 cities
sacked." The slaves were sold to the wholesalers for about a dollar a head and the gold carried to the capital.

Paulus Aemilius returned to Rome with the riches of Epirus
and Macedon—such a wealth of plunder that republican Rome
never again had to tax her citizens. It took three days to bear it
all through the city. The third day was reserved for the gold.
Leading the triumphal procession were 120 white sacrificial
oxen. Following them came 308 men bearing seventy-seven containers filled with gold coins. There were twenty-seven large vessels of beaten gold, gold cups which had belonged to Alexander's
generals Antigonus and Seleucus, the gold plate which had once
graced the tables of Macedonian kings, four hundred crowns
from fallen cities, and countless chests of gold ornaments and
jewelry and at the very end was King Perseus in chains with his
children.

The national wealth was further multiplied by the heavy indemnities paid by the Celts of Galatia and other conquered
states. Gold-rich Pergamum, in the western part of Asia Minor,

was ceded to Rome by its dying King. Spain, however, remained the most productive and dependable source of gold. By the mid-second century B.C. the auriferous rivers of southern and central Spain, including the Guadalquivir area, were being washed for gold. There was so much of it at that time that mining wasn't necessary. Strabo, who visited placers in Spanish rivers such as the Tagus and Douro 150 years later, described the process, which was unchanged. Women as well as men worked the alluvial deposits.

"The gold is not merely got by mining, but is also washed down. Rivers and torrents carry down the golden sand; it is also to be found in the waterless districts, though there it is invisible, but where the water flows over the sand the gold-dust shines out. They lead water to the arid spots and thus make the gold dust glitter. They also get the gold out by digging pits and by other methods of washing the sand. . . . Nuggets of up to half a pound in weight are said to be found sometimes in the gold dust. . . . In the river beds the sand is carried along in the stream and then washed in troughs by the river."

Roman requirements for gold, silver, and other metals were enormous and led to large-scale industrial exploitation of the empire's vast mineral resources. The Romans were great engineers and superlative administrators—a potent combination. Unlike the Greeks, who considered the practical applications of technology vulgar, the Romans eagerly adopted and perfected the mechanical devices of others.

Under Augustus, the first Emperor, Rome began to tap a new source of Iberian gold which made the rich placer deposits of southern Spain look pale in comparison. The mines of northwestern Spain were organized after the area was subjugated in 31 B.C., and Pliny figured their output at seven tons a year, some twenty thousand Roman pounds.

In some of the gold mines shafts were sunk as deep as 650 feet, an extraordinary depth for that time. Miners faced recurring problems with underground water which flooded the workings. To combat the problem slaves were assigned to bail the invading water with tar-covered baskets which held about two gallons. The Archimedian screw pump was used, and the richest mines merited the introduction of the more effective but costly and cumbersome cochlea and water wheel. They remained, until the late eighteenth century, the most successful machines for coping with the endemic problem of mine drainage.

Roman mining engineers were trained at a government school in Spain where they learned to recognize gold-bearing earth by the presence of quartz gravels or various copper ores, the oxidized layers of which often contained a profitable amount of gold. Liquation, a method of separating gold from its matrix of copper ore, was a Roman innovation of the first century B.C. and added substantially to the amount of gold recovered as a by-product of copper smelting.

Apprentice mining engineers learned how the mercury from Spanish mines was mixed with crushed ore and the amalgam pressed through leather sieves to separate the mercury and its clinging gold from the worthless detritus. Cupellation, the salt and sulphur process for refining gold, and assaying were taught. The men were instructed in the design and construction of the engineering works employed in the hydraulic crushing of gold-bearing strata.

Roman gold production made a great leap with the introduction of hydraulic mining, which was a quick, effective, but devastating way of using great jets of water to break down relatively soft rock beds and expose auriferous earth. This system was later adapted in the California gold rush and called hydraulicking.

Whole mountains were washed away, the landscape changed beyond recognition, farm lands destroyed, and rivers and harbors silted up before legislation outlawed the practice.

Hydraulic mining made it possible for the Romans to process a colossal volume of rock in northwestern Spain—estimates run as high as 500 million tons. Strabo writes more gold was won this way than from underground mines. It was practiced in central Gaul, in the Welsh tin mines (according to Pliny), and other places as well. Canals were channeled from rivers to huge artificial ponds or holding tanks overlooking the site. The water was discharged in a controlled flow from heights not uncommonly of four hundred to eight hundred feet. The force of the water crushed the relatively low grade ore, freeing the gold, which was then washed in sluices lined with shrubs.

The shrubs' foliage trapped the heavier gold particles, which were removed by hand. From time to time the shrubs were removed from the sluices, dried, and burned. After the visible gold had been picked out the ashes were washed on a bed of turf to catch the finest gold dust. The detritus, great amounts of crushed rock, was carried off by the flow of water into the nearest stream below the level of operations, causing terrible silting. As early as the end of the first century A.D. rivers carrying the wastes were clogging up at their mouths, the coast line was altered, and harbors filled in completely, turning port towns into inland settlements.

Roman mining, like Greek, was one of the few industries which drew its work force almost entirely from slave labor. Diodorus aptly called the mines "golden prisons." Throughout the Roman domains slaves and prisoners of war, naked and poorly nourished, labored and died in clammy subterranean darkness. Great numbers of human bones have been found in Roman mines along with iron rings where the miners were shackled to the walls at night. A mine which archaeologists have explored at Aramo was littered with skulls and had a vertical shaft entrance to prevent escape. Generations of Spanish slaves, whose fathers had labored for the Carthaginians, were augmented by great numbers of Africans who worked the Roman mines as their descendants did those of Spain in the New World eighteen hundred years later.

Pliny in A.D. 79 gave full account of imperial mining in Spain in which he describes washing of the rivers for alluvial gold, shaft mining, and in the following passage "gold gained by the destruction of mountains."

The third method of mining may seem to surpass the achievements of the giants. For by the light of lanterns mountains are hollowed out by galleries driven deeply into them. Lamps are also used to measure the length of the miner's shifts, for many of them do not see daylight in months together. Mines of this kind they call "arrugiae."

Fissures can suddenly open up and crush the miners and so arches are left at frequent intervals to hold the

mountains up. In these mines—and in the mine shafts
too—flint is met with, and the miners break it up with
iron rams of 150 pounds weight. The pieces are carried
out night and day in the darkness along a human chain:
only the last in the chain can glimpse daylight. When
all is ready they cut the "keystones" of the arches, beginning with the innermost. The earth on top subsides,
and gives a signal, and a solitary lookout on a peak of
the hill observes it. With shouts and gestures he orders
the mine to be evacuated and he himself speeds down
as well. The mountain then breaks and falls apart with
a roar that the mind can hardly conceive and with an
equally incredible blast of air.

Seldom have gold and murder been so brazenly employed as
political weapons as in the ailing Roman Republic, which choked
to death on corruption and bloodshed. During the republic votes
were openly bought with gold. Roman generals were the first to
take advantage of gold's link with the economics of political
power. The first Roman gold coins issued in any numbers were
minted by generals in the field to pay their troops. The Senate
permitted the imperator, or general in command of a legion, to
strike coins from seized bullion.

The first military issue was struck about 80 B.C. by Sulla, commander of an army in Asia Minor, to commemorate his victory
over Mithridates VI, King of Pontus. The coin's denomination
was an aureus, which became the standard gold coin of the empire. The reverse of the coin portrays a small Winged Victory
placing the victor's crown on Sulla's head. The obverse bears a
helmeted personification of Roma and the name of Sulla's chief
financial administrator, L. Manlius.

The Senate was alarmed at the tremendous power of the commanding generals who had gained so much wealth and enjoyed
the fierce loyalty of their armies. Legislation to curb their
influence in the city was generally ineffective. Ambitious generals, heady from their triumphs, used their captured gold without restraint to satisfy political aims. Backed by their loyal
troops, they precipitated the bloody struggles which culminated
in the establishment of the empire.

Sulla, one of Rome's first dictators, came to power on a wave of conquered gold and Roman blood. An unassuming figure with a splotchy face like "a mulberry dusted over with flour," he never lost a battle. As a general in Greece he looted the temple treasuries of Delphi, Olympia, and Epidaurus. He sacked Athens and ravaged Greece. He returned from his victories in Asia Minor with the huge sum of 20,000 gold talents in indemnities and taxes. To raise this amount the cities he took had to borrow from Roman bankers, incurring a grinding burden of debt. In addition he brought back 15,000 pounds of gold and 115,000 of silver for the state treasury, not to mention enough for himself to eventually buy the dictatorship.

Sulla, known as Sulla Felix because of his sense of humor and love of wine, women, and song, was born a penniless patrician. He allied himself with the archconservative cause. While he was waging war abroad Rome was a battleground contested by the conservatives and their various enemies. In one day in the center of the city there was a pitched battle in which ten thousand were killed. Rebel terror gripped the capital for a year as Marius, Sulla's archenemy, ruled. At a nod of Marius' head, men were cut down on the spot and their property confiscated. Life in the eternal city was never secure for either rich or poor.

When he returned, Sulla found his supporters had been murdered and his estates seized. He used his 40,000 veterans and gold to overcome the democratic forces which had made some effort to enfranchise the poor and reduce slavery. His revenge was cold-blooded and thorough. In 81 B.C. he was named dictator, and his first act was to issue a proscription list calling for the deaths of 90 senators and 2,600 of the hated equestrians. He offered golden rewards to their murderers, and soon the Forum was adorned with ghastly severed heads.

Proscription condemning Romans to death or exile became common. Men lived in dread and assassins murdered with impunity. "Men were butchered in the arms of their wives," wrote Plutarch, "sons, in the arms of their mothers." Sulla even had men of his own conservative party proscribed to obtain their gold and estates, which he auctioned to his favorites at ridiculously low prices.

The happy Sulla offered up to $10,000 a head for his enemies. Forty years later, during the Second Triumvirate, assassins could expect as much as $15,000. Generally, however, the cost was far lower, and many aspiring politicians found it cheaper and more expedient to have their rivals murdered than to buy favor. Gold was the end and the means of Roman politics.

Some of the gold that came back with the armies in the first two centuries before Christ filtered down to the populace in the form of bribes in bitterly contested electoral campaigns. Candidates openly handed out coins; Cicero describes the dispensing of bribes on the Field of Mars. Whole segments of the electorate were purchased with mass bribes, and extravagant entertainments were offered free to the public as contenders vied for votes.

The Senate seldom did more than protest the most outrageous abuses, since each solon did exactly the same given his "golden opportunity." The sure winners at election time were the temple bankers and the money-changers, whose shops huddled in a crooked row leading from the Forum. They lent colossal sums at outrageous rates to aspiring politicians who weren't fortunate enough to have either gold or a rich patron.

Caesar's patron was Crassus, one of the richest of Roman tycoons, who died with a throat full of gold at Carrhae. He made his first millions as a slum lord. He organized the city's first fire brigade, which turned up at the scene of disaster and quenched a fire only if paid at once. Otherwise he bought the burning building for a pittance as well as those adjoining it and only then moved to put out the flames. He bought thousands of tenements this way, which he let at high rents. Sulla, who had been a friend of his father's, sold him confiscated estates at special prices, and when the dictator denationalized the state mines, Crassus was there to snap them up. In a short time he increased his worth from 7 million sesterces to 170, more than $25½ million, which nearly equaled the annual revenue of the state.

Crassus lent the young Caesar gold to further his political career in the accepted fashion by handing out bribes and financing public games. Caesar once owed him almost $3 million. Such debts were not unusual. They were considered campaign contributions by men sure to profit at the success of their candidate. Crassus was rewarded by being made a member of the First Triumvirate with Caesar and Pompey in 60 B.C.

Julius Caesar became an exceedingly rich man in a way that became standard Roman practice as a provincial official. Not only generals but governors made fortunes in the provinces. They served without pay and one year sufficed to enrich a man for life. Verres, governor of Sicily, frankly admitted that a three-year term as provincial administrator was quite enough. He told Cicero that "in the first year he could secure plunder for himself, in the second for his friends, and in the third for his judges."

When Caesar came back from his first stint in Spain as quaestor, he brought enough booty to pay off part of his debts. He even borrowed more from Crassus to buy his election of commissioner of public works. He wooed the citizens with circuses and moved up the ladder. When he was appointed governor of Spain, he owed, by his own admission, some $7½ million to various creditors. He departed a debt-ridden man with many enemies, both political adversaries and cuckolded husbands. A year later he returned from the gold-rich province with so much of the precious stuff that he paid off all his debts and filled the treasury so copiously that the Senate voted him a triumph.

The Spanish gold bought him a part in the triumvirate with Crassus and Pompey, the two richest men in Rome. Pompey was his ally in the First Triumvirate and ultimately his foe in the struggle for power. When Caesar reached Egypt, he was handed the severed head of his fellow Roman by the eunuch vizier of young Ptolemy XII, Cleopatra's brother and rival. It was said he wept at the sight of his former friend but recovered quickly to administer the ancient kingdom and succumb to the charms of the princess.

Despite his previous successes, it was Caesar's conquest of Gaul which brought him the greatest riches and fame. Plutarch says that the object of his Gallic wars was clearly less to subdue the population than to gain gold.

Whatever his motives, Caesar's conquest of Gaul added to the Roman Empire a country twice as large as Italy, which acted as a buffer between the Mediterranean world and the northern barbarians for another four hundred years. For the first time the values and culture of the classical world reached the peoples north of the Alps. The immediate cost to the Gauls was great. Plutarch reckoned a million perished in the wars and another million were enslaved. Yet centuries later when the glittering Roman Empire was spent, medieval France shone as a beacon of Western culture in the darkness of barbarian Europe.

Caesar made two armed reconnaissance missions across the Channel invading England as far as the Thames, where he negotiated with British chieftains for tribute payments. Contemporary sources insisted his forays into Britain were not for the good of the empire, but for a share of the gold and pearls he had heard abounded there.

In fact, gold was then relatively scarce and Britain was incapable of substantial payments in the precious metal, although a century later Tacitus could say, "It yields gold and silver as the prize of victory." Tales of gold money may have originated with the Irish gold which had long been traded on England's southern coast. The gold rings which had circulated as currency in Ireland since about 1600 B.C. had been introduced into England, where money was chiefly in the form of rings of brass and iron, but they were very rare.

Irish gold deposits, particularly in county Wicklow, although not the equal of those of Egypt or Spain, were productive until the nineteenth century A.D. and furnished the material for much of the beautiful and dramatic Celtic goldwork. The Romans later worked deep gold mines in Wales using hydraulic methods, and Welsh gold accounted for the bulk of British production.

Caesar did see gold coinage in England which had been adapted from the rude imitation staters introduced about 75 B.C. by Belgic tribes fleeing from the Romans. The Celts issued these staters until Britain became a province when a mint was established at London and regular Roman issues replaced them.

Caesar got a portion of his gold from the diggings at Aquileia, a Roman town at the head of the Adriatic where he had established headquarters. In the second century B.C. the Romans had founded a settlement to work the gold deposits discovered there. Polybius, quoted by Strabo, said that the area produced so much gold at that time as to cause a fall in gold of one-third its value. The golden booty Caesar sent to Rome from Gaul also precipitated a sudden fall in the value of gold. However, since gold coinage was not yet part of the monetary system, the ratio soon widened again.

Caesar after nine years in Gaul was responsible for making gold readily available as coinage. The upper classes had long accumulated the precious metal in the form of ornament and table plate, and veterans returned from abroad with gold spoils and some coins. But with Caesar's aurei gold ownership spread to a larger segment of the population. Caesar struck the coins to pay his troops, an aureus equaling two weeks' pay for the common soldier.

Caesar described the Gauls as tall broad-shouldered men with thick blond hair and great curling mustaches. They had a passion for gold and wore abundant gold ornaments into battle "even if they wore nothing else." The proud Gauls had a long tradition of working in gold. They were skilled in the manufacture of bronze and iron, diffusing knowledge of ironworking through much of northern Europe.

During the first century before Christ many barbarian tribes of Eastern origin were pushed westward in the shock waves of disruption emanating from central Asia and flowed through the Danube Valley, the natural highway to new lands in the West. It was there that they first saw Hellenistic gold staters. Various Celtic tribes imitated the Greek coins, giving them a fresh barbaric verve which was attractive, although quite different from the refined beauty of the originals.

The Celtic people were politically divided but shared a common culture, although those living closest to Italy had been civilized through contact with the south. Archaeologists call their culture La Tène after the Iron Age settlement at the eastern end of Switzerland's Lake Neuchâtel, which provided an abundance of Celtic artifacts. The La Tène culture evolved out of the earlier Hallstatt culture in the mid-first millennium B.C. on the Middle Rhine and is distinguished by the use of torcs, the heavy neck pieces of gold or bronze. La Tène artistic tradition incorporated elements from the Etruscans and Scythians, as well as early indigenous groups.

The Celtic goldsmiths fashioned some of history's most remarkable jewelry in the form of torcs, brooches, helmets, bracelets, and rings. They were adept at a wide range of techniques including casting and filigree. Celtic influence ranged from Ireland east to Hungary, where goldwork has been excavated decorated with characteristic spirals and scrolls, similar to Celtic ornaments found in Britain.

Caesar's ambition, nourished in the lucrative years in Spain, Gaul, and Egypt, brought him to the dictatorship of Rome. But his foes and many of his former friends found his rule intolerable and he was stabbed to death on the Ides of March in 44 B.C.

With his murder the republic came to an end. Rome, long accustomed to violence and bloodletting, was plunged into thirteen years of monstrous civil war before Octavian, known as Augustus, emerged triumphant over Mark Antony, Caesar's trusted general.

Mark Antony, presuming himself Caesar's heir, at once seized his papers from the slain ruler's stunned wife. He also took Caesar's will from the Vestal Virgins, to whom it had been entrusted. He discovered that it named not him but Octavian as his posthumous adopted son and heir to three fourths of his fortune. Caesar also left each Roman citizen three hundred sesterces (about sixty dollars) and designated his gardens as a public park.

Antony acted quickly to make the most of the private papers, claiming to find therein appointments for his friends and privileges for himself. Within two weeks he was a very rich man. He managed to remove some $25 million Caesar had on deposit at the Temple of Ops, goddess of wealth. He also helped himself to a further $5 million from Caesar's private treasury. His greed not yet satisfied, he had himself named to the lucrative governorship of Cisalpine Gaul.

Antony and Octavian initially formed an alliance of sorts to avenge Caesar's death. They formed the Second Triumvirate with Lepidus and promptly proscribed three hundred senators and two thousand equestrians. The ensuring bloodbath was partly motivated by a desire to settle the score with Caesar's conservative assassins, but primarily the three men needed gold. Without gold they could not pay their armies. Without their armies they would have no power, and without power they could gain no more gold.

The mere possession of money became criminal. Children who had inherited estates were executed. Fifteen thousand dollars was paid in gold to any freedman and ten thousand to any slave who brought in the head of a person on the proscription list. The three triumvirs had their troops block exit from the capital. The condemned vainly tried to hide in sewers and chimneys. Men and women starved themselves, jumped off roofs, and even hurled themselves into fires. Many who were not on the list were slain in error. Adulterers and jilted lovers revenged themselves. Many slaves were cut down as they protected their masters. One disguised himself as his owner and died in his stead. Many others betrayed hard masters.

The head of Cicero, who had acted bravely to oppose the rise of a new dictatorship, was nailed to the rostra in the Forum. As it hung there Antony's wife scornfully stuck a gold pin through the tongue of the great defense attorney and statesman who had devoted himself in vain to achieving "a concord of the orders."

The provinces suffered too in this chaotic period. Brutus and Cassius, opposing the Triumvirate, marched through the East exacting ten years' gold tribute, in advance, to support their troops. When the island of Rhodes hesitated, Cassius stormed the port, demanding that all citizens surrender their gold. He slew those who were not immediately compliant and in this way added an additional $10 million to his chest.

In Cilicia the inhabitants were forced to melt down all the gold that had lain for centuries in their temples and public buildings along with all their personal gold in an effort to meet a ransom demand of $9 million. It wasn't enough and eventually they were forced to sell men, women, and children into slavery. In Judea, Cassius demanded over $4 million in gold and silver and, when he didn't get it, sold the people of four towns as slaves. Cassius and Brutus were killed battling the forces of the Triumvirate, but the East was not left unmolested as opposing armies locked in combat for supremacy of the Roman world.

Mark Antony, who was driven by a relentless need to establish his legitimacy, advanced through the East forgiving the cities the gold they had paid to his enemies—on condition they come up with ten years' taxes in advance for him in the space of a year. He believed that if he could bring gold-rich Parthia into the Roman fold, a feat which had stymied Crassus and Caesar, then the contest would be his. Once again, the Parthians eluded the Roman net. Their cavalry routed Antony's army, and he retreated to Egypt leaving twenty thousand dead Romans on the battlefield.

Antony himself was snared in the East by the clever girl Queen of Egypt. He was drawn to the Nile Kingdom by a hunger for gold and succumbed to the twofold lure of treasure and love.

He ordered Cleopatra to come to him to answer the charge she had abetted his enemies. He sat in the forum at Tarsus waiting for her. She appeared, not before him, but on the river dressed as Venus in cloth of gold. "The barge she sat in, like a burnished throne, Burn'd on the water: the poop was beaten gold." She did not plead with him or answer his accusation but invited him to dine aboard her golden ship. The rest is history.

Cleopatra was a woman of great acumen. She was aware that Ptolemaic Egypt lay vastly rich but mortally vulnerable to greedy Rome. Marriage with Antony was expedient. She made "hungry where most she satisfied," exacting large parts of the eastern Roman domains for her children by Antony in return for Egyptian gold. The Romans resented the partition of Roman territory and were hostile to Antony's connection with the Oriental Queen. At the naval Battle of Actium in 31 B.C. the forces of Antony and Cleopatra met with Octavian's. Cleopatra and her squadron turned during the engagement and sailed toward Egypt. Antony abandoned his fleet and sailed after her. His troops surrendered and Octavian was crowned Caesar's heir.

The ancient kingdom of Egypt with its gold was reduced to an estate directly administered by the Roman ruler who became heir to the pharaohs and the Ptolemies. When Octavian mounted the throne as Augustus, Rome was discouraged by the buffets of so many years of civil war; cynicism and childlessness were in vogue. The Egyptian treasury and the spoils of Cleopatra when they came to Rome infused new life in the stagnant economy. Egyptian gold was added to the Spanish and Gallic supplies, furnishing the material for reformation of the monetary system.

Money became so abundant, wrote Suetonius, that the interest rate fell from 12 to 4 per cent and the value of real estate rose fantastically. With Augustus' affirmation of the right of private citizens to amass wealth, the gold which had been in hiding since Caesar's death emerged. It stimulated trade and investments as it began to circulate. Life improved for everyone, even the masses of poor. The privileged classes embarked on an era of opulence. The homes, appointments, and ornaments of the rich rivaled the magnificence of Oriental potentates.

One of Augustus' first acts had been to put Rome on a bimetallic system based on the gold aureus. He issued gold aurei in great numbers. For almost the next thousand years gold remained the predominant metal for European coinage. The Romans had developed coinage rather late. Cattle were acceptable in trade in the agricultural society until the fourth century B.C. when the expansion of the state brought the Romans into contact with the Greek commercial cities of southern Italy. By 350 B.C. increased trade demanded a more convenient medium of exchange than barter. Bulky one-pound copper pieces called asses were issued, the choice of material determined by availability. The first copper coins bore figures of cattle, sheep, or hogs and were called *pecunia,* from the word for cattle.

Early Rome had no gold to mint and very little silver. For developing overseas commerce, however, she was forced to mint silver denarii, which were almost exact replicas of current Greek coins to make them acceptable to the Hellenistic world.

Italy's first gold coins had been struck by the southern Tarentines as early as 340 B.C., but the first Roman gold coin was an emergency stater struck during the Second Punic War about 217 B.C. The republic had amassed fantastic amounts of gold in the course of conquest but rarely issued gold coinage, preferring to maintain bullion reserves. The empire adopted a reverse policy.

From Augustus' reign on, a staggering variety and volume of coins were issued from some six hundred mints in the Western and Eastern empires. The Roman mint was housed in the Temple of Juno Moneta (from which came the word "money"). The extraordinary military coinage of Sulla, Caesar, Brutus, and other generals was the model for imperial coinage. The emperors portrayed themselves on one side of a coin, their achievements on the other. They were splendid propaganda devices. In Asia, Africa, and the wild north of Europe people came to recognize an emperor, his family, his public works and victories through commemorative gold coins. Roman engravers were particularly talented portraitists working on gold, cameo, and stones, and their superb coins were considered the empire's finest artistic achievement. The Romans themselves were great coin collectors and appreciated the beauty of the imperial issues. Counterfeiters were not tolerated. When caught they were thrown to the lions or hanged. The milled edge on coins was a Roman innovation designed to discourage shaving off bits of precious metal. Clippers continued to remove gold by washing and sweating the coins, and in the late empire the beaded or serrated edge was abandoned.

Being emperor was a risky business. Few died peacefully and even fewer enjoyed reigns of any length. In A.D. 238, for example, six emperors were named; four of them were murdered or committed suicide and one fell in battle. Vanity, the desire for immortal fame, as well as economic considerations, stimulated emperors to order coins bearing their portraits the minute they came to the throne. Virtually every emperor had at least one type of gold coin minted. In the third century A.D. a father and son, Gordian Africanus I and II, reigned about a month before the son died fighting political enemies and the father killed himself. However, they had not neglected to provide posterity with several issues minted at top speed. Their coins became choice items with contemporary numismatists. The demand far outran the supply, so some years later a number of coins minted by the grandson of Gordian I, who became Emperor, were tampered with by *falsarii* to resemble the numismatically valuable coins.

Under Augustus' steady rule of forty-one years, gold borne over the stone-paved roads that crisscrossed the empire flowed into the two Roman temples which served as treasuries. The National Treasury was controlled by the Senate. The Imperial Treasury, the fiscus, was owned and controlled by the Emperor. It was to the fiscus that the sealed baskets, called fisci, containing the provincial money tribute came as well as a share of mined gold and booty. There too the emperors kept their own store of gold which increased through legacies and gifts from "well-wishers." Augustus, who lived simply and had returned the 35,000 pounds of gold offered by the municipalities as a coronation gift, accumulated 1.4 billion sesterces in such bequests during his lifetime.

Massive annual tribute payments in gold and silver were one of the empire's chief sources of revenue. But there never seemed to be enough gold. Augustus sent unsuccessful expeditions to vanquish the gold countries of Ethiopia and Arabia. Nero was always looking for more gold. He tried and failed to get it from the Black Sea area and from central Asia. He sponsored an exploratory group to the wilds of Ethiopia to investigate the possibilities of acquiring the gold of that African land. The Roman officers he sent penetrated closer to the headwaters of the Nile than any Europeans would for the next eighteen hundred years but came back with no gold.

Nero was gleeful when he received reports of a newly discovered vein of gold in Dalmatia. It gave him another fifty pounds a day for his legendary excesses. By his time the empire received gold from Spain, the southern part of central Gaul, Greece, Egypt, Arabia, the Balkans, and on an irregular basis from various Asian sources.

Nero was under constant pressure to make money go further to finance not only his degenerate extravagances but also his ambitious public works program. He was not deterred by the fact that the treasury was often empty and that there was widespread misery in Italy. He ruthlessly proscribed the rich and seized their property. When oppressive new taxes and confiscated riches didn't cover his bills, he debased the coinage, permanently reducing the weight of the gold aureus, but not its purity.

The Greeks had preserved the integrity of their currency believing it should equal the value of what it bought. The Roman emperors, however, treated money as a medium of exchange the value of which could be altered at will. Following Nero's lead, successive rulers tampered with the currency trying vainly to enrich the empire by stretching the money supply. The silver denarius was sometimes as much as 50 per cent zinc or lead.

By the mid-third century A.D. the empire was drowning in a sea of silver-washed copper coins over which gold lost its steadying influence. Inflation mounted as more and more of these almost worthless billon coins circulated. Two hundred years after Augustus the silver denarius was worth less than one fiftieth of the Augustan coin. By contrast the gold issues maintained their high quality throughout most of Roman history, although they were lightened several times.

Nero's reign marked the zenith of Roman extravagance. The Emperor led the way, laying out as much as 4 million sesterces for a Babylonian gold-embroidered fabric and 800,000 for a gold brocade from Alexandria. In the Neronian period silks brought overland from China were worth their weight in gold. Women of fashion paid even more for costumes of gossamer veils of silk made on the Greek island of Kos by unraveling Chinese silk fabric and reweaving it.

Neronian mansions were a parvenu's dream. Inspired by the Emperor's Domus Aurea, palatial mansions boasted walls plated with gold and paved with gems, ceilings coffered in ivory and gold. Philo, the Jewish philosopher from Alexandria, wrote that "the couches upon which the Romans recline at their repasts are splendid with purple coverings interwoven with gold and pearls." Tables and chairs of rare woods rested on gold legs inlaid with ivory, and beds and couches were embellished with gold, silver, gems, ivory, and tortoise shell. Gold bought statuary from Greece, paintings, ornate candelabra, gilded bronze vases from Corinth.

The first five years of Nero's rule were good ones for the empire. As a modest seventeen-year-old he dissuaded the Senate from erecting life-sized gold and silver statues. Initially he loathed signing sentences of death or exile. Following the sage advice of his childhood tutor, Seneca, he lowered some taxes and abolished others. Frontiers were secured and corruption somewhat reduced. However, venal advisers encouraged him to indulge his penchant for debauchery in an effort to keep him from involvement in government and he soon lost all interest in affairs of state. "At a time when vice had charms for all orders of men," wrote Tacitus, "it was not expected that the sovereign should lead a life of austerity and self denial." In an era of relaxed morality his sexual license shocked Rome's patricians far less than his indecorous public performances.

Hungry for applause from the mob that loved him, the satyr-prince sang, danced, and played the lyre. He went on tour in

Greece where he appeared in the Olympic and Delphic games, winning the laurel in every event for obvious reasons. When he gave a concert the theater doors were barred. No one was let out "even for the most urgent reasons," noted Suetonius; "And so it was that some women gave birth there, while some feigned death to be carried out."

The Domus Aurea, Nero's Golden House, was built after the nine-day fire storm which razed much of Rome in A.D. 64. He appropriated a large part of the burned city for his palace-park complex, giving rise to speculation he had started the fire. In fact, he was at a seaside resort at the time. Eventually the Christians, a relatively new sect, were blamed. Nero had a number of them horribly tortured and killed—some set on fire to serve as nocturnal torches.

The treasuries were drained for the reconstruction of the capital and for the gaudy pleasure dome he built for his third wife. He had murdered his mother and then his first wife in order to marry his mistress, a married woman named Poppaea. Regrettably he killed her with a kick to her pregnant belly. He sought a new wife to replace his dearly beloved and finding a young boy who resembled Poppaea, had him castrated and wed him in a great public ceremony. The Domus Aurea was his bride's wedding gift.

The buildings of the Golden House covered 900,000 square feet of a mile-square park which was a wonderland of gardens, meadows, orchards, lakes, and a pool Suetonius described as "more like the sea" upon which gilded imperial galleys floated.

The walls of the fabulous palace were ablaze with gold, mother-of-pearl, and gems. The bathrooms had gold fixtures which controlled mineral water, salt and sweet water of various temperatures. He had a 120-foot gilded bronze statue of himself raised at the entrance. This colossus gave its name to the Colosseum, which was later built on the site of the palace. When the Golden House was completed, Nero remarked, "At last I can begin to live like a human being!"

The Praetorian Guard, an influential body of three hundred men which made and unmade emperors according to the amounts of gold they were offered, let it be known they were willing to abandon Nero. The Senate hastily proclaimed Galba, a balding man of modest attainments, as Emperor. Nero fled from his Golden House. Not one guard or friend would accompany him. He tried to take poison but lost his nerve. He went to throw himself into the Tiber but again lost courage. Finally, after a night spent cowering in the dirty cellar of one of his freedmen, he attempted to stab himself. As he wavered the freedman mercifully guided the blade to his throat, ending the life of the pleasure-rotted egomaniac.

His successors fared little better. Nero's thirty years of misrule were followed by a series of civil disorders which threatened the empire and brought widespread famine and suffering to the masses. In the year following Nero's death the all-powerful soldiery enthroned four emperors. Galba, the first, was undone when he decreed that those who had received gifts or pensions from Nero must return nine-tenths to the treasury. Not only that, he wasn't forthcoming with the gold donative as he had promised the Guard. Galba and his two successors died violently.

Vespasian, who ruled next, received $44 million in revenue from the Spanish gold mines annually, but it was not enough to bring the empire out of bankruptcy. He resorted to heavy taxation, levying taxes even on the public urinals. His son, Titus, who later destroyed the Temple at Jerusalem in the Jewish War, flinched at such revenue, but his father held a couple of gold coins under his nose saying, "See, my child, if they smell."

In the first century A.D. the fantastic placer deposits of southern and central Spain were showing signs of depletion, producing less than the ten thousand pounds of gold a year they had formerly. The yield had also dropped off from the workings in Gaul. The number of lands which could be stripped of temple treasure and booty was growing smaller. Yet the empire needed ever larger and more dependable sources of supply of gold to support the armies, keep the frontiers strong, and pay for the overwhelming amount of luxury imports that had become essential to the Roman life style.

With the capture of Dacia, comparable to present-day Hungary and Romania, at the beginning of the second century A.D., the empire got a much needed injection of gold. The most immediate gain was the colossal royal treasure which some chroniclers put at 5 million pounds of gold and 10 of silver. Such figures seem inconceivable; it has been suggested the actual spoil must have been multiplied by ten. Even so, 500,000 pounds of gold and a million of silver would have enabled the Roman mints to strike 22½ aurei and more than 90 million denarii.

In any case the gold and silver from the Dacian treasury was the last great war booty that came to Rome. When the conquering Emperor, Trajan, returned to Rome from his brilliant campaign, he was accorded a triumph which lasted 123 days. Trajan, Spanish-born and the first provincial to attain the principate, used the treasure to fund the greatest program of public works since Augustus, building roads, harbors, and aqueducts. A portion of it he shrewdly used to strengthen his position with the population of Rome, doling out about $260 to every citizen who applied for the gift.

In the long run the Dacian gold mines of Transylvania were to prove even more valuable to Rome than the royal treasure. The Carpathian area had produced gold from prehistoric times and its riches were well known to the classical world. Rome had long coveted Dacia's mines but prior to Trajan had not felt strong enough to bid for them.

The mines, under Roman control, were organized and run by a state-appointed procurator. Dacian gold added so much of the precious metal to the imperial supply that between A.D. 97 and 127 the price of gold fell 3 per cent in spite of government control of mining. The maintenance of a fairly steady ratio of gold to silver was fundamental to Rome's bimetallic system. To make up for the influx of gold and keep the gold-silver ratio at 1 to 12½ or 13, Trajan increased the proportion of dross metals in his silver coins, furthering the debasement of the currency which plagued Rome throughout its history.

From the mid-second century A.D., the period of great conquests was past. Soldiers no longer counted on bringing back gold, silver, and slaves. There was already a considerable number of emancipated slaves in Rome and the provinces. Many bought their freedom with a small accumulated store of money called *peculium;* others had been released at the death of their owners. Many of these freedmen were skilled in administration, banking, and commerce, having performed these services for their senatorial masters.

Gradually the manumitted slaves and freedmen gained prominence in commercial affairs and entered the imperial bureaucracy. When Hadrian became Emperor, he revamped government administration, taking most of his officials from the class of freedmen. The patricians, who had disdained the day-to-day workings of business, although they appreciated the golden profits, viewed with alarm the freedmen's growing power. They participated in every trade and profession, managed the vast landed estates, and directed business ventures of every nature for themselves or their aristocratic patrons. The patricians despised the former slaves but found them indispensable for the conduct of private and state affairs. Eventually the commerce of the empire was largely in their hands.

The gold and silver which made large-scale coinage possible had stimulated the acquisitiveness of the Romans, who had never developed strong domestic industries to offset their terribly lopsided balance of payments. Italy's exports were negligible, her imports overwhelming. "Whoever wishes to see all of the world's goods," wrote a third century A.D. author, "must either journey throughout the world or stay in Rome." Never before had so many people demanded so many costly luxuries. Thousands of varieties of manufactures, delicacies, and raw materials poured into Rome. The provinces too began to covet and purchase the precious items that earlier had all gone to the capital.

Large Roman merchant fleets sailed from the Red Sea ports of Egypt for southern Arabia, Ceylon, and India: more than 120 regularly scheduled sailings from one port alone. Wheeled traffic moved smoothly over the intricate network of roads leading to the heart of the empire. Free barbarians and Romans traveled to and from the capital and the fringes of northern Europe bringing blond hair, slaves, amber, and furs. Parthia grew fat acting as middle man in the overland China silk trade. Camel caravans crisscrossed the Saharan wastes bringing gold, ostrich eggs, and rare essences for Roman consumption.

Among other wares peddled in Rome were wild beasts for the Arena, gold, rare marbles, pearls, and slaves from Africa; jewelry and statuary from Sicily; slaves, pearls, and oysters from Britain; and from distant Belgium, flocks of geese driven to Rome so that their fat livers might grace Roman banquet tables. Greek emeralds, Tyrian purple, the list was endless. Rome opened her pocketbook and the gold flowed out since most imports were paid for in gold. This was especially true as material prosperity declined after the second century A.D. and the empire slid into insolvency.

The imperial policy of ad hoc currency manipulation caught up with the Romans, who had long ignored Gresham's law that cheap money drives out dear. Progressive debasement and the exhaustion of the silver mines eventually made it impossible to re-establish the old gold-silver ratios. Silver coins had been so watered that they were no longer acceptable in Italy or abroad. As a result there was an increased drain on gold—the only acceptable medium of exchange.

Roman coins traveled far. They have been found in China, Tibet, Vietnam, and Ceylon. The largest number of Roman gold coins found outside the empire's boundaries have come from India, which provided more imports than any other area save Spain. The Indian luxuries were the most sought after by the opulent and the most railed against by the moralists. Pliny the Younger complained in the first century A.D. that ". . . at the lowest reckoning Arabia, India and China drain our Empire of one hundred million sesterces every year—that's what our luxuries and our women cost us!" More than twenty thousand pounds of gold went East for luxuries, although the outflow of bullion and coin slowed somewhat as Rome and especially the provinces began exporting some of their merchandise to the Eastern countries. Syria sent fine glass; Italy, bronze; Egypt, linen; and Asia Minor, wine and oil.

The Indians had a long history of gold use and of veneration for the yellow metal which was quite foreign to the less spiritual Romans. In remote times India had exploited native sources of gold and imported some in the form of dust from the Siberian area. Princes and traders stockpiled it in the form of cakes or balls and commissioned legions of goldsmiths to make gem-set gold ornaments, ornate gold-embellished furniture and accessories, and glittering fine-drawn wire which was woven into sumptuous brocades. Herodotus mentioned the enormous tribute in gold dust India paid to the Persian Empire, along with a tribute in cotton, "a kind of wool on trees."

Archaeology once again provides the evidence for early gold

use. Excavations at Mohenjo-Daro and Harappa in the Indus Valley have uncovered minute gold beads, rings, brooches, necklaces, and unique conical head ornaments made as early as 2500 B.C.

Gold was collected from the auriferous sands of the Ganges and the Indus from time immemorial. Pliny in A.D. 77 noted that "in the country of the Nairs [India] there are numerous mines of gold and silver." These may have been in the area of Mysore and Hyderabad. Although there seems to have been a long hiatus in Indian gold production, the southern area of Kolar still produces gold today. The period of greatest mining activity was probably over by A.D. 1000, and the ancient mines were evidently soon forgotten. The voluminous records of Mohammedan rule from A.D. 1300 to 1600 make almost no mention of gold mines.

Gold washing in the rivers appears to have been a recognized profession in ancient India; the Mahavastu mentions a guild of such men. Other ancient texts describe how alluvial deposits were worked and how vein gold was extracted from stone.

The Kala-vilasa is a fascinating eleventh century A.D. treatise detailing the implements and procedures used by Indian goldsmiths. Not all of them were honest, for, as Kshemendra, the author, describes, double-sided crucibles were made so cleverly a customer's gold could be surreptitiously mixed with an alloy even as he watched. Deceitful smiths had an amazing number of tricks to manipulate the scales including the use of mercury to make the pan heavier. The keen eye of Kshemendra noted that at times a goldsmith's fire burned with flames that were unusually "ringed, smoky, crackling, slow," indicating that copper powder had been added. Indian smiths knew how to impart a false shine to diluted gold by putting salt and soda in a slow fire and heating the gold object in it. The Indians used touchstones to test the purity of gold, but the dishonest smith had various hard and soft stones to dupe the unwary.

The only known Indian goldsmith's implements to have survived antiquity are some molds and matrices made of steatite, limestone, or clay. The earliest date from the fifth century B.C. and like the others were used in the casting of secular and religious objects. Archaeologists have found gold votive plaques and religious statuettes made in such molds.

One man more than any other embodied the cancerous decadence which preceded the fall of Rome. In A.D. 219 the gold of
Julia Maesa bought the throne for her fourteen-year-old Syrian
grandson, Elagabalus. During the four-year reign of this utterly
depraved boy-priest Roman debauchery reached its peak. Not
even Nero or the insane Caligula matched his adolescent bisexual excesses, which were detailed by his biographer, Aelius
Lampridius, who indicated that advancement in rank was based
solely on the proportion of one's genitals and buttocks.

Elagabalus had been trained as a priest of the Phoenician god,
Baal. He brought a priapic black stone worshiped in Syria as the
symbol of his god and attempted to supplant Roman pantheism
with the worship of one god, something that did happen in the
following century when Constantine converted to Christianity.
He housed the jewel-encrusted stone in a temple embellished
with tons of gold and showed his devotion by considering castra-
tion in its honor.

He decided against that drastic measure, however, and devoted himself to the worship of pleasure, leaving the government
to his ambitious grandmother.

He was popular with the city mob. Romans of all walks of life
were welcome at his palace. He sometimes amused himself by
distributing lottery tickets among his visitors. The prizes might
include a set number of a variety of things: flies, hen's eggs, or
gold pieces. He gave public games. One of his favorites was to
have gold and gems thrown among milling cattle. He watched
with delight as greedy Romans were crushed beneath the tram-
pling hooves of the frightened beasts who plunged into their
midst. He also enjoyed watching from the Basilica Julia as great
throngs fought for handfuls of coins he tossed down, cheering as
men killed each other for the gold.

At his orders slaves frequently dusted gold and silver about
the palace porticoes. His chamber pots were gold, as were almost
all the royal accessories. Dressed in gold and dripping jewels,
his cheeks rouged, and his eyes rimmed with kohl, the satyr
made a mockery of the ideals upon which the might of Rome
had been founded.

The acme of his degeneracy was the banquets held in gold-
and-ivory-paneled halls. Lampridius wrote that he rarely spent

less than 100,000 sesterces on a repast and often as much as 3 million ($450,000). His guests reclined on couches of gold and silver covered with the golden couch spreads which had been prohibited by sumptuary laws at a time when Rome's leaders had the greater good of the state at heart.

Parasites surrounded the Emperor in hopes of benefiting from his largess. The guests at Elagabalus' banquets came knowing they were bound to be the butt of his perverted humor but were unable to resist the prizes he often handed out. There was always the chance that the evening's meal might include such specialties as gold pieces mingled with the peas, pearls in the rice, or amber beads in the beans.

The invited never knew what to expect. Some evenings Elagabalus would have their gold and silver plates heaped with carved food of wood or wax. They watched without commenting as he ate exotic dishes of nightingale tongues or flamingo brains and washed their hands with him as he finished each course. At the end of the tantalizing meal he might, or might not, present his guests with the gold plates, some chased with lewd designs. Sometimes each diner found a gold spoon at his place with a prize inscribed on it.

He distributed such favors as eunuchs, four-horse chariots, a thousand aurei, or gold plate. Performers who pleased him were richly rewarded. Those who did not might be given a dead dog. He once promised a group of banqueters that he would either produce a phoenix or give them a thousand pounds of gold. When he couldn't come up with the mythical bird, he made good with the gold.

Syrian priests had predicted the Emperor would die violently. He prepared by building a high gold tower from which to hurl himself. Elagabalus declared no one would ever die in as luxurious a fashion as he and adorned the tower with precious gems. Despite his elaborate arrangements, which also included collecting implements for a worthy suicide—a gold sword and poisons in containers of hollowed sapphire—he died as ignobly as most of the Roman emperors. The Praetorian Guard cut him down in a toilet, dragged his body through the filth-clogged streets, and flung it into the convenient Tiber.

As the years wore on, the provinces recovering from the oppressive exploitation of earlier times grew prosperous. The gold robbed from half a hundred countries that had gone to gild the life of the captial now made its way to the provinces, which grew wealthy as Rome sank into a state of torpor. At the close of the second century A.D. the constellation of a thousand Roman cities far outshone the dying star of Rome, for whose benefit they had for so long been mulcted. They became self-sufficient, vital centers which furnished Rome with emperors, military leaders, intellectuals, and artists in increasing numbers. The military center of gravity shifted east because of continued barbarian incursions and because the Balkans supplied most of the soldiers to keep the tribesmen at bay.

The seeds of destruction planted in the preceding era took root in the soft rot of third-century Rome. The empire, plagued by bankruptcy and barbarians, was convulsed in a maelstrom of economic and political upheavals. People were on the run before the hordes that breached once invulnerable defenses. Frequent modern finds of Roman gold coin hordes attest to such incursions in the Balkans, Greece, Italy, Asia Minor, and Mesopotamia.

The Army maintained its supremacy by virtue of the vital need to defend the empire's far-flung frontiers. The officers took bids for the throne and collected from the man who gave them the most gold. The dying words of one such Emperor, Septimius Severus, were befittingly cynical. "Make your soldiers rich, and do not bother about anything else," he told his sons Caracalla and Gaeta (Caligula). For the following eighty years every Emperor met a violent end.

Imperial rule was often a travesty. Military anarchy reigned and the political chaos hastened economic decay. Trading suffered, production faded, and the currency collapsed. By the mid-third century the silver denarius contained a mere 2 per cent silver and the golden aureus was reduced to a third of its original weight.

Coupled with government insistence that coins circulate at face value was the refusal to accept taxes in anything but gold or kind. Prices ran wild. Inflation paralyzed industry, disrupted trade, and robbed the middle class of much of its wealth. Unchecked inflation between the first and third centuries, for example, caused a 1,000 per cent rise in prices in Roman Palestine. A large part of the capital once available for the trade and industry was wiped out.

In addition, gold production began to ebb. No new sources were added and the old ones yielded less and less. Some were no longer available. Under Aurelian, Rome surrendered the rich mines of Transylvania. Parthia grew stronger absorbing gold from scattered central Asian sources which had once gone to Rome.

Great amounts of gold had gone for vanished frivolities. A great deal more was immobilized in ornament and art objects. Toward the end of the empire men hid what gold they had to escape taxation, which was more oppressive than ever. The state, faced with mounting military expenditures and payments to the threatening barbarians, was desperate for precious metal. The mints continued to turn out volumes of worthless coins in a vain effort to finance the empire, which had been living dangerously off its fat for a long time. No one wanted the copper coins with a wash of silver. Despite several attempts at monetary reform, notably those of Diocletian, the situation worsened. Gold was acceptable but subject to weighing and assaying, and there was a large-scale return to barter.

When Roman expansion slowed, various barbarian groups had stepped up their attacks on the fringes. Disorganized at the first, they gained effectiveness by uniting to attack the empire's weakest spots. Roman citizens began to abandon those parts of the empire under continuous assault. At one point in the mid-third century the Emperor Valerian was actually captured by the Sassanians as he led a military campaign, the first time such a thing had happened.

For centuries a growing volume of Roman gold had been siphoned off as bribes to the barbarians. Domitian had set a precedent by offering subsidies in gold to the Dacians toward the end of the first century A.D. At the beginning of the third century so much gold was being paid to barbarian extortionists that it equaled the annual payroll of the Roman Army. The subsidies mounted during the century and were a fatal drain on Rome's dwindling stockpiles of gold, but there is no way to accurately determine how much they totaled before the dike burst and the barbarians of central Europe poured into Italy collapsing the Western Empire.

In the final century of the empire the bribes to the hovering tribes took several forms. Gold coins accounted for much of it, and officially marked gold bars such as those found from the Balkan mint at Sirmium accounted for a part. The largest share of these huge bribes seems to have been paid in a form that allowed the Emperor to save face. Splendid gold medallions were struck, masterpieces of the engraver's art, which have been unearthed in Poland, Yugoslavia, Romania, Germany, and other areas where the gold-loving Germanic tribes bided their time waiting to swoop down on Rome. If the imperial annual payment was late, they swarmed across the borders to collect.

Many barbarians settled on uninhabited or abandoned Roman land and were enlisted as mercenaries in the Army. By the end of the fourth century almost the entire Western Army was barbarian, both soldiers and officers. In addition to the troops drafted from barbarian settlers, the Army drew on battle captives, and men sold by tribal chieftains in exchange for Roman gold.

Another drain on what was left of Roman gold was the soldiers who proclaimed the series of "barracks emperors." The man they raised to the principate was fully aware his survival depended on the favor of the Army. Consequently there were frequent ill-advised pay raises and donatives in the form of beautiful gold medals bearing the portrait of the current emperor.

When Aurelian came to the throne in A.D. 270, the empire was in a precarious state, weakened by plague and famine, torn by internal dissension, and reeling from the unrelenting blows of the Germanic hordes. The cities were emptying as men seeking refuge from barbarian pressure and Roman taxes huddled in walled towns or rural strongholds. He set out to restore imperial unity. The foes of the empire were driven back everywhere but the Danube; the territories of Gaul, Spain, and Britain were restored to the rule of Rome. At home he built the Aurelian Wall, encircling ancient Rome, part of which still stands.

He carried on the Orientalizing of the monarchy which Elagabalus had begun. He built a dazzling Temple of the Sun to encourage monotheistic worship which he thought could unite the empire. Aurelian proclaimed himself the earthly representative of the sun and assumed the trappings of an Eastern god-king. Men at court knelt before him as he sat resplendent in gold, gems, and furs, crowned with a brilliant diadem which "shone like the sun itself." He was hailed as *resitutor orbis*, "restorer of the world."

Gold, the means and the end to so much of Roman effort, shone everywhere. The effect was magnificent and heady, but the superficial brilliance masked a disintegration beyond repair. However, under the deft administration of Diocletian and subsequently the fourth-century reforms of Constantine the weary empire took heart. In a final struggle for survival the empire was divided into two parts to better deal with threats from Sassanian Persia to the east and the barbarians to the north. The nominal capital of the Western Empire was Rome, but for strategic reasons, the actual seat of power was nearer the vulnerable northern boundaries.

In A.D. 284 Diocletian officially abandoned Rome and established his court at Nicomedia in Asia Minor. Soon after he transferred it a few miles north to Byzantium. Under Constantine the city was rebuilt as the great Christian capital of Constantinople, a magnet for gold in the Byzantine era.

Diocletian was a consummate bureaucrat whose last-ditch reforms temporarily bolstered the sagging empire. The son of a former slave became an Oriental despot, cloaking himself in the golden paraphernalia and ceremony that came to be associated with the Byzantines. Men approached him on their knees, kissing the hem of his robe.

He coupled the elevation of the monarchy with reformist policies which included currency reorganization and state decrees which vainly attempted to replace the laws of economics with a tightly managed economy. Most famous of these was the Wage and Price Edict, repealed by Constantine. Merchants and traders were blamed for many of the state's ills. A five-year tax in gold and silver was levied on both merchants and craftsmen, which destroyed many of them.

Most successful was his currency reform, which restored value to Roman coinage. He established gold coins of reliable weight and purity. The gold solidus weighed a $\frac{1}{60}$ of a pound. Constantine reduced it to ⅟₇₂ of a pound. The solidus and its third, the tremissis, were retained by the Byzantine Empire and circulated on both sides of the Mediterranean until the fall of the Eastern Empire in 1453. They were copied for Europe's early gold coinage by the Vandals, Lombards, and Ostrogoths, who inherited the Western Empire after Rome fell.

When the Arabs conquered Byzantine Syria in the seventh century A.D., they adopted the solidus as their unit of gold currency, giving it Muslim types, since the Koran forbade portrayal of the human figure. The dinar, so called from denarius aureus, remained the basis of the Arab world's monetary system for half a millennium.

Diocletian's gold coins were good, but they were limited in quantity. The shortage of gold was more acute than ever. In the late fourth and early fifth centuries A.D. hoarding was at an all-time high. The civil populations of Roman territories were subject to repeated plundering by the military under the guise of requisitions. Taxation was crushing and thousands of functionaries in Diocletian's complex bureaucracy managed to rake off gold that should have gone to the government. From his reign on, Roman cities were compelled to sell their gold stocks to the state to furnish gold for the escalating bribes of the barbarians.

The empire was moribund, but there were still wealthy men and women. These were predominantly people who had vast land holdings cautiously spread over the empire to avoid total loss in the event of barbarian take-over. Smaller landholders, ruined by brigandage, taxes, and debt, placed themselves under the protection of the large estates. Slaves, tenant farmers, and the sons of serfs, unable to leave the land, swelled the populations of these estates. Many men made illicit fortunes in gold through government service and used their ill-gotten gains to buy landed estates. The cities emptied.

According to contemporary sources there were senators who, even in the late empire, had annual incomes in gold of 1,000, 1,500, or even 4,000 pounds in addition to income in kind. The consul Summachus had enough gold to spend 2,000 pounds of it when his son became praetor.

Constantine carried on Diocletian's reforms, adding to imperial revenues by continuing the tax levied in gold on artisans and merchants. After A.D. 331 the mints suddenly began to pour out an accelerated volume of gold coins. The source of the metal was probably confiscated treasure from the thousands of pagan temples which the Emperor, having become a Christian, felt free to appropriate.

The state used every possible means to extract gold from Romans everywhere. Certain taxes formerly payable in kind were demanded in gold. There were severe penalties for trading gold across the borders with the barbarians. The very need for such prohibitions indicates the existence of such a traffic between private citizens and the tribesmen, which deprived the state of critically needed gold. Military officers refused to be paid in anything but gold and military costs skyrocketed.

Men of means were coerced to present gifts of gold to the Emperor to celebrate various occasions such as his birthday. In the late fourth century Valentinian II extorted such a golden "gift" in the form of sixteen hundred pounds of bullion and coin.

The respite the empire enjoyed under Diocletian and Constantine was a mirage. Province by province the West, too weak to withstand external pressure any longer, fell to the shaggy barbarians.

Once again, as in the earliest Greco-Roman period, the world was shaken by the thunder of hard-riding nomads sweeping across the steppes as the Huns poured into the Eastern Empire. "They filled the whole earth with slaughter and panic. . . . By their speed they outstripped rumor and they took pity neither upon religion nor rank nor age nor wailing childhood," wrote St. Jerome.

Attila, the "Scourge of God," ruled a territory from the Alps and the Baltic to near the Caspian Sea. The Eastern Empire paid him an annual tribute in gold which in A.D. 434 was raised to 700 pounds a year. His Huns ravaged the East, capturing one hundred cities, looting and terrorizing. When they threatened Constantinople, the Romans signed a treaty with Attila which stipulated they owed him 6,000 pounds in back tribute and henceforth agreed to pay him 2,000 pounds of gold annually.

The wild Hun led his horsemen into Italy. They ravaged as far as the Apennines before retiring in the face of the invincible plague. When the new Eastern Emperor refused to continue the gold payments agreed upon by his predecessor, Attila made plans to attack Constantinople. But he died, quite out of character, in his sleep on the night of his marriage and was buried with a truly vast treasure of gold and jewels. Those who interred him were murdered so that no one might find and violate his tomb. Temporarily the pressure on the East subsided.

Rome, however, despite two payments of gold and peppercorns, worth their weight in the precious metal, did not escape. Inviolate for eight hundred years, the greatest city in the world was sacked for three days in A.D. 410 by Alaric's Visigoths, who had been shoved south of the Danube by the invading Asiatic Huns. All pretense of power and glory was irretrievably gone. In 455 the Vandals took and sacked a shrunken, impotent Rome.

The Western Empire, long in dying, expired in 476 when the Army, now entirely Germanic, elected one of their officers, Odoacer, as King. The last Roman Emperor, Romulus, stepped down for the German and went meekly into country retirement having accepted a generous handout of gold. In the Dark Ages that followed gold was to bypass once glowing Rome and concentrate in other hands. The spotlight moved East to focus on the celebrated gold of Byzantium.

CHAPTER TEN *Medieval Gold*

In 476 the enfeebled Western Empire, shorn of her golden wealth and majesty, expired as the apocalyptic hordes swept down from the north. Europe melted into chaos during the tenebrous centuries of the *Volkerwanderung*, the wanderings of the barbarians. The suddenness with which the West was plunged into darkness was unprecedented. Economic development ground to a standstill. The excellent Roman network of roads and bridges that had linked the flourishing towns and cities of the provinces fell into disuse and disrepair. Urban life and organized society in the Greco-Roman tradition which had supported a gold-loving and gold-using population of merchants, bureaucrats, and nobles all but disappeared. People cringed in self-sufficient rural enclaves beset by fear and uncertainty, defenseless before waves of invaders. During the early medieval period Germanic tribes, Magyars, Norsemen, and Arabs kept the West alternating between torpor and chaos.

Without the great sponge of Rome to absorb and distribute provincial goods and without urban centers, highways, and the competent civil and military administration which had been a bulwark of the empire, trade and industry withered and markets disappeared. The West slid back into an agrarian society. The severe economic and cultural dislocations were matched by an almost total loss of technical and engineering knowledge. Until the eighth century, for example, roads, bridges, and even harbors were hardly used. The art of bricklaying was lost, and only a handful of stone buildings were constructed in northern Europe. Mining for gold virtually ceased following the loss of Roman technical and organizational skills. The Spanish mines were abandoned to seeping ground water and the haphazard efforts of free-lancers, who washed surface ores and gleaned the tailings of deep mines and hydraulic workings. Some men dug in crumbling galleries, heedless of the threat of collapse, and undoubtedly many continued to work river placers in Spain, France, and in the Alps.

Gold, which had been a barometer of civilization for at least four thousand years, all but vanished from Europe after the Fall of Rome. From the fifth century to the twelfth there was a great gold famine, precisely at a time when world stocks were at an all-time high. The yellow metal had been discovered by men in many parts of the earth. For millennia men had prized gold as a measure of wealth and an economic indicator. Gold was the object and reward of international struggles for power, attracted to the victor. The spotlight on gold shifted with the vagaries of fortune—Egypt, Mesopotamia, Persia, Greece, and then Rome, with its dazzling displays tempting the barbarians. During the height of the Roman Empire gold had circulated in prodigious amounts in the West. It had been more widely available than in any previous era. But after the Fall extinguished the light of Greco-Roman civilization it was drawn away from Europe to brilliant Constantinople, capital of the still flourishing Eastern Empire.

Although it was very scarce indeed, gold continued to play an important role in the European Dark Ages, particularly following the ephemeral Carolingian renaissance in the ninth century. It never ceased to be the ultimate symbol of divine grace or worldly power. Charlemagne's rule initiated a period of general awakening and more stable conditions. The darkness faded, and after the millennium European trade and urban life revived strongly. As a corollary some gold in the form of coin, ornaments, and jewelry became available to well-to-do men and women. Gold ownership was not limited as it had been in the previous centuries to kings and the Church.

The Dark Ages were not as bleak as the name suggests. The term fails to reflect the part the Christian Church played in keeping alive the spark of classical learning and the skills inherited by Rome from Mesopotamia, Egypt, and Greece. The one strong link among the shattered groups in Europe was the Church. The monastic schools lit up the Dark Ages, training goldsmiths, jewelers, illuminators, and copiers of manuscripts. In scattered, isolated cloisters on bleak, wind-swept islands in the North Atlantic and rocky crags overlooking the Mediterranean, artisans practiced the ancient pagan goldsmithing techniques, infusing their work with Christian spirit. Throughout the medieval period religion furnished the dominant theme for every aspect of life.

Most of what gold there was gravitated to the Church. The atavistic feeling that gold had magic power and was symbolic of the ideal and eternal endured into the medieval period, making a painless transition from the sacred metal of paganism to Christianity. Shocks battered the Continent and Great Britain. The churches, regarded as the only sanctuaries from violence, became the repositories for ecclesiastical and princely gold. Under the patronage of Christian kings the Church became wealthy and powerful. Gold accumulated in crypts, treasuries, and sacristies, and golden gifts gleamed in the dim interiors of abbeys and monasteries. Gold visible in glowing church ceremonies brought what richness and color there was to lighten the drab life of most of medieval Europe.

The history of gold in the Middle Ages was closely knit to the rise and spread of the Christian Church. Churches were the beneficiaries of gold given by princes, nobles, and later by pilgrims and Crusaders. They became the mightiest financial power in Christendom. They replaced the pagan temples as banks where secular wealth was deposited for safekeeping and even loaned money from their store of liquid capital. Loans were made to the free peasantry for agricultural equipment and, from the late eleventh century on, to feudal barons who mortgaged their property to the Church.

There was no significant European gold production in the early Middle Ages. From the Fall of Rome to the seventh century there seems to have been enough gold, however, to allow the barbarians to coin gold even though they had killed the Golden Goose. In the Anglo-Saxon ship burial found at Sutton Hoo in England there were thirty-eight gold coins—each from a different Frankish mint. While the mines no longer produced and no new sources of gold were discovered, some gold was washed from auriferous river sands in Spain and parts of France.

This must have been particularly easy in Spain where alluvial river deposits were so rich that even in the nineteenth century, after more than three thousand years of exploitation, nearly half a ton of gold was produced in a year.

The rivers and the slag heaps of flooded Roman mines were not the only sources of treasure. The various barbarian groups cherished gold and had long been familiar with it, finding it first in the rivers of central Asia and then, as they moved westward, in eastern and central Europe, Gaul, and Spain. Iron Age burials found in many parts of Europe from eastern Bohemia to France contain gold artifacts of barbarian workmanship. The aristocracy of the powerful Hallstatt and La Tène cultures loved the yellow metal. Nobles were entombed with native goldwork and sometimes with articles of Etruscan, Celtic, or classical craftmanship such as a gold diadem of supposed Greco-Scythian orgin found in the chariot grave of a young princess at Vix in France.

The hordes that battered all of Europe had been accumulating gold in the form of Roman subsidy payments for many years before Rome fell. That stockpile had been supplemented by gold received in private transactions with Romans who defied the fourth-century prohibition on exporting gold to barbarian areas.

All those supplies plus gold looted after Rome fell provided the gold for barbarian coinage which imitated Roman issues. A study of early medieval gold currency furnishes the best indication of the extent and range of gold usage, since almost no jewelry survived and there are few literary references. The barbarians, who soon converted to Christianity, took over Roman mints and the Roman system of currency. Rulers, civic leaders, nobles, and prelates issued coins which were often of surprisingly good quality, although barbarian die cutters sometimes botched an inscription so that unfamiliar Latin letters were reversed or turned upside down. The barbarian coins usually imitated the famous Byzantine solidus but were a third the size and denomination. These small tremissis (or triens) coins copied, more or less faithfully, the portrait of the current Byzantine Emperor.

The powerful Visigoths in their gold-rich kingdom in Spain and the Burgundians in France were the first to coin gold after Rome fell, turning out considerable quantities in the late fifth century. Britain had been abandoned by the Romans early in the fifth century, and by the sixth century the pleasant life of the prosperous landed aristocrats who had grown wealthy in the wool trade and enjoyed villas with central heating and window glass was a dim memory. The island retreated into isolation and lethargy. British life was paralyzed by Saxon and Jutish invasions, yet in the mid-sixth century gold began to come into Britain. When the Christian princess Bertha from Paris married King Ethelbert of Kent and dedicated a shrine to St. Martin at Canterbury, she was able to offer gold coins and medallions, one of which bore the likeness and name of her confessor, Bishop Leudard. An ecclesiastical mint in London was issuing gold coins soon after 600 and by mid-seventh century mints in Kent, London, and other places were turning out Anglo-Saxon coins.

The Visigoths in Spain established a magnificent capital at Toledo. Visigothic royalty enjoyed Europe's greatest wealth, partly derived from washing Iberian rivers for gold. When the Moors took Toledo in the seventh century, they marveled at the richness of the city, the luxury of the Visigothic court, and especially the treasures in the churches. Arab chronicles record such marvels as a "table of emerald inlaid with gold and silver," gold fabrics, gold and silver vases filled with jewelry and swords and armor inlaid with gold and encrusted with jewels. Such dazzling treasures attest to the availability of gold and gems at a time the rest of Europe had very little.

Moorish historians wrote of the twenty-five gold and jeweled crowns which hung as votive offerings before the Toledo Cathedral's high altar. The crowns and all the other Visigothic treasure the Moors seized were melted and transformed. We might not know what Spanish goldwork of the Dark Ages looked like had not a buried treasure been discovered in 1858 at Guarrazar in the countryside near Toledo. Perhaps the cache, found by Spanish peasants, was hidden by a priest fleeing the implacable warriors of Islam, since it included eleven gold votive crowns as well as other Visigothic goldwork.

The Guarrazar Treasure, now in the Museum at Cluny, has an elaborate votive crown that belonged to King Recceswinth (649–72) and another inscribed as a gift from King Swinthila (621–31). The donors' names appear as gold letters hanging from the massive crowns which are set with cabochon gems, sap-

phires, and pearls. The dangling Visigothic letters are inlaid with
cloisonné enamel and have jeweled pendants dangling from
them. Gold chains embellished with filigree were attached for
hanging. One of the crowns had a magnificent gold cross affixed
to it which measured 4½″ long and 2½″ wide and was set with
the finest pearls and sapphires.

The words "Barbarian" and "Dark Ages" invoke images of disruption and ignorance. Yet the pieces in the Guarrazar Treasure
are not crude but highly refined, the work of master goldsmiths
trained in the classical tradition. Rare finds of early medieval
goldwork from other parts of Europe such as the treasure buried
with Childeric, founder of the Merovingian dynasty in Gaul who
died in A.D. 481, and the Anglo-Saxon ship-burial horde found in
1939 at Sutton Hoo also illustrate the continuation of Greco-
Roman techniques. The preservation of high-quality work in precious metal is in sharp contrast to the loss of skill and finesse displayed in the bronze or gilt-bronze ornaments which were all
most people, whose ancestors had enjoyed gold rings and bracelets, could afford. Gold was very scarce. After about A.D. 700
even kings and the Church suffered a critical deficiency which
lasted until the millennium save for a short period of renewed
mining in central Europe during Charlemagne's reign. Because
the precious metal was in such short supply, ownership, as in the
most ancient times, was the privilege of rulers and priests who
meted it out to goldsmiths.

So little jewelry and church plate has survived that it is
difficult to trace the history of early medieval goldwork. The
Moors seized Visigothic gold and the Vikings seized the Irish
treasures when they surged down out of their icy fastness at the
top of the world. For two and a half centuries the Norsemen
in their dragon-prowed ships, lured by the rich lands to the
south, battered Europe. They looted craft shops, libraries,
churches, and palaces, multilating their contents, and carried
back bright warm gold. Christian Europe prayed, "Libera nos a
furore Normanorum," as the Norsemen established themselves in
Normandy, the Danes swept into England and the Norwegians
into Ireland. Norse fleets of hundred-oared ships plundered
Italian cities, raiding Rome and Milan which had remained goldworking centers even after the Fall of Rome. During the ninth
and tenth centuries not only Norse incursions but raids by

Magyars and Saracens revived the terror and insecurity of the barbarian wave four hundred years before. The Saracens took Corsica and Sardinia and gained control over the Mediterranean coast of France until almost A.D. 1000.

The tribal influence provided an important element in early medieval jewelry. In early Ireland, which had been settled by Celts about 600 B.C., goldsmiths were honored as the *Aes dana—men* of special gifts. The Germanic Teutons and the Celts, both on the Continent and in Great Britian, had a preference for cloisonné jewelry. Inlays of garnets, red glass, or other semiprecious stones were set in individual gold cells and then ground down flush with the gold walls. Celtic goldwork with its simple, strong rhythms in spirals, curves, and whorls, echoed the ancient tribal motifs of beasts and monsters. It featured stylized human and animal figures in ornaments inlaid with garnets, turquoise, lapis lazuli, mother-of-pearl, or colored glass paste. Gold was used in conjunction with stones and glass, enamel, crystal, and niello partly to create effects of color, light, and shade but primarily as an economy measure designed to conserve the precious metal.

England and Ireland, which came under Celtic domination, both had indigenous traditions of goldwork. As early as 2000 B.C. Neolithic smiths in Great Britain created ornaments from cut sheet gold and made crescentic neck pieces. Somewhat later goldsmiths made more sophisticated articles such as the Mold cape, which is a magnificent repoussé covering for back, chest, and arms, with narrow bands of various repeated geometric designs.

Anglo-Saxon poets saw in gold a symbol of perfection and made frequent use of golden metaphor. The following few lines by a bard evoke the age-old excitement of the victor surveying the spoils:

> There once many a man
> Mood-glad, gold-bright, of gleams garnished
> Flushed with wine-pride, flashing war-gear,
> Gazed on wrought gemstones, on gold, on silver
> On wealth held and hoarded, on light-filled amber.

A Roman in Ireland wrote, "The natives accumulate large quantities of gold and make use of it for personal adornment, not

only the women but also the men. For they wear bracelets on
wrists and arms, and round their necks thick rings of solid gold,
and they also wear fine finger rings and even gold tunics. On
occasion chieftains marched into battle naked save for gold
torques."

Celtic tradition, with its legions of demons and dragons brought
from the long-ago migration westward, blossomed in sumptuous displays of goldwork. Monastic artisans produced for their
ecclesiastical patrons illuminated gospels, such as the *Book of
Kells* and the *Lindisfarne Gospels,* croziers, vestments, pins, chalices, shrines, and myriad other devotional objects. Ireland in the
eighth century was the "Land of Saints and Scholars," an outpost
of Christian learning where missionaries were trained for conversion of the continental barbarians. St. Patrick's island was also a
haven for many who fled the shadow of Islam, which passed
over much of the East. In A.D. 550 a ship had brought fifty
scholars to Cork. They were followed by scores of learned men
and skilled craftsmen who formed a close international monastic
society, as they did in Wales and England. Goldwork benefited.

Within the cloister, goldsmiths blended Christian iconography
with refined classical technique, barbaric love of stones, and
stylistic elements imported from Byzantium. By the sixth century
the production of goldworks was the chief vehicle for expression
of the Christian faith. The goldsmiths were the great artists of
the centuries before the millennium when there was little scope
for the sculptors, painters, and architects who came into their
own in the twelfth century during the Gothic period.

During the sixth century gold from the Eastern Empire had
trickled into Europe in trade in spite of imperial prohibitions
which were issued from time to time by Byzantine emperors.
There was traffic in gold which was partly motivated by the lucrative trade in northern European slaves which more than offset
the limited import into Europe of such luxury items as spices and
textiles and even a bit of jewelry. The focus of this trade was
Merovingian France, where the Teutonic Franks occupied an
area which under Roman administration had been the most prosperous and civilized part of Europe.

Early in the sixth century Merovingians started minting relatively large numbers of gold coins. King Theodebert I (534–47)

even felt strong enough to depart from tradition and substitute his own portrait for the Byzantine Emperor's. Frankish kings occasionally received considerable quantities of gold in payment for military aid they gave the Byzantine Emperor.

In the mid-sixth century the Lombards, a powerful coalition of Germanic tribes, swept across the Alps, uprooted by conflict between the Avars, yet another group of Steppe nomads, and the Slavs. The Lombards, 130,000 strong, took over a large portion of northern Italy. This effectively severed Byzantine northern contacts, an intolerable situation which they paid the Franks to remedy.

In return for military expeditions against the Lombards the Franks received enough Byzantine gold to keep their mints working. Gaul enjoyed a period of prosperity as Oriental merchants—Jews, Greeks, and Syrians—set up in Marseilles and other Gallic cities. Byzantine coins, although officially banned from export by the Eastern Emperor, circulated. They have been found by archaeologists as far afield as England and Friesland. The Byzantine mints in the sixth and seventh centuries minted coins of absolute purity but light in weight especially for trade with the north. Despite the colossal amounts of gold piling up at Constantinople, the emperors were unwilling to export more than was necessary. During the reign of the Byzantine Emperor Maurice (582–602) an exceptional number of gold coins were struck. There is evidence to suggest that many of them went to support the bid of a rebellious Merovingian pretender who was supported by the Byzantines.

Emperor Maurice sent Childebert II 50,000 gold solidi when the Franks intervened against the Lombards for him in Italy and another 3,600 as compensation for the murder of two Frankish ambassadors in Carthage. Usually, however, the Byzantine gifts took the form of wrought gold. King Chilperic I had a fifty-pound gold bowl and a number of gold portrait medallions weighing a pound each that had been sent to him by the Emperor. Most often the Byzantines presented their allies ecclesiastical goldwork. It was in this way that the Byzantine style, with its devotion to detail and emphasis on color and line, came to the attention of the monastic goldsmiths of the West. They studied reliquaries, embroidered vestments, and church plate. In their turn they produced enamels and jewels the technical equal of the Eastern pieces but infused with a distinctly European feeling.

The Lombards also gave gold to the Franks. They paid Clotaire III an annual tribute of 12,000 solidi. In the reign of Dagobert (628–39) there was sufficient gold in Gaul so that abbeys buying land paid for it in gold coins. Dagobert's court, although far smaller, vied with Constantinople in splendor. He sent his talented monk-goldsmith and mintmaster, Eligius, to Constantinople to learn Byzantine enameling and other Oriental techniques. When Eligius returned he made his famous gold and jeweled reliquaries and crosses. He was raised to a bishopric, and eventually canonized as St. Éloi, the patron saint of goldsmiths to this day. He was one of three sainted Frankish goldsmiths produced by the same century—Éloi, Alban, and Theau, who made the reigns of Dagobert and Clotaire III the era of magnificent jewel-encrusted gold shrines.

During the seventh century the flow of Byzantine gold into Gaul slowed. There was no longer enough of it to support a gold coinage for the Franks or other states with consolidated rule and expanding economies. Much of the stocks which had been held immediately following the Fall of Rome had been siphoned into ecclesiastical treasures where the gold was immobilized. The volume of coins in circulation was no longer adequate to meet the demand in spite of the fact that an overwhelming majority of people in Europe lived at a bare subsistence level and never held a gold coin even though they were exposed to imposing displays of the gleaming metal in their churches. The Franks toward the end of the century were forced by circumstance to switch to a silver-based economy. From that time on Europe minted silver for more than five centuries, although a token amount of gold was occasionally minted. Extremely unusual coins in the form of Arab dinars were struck by Offa, King of Mercia in eighth-century Britain, and very small numbers of coins were issued by several English kings and prelates into the twelfth century, which were destined for payment of the "Rome-scot" to the Holy See or for presentation. The Lombard kings in Italy continued to issue gold coins, taking advantage of gold washed from the Alps.

There was brief respite from the five-hundred-year gold shortage preceding the millennium during the reign of Charlemagne, King of the Franks and Holy Roman Emperor, when old gold mines in central Europe were reopened and new ones dug. During the relatively stable eighth century mines in Saxony and Silesia yielded gold for the Holy Roman Emperor's goldsmithing center at Aachen, where he founded a new "Rome." The six-foot-tall King, who understood Greek and spoke Latin, but never learned to write, lent his patronage to all manner of artistic and cultural activity and gave his name to the ephemeral Carolingian renaissance which foreshadowed the achievements of Romanesque and Gothic art and architecture.

He instituted reforms in industry, agriculture, finance, and education, relying on a powerful hierarchy of landholding vassals to render the serf-troops he needed for the constant wars waged throughout his reign. He rewarded the landed aristocracy with royal bequests of battle spoils and more land. When the Franks triumphed over the monstrously brutal Avars in a savage war that lasted seven years it took fifteen huge wagons, each pulled by a team of four oxen, to carry the gold and gems belonging to the nomadic Avars' Khankhan, or king, to Charlemagne.

Charlemagne surrounded himself with imperial grandeur imitating that of Constantinople. He dreamed of establishing a new Rome, of reviving the Western Empire. His court at Aachen, the site of warm mineral springs where he loved to swim, was filled with golden furniture, regalia, and accessories which blended the sensuousness of the Byzantine court with a northern love of bold display. A great golden desk, its top etched with a map of the universe, was one of his prized possessions. He imported Byzantine goldsmiths to teach his own workers their secrets.

He also initiated the revision and copying of Christian manuscripts. The handwritten books were as rare as jewels and were treated as jewelry, adorned with gold and bound in wrought gold set with gems. Throughout the ninth century monasteries were constructed where men spent their entire lives in the libraries, illuminating the capital letters with gold, entwining them with vines, flowers, and creatures of land, water, and air. Illustrating the manuscripts with miniature paintings and elaborate linear decorations was an exacting art which had its genesis in Egypt, passed to Greece and Rome, and thence to the Eastern Empire, where it was perfectly suited to the Byzantines' love of the minute and brilliant jewel-like color. Backgrounds of burnished gold were favored by the miniaturists who loved its reflective qualities and symbolic associations.

An illuminator, in the relative tranquillity of the cloister, easily spent a day on an initial, a week on a page, or a lifetime on one Gospel or Psalter. Preparing the sheet gold was a demanding procedure. One recipe for the preparation of size or glue mixed with gold, called for slowly cooking the dried head bones of a wolf fish with the skin of an eel and an egg dipped in the latexlike milk of a fig tree. The gold, once applied to parchment or vellum, was burnished to a high sheen with a carnivore's tooth or precious stones.

Charlemagne was the first great man of action to rise from the ashes of Rome's collapse, and he took the role of Christian king very seriously. He was the first European monarch to visit Rome since the Fall, and in 800 on Christmas Day, Pope Leo III crowned him Emperor in a ceremony in St. Peter's, nominally reviving the Roman Empire in the West. Christian doctrine taught men that earthly wealth would be of no use in the life eternal, so very few Christian rulers were buried with the rich assortment of grave goods which proved so illuminating to archaeologists and students of earlier times. Charlemagne, however, chose to be entombed like a pharaoh. His embalmed body was placed on a massive gold and ivory throne which had come from Constantinople. He was buried as splendidly as he lived, dressed in richly embroidered robes, heavy with gold and gems. A gold chain and reliquary containing a piece of the "True Cross," a gold scepter, shield, and sword accompanied him.

He fared little better than the pharaohs. His gold-filled tomb was plundered by his successors, and within two generations his great empire and reforms disintegrated. But for half a century the greatest of medieval kings had forged most of the continent into a united empire and inspired Europe with new hope and energy. Charlemagne had loved gold and gems, lavishing them on his many children, surrounding himself with them, and stipulating that each of the many royal villas which supplied his court and army be self-sufficient with its own goldsmith. Yet there was not enough gold trickling into his treasury, despite the burst of new mining activity, to institute a regular gold coinage.

The gold coin that circulated throughout Europe, indeed throughout the world, in a vacuum of local issues was the Byzantine solidus. Known to the West as the bezant, it was the basic unit of international trade and the foundation of Byzantium's continued power. The gold solidus was established by Constantine the Great in the fourth century A.D. and for seven hundred years maintained its amazingly high purity of twenty-four carats.

While Europe struggled, the Eastern Empire thrived, attracting the world's gold. Constantinople was the seat of unrivaled opulence. Despite his Roman background, Constantine in the early fourth century had adopted the Eastern attitude of investing gold with great symbolic value. He was the first Roman to wear a crown at all times. His gold crown studded with pearls and his golden helmet set with precious stones were adapted from Persian regalia. The Byzantine court was given over to the sensuous Eastern love of splendor and pomp.

The zenith of Byzantine splendor came under Justinian and his Empress, Theodora, a former prostitute who became an exemplary Christian queen. Justinian early in the sixth century inherited 320,000 pounds of gold in the Royal Treasury and managed to exhaust it completely. When the imperial gold was gone, the Emperor taxed his resentful subjects mercilessly to pay his mercenary armies and finance grandiose public works. When the prospect of victory seemed dim, Justinian used gold to buy off his adversaries. When dispute flared between Sassanian Persia and Constantinople over control of the ancient luxury trade route to central Asia and India, Justinian deemed it wiser to give the Persians gold than fight an inconclusive war. A treaty called the Endless Peace with Rome was signed, and Justinian handed over 11,000 pounds of gold. Seven years later the "endless peace" was broken, and it cost him an additional 1,000 pounds annually to sign a treaty the Persians labeled the Definitive Peace with Rome.

Byzantine civilization created a state that endured eleven hundred years and Byzantine art, which fused classical, Oriental, and Christian elements into an inspired style dedicated to the glory of God and the instruction of the faithful. Byzantine art moved away from Greco-Roman naturalism and emphasized more abstract expression which relied for effect on strong color and richly ornamented surface. The enamels, brocades, jewelery, mosaics, and manuscript illustrations of Byzantium employ gold in a uniquely colorful and brilliant art.

The exterior of the early Christian churches, adapted from the pagan basilica, was austere, but within they blazed with the shimmering light of hundreds, even thousands of candles reflected from gilded walls and domes. Rich mosaics of brilliant glass and gold tesserae and golden appointments set with precious stones were designed to awe worshipers. For centuries Constantinople was the center of craftsmanship in all work relating to gold and jewels. In the Byzantine churches the glowing metal proclaimed the mystery of the faith and its power. Crafting ecclesiastical gold was an art of worship in itself.

Justinian alone built twenty-five magnificent churches on which gold was lavished in a multiplicity of forms. The basilica of St. Sophia stands as Justinian's supreme achievement. He poured his energies and all his funds into the building, which is the great exemplar of Byzantine art. He participated in the design and construction of what was called from the beginning the "Great Church." He oversaw the collection of gold, silver, precious gems, and ivory and ordered provincial officials to scour the countryside for antique relics and precious objects. For almost six years ten thousand men labored as Justinian, garbed in white linen, directed them, addressing himself knowledgeably to masons and goldsmiths alike. He dedicated 32,000 pounds of gold to the building and when it was completed exclaimed, "Solomon, I have surpassed thee!"

The shining gold dome, which rose a towering 180 feet over a ground plan based on the Greek cross, was supported in such a way that it seemed to "float on air as if suspended from Heaven on gold chains," wrote Procopius, adding that "sunlight seemed to grow in it." Justinian had the interior embellished with great gold plates and lined the aisles with silver rails. The altars were filled with gold chalices, pyxes, and reliquaries. The whole interior was a testament to faith in luminous splendor created by the play of light and shadow on a harmonious assembly of frescoes, mosaics, precious metalwork, sumptuous brocades, sculpture, and colored marbles.

The Constantinople workshops also turned out orders for Christian monuments in the West as Europe gained ground. Byzantine smiths traveled to Europe to work on such projects as the resplendent mosaics of St. Marks in Venice in 1071, the world-famous mosaics of San Vitale in Ravenna, and a gold candelabrum for St. Peter's which held 1,465 candles.

The mid-Byzantine period produced magnificent cloisonné enamels. The art of cloisonné, the oldest form of enameling, had come to Greece from the Orient. It vanished in the third century B.C. and reappeared six hundred years later. Byzantine craftsmen learned cloisonné enameling from the Sassanid Persians and used it to enhance icons, book covers, medallions, and even horse trappings. Early Byzantine secular jewelry reflected a continued fondness for the Greco-Roman love of gold surfaces. Abundant gold made such generous use of precious metal possible. Heavy pieces in the opus interrasile or cutwork style or decorated with filigree became less prominent as the Church became paramount in life and secular goldwork began to reflect ecclesiastical gold with its colorful, rich adornment of gems and enamels. Western Europe imitated the polychromatic Byzantine styles which were particularly suited to Europe, where gold was so terribly scarce. The northern countries had almost no access to gems and replaced them with garnets, rock crystal, and colored glass. Spain, because of her favored position in regard to the Mediterranean sailing routes, was the only European area to have enjoyed a continued supply of Eastern stones, although some filtered into France on an irregular basis.

The Dark Ages was not a time of hermetically sealed cultural compartments. In the eighth and ninth centuries English monastic goldwork was famous on the Continent. The Vatican's Liber Pontificalis records a number of orders for English goldwork which was a unique blend of Eastern, continental, Celtic, and even Scandinavian motifs. Alfred the Great set up a school of crafts for goldsmiths, jewelers, and embroiderers at Athelney. He imported skilled foreign craftsmen just as Charlemagne had at Aachen. English embroidery, the opus anglicanum, was prized throughout Christendom for its magnificent richness of detail and color. In the echoing dimness of the medieval churches candlelight flashed on gorgeous gold-and-silk-embroidered jeweled robes, altar cloths, and banners which rivaled the sumptuous fabrics of the East.

In 1693 a peasant in Somerset, where Alfred the Great in 878 hid from a Danish invasion, dug up an Anglo-Saxon jewel of consummate beauty and execution. The Alfred jewel, as it is known, reflects the influence of Byzantine and even Persian forms on the ninth-century English goldworker, who was innately skilled and discriminating. It is an impressive pear-shaped ornament, 2½ inches long and 1¼ inches across at the broadest point, with a cloisonné figure resembling Christ covered by a plate of rock crystal and framed with gold filigree. Around the border is an inscription reading "alfred ordered me made." The reverse side is a gold plate chased with a floral design. At the narrowest point is a gold boar's head, finely granulated, which terminated in a socket. The ornament, now in the Ashmolean Museum at Oxford, was most likely the handle of a pointer such as those used in reading a manuscript.

Such a jewel was very rare in Great Britain at a time when all Europe was at lowest ebb. In contrast, Byzantium overflowed with golden wealth. Constantinople was the chief gold market and commercial center in the world. Like Rome before her, Constantinople commanded colossal volumes of gold which she used to pay for imports of furs, spices, amber, Persian carpets, and ivory. Such a large portion of the gold and silver work turned out by Byzantine craftsmen remained within the empire that it did little to alter the deficit budget. Even exports of the famous cotton, linen, and silk textiles brought in relatively little revenue. The eminent Byzantine historian Procopius recounts how Justinian received Chinese silkworm eggs from two smugglers and set up a silk factory within his palace, establishing a state-run industry which became Byzantium's most profitable export.

The gold for coin and ornaments came from trade, from mines, from taxation, and from conquest. Neighboring Persia, a very rich kingdom under the Sassanian monarchs, had intimate connections with Constantinople. The Sassanid kings, who gave Persia its first taste of prosperity since the Achaemenid defeat by Alexander, produced a creditable gold coinage with exceptionally fine issues struck in the reign of Shapur I, the King who captured the Roman Emperor Valerian in battle in A.D. 260.

Sassanian goldsmiths were renowned for their work, producing over-sized gold and silver jugs, ewers, bowls, and cups on a lathe and decorating them with elaborate repoussé or chased designs. Characteristic pieces are illustrated with hunt scenes and have handles and spouts in the form of animals and birds. They excelled at cloisonné work but reached their highest expression in textile art. The Crusaders made off with numberless gold-embroidered silks, brocades, damasks, tapestries, and carpets, many encrusted with gold and precious stones. Persian poets celebrated their love of such carpets in poems and songs. One king commissioned the renowned "Winter Carpet" woven with scenes of spring and summer to drive away the penetrating cold of the Persian winter. Rubies, pearls, and diamonds were placed on the carpet to form fruits and flowers bordering streams of pearl and silver on a gold ground.

The treasury of the Persian King was often larger than that of the Emperor, thanks in part to Byzantine payments to the Persians. Khosrau II, the last famous King of the Sassanid dynasty, had an annual income of more than $200 million. In A.D. 626 when Heraclius defeated the Persian King he seized almost a billion dollars' worth of gold from his coffers, in addition to great amounts from the treasuries of the temples sacred to the Persian god of light, gold tables, plate and ornaments from the palaces of the nobility, and manuscripts which were works of art incorporating gold and gems. When the sacred books of Mani were burned, tradition says that gold and silver showered from them.

In the eighth and ninth centuries gold seized from Byzantine Christian churches during the iconoclast period in the form of proscribed images and icons of precious metal furnished metal for the mints. Leo III, crowned in A.D. 717, had initiated the great iconoclastic controversy professing, like many devout persons, disapproval of widespread image worship. In fact, he was also motivated by alarm at the spread of monasticism and the increasing concentration of wealth and power in the hands of the orders which withdrew men of talent, learning, and means from active economic life. During the decades of strife, monasteries and convents were closed, men and women were tortured and killed. Most early Byzantine goldwork was mutilated and destroyed by iconoclastic zealots.

The Byzantine emperors, some of them brilliant administrators, many of them able, and others abysmally incompetent, taxed their subjects unmercifully making every effort to separate the citizen from his gold. Eventually gold-encrusted life at home, costly wars abroad, subsidy payments to foreign powers, and the outflow of gold to pay for luxury imports caught up with the lopsided Byzantine consumer economy. The situation was aggravated by the disruption of the traditional sources of newly mined gold. Fresh gold had come to Constantinople from two main areas where it was obtained on advantageous terms—central Asia and Africa. Military expeditions often included specialists who surveyed for gold-producing areas.

Until much of the Byzantine Empire fell to Islam the gold trade of Africa was controlled by Egyptians who handled gold from Nubia, Ethiopia, and the Zambezi area to the south. The Kingdom of Axum, identified with the Queen of Sheba, in Ethiopia had diplomatic relations with Byzantium since both had Christian rulers. The Axumites issued a gold coinage starting in the mid-third century A.D. Even after Ethiopia was cut off from the rest of the world following the Islamic conquest of Egypt in A.D. 640, the Axumites struck gold coins on a fairly regular basis until Muslim forces overwhelmed the remote country in the early tenth century. During the Middle Ages and Renaissance Ethiopia became the focus of the search for the mythical Prester John, the mysterious benevolent Christian King whose streets were paved with gold.

Ships of the Axumite traders carried Zambezi gold to Egypt, and camel caravans bore the gold of Nubia and the southern highlands northward to Egypt and Syria. Much of the African gold remained there since both areas were commercially active with wealthy inhabitants whose life styles and consumer habits matched those of the Byzantines at Constantinople. Even after the disruptions caused by Islamic take-over of Egypt and Syria some of the African gold still reached Constantinople by a circuitous route. The gold supplies followed the spread of Islam along the North African littoral and into Moorish Spain. In that way gold in increasing amounts reached the Western courts, which traded it back to Constantinople for Byzantine goldwork and textiles. This pattern is substantiated by scores of discoveries of Islamic coin hoards in various parts of Europe.

The preponderance of new gold entering Constantinople came from the Caucasus and central Asia, which seem to have been inexhaustibly rich in gold. The gold of the Caucasus was traded via Trebizond and Colchis on the Black Sea. Gold from the Ural Mountains was marketed in the Crimea. Although the steppe nomads occasionally interfered with these Asian supplies, they were less precarious than those from Africa.

For five hundred years the integrity of Byzantine gold currency was maintained, surviving the Arab take-over of Egypt and the Persian capture of Syria. The stability of the empire rested on gold coins just as the opulent standard of living rested on ample personal stocks of the precious metal. Not only did the imperial circle hold great amounts of gold in the form of plate and ornament but also Church institutions and the frightfully rich landowners called *dynatoi*, or "powerful men." While the landowners reveled in Oriental magnificence within city palaces and behind the wall of suburban villas moving through days of sensuous ornate ceremony, hopeless serfs worked the lands having no share in the glittering ornate life of Byzantium.

The veneer of gold and jewels covered the sweat of serfs and slaves, the blood and cruelty of conquest and exploitation. Constantinople at its zenith surpassed antiquity's great cosmopolitan centers in wealth, luxury, and artistic refinement. Basil I, a groom of Armenian stock who became Emperor, in the ninth century added a chapel to his labyrinthian palace complex, all "adorned with fine pearls, shining gold, silver, silk, mosaics and marbles in a thousand varieties." Each emperor thereafter added his touch to the complex of royal apartments, gardens, baths, and factories. Theophilus built a Hall of Pearls and the Kamilas. This last was an apartment roofed in gold with ornate columns of green marble. The outer limits of Byzantine ostentation were reached in his palace at Magnaura where he had the renowned tree of gold created for Harun al-Rashid in Baghdad. Theophilus had his goldsmiths and artificers fashion a plane tree of gold and gems which shaded his gold throne. Both the tree and the throne were decorated with golden birds. Gold lions kept watch at the base of the throne and gold griffins flanked it. When he wished to impress a visitor, the mechanical lions swished their tails and roared and the cunningly contrived birds opened their beaks to warble a greeting.

Basil II, the strongest ruler since Justinian, was reputed to have over 200,000 pounds of gold in his coffers and more stashed in secret subterranean chambers specially built to handle the overflow. Anastasius left a personal store of 320,000 pounds of gold, and the Empress Theodora handed over 109,000 pounds to her successor. These staggering amounts of gold were only part of the treasure that was drawn to Constantinople during the high watermark of the Byzantine Empire. Private individuals, the *dynatoi*, often had reserves of 2,000 or 3,000 pounds each and the Church had an incalculable amount. During one of the periodic campaigns to stem corruption, bureaucratic officials were forced to surrender embezzled gold. A chief minister turned in 5,300 pounds which he had secreted in a deep well.

Displays of such colossal wealth naturally aroused the hatred of the masses who were placated with doles of oil and wine and calming religious propaganda. Great cruelty went hand in hand with great piety. Children were made eunuchs to serve in harems or administration, and the poor sometimes starved as landowners sat down to feast at gold-covered tables.

In the eleventh century the cumulative effects of so many centuries of extravagent living, the drain of constant warfare, and subsidy payments to powerful adversaries was reflected in the sudden watering of the bezant with as much as 25 per cent alloy. There was a sharp reduction in the volume of coins issuing from the mints. As Arab conquests interrupted the flow of African gold and the fluidity of Byzantine trade, Arab coinage began to appear in the international market place edging out the bezant. The purity of Byzantine gold coins was lowered from twenty-four to eighteen carats during the reign of Constantine IX in mid-century when the Seljuk Turks wrested considerable territory in Asia Minor from the Byzantines. Later in the eleventh century the value of the bezant, or nomisma as it was then called, had sunk to between fourteen and twenty-four carats. It was a time when, in the words of a chronicler, "Gold flowed from the public treasury like a stream bursting up from inexhaustible springs." In the fourteenth and fifteenth centuries the imperiled empire issued carelessly struck coins of electrum or even baser alloy. The last Byzantine Emperor, Constantine XI, struck no coins at all. Following the capture of Constantinople in 1453 by the Ottoman Turks, gold dinars from the Islamic states, which had been gaining ground as the Eastern Roman Empire deteriorated, became the preeminent international currency.

In the seventh century Islam had erupted into the Byzantine consciousness. Syria and Egypt, the empire's richest territories, had fallen before the implacable zeal of austere desert tribesmen who whirled out of the Arabian wastes united by the Prophet Mohammed. The warlike faith of Islam launched the most amazing phenomenon in medieval history. Within a hundred years of the death of Mohammed, prophet warrior and organizer, Islam had overrun North Africa, Egypt, the Arabian peninsula, Byzantine Asia, Spain, and much of France.

The ascetic Moslems changed the course of gold history. They came into stupendous amounts of gold in Egypt, Syria, and Persia which had belonged to sybarites steeped in unprecedented luxury. They also came into control of some of the world's richest gold-producing areas in Arabia, Africa, Asia, and later in Spain. The sons of the Prophet shunned, initially at least, indulgent personal use of gold. Unlike Christian aristocrats Moslem leaders did not scorn commerce. They took to trade with a natural flair which recalled the astute Phoenicians. Arab merchants were adventurers who acted as intermediaries between the civilizations of the Mediterranean and Europe and those of India and the Orient. They were willing to travel for months on end through infinite emptiness, steering by the stars as far as China. Arab caravans endured untold danger and discomforts because profits were huge for rare and costly merchandise from distant lands. Investors bought stock in dhows, which penetrated down the African coast to Madagascar and sailed east to India, Ceylon, the Moluccas, and China, where a colony of Moslem and Jewish merchants was entrenched by the eighth century. From the seventh to the ninth centuries Arabs controlled the islands of the Mediterranean from Sardinia and Corsica down to Sicily and across to the Balearics, Malta, Crete, and Cyprus. Until the Normans seized Sicily from the Saracens in the eleventh century the force of Islam had no opposition in the Mediterranean.

Traveling up the great river highways of Russia and into Finland and Scandinavia, where hordes of dinars have been found, Arab merchants traded gold, silks, gems, spices, and wine for furs, amber, honey wax, and slaves—goods that had been coveted by southern peoples since prehistoric times. Moslem commerce and industry were free of government control, and merchants making up to 800 per cent profits grew enormously wealthy.

The bold Arabs financed their trade with the precious metals inherited from the vanquished. In Syria they garnered great reserves in coin and treasure which represented the riches of generations of diligent Levantine traders. In Egypt the mountains of gold they gained beggar description; not only was there the gold of the living but the treasure of the pharaonic rulers, whose tombs were sought out and plundered. In the ninth century one looted tomb yielded nine thousand pounds of gold. The Moslems were not skilled mining engineers, but they managed to exploit the ancient alluvial placers in Egypt, Nubia, and the Ethiopian highlands and sought out new areas where gold could be washed.

The splendor of the pharaohs was reborn in Fatimid Egypt. The overwhelming amounts of gleaming gold seduced the Islamic rulers into an effete life style that would have appalled their ascetic forebears. At the newly built capital of Qatai kings lived in gold-walled palaces and took their ease on inflated leather cushions which floated on a pool of quicksilver. The Fatimids, in the fortuitous position of being the commercial link between Asia, Africa, and Europe, became the world's richest sovereigns in the tenth century. When the sister of King Mu'izz died, she left 2.7 million gold dinars and 12,000 robes, many of them elaborately woven or embroidered with gold thread and sprinkled with jewels and pearls. Another sister left a collection of gold jewelry, 400 swords damascened with gold, 30,000 magnificent textiles, and 3,000 silver vases.

It was in the reign of Mustansir, son of a Sudanese slave, that Fatimid wealth reached its apogee. Cairo eclipsed Baghdad in power and splendor. Merchant fleets coming from the East sailed up the Red Sea and the Nile with their precious cargoes and camel caravans brought the gold of the eastern desert, Nubia, and Ethiopia to the capital. An Arab visitor to Cairo in 1047 marveled that some twenty thousand shops were so filled with gold, jewelry, embroideries, and satins that there was no room to sit down. The Egyptian merchant princes led gilded lives filled with sybaritic luxury, wine, and music. They salved their consciences by building mosques, libraries, and schools. In pursuing such an existence Fatimid voluptuaries emulated their ruler. Mustansir avowed his life of pleasure was "more pleasant than staring at the Black Stone, listening to the Muezzin's drone and drinking impure water [from the holy well at Mecca]." It was difficult to recognize in him the Carrier of the Seed of Islam. His Turkish troops rebelled in 1067, looting his palaces, and burning his priceless manuscripts to warm themselves. With the death of the corrupt King the Fatimid Empire fell apart, corroded by the fatal power of gold.

During their early expansion the Arabs had contented themselves with using Byzantine coins. The first Arab mints quite naturally copied the internationally known currency. Having chosen to concentrate on commercial expansion rather than personal opulence, the Ummayad caliphs at Damascus in the seventh century began to mint coins which imitated the bezant. The mintmasters copied Christian coins making subtle alterations such as removing the horizontal bar on a cross and changing the inscriptions from Latin to Kufic. One dinar, as the Arab coins were called, was based on a solidus of Heraclius' reign. The prototype bore a full-length figure of the Emperor flanked by his two sons holding small crosses. The Ummayad version struck about A.D. 693 in Damascus replaces the Christian symbols with swords. Very shortly, the gold of Egypt, Persia, and Syria was minted in purely Islamic forms.

Within several years the characteristic severe, nonpictorial style of the beautiful Islamic coins had been well established. The dinars, stamped with legends proclaiming the truth and power of Allah, were continued under the Abbasid dynasty of Persia which overthrew the Ummayads. The capital and mint were transferred to Baghdad, whence the dinars penetrated the Levant, Africa, and began to circulate in Europe as well.

Eighth-century Baghdad was the inspiration for *The Thousand*

and One Nights. The reign of Caliph Harun al-Rashid, hero of the Arabian nights, was the most famous in Islamic history; his court the most splendid and voluptuous. His caliphate covered all southwestern Asia and he exchanged gifts with Charlemagne and ambassadors with T'ang China. He attracted not only alchemists and astrologers to his brilliant court but the world's finest goldsmiths, artists, philosophers, musicians, and poets. He provided them with workshops and retreats within his palace complex, which occupied a third of the city. He loved poetry so passionately that he forgave a poet's crimes and showered lavish rewards on the author of a fine verse. For a brief laudatory poem he gave the poet Merwan 5,000 pieces of gold, ten Greek slave girls, a fine Arabian horse, and a gold-embroidered robe of honor. The Prophet Mohammed had forbidden the wearing of rich robes of silk and gold. His followers, however, not only valued them highly for themselves but became the medieval world's leading silk merchants. The archives of Caliph Harun al-Rashid record that he paid 400,000 pieces of gold for a robe of honor for Jafar, his favorite courtier.

The palace of the Baghdad caliphs was called the Golden Gate for its gilded entrance. Within were walls of gold and ivory, 22,000 magnificent carpets, and 38,000 tapestries. The Hall of the Tree with its artificial tree of gold and silver weighing 500,000 drams inhabited by musical birds contrived of gold and carnelian with ruby eyes and ivory beaks was the inspiration for the trees at Constantinople and a similar fantasy in gold, silver, and rubies immortalized by Firdausi, the Persian Homer. The wealth of the Islamic Persians was so immense that a specialized group of artisans called *nakhalband* created gold trees with leaves and fruits of turquoise, pearl, sapphires, emeralds, and rubies. Artificial birds of enameled gold perched on their branches or trilled in golden cages.

When Harun's son married a very wealthy girl, the bride's grandmother literally showered priceless pearls on the youth. His father-in-law tossed gold balls among the wedding guests. Each of the hollow perfumed globes contained a ticket redeemable for a prize—a piece of jewelry, a slave, a horse, or even a large estate. When Caliph Almunum married, the road to Baghdad was laid with cloth of gold. The bride, adorned with a headdress of gold and a thousand priceless pearls, was carried over the carpet to the Caliph. The great mercantile city on the Tigris attracted the riches of the whole world and made possible unrestrained luxury. The caliphs had as many as eleven thousand eunuchs in their households, harems of international beauties, dwarfs, jesters, spies, poets, and musicians. There was a proliferation of vast estates tended by armies of slaves. Men, whose forefathers had slept under the desert stars and subsisted on dates, died leaving as much as $100 million in gold. Not all the magnates were caliphs or traders. The investors and international traders who had such vast fortunes supported a legion of goldsmiths and jewelers who themselves became rich men. The famous jeweler ibn-al-Jassas remained an immensely wealthy man even after the Caliph confiscated 16 million dinars from him.

Each year millions of dinars in revenue from trade, from the provinces of the empire, and from tribute poured into Baghdad. In the tenth century it was the largest city in the world with the possible exception of rival Constantinople. In A.D. 784 Harun had pressed so hard at the gates of the Byzantine capital that the Empress Irene had been forced to pledge a yearly tribute of seventy thousand gold dinars to the Caliph. Gold from victories in Asia Minor, India, and Turkestan poured into Baghdad supplementing the flow of gold from trade.

Moslems gained control over Iberian gold as well. Most of Iberia had come under Islamic sway early in the eighth century when the Moors, a mixed force of Arabs and Berbers, led by a freed slave, defeated the Goths. When the Ummayads were overthrown at Damascus, the lone survivor of the dynasty moved westward until he established an emirate in Spain that lasted until 1031. Thanks to the gold of Iberia, the caliphate of Córdoba, as it was called, issued gold coins in great number which circulated in Iberia, Italy, and Sicily. Gold helped make it the richest and most cultivated part of continental Europe. It was known as the "Athens of the West." Islam prospered fostering the growth of a wealthy upper class and a capital which was the "jewel of cities." Tenth-century Córdoba was a beehive of intellectual activity filled with libraries, universities, and majestic buildings. Visitors from Christian Europe were struck by its grace and beauty. The city, second only to Constantinople and Baghdad, boasted ten miles of lighted streets at night, six hundred mosques, more than sixty thousand mansions which rivaled those of Neronian Rome with gilded ceilings, mosaic floors, forests of graceful columns, and surfaces overflowing with the graceful arabesques and swirls characteristic of Islamic art. Hangings of glistening gilded leather—the famed Cordovan leather gilt, later imitated in the rest of Europe—decorated walls, doors, and screens. The city's crown jewel was the Blue Mosque, which exceeded all other shrines to Allah in scope and magnificence.

The Moslem world from India to Spain loved gold ornaments despite Mohammed's warning that "he who drinks from gold or silver drinks the fire of Hell." There were a few like the thirteenth-century Persian cosmographer Qazwini who believed with justification that gold ornaments thwarted the divinely ordered application of gold in commerce and as currency. Despite the prohibition on depicting the human figure a number of fascinating Islamic gold medallions have been found illustrating tenth-century caliphs drinking forbidden wine out of forbidden golden cups and listening to forbidden music. The aristocracy commissioned gold accessories inlaid with gems or embellished with profuse surface decoration. At Damascus smiths refined the art of inlaying highly elaborate incised designs—gold and silver wire in metal base. Damascened swords of highly tempered steel filled with script or swirls in gold thread made Toledo in Spain world-famous. Toledo artisans still make jewelry in the time honored fashion which had its origins in Damascus.

Flowing Kufic script was incorporated into gold jewelery or accessories such as mirrors, chessmen, caskets, or jugs, in the form of etched bands or niello inlays. Other popular motifs included lavish, swirling adaptations of Persian animal and floral designs. Jewelry was adorned with granulation, filigree, and precious stones; later colorful enameling became popular. The Fatimids had revived a fashion for vessels with designs in gold leaf enclosed in glass. Later gilding the exterior of glass became common, reaching its highest expression in thirteenth-century Syria.

It is interesting that much of the goldwork the followers of Islam coveted appears to have been manufactured by Jewish goldsmiths for Moslem clients in North Africa and southern

Arabia. The Jews played a remarkable role in the medieval world, leading a perilous existence in both Christian and Moslem lands. They performed a vital function linking East with West. Jews held honored positions in the administration of courts such as Cairo and Baghdad. A Jew was the superintendent of customs at Córdoba; another was governor of Siraf, the Persian Gulf terminus of the treasure convoys from China and India. Jewish traders ranged far and wide. On the Volga River, the Khazars, whose district was on the international trade route over which Caucasian gold and Turkestan silk traveled to Constantinople were converted to Judaism by traders. Jewish wholesalers by the eighth century were established in many of the world's most distant entrepôt ports, trading gold in Africa, India, and China.

It was chiefly Jewish physicians who kept the spark of medical knowledge alight in the West during the Dark Ages. Jewish doctors were deeply involved in alchemical research. Trained in the Greco-Arab tradition and active in Spain and North Africa, they enjoyed freedom of circulation throughout the mutually hostile worlds of Christendom and Islam. In the twelfth century at Salerno was the West's first scientific school of medicine where Arab and Greek texts were translated into Latin. Physicians gathered there to study 130 eye diseases, obstetrics, and almost every other branch of medicine. One Arab treatise describes six types of cataract operations including one which used a golden needle to remove the blinding film. Gold in solutions, *aurum potabile,* was prescribed for a gamut of ailments, and powdered gold was used in making false teeth and in frames for spectacles.

In southern Europe and the East Jewish craftsmen were renowned. They often built up large factories such as the glassworks at Tyre and Antioch. They established important embroidery and dyed-textile factories in Egypt and Greece. In thirteenth-century Sicily Frederick II engaged Jewish artisans to manage the state-controlled silk industry. Jewish goldsmiths often acted as transmitters of techniques from Byzantium and Islamic lands to Christian Europe. In southern Europe Hebrew metalworkers were organized into guilds which competed with Christian guilds. Eventually, however, Jewish craftsmen in Europe were prohibited from serving Christians and turned increasingly to trade.

Despite bitter afflictions the Jew managed to survive and gain strength and gold. In medieval Europe Jews, whose survival depended on royal whim, were sometimes protected by the reigning prince or lord as a source of capital and revenue. English Jews in the twelfth century made up a quarter of 1 per cent of the population yet they paid 8 per cent of the national taxes, raised a quarter of the levy for the Crusade of Richard I, and gave five thousand marks, three times the sum given by the city of London, for his ransom from Germany. To finance the Fourth Crusade, the Pope in 1198 had all Christian rulers everywhere remit all interest owed to Jewish moneylenders by Christians. The short-changed dared not complain. Henry II in 1187 ordered a special tax on the English—Christians were stripped of one tenth of their wealth, Jews of 25 per cent.

Gold was by far the safest investment for a Jew. The constant threat of attack, expulsion, revocation of land grants, or seizure of property induced European Jews after the ninth century to abstain from holding assets which could not be hidden, immediately turned into cash and easily transported. Jews elsewhere fared better for a time, but in the eleventh century Jewish leadership in international commerce was eclipsed by the Venetian and Genoese conquest of the Mediterranean and the capture of Jerusalem by the Crusaders and they were closed out of the burgeoning Hanseatic League trade on the Baltic and North seas. By the twelfth century Jewish commerce had been further strangled by severe restrictions extending to domestic commerce.

When they were excluded from international and even large-scale national trade, Jewish traders and investors turned to finance, serving first as money-changers and then as money-lenders. Although the Talmud forbade lending money at interest, the restriction did not apply to a transaction between a Jew and a Christian. Thus in the years before the thirteenth century when there were few Christian moneylenders, princes, churches, and Moslems all applied to Jewish usurers for loans.

Jews had a tradition of keeping their wealth in gold, the most liquid and durable store of value. They were often suspected of not reporting their full worth and sometimes tortured to reveal supposed hidden caches of gold. The rich Jew was understandably wary of indulging his Oriental love of golden display.

He lived in fear of humiliation, attack, and expulsion and dared not adorn his women in the gold and jewels so dear to his ancestors lest he draw attention to himself.

By the tenth century the gold booty of victory, the gold from tributes, taxes, and the production of Ethiopia, Arabia, Egypt, Nubia, and Spain no longer sufficed the Moslem world for the increased needs of gold for coinage, trade, and luxury items.

The Fatimids of Egypt based their copious production of gold coins on supplies collected at Dongola, south of the Nile's Third Cataract and the terminus of Sudanese desert routes. However, far more gold came from two other areas of the vast continent. Arab seafarers and traders braved the Mozambique Current to probe down the east coast as far as Sofala. There they traded with the Zandj, as they called the natives, for raw gold which came from some mysterious place in the interior. The source of the gold was the inland mines long associated with the Monomotapa where the medieval ruins of Zimbabwe lie. This area in southern Rhodesia was a central gold-mining area of long standing. Modern excavations there have yielded trade goods including Indian and Indonesian beads and Chinese porcelain which were exchanged in coastal towns for the produce of the mines. Local rulers controlled the open-shaft mines, levying export duties and posting guards over the workings. There were resident communities of Arab traders at coastal towns like Sofala and Kilwa. Africans brought their gold there and bartered it for textiles, beads, and shell money. During the Renaissance the Portuguese attempted to wrest the gold monopoly from the Arabs but with little success.

The Arabs in control of North Africa began to tap a source, new to them, but known a thousand years before to the Phoenicians—the gold of Nigeria and the Gold Coast. Unlike the Phoenicians or the Portuguese who were to muscle in on the trade in the fourteenth century, the Arabs brought the gold overland across the great trans-Saharan caravan routes.

The Arabs established market towns along the North African littoral beginning with Tunis at the end of the seventh century. Inland market centers were founded as far west as Marrakesh, beyond and south of the Strait of Gibraltar. The trans-Saharan route over which the gold was carried ran from Timbuktu on the northernmost bend of the Niger north to the oasis in northwest Libya at Gadàmes, across fifteen hundred miles of desert wastes. The distances were awesome; from Timbuktu to Marrakesh, for example, was one thousand miles of unrelenting desert, but the profits were phenomenal. In spite of the vast distances involved and the expense of refining and minting, the gold trade, because of the volume and exceptional quality of the gold, was well worth the effort.

The Arabs appear to have collected some gold from West Africa as early as the eighth century. A few centuries later they were bringing as much as nine tons of raw gold a year across the Sahara by camel caravans which funneled it to Tripoli, Tunis, Algiers, Mahdia, and other centers, whence a great deal of it made its way eastward or into Europe via Spain.

The area which the gold came from was called Wangara and covered two zones—the region in modern Mali and Guinea between the confluence of the Niger, Senegal, and Falémé rivers and the Lobi area of the Upper Volta. Most of the gold was washed from the upper reaches of the rivers, from estuaries along the seacoast, or from adjacent alluvial terraces. The yield was highest at the season of the annual floods and was found as extremely pure, fine dust. Some gold was refined from auriferous ores dug from large shallow pits. The dust, packed tightly in tubes, was taken to the places where the Tuareg-controlled salt caravans assembled. The foremost of these collection centers was Timbuktu, which was known as the City of Gold, because of the great quantities of gold that passed through it.

The gold was gained primarily through trade. The southerners were eager to trade their gold for silks, swords, horses, trinkets, and above all salt, the most coveted item among the peoples of the Savannah. Even today imported salt brings a high price in the area. Salt was so highly valued in the south that it was often exchanged for its weight in gold. The blocks of salt were mined by black slaves of the Berber Tuareg in the far-off northern desert where it was so abundant houses and mosques were built out of great dingy slabs of it. The wretched slaves who mined the gray coarse salt were sometimes blinded by the fierce desert winds. They subsisted on palm dates and occasional bits of camel meat brought by the traders who came to the desolate region to collect the salt.

In the ninth century the powerful kingdom of Ghana controlled production of West African gold. Ghana dominated an extensive area that reached south into the Wangara gold fields. The commercial city of Kumbi Saleh was the seat of the royal court, which was so splendid that even the domestic animals sported gold jewelry. The royal treasury was overflowing with gold, but by the mid-eleventh century a Moslem holy war led by the fanatic Almoravid sect fractured the power of the Ghanian Royal House.

In the thirteenth century the Kingdom of Mali controlled the gold of Wangara. Mali came to the attention of Europe in the fourteenth century when the devout King Mansa Musa made his celebrated pilgrimage to Mecca and tour of the Middle East. Contemporary sources describe his dazzling retinue of five hundred richly clad slaves, carrying staffs of solid gold, and his caravan of one hundred camels, each laden with three hundred pounds of gold. The extravagant African King bought so much in the tempting bazaars of Cairo that the price of gold fell precipitously on the Cairo exchange.

In the thirteenth century the bulk of the world's gold production was in Islamic hands. The Byzantine Empire was under constant seige and attracting less and less gold. The long dependable purity of Byzantine gold currency was consequently contaminated. A number of European states during this period began to issue gold coins, after a hiatus of more than four hundred years.

In the tenth century, as the millennium of Christ's birth approached, Christendom had been tinged with dread that the world might come to an end. Secular activity slowed as Europe's few rich men, spurred by panic and penitence, heaped their worldly treasures on church altars, offering gold in every form and relinquishing priceless illuminated books. When the year 1000 passed with no Apocalypse, a new burst of energy, a wave of confidence, swept the Christian world. Men celebrated life and renewed their faith, launching the age of the Romanesque and Gothic when attention to the soul reached its zenith. In France alone in the eleventh century some 1,587 churches were constructed, most of them on the routes to holy shrines. Pilgrimages to the great shrines were apart of the life of high- and low-born alike.

Europe's goldsmiths and jewelers welcomed the new era. Through the contributions of the faithful and donations from pilgrims prelates of the High Middle Ages were able to fill the holy places with the outpourings of the goldsmiths' workshops. People gave their gold, jewels, and labor to raise hymns in stone, glass, and gold to the glory of God. The greatest source of information on medieval European metalworking is a treatise published about 1190 by a monk named Theophilus the Presbyter. His great compilation on medieval crafts, the *Diversarum Artium Schedula,* devotes seventy-nine chapters to the goldsmith's art. Written during the aesthetic awakening that stirred Europe, it is addressed to craftsmen who wished, "by the practical work of their hands, and by pleasing meditation of what is new," to learn "all that Greece possesses in the way of diverse colors and mixtures; all that Tuscany knows of the working of enamels . . . all that Arabia has to show of works ductile, fusible, or chased; all the many vases and sculptured gems and ivory that Italy adorns with gold; all that France prizes in costly variety of windows, all that is extolled in gold, silver, copper or iron, or in subtle working of wood and stone." No fine art was untouched by gold in the High Middle Ages when goldsmiths were called upon to work on such monumental projects as the abbot Suger's reconstruction of St. Denis, the first of the Gothic churches, which became the focus of European life, serving as library, art gallery, school, and entertainment center.

Suger was a brilliant Benedictine abbot and regent of France. His object was to make the abbey the resting place of kings and a fitting home for the patron saint of France. Suger pursued his vision with all his being, overseeing every detail, as Justinian had during construction of St. Sophia. He brought the most gifted goldsmiths from Lorraine and other goldworking centers providing them with fur cloaks, free housing, and exemption from taxes.

St. Bernard criticized the lavish project and Suger replied, "If the ancient law ordained that cups of gold should be used for libations and to receive the blood of rams . . . how much rather should we devote gold, precious stones and the rarest of materials to vessels designed to hold the blood of Our Lord?" To pay the exorbitant cost of the gold, jewels, silver, and enamels he needed, Suger persuaded King Louis VII and the aristocracy to subscribe their funds. "Following our example," he wrote, "they took the rings from their fingers" to finance the restoration, which was begun in 1137.

By the thirteenth century there was enough gold in Europe to initiate gold currency. The gold came from melting Arab coins which circulated in large amounts and from supplies returning with the Crusaders from the twelfth century on. Florence and Genoa, two vigorously growing commercial states, issued gold coins in 1252, followed by England, which produced a short-lived issue in 1257. France struck gold coins in 1266, Sicily and Naples in 1278, and Venice in 1284. The florin of Florence and the ducat of Venice, destined to play a leading role in the Renaissance, soon ranked as internationally exchanged currency. Expanding European economies supported gold coinage and created a demand for yet more gold.

In addition to gold from the Islamic world and some from crumbling Byzantium, thirteenth-century Europe drew on newly exploited zones of alluvial gold in Bohemia, Thuringia, Silesia, the Black Forest, and especially the Rhine Valley. But it was not until the fourteenth and fifteenth centuries that European gold production peaked with a shift in emphasis from the washing of placer deposits to mining. The excitement of mining activity, the working of hundreds of sites from the Rhine to the Carpathians, helped accelerate the extraordinary economic social and cultural progress which fed the viable economies of the Hanseatic cities and Italian states and culminated in the glorious burst of the Renaissance.

Hungary soon outstripped all other European areas in gold and silver production. It remained the chief source of bullion until the Spanish conquest of the New World in the sixteenth century. She produced between two and five thousand pounds of gold a year, about half of Europe's total yield. Within seventy-five years of the striking of the first florins, Hungary initiated a gold currency. A quarter of a century later, Germany was minting gulden, gold coins which, like those of Hungary, closely imitated the Florentine currency which had become familiar along the trade route north on the Rhine where it paid for manufactures. By 1500 Europe was well supplied with gold.

Medieval European mining was not technically superior to that of the Romans; in fact, it was less sophisticated. During the early stages serfs did the work for the benefit of landowners. By the mid-twelfth century the Holy Roman Emperor Frederick Barbarossa put all mining under state control and decreed the output of the mines a royal monopoly. So did the rulers of most other auriferous areas.

Medieval mines were subject to flooding which had always plagued miners. The only remedy for flooding was hand bailing or the employment of the same cumbersome arrangements of water wheels and water snails the Romans had used. Open pits were more common than shaft mines, which rarely exceeded eighty feet in depth as compared to Roman mines, which had frequently plummeted five hundred feet or more.

During the mid-fifteenth century the most famous of all books ever written on mining and metallurgical techniques was written by a Saxon named Georg Bauer, who signed his work Georgius Agricola. Agricola's *De Re Metallica* was published in Basel in 1556. It was not the first such book. A comprehensive volume on the subject had been published in 1540 by the Italian Vannoccio Biringuccio. However, Agricola's exhaustive treatise was profusely illustrated and was the first work based on research rather than imagination and superstition. Agricola denied that gold grew underground or could be found with divining rods but hedged a bit on the subject of demons, writing that "prayer and fasting will keep them at bay."

Agricola had a medical degree from Italy and like many other young men in the sixteenth century made his way to the gold fields of Bohemia. While he was a doctor at the Joachimsthal mining camp he tried his hand at mining and learned all he could from seasoned miners. His book traced the history of mining and refining from ancient times, detailed the various methods of draining underground workings, and dealt with the vexing problem of subterranean ventilation. It described superior drainage machines, one of which sucked water by piston action and another which was operated by a team of eight horses. Agricola's drawings illustrate winch-operated elevators, systems of underground haulage including wheelbarrows and small sledges pushed along a track of grooved planks.

The twelve-volume work was not translated into English until 1912 (by the future President Herbert Hoover and his wife, Lou), but it was a sixteenth-century best seller. It had ten printings, was translated into three languages, and had universal influence.

A new force, that of the bourgeoisie, had entered the feudal world by the fourteenth century. They prospered with the growth of industry and competed for power and status-enhancing gold. The knights and the churchmen had to recognize the bourgeoisie of the growing towns throughout western Europe. Traders, merchants, and craftsmen formed guilds through which they made their influence felt in cities like Paris, the largest in the West with a population of 200,000, Venice, London, the wealthy cities of Flanders, Strasbourg, and Mainz in Germany, and the independent states of Florence, Milan, and Pisa. All had powerful guilds. In almost every city the goldsmiths appear to have been among the first to organize to satisfy their group interests and regulate their profession.

Goldsmiths of the Western Roman Empire had belonged to a type of guild which did not survive the dissolution of the West. In the East the organization remained strong, and through the fifth and sixth centuries Byzantine goldworks were marked with city and maker's marks. The goldsmiths of Europe responded to the gradual increase in gold supplies after the millennium by forming guilds, which produced objects of great beauty for princes, the Church, and once again for well-to-do citizens. In Paris at the turn of the thirteenth century the goldsmiths had their shops, *sur le grand pont,* and by mid-century had regulated their guild.

The goldsmiths of England were incorporated by royal charter in 1327 into the Worshipful Company of goldsmiths. The goldbeaters had a separate guild. By 1500 there were fifty-two workshops in London's Strand. English goldsmiths acknowledged St. Dunstan, the tenth-century goldsmith and archbishop of Canterbury, as their "blessed patron, protector and founder of the goldsmiths of London." The Ponte Vecchio over the Arno in Florence was the site of over forty goldsmiths' shops by 1350. The goldsmiths were among the first to form a guild in Venice in the early thirteenth century. The guilds regulated all work in precious metal. They controlled admission and supervised decrees stating that all work be carried out in full view of the public to assure no fasification or adulteration of gold or silver. Over the years scores of edicts were issued regulating goldsmiths' work. Their varying subjects reflected current political and economic tensions—restricting the export of gold or silver: for example, controlling quality, standardizing plate, or dealing with cases of fraud.

The reappearance of gold in western Europe removed the exclusivity of patronage from the Church and royal houses. Goldsmiths organized in secular workshops as wealthy clients began to order goldworks for their houses and for personal adornment. During the Gothic period reliquaries, tabernacles, and other devotional objects were constructed on Gothic architectural principles, turned into exquisite miniature gold shrines turreted and adorned with architectural elements in miniature. By the mid-thirteenth century patronage passed out of the hands of the great churchmen back to the courts, which were becoming increasingly luxurious, and the nobles, who desired a wide range of ornaments and accessories.

Although the change in patronage did not immediately decrease the emphasis in goldsmithing on the religious, during the late medieval period there were a significant number of wealthy people, both nobles and commoners, who ate from gold plates, drank from gold goblets, and decked themselves in gold jewelry. Less wealthy burghers aspired to silver-gilt table plate and jewelry or even iron jewelry washed with gold. Members of the wealthiest households reserved silver for penance during Lent setting their lordly tables with gold the rest of the year—a far cry from the austerity of the preceding centuries.

Sumptuary decrees were issued from time to time restricting the wearing of fine jewels which were regarded as a badge of rank. In 1283 the bourgeois men and women of France were forbidden to wear belts of gold, precious stones, or coronals of gold or silver. In the fourteenth century costume changed radically for both men and women. The simple, draped medieval woolen robes which were decorated with fur gave way to much richer and more structurally complicated costumes made of gorgeous brocades and subtly dyed cloth. Gold was employed in brocades and sumptuous embroidery. Jewelry too became much more elaborate. Enameling was popular because of the rich colorful effects which could be achieved either with gold alone or with gold and stones. A new technique called basse-taille was developed in which a design engraved on a gold surface was covered by a brilliantly colored translucent enamel. Later, goldsmiths did away with the gold backing to make plique-à-jour enameling in which gold strips held enamel or stones open on both sides. Men and women of royal or noble blood boasted jeweled crowns, clasps, brooches, and collars. Women's hair styles became more and more intricate giving new scope to goldsmiths, who fashioned golden hair nets studded with gems and elaborate heavily jeweled headdresses such as appear in so many portraits of the period.

At the same time the right to wear such lavish adornment became ever more restricted. Craftsmen and yeomen were the object of a 1363 statute of England's Edward III. They and their families were forbidden to wear "cynture, cotel, fermaille, anel, garter, nouches, rubaignes, cheines, bendes, sealx u autres chose dor ne dargent." The same statute forbade knights to wear gold or jeweled rings or brooches. Only esquires with land or rent of two hundred marks a year and merchants with assets of five hundred pounds sterling might wear costumes adorned with silver and their wives and daughters jeweled headdresses. The King of Castile in 1380 passed a much more severe ordinance: no Spaniards were to wear cloth of gold or silk, gold jewelry, or precious stones save for queens and princesses. The very fact that such sumptuary decrees were issued again and again indicates that they were not more effective than those of the Romans. The love of gold and gems worn to enhance one's beauty and station in life is too deep-seated to legislate away. During the Renaissance, gold from new lands multiplied Europe's supply. Gold in abundance became available to a sophisticated middle class who dedicated it not to God, but to the glorification of man on an unprecedented scale.

CHAPTER ELEVEN *Alchemical Gold*

The history of alchemy, also known as the Hermetic art, is one of the most colorful chapters in the history of gold. The ancient practice of alchemy was introduced to Europe in the Middle Ages. Returning Crusaders brought home tales of exotic sun-drenched lands and brightly gleaming gold which lit up the dark, huddled world of the Middle Ages. With bloodied cross and sword they won golden treasure, and once again the gold of the East exercised a profound influence on European economics and goldsmithery. The "awesome hunger for gold," which Virgil noted, fed on plunder and fattened on exposure to the golden opulence of the East, but could not be appeased. Expanding western economies and reviving trade required ever greater supplies of the precious metal. Kings needed it to prop up their authority, the Christian God needed it for his powerful church, and the men who had tasted the gold of conquest craved more.

The Crusades opened the medieval world to new currents of thought and experience. With the fresh winds of Islamic, Nestorian, and Coptic learning that warmed the intellectual chill of Europe came alchemy, popularly known as the search for the philosophers' stone, which would transmute base metals into gold and unlock the secret of eternal life. Alchemy was born in Hellenistic Alexandria and practiced for at least a thousand years in the eastern Mediterranean and almost as long in China, before the alchemical texts of the Arabs came to the attention of European scholars. Alchemy caught fire in Europe, and during the Middle Ages, the Renaissance—in fact, right up to the twentieth century—it numbered among it practitioners a mixed bag of genuine seekers of knowledge, scientists, crackpots, and charlatans. Alchemy, which is in bad repute today, classed with astrology, numerology, and various occult practices, has a most engaging and meritorious history.

Through the ages men labored among smoking retorts and belching furnaces to make their golden dreams come true. In pursuit of the philosophers' stone and the divine gold, alchemists learned the laws governing motion, gravity, and heat. They laid the foundations for chemistry discovering new elements, compounds, and chemicals. Magic was the precursor of science, and alchemy, the marriage of magic and controlled observation and experimentation, produced significant developments not only in chemistry and physics but in metallurgy, medicine, optics, biology, and psychology. "Alchemy," wrote Francis Bacon, the English essayist, "may be likened to the man who told his sons that he had buried gold in the vineyard; where they by digging found no gold but by turning up the mold about the roots of the vines procured a plentiful vintage."

There were two categories of Hermetic scientists. The adepts were theoretical alchemists who through the centuries surrounded themselves with an impenetrable cloak of mysticism and arcana. The aim of these philosophically oriented men was expressed in a 1636 work, *Secrets Chymiques,* by the Parisian Fabre. "Alchemy," he wrote, "is not merely an art or science to teach metallic transmutation so much as a true and solid science that teaches to know the center of all things, which in divine language is called the 'Spirit of Life.'"

The empirical puffers, as opposed to the adepts, experimented with material things. Called puffers because of their penchant for the bellows, they were the men and women primarily responsible for alchemy's "plentiful vintage." Among the puffers, however, was a host of quacks and charlatans whose sole objective was to enrich themselves at the expense of others. Taking advantage of the traditional secrecy and obscurantism of the Hermetic science, these characters immersed themselves in mumbo jumbo. Often, they performed convincing transmutations by sleight of hand, and not infrequently they poisoned themselves or others.

Renaissance puffers found a ready market for their questionable concoctions which they advertised as promoting long life and everlasting beauty. *Aurum potabile,* gold dissolved in an acid or gold powder mixed in a liquid, was a favorite remedy for almost every condition. Gold bromide was reputed to have aphrodisiacal powers (and is still sold in some parts of the East), and gentle-born ladies applied gold leaf or salve containing gold to their smallpox-ravaged faces. The cure was sometimes worse than the ill. The gold leaf was supposed to prevent scarring, but since it had to be removed with needles, it was often difficult to judge its effectiveness on women who looked as disfigured as those who had been unable to afford the treatment. Patients who imbibed aurum potabile containing traces of mercury were often stricken with falling hair and teeth, kidney disease, and nerve damage.

The red powder so prominent in phases of the Great Work, as the pursuit was called, may have been fulminate of mercury, and another favorite mixture, sulphur nitrate and charcoal, came close to being gunpowder, so it is not surprising that more than one puffer literally exploded. Legend asserts that Friar Roger Bacon, the thirteenth-century English alchemist who lectured in Paris and Oxford, blew himself up and was carried off in the talons of the devil.

A late-sixteenth-century alchemical work, *Memoirs of the New Atlantis,* by Mary Manley, describes the misadventures of one puffer who spent two years holed up in a large, specially equipped laboratory on his noble patroness' estate. He assured the wealthy lady he could turn lead into gold provided he was left to his "high thought" and in no way disturbed. He saw no one, not even his hostess, who spent a large part of her fortune in supplying his frequent demands for enormous quantities of lead, charcoal, alembics, and other items. No gold was forthcoming, and finally the lady "subordinated the flights of her imagination to the counsel of wisdom," and demanded access to his sanctum. "When at last she was admitted she looked with awe at the alembics, the enormous cauldrons, long tubes, forges, furnaces and three of four scorching fires blazing in various parts of what felt like the interior of a volcano." With no less veneration she observed the smoke-grimed face of the physicist, pale, emaciated, worn by daily labors and nightly vigils. He told her in unintelligible jargon of such successes as he had obtained. The forbearing lady spoke of her disappointment. The scientist assured her he would step up his efforts and would reluctantly attempt a particularly challenging operation he had hoped to avoid. The patroness left with "hopes and golden visions revived." A few days later as the household was at dinner, a piercing shriek was heard followed by a tremendous explosion. The lady and her servants rushed to the laboratory only to find the building in flames and the poor puffer a cinder.

Such men gave a bad name to alchemy which claims such distinguished luminaries as Avicenna, Roger Bacon, Albertus Magnus, Thomas Aquinas, Paracelsus and Goethe. Even Isaac Newton was familiar with alchemical literature in the eighteenth century before there was a clear distinction between alchemy and chemistry.

Like so many alchemists Albertus Magnus was the son of a wealthy family and a cleric. He was born in Germany and studied at Pavia before becoming a member of the powerful Dominican order. In the mid-thirteenth century he taught at the Sorbonne, where he gained fame as a great teacher. The Catholic Church denied that he had ever been an alchemist when he was canonized at the beginning of the twentieth century. But European libraries contain manuscripts in his own hand detailing his alchemical experiments, and he wrote at least five books on the subject as well as works on chemical mineralogy and the history of metals. He left sound advice to the gold makers in his *De Alchimia:* "An alchemist should be reserved and discreet, work in seclusion and tell no one of his results. He should be patient, persistent and unwearying, faithfully following the long and difficult path of the Great Work and above all, he should not get involved with princes and lords." Any such association was doomed to failure, he wrote, because such men were impatient and forced the alchemist to accelerate his pace. Moreover, in the event of nonsuccess the alchemist would be tortured, and should he succeed he would be imprisoned.

Thomas Aquinas was a student and associate of Albertus. They are said to have created a head which could talk and answer the most abstruse questions often at very great length. One day Aquinas, tired of the constant babbling, smashed it with a stick. Aquinas also wrote several works dealing with the Hermetic art. In one he debated whether the use of Hermetic gold is

lawful and concluded that natural gold is not superior, stating he
had always used both.

Leonardo da Vinci, himself a scientist, took the Renaissance
alchemists to task for their obsessive experimentation to repro-
duce "the most excellent of nature's products." He urged them to
"observe gold in the mine where none of the things the magician
uses will be found: no quicksilver, no sulphur, no fire." But he
echoed the prevalent belief that gold grew underground, adding,
"You will see that the extremities [of the gold vein] are continuously expanding in slow movement, transmuting into gold
whatever they touch; and note that therein is a living organism
which it is not in your power to produce."

It was generally agreed that not only did gold grow and ripen
underground, expanding dendritic fingers throughout the rock
matrix, but also "seeds of gold sown in the earth would mature
and turn into more gold." Each metal was associated with a
planet—gold, the noblest, naturally with the sun. Silver was linked
to the moon, copper to Venus, iron to Mars, mercury to Mercury,
lead to Saturn, and tin to Jupiter. Planetary influences caused
each metal to progress upward until it was transformed into the
most perfect substance of all—gold, the dew of the sun. However, men believed if not harvested from the earth at the opti-
mum moment overripe gold was subject to wither into worthless
earth.

The alchemists sought to hasten the transmutation within their
laboratories in a series of controlled, prescribed processes. The
philosophers' stone was analogous to the stone of the wise, the
magisterium, and the universal essence. It was conceived of as
being a stone, a liquid, or a powder and was the key to effecting
transmutations of lesser metals into gold. A number of reagents
were employed to treat materials such as hair, blood, earth, eggs,
and urine, which were then subjected to calcination, albification,
sublimation, fire, and exposure to sunlight.

The growing emphasis on mysticism and allegory in European
alchemy coupled with the proliferation of dishonest puffers who
tended to wander from one rich city or estate to another in
search of victims made the alchemist a figure of derision.
Chaucer in his fourteenth-century *Canterbury Tales* cast a satiri-
cal eye on the Hermetic art in his "Canon's Yeoman's Tale,"

which is recited by the servant of a clerical puffer. He recounts his learned master's sorry history of failures and tells how the canon, once a wealthy man, ran through his fortune and was eventually reduced to perpetrating a number of swindles to get more gold to finance his work.

Chaucer had spent most of his life connected with the English court, which was a magnet for alchemists of all persuasions, so he knew them well and shows a detailed knowledge of alchemical equipment and procedure. He quotes from a medieval treatise containing the instructions for transmutation allegedly passed down from Hermes, which Aristotle passed on to his pupil Alexander the Great. The portrait Chaucer paints of the alchemist is a sorry one, but probably accurate. In the closed and stifling atmosphere of the windowless laboratory even the freshest complexion faded leaving a man bleary-eyed and of "a leden hewe." The typical practitioner was surrounded by a mass of clay and glass vessels, vials, urinals, and sublimatories in which he concocted mixtures of metals, bull's gall, arsenic, sal ammoniac, brimstone, agrimony, valerian, and other herbs, dyes, and chemicals. Various solutions such as rubifying water and a special blend of chalk, unslaked lime, and white of egg were used for albification. Chaucer mentions other ingredients— "burnt bones, ashes, donge, piss and cleye." No wonder that the alchemist even when away from the scene of his mysterious labors was shunned. "For al the world they stynken as a goot; Hir savour is so rammyish and so hoot, that thought a man from hem a mile be, the savour wole infecte hym, trusteth me."

The word "alchemy" has been attributed to several sources. One theory proposes that it came from the Greek *cheo*, "I pour" or "cast," which shows the close tie between alchemy and the Alexandrian metallurgists who were its first practitioners. However, it seems more likely that it was derived from *khem*, the ancient Egyptian name for their fertile "Black Land." The Arabic article *al* was added during the Islamic period to make the word "alchemy," from which comes the word "chemistry." The first appearance of the word "chemistry" is in a work by the tenth-century lexicographer Suidas, who uses it to refer to an alloy of gold and silver. He also writes that the Roman Emperor Diocletian had all the alchemical texts in Egypt burned when the Egyptians revolted at the end of the third century A.D. His aim, according to Suidas, was to punish the rebellious Egyptians by keeping them from the lucrative practice of goldsmithing. Among other riveting tidbits in the lexicon is the note that the Golden Fleece was actually a papyrus with the ancient secret for producing alchemical gold.

Tradition credits the mythical Hermes Trismegistus with the first treatise on the Great Work and with the Hermetic seal which he supposedly discovered while trying to fasten the halves of the philosophers' egg so he could hatch it into gold. Hermes is identified with Thoth (Tehuti), the Egyptian embodiment of the Wisdom of God, who is depicted in an Egyptian papyrus drawing about 1000 B.C., as a creature with the head of ibis bearing the symbols for creation. Hermes' treatise the *Emerald Table* was supposed to have been graven with a diamond stylus on a huge emerald which was found in his tomb by the soldiers of Alexander at the Great Pyramid at Gizeh.

Alchemy's hazy origins are hard to pinpoint. There may well be an analogy between the fundamental alchemical concept of all matter arising from a primeval mass and the ancient Egyptian perception of the annual generation of plant and animal life by the sun and the rich silt deposited by the Nile floods. Western alchemy began in Alexandria, the pulsating Hellenistic cultural center founded by Alexander at the mouth of the Nile. The teeming cosmopolitan seaport of the Ptolemies was a city famous for its master metalworkers, dyers, and glassmakers. It was also an intellectual mecca to which scholars were drawn from Asia Minor, the Levant, Europe, and Africa. They gathered in the great library and the Museion established in the third century B.C. by Ptolemy Philadelphus to read, copy, study, and compare.

From this ferment alchemy was born in the fourth century B.C. The Hellenistic Greeks, who blended the contributions of Eastern mysticism, Greek philosophy, and Egyptian technology and myth, brought it to full flower. The Egyptians had a tradition of empirical craftsmanship, and the intellectual climate of Hellenistic Alexandria encouraged technicians and philosophers to speculate about the physical world and changes they observed in it. The early alchemists were primarily concerned with color. A third century B.C. Egyptian work dealing with the making of gold, silver, gems, and dyes and emphasizes the importance of color changes. One of the first alchemical texts written in the fourth century A.D. incorporates material from the earlier technical work and also deals with gilding and the preparation of alloys.

Metallurgists, who were often dyers as well, observed that some of the reagents used in dying produced surface color changes on metal. They had also seen the apparent transmutation of malachite ore into shining copper and of lead into silver when galena ore was smelted. They had discovered millennia before that earth could be heated to produce shining gold and that two metals in liquid form could combine to produce a third which had the appearance of gold, yet contained none. The early alchemists-metallurgists made much of the iridescence which danced over the surface of molten lead and the color changes of metals when they were heated or treated with substances such as sulphur. They learned how to distill mercury from the heavy bright red cinnabar ore and marveled at the magic which made liquid quicksilver combine with other metals and then separate them.

The Alexandrian alchemists were sure they could transmute inferior metals, step by step, bringing them up through a sequence of color changes until they matured into gold. They were supported by astrological theories from Mesopotamia which propounded the interchangeability of matter and the coexistence of the great macrocosm of the universe and the microcosm of man. The influence of one was felt upon the other. Growth and development were characteristic of the microcosm; thus, it followed that if the human soul could elevate itself to perfection as it passed through death and rebirth, so metals could progress in the earth from base to sublime. And if this happened slowly in the bosom of mother earth, why could the process not be speeded in the laboratory? A change of color rather than a change of form was considered by early alchemists to be the goal, since the color of the metal revealed its real spirit. Later, at any given point along the way, the color of the material being subjected to transmutation was evidence of the stage the Great Work was at.

The fledgling art was nourished by contributions from many

sources—Zoroastrian, Manichean, Babylonian, and Syrian—but the most profound influence was Greek. The alchemists at Alexandria had access to Aristotle's works and even his own library. The Greeks had no fondness for manual labor or applied theory. They were philosophers, concerned with such questions as the nature of the universe. Aristotle, who died in 332 B.C., only ten years after the founding of Alexandria, formulated an explanation of the universe which was the culmination of Greek thought and formed the basis of alchemical and scientific speculation for almost two thousand years.

All material objects, according to Aristotelian theory, were composed of combinations of the four elements—earth, air, fire, and water—in varying proportions. Each element had two qualities, one of which predominated. A solid object, for example, had a preponderance of earth. A liquid or liquefiable object was composed chiefly of water. Fire represented the principle of combustion and air was thought by the Stoics to equate with the soul. Any two elements could be combined to make a third, and all four were present in every substance. To the alchemist this meant that any substance could be changed to another if its elemental proportions were brought into balance with the proportions of the other.

From the outset there were men and women of a philosophical bent who applied theories governing the transmutation of metals to the human soul and had no interest in mucking about in the laboratory. There was a marked dichotomy between the mystically oriented who moved along an inward path toward the purifying fire from which they hoped to emerge reborn as spiritual gold and the practical Alexandrian alchemists who aimed at creating material gold. These latter practitioners developed the flasks, beakers, water baths, stills, and furnaces still in use today to facilitate their experiments with chemical reactions.

Meanwhile in China, Taoist philosophy, which sought to penetrate the nature or "way" of matter, stimulated alchemical pursuits which were almost wholly spiritually oriented. The Chinese word for alchemy, *kem-mai,* means "gone astray in search of gold." The Chinese alchemist added a "medicine" to metals to bring about transmutation. He valued the gold not for its intrinsic worth, but because it had the power of conferring immortality on whoever ingested it or ate from plates of the magical gold. In some cases the "gold" couldn't guarantee eternal life but could cure illness and prolong life.

The first mention of alchemy in Chinese history is a story from the second century B.C. A certain Li Shao-chün appeared at the court and assured the Emperor, Lui Ch'e, that he could make the dishes of divine gold which the ruler craved. He said that he had been shown the secret by a lovely woman robed in scarlet, the Taoist goddess of the furnace. The account says the confident alchemist was provided with a laboratory and cinnabar but there is unfortunately no mention of the results.

Chinese alchemy eventually withdrew almost completely from the laboratory and became a hodgepodge of obscure mystical allusions regarding the path of enlightenment. Interest faded but not before the experiments of the Far Eastern alchemists had made many contributions to pharmacology. The most celebrated of the Chinese alchemists was Ko Hung. In the late fourth century A.D. he wrote a book in which he outlined the requisite steps for producing the powerful gold. Ko Hung describes some of the alchemists' products which were chiefly gold alloys and amalgams of copper, arsenic, and lead with mercury derived from cinnabar. The very first mention of "mosaic gold," a sulphide of tin, appears in his book.

Alchemical works have been attributed to Isis, Moses (who, according to the Bible, gave the idolators *aurum potabile* to drink), Aaron, Solomon, and many others. One of the most famous of Alexandrian alchemists was Maria Prophetessa, a Jewess who has been associated with Miriam, the sister of Moses. Legend credits her with a large number of discoveries and treatises. Despite some confusion it seems there actually was a brilliant Jewish woman who invented a number of pieces of equipment still found in scientific laboratories. An illustration in a Egyptian papyrus called "The Gold making of Cleopatra" depicts the type of distillation apparatus she developed which is known as "bain-marie," or water bath.

To hinder those who lusted after easy gold, the initiates purposely couched their written works in the most obscure and deceptive terms. Materials were not what they appeared to be. Mercury was not chemical mercury, and the green lion was aqua fortis, the mixture of acids which can dissolve gold. Flaming chariots, dragons, salamanders, naked kings and queens enliven the profusely illustrated pages of the alchemical works of the Christians. The Arabs, who provided the link between the birth of alchemy in Egypt and its introduction to Europe, were forbidden to use pictures and restricted themselves to text and elaborate symbols.

In the fifth century A.D. the center of alchemical activity was in the Byzantine Empire. The schismatic Nestorian Christians, who had splintered from the Byzantine Coptic Church, translated Greek alchemical manuscripts into Syriac. They founded schools at which Hellenistic theories of the Hermetic science were taught, and in the eighth and ninth centuries these deeply influenced the Arab caliphate at Baghdad. This city of intellectuals and sybarites took the place of Alexandria as an academy; from the seventh century to the eleventh as Islam spread, alchemy took root and was introduced into the conquered territories.

The Arab physicians and druggists who practiced alchemy made myriad improvements in laboratory equipment and techniques. They made chemical discoveries such as the caustic alkalis and gave the world such words as "elixir," "alcohol," "alkali," and "alembic." They practiced controlled observation and experimentation and kept detailed records. Onto Alexandria root stock the Arabs grafted Chinese theory, adapting the idea of adding a "medicinal" element to the base metal to precipitate the transmutation into gold. Not all of them were dedicated chemists. According to one Arab wit, Moslem alchemists knew "300 methods of making fools." There is a story that in the twelfth century the Sultan Nureddin underwrote the researches of a very persuasive puffer giving him a veritable fortune in gold all in one lump sum. Not surprisingly, the golden-tongued alchemist vanished overnight, and the following day an anonymous hand posted a list of fools with the Sultan's name at the top and a note at the bottom which stated the Sultan's name would be removed if the alchemist returned to replace it with his own!

The man regarded as the father of alchemy was the Arab Jibir ibn-Hayyan, revered in medieval Europe as the Great Geber. He was alchemist at the court of Harun al-Rashid, Caliph of Baghdad, Charlemagne's erstwhile correspondent. In Baghdad learned men persecuted elsewhere were encouraged to pursue their researches in the caliph's libraries, laboratories, and observatories.

Geber, the most outstanding of all Islamic alchemists, was born in an Iraqi village and sent to be educated in Arabia after the execution of his druggist father, who had plotted to overthrow the Umayyad caliphs. Geber studied mathematics, astrology, medicine, and Arabic—the classic preparation for an alchemist. He became famous as the most learned man of his time and worked until he was over ninety making discoveries which included the first known preparation of nitric acid.

According to tradition, some two hundred years after his death in the little village on the Euphrates where he had been born, the site of his laboratory was uncovered by men preparing ground for a new house. One story says among the buried rubble they found his notes, textbook translations from many sources, including Byzantine Greek, and all of his laboratory apparatus: bellows, retorts, vials, stills, crushing and rolling machinery, and so on—but no gold. Another version of the tale says they found nothing in the ruins save a mortar cast out of pure gold.

Geber was a prolific writer but hardly able to have written the hundreds of works attributed to him which were found in the libraries of Europe, North Africa, India, and the Levant. Many of the works bearing his name were probably written by members of the Ismaili sect a century after his death. Many more were undoubtedly the work of some of Europe's first practical alchemists who signed Geber's honored name both to cash in on his reputation and because the church officially censured the practice of alchemy.

Spain, under the rule of the Moors, was almost the only place in Europe where alchemy was studied during the Dark Ages. It was really only after the millennium that the great era of European alchemy was launched. There had been a few practitioners before but the climate of repression and uncertainty hindered men from traveling to the centers of learning. It is interesting that despite the antagonism between Islam and Christianity the learned men who met together in the name of alchemy were religious scholars of both persuasions. The cradle of European alchemy was the University of Montpellier, founded in 1181. Although alchemy was not taught formally, the university turned out a constellation of brilliant thirteenth-century alchemists including Albertus Magnus, St. Thomas of Aquinas, Roger Bacon, Arnold of Villanova, and Raymond Lully. Later graduates were Nostradamus, Erasmus, and Rabelais, whose *Pantagruel* contains allegorical paraphrasing of alchemy's Great Work. In 1307 the Church condemned alchemy as a diabolic art, but the gold seekers and life seekers continued their research.

Roger Bacon, the most renowned of all medieval scientists, was a Franciscan who studied at Oxford before 1240, numbering alchemy among his many interests. In 1267 Bacon wrote that he had spent the astonishing sum of more than two thousand pounds "for purchase of secret books and instruments." His genius made signal contributions in many fields, notably optics, physics, medicine, and calendar reform. He used saltpeter in the manufacture of gunpowder and foresaw both the airplane and steam-powered ship. During his lifetime, however, he was imprisoned for heresy, denied all books, and regarded with suspicion as a powerful magician.

Bacon recognized Geber as his "master" and echoed the Arab's belief that "the Sun [gold] is composed of a very subtle mercury together with a small amount of very pure, homogenous, limpid sulphur, of a clear red tint: and since sulphur is not always of exactly the same shade but may vary in depth of color, so gold may be yellow to a greater or lesser degree." Thirteenth-century European scientists like the Arabs believed all metals wore a combination of mercury and sulphur in varying proportions. This hypothesis was based on the fact that sulphur was often found in association with gold in the earth and mercury had the miraculous power to extract gold from crushed ore.

European courts were a mecca for alchemists, both sincere and fraudulent. English monarchs, for example, were perennially short of currency and almost always involved in costly wars. They resorted to several solutions. To protect the gullible but leave the door open for transmutations that could fill the campaign chests for the Hundred Years' War, English law in the late Middle Ages restricted the practice of alchemy to the holders of a royal license. Laws regarding the Great Work were subject to change. In 1461 Henry VI, for example, repealed a law making alchemy a crime and demanded that the alchemists come up with gold coins to pay his troops fighting the French wars.

Counterfeiters and alchemists found ample room to maneuver, despite severe penalties for tampering with the coin of the realm. Kings routinely had court alchemists, and some such as James II of Scotland dabbled in the Great Work themselves. The Anglo-Saxons had prided themselves on the fineness and true weight of their coins, but with time there were increasing abuses of English currency. In 1002 laws had been passed prohibiting the mintmaster striking coins without official witnesses. Apparently this was done to stop moneyers from recoining debased bullion or foreign currency brought to them by merchants. After the Norman Conquest English currency suffered a marked decline in quality. Henry I sought to establish a sound money policy. To punish dishonest mint workers he issued a decree in 1124 commanding that all moneyers should be deprived of their members. The chronicles recount that ninety-four men were mutilated with the result that the following year money was very scarce indeed.

In the thirteenth century a ceremony was instituted to discourage counterfeiting and bolster public confidence in the coinage by requiring that it undergo periodic assaying. Under Edward III in the fourteenth century the "Trial of the Pyx" was formalized as an annual assay observance, during which randomly selected coins were put in a "pyx" or box and then tested by a jury of goldsmiths. The three-month process is still carried out today in Goldsmith's Hall in the City of London. Today malpractices are as rare as they were common in earlier times. Knavish characters were quick to shave and clip coins or to "sweat gold" by shaking coins in a chamois bag until some dust was exuded from the soft metal. The Mint tried to halt clipping by milling the edges, sometimes a holy legend was run around the outside edge in the vain hope that God-fearing men would not dare deface Scripture. That reasoning also prompted coins on which the arms of a cross were extended to the coin edges to discourage clipping. In the reign of Henry VIII possession of a gold piece lacking one eighth or more of its original weight was prima facie evidence of clipping, and the punishment was severe. "This yere," recorded the Clerk of the Assizes in 1456, "in

Februarie should a woman have been brent at Smythfield for the clipping of gold, but the Kynge's pardon came, she beyeing at the stake ready to be brent."

English monarchs all too often set a poor example for their subjects. Charles I seized all the bullion and coin in the Tower Mint, much of which belonged to private citizens. Thereafter, the English, who had traditionally entrusted their treasure to goldsmiths for safekeeping, were even more skeptical of the crown. From the fourteenth century on, although there was a dramatic increase in European gold supplies over the centuries following 1500 A.D., less and less of it concentrated in royal hands. The ancient royal monopoly on controlling gold stocks was eroded, undermined by the rising power of the merchant bankers. Goldsmiths, acting as bankers and merchant bankers, wielded such power in the mid-seventeenth century that they were able to wrest control of the bullion market from Charles II and his government.

When Charles II came to the throne, the treasury was bare—only eleven pounds sterling remained in the royal coffers. In hopes that magical gold could solve his problems, the King not only supported alchemical research but had his own laboratory, reached by a secret staircase in his bedchamber. Henry VIII was responsible for drastic watering of both gold and silver coins. His father, who was crowned in 1485, took a great interest in the coinage and issued a magnificent gold piece called the sovereign. It was a beautiful coin, an impressive 240 grams twice the weight of the first English gold coin, the 120-gram noble struck in 1351 and later reduced in weight by Henry IV to compete with foreign coins.

Henry VIII, King at age eighteen, showed little interest in anything but sport and sensual pleasure. He spent his father's gold so lavishly that he was forced to debase the splendid and sound currency introduced by his father. He reduced the weight of the sovereign and introduced a smaller gold coin. He watered the gold from 23 carats and 3½ grams to 22 carats and when the budget still wouldn't balance added even more base metal to make it 20 carats.

During the brief reign of Henry's son, Edward VI, who was only nine when his father died, the Council of Regency made an effort to restore the integrity of English currency. This required more gold than was available, so they resorted to issuing good gold coins bearing Edward's likeness and simultaneously minting watered gold coins bearing the dead Henry's portrait. Queen Elizabeth inherited a currency that was frightfully debased and underweight. She accepted the proposal of a former employee of the French Mint to set up a mechanical screw press powered by horses at the Tower Mint. In 1561 under the direction of Eloye Mestrel hammered coins were replaced by England's first milled coins. After two years of fevered activity the government had an ample supply of the new coins and slowed production. The mint workers complained of a lack of work. They feared that the Frenchman's new system would make their jobs obsolete, and Mestrel was forced out of his post and six years later hung for counterfeiting gold coins.

He might have been slightly better off in his native France, where counterfeiters were branded on the forehead with F.M. (*falsator monetas*), shaven bald, but left alive. He had left Paris because the water-powered press which he had helped install aroused such opposition from the mint workers. Like the English, they feared this example of early automation meant an end of their livelihood and prevailed upon Henry II to issue an injunction against milled coinage.

In the fifteenth century Charles VII of France financed the wars against the English with the gold of his Finance Minister, Jacques Coeur, the richest man in Europe. When even Coeur's Croesus-like resources proved unequal to the colossal demands of war, the King turned to his alchemists. They couldn't produce genuine gold, But the King was pleased with their ersatz substitute which, incidentally, was approximately the same as the bogus gold being manufactured by Henry VI's alchemists across the Channel. Both the French and English kings issued great amounts of counterfeit gold coins made of copper and silver alloy and color treated with cinnabar to resemble gold. They paid their armies with them. Soldiers of the opposing sides exchanged their bogus coins and were chagrined to find themselves still holding worthless currency. The English, with no Joan of Arc to lead them, lost the war but managed to strip the country of most of her gold bullion, plate, and jewelry as they retreated.

France was left awash in counterfeit currency of both countries. The public directed their rage at Coeur, who had been mint-master and was held responsible for the nation's economic chaos. He was tried on counterfeiting charges and acquitted but sent into Roman exile.

Counterfeit gold notwithstanding, most people had absolute faith in the power of the alchemists to produce gold. When Pope John XXII died in the fourteenth century, a massive golden fortune was discovered hidden in his palace which could only be explained as Hermetic gold. It was popularly thought to have been manufactured for the Pope by the famous alchemist John Dastyn, who was, like so many other practitioners, a monk and respected scholar. When the Hapsburg Emperor Rudolf II died in 1612, there were four tons of small gold ingots and three of silver stacked in his vaults which had never been entered into the ledgers. Only three generations earlier the gold and silver of the New World had begun to pour into the Hapsburg treasuries, and there was much speculation whether this secret treasure was American gold and silver or alchemical gold.

Ferdinand the III, who became Holy Roman Emperor twenty-five years after Rudolf's death, coerced alchemists to labor for him, as did his son, Leopold I, who pronounced himself most pleased with a goldlike facsimile that came out of the royal alchemist's laboratory. The practical alchemist faced persecution as a magician, imprisonment at the hands of the King or Church, and yet men, many of them men of means, scholars, and clerics, continued to be fascinated by the ancient pursuit.

Occultism flourished in the turmoil of the war-torn seventeenth century, and the alchemist was never more in demand nor more endangered. He was hired or seized by governments who wanted him to conjure up alchemical gold. The dichotomy between the puffers and the philosophical alchemists was sharper than ever. The adepts withdrew almost completely from experimentation, interpreting the mass of earlier texts as purely allegorical works. The puffers were under great pressure to produce Hermetic gold, and when they failed some lost their freedom or their lives.

Fredrick, Duke of Württemberg, was one ruler who had little patience with unsuccessful puffers. He had them tortured and then executed on a gallows made of the iron they had not been able to turn to gold. He watched with his court, seated in a gold-covered grandstand.

An alchemist of great renown who ran afoul of the duke was a certain Sendivogius, a Moravian who had been left a bit of powdered philosophers' stone by an alchemist named Alexander Seton. According to the story, Seton, or Suetonius, a Scot, had discovered the secret of the philosophers' stone and offered proof of transmutation at public displays in cities all over Europe, where his Hermetic gold was tested by specialists and pronounced genuine.

In Switzerland in the summer of 1602 a passionate enemy of the alchemists, the distinguished Professor Dienheim of Fribourg, and the famous physician Jacob Zwinger witnessed Seton carry out what has been called the first historically verified account of transmutation. These two irreproachable men went with Seton to a goldsmith's laboratory in Basel. Dienheim wrote,

> We took with us some slabs of lead brought by Dr. Zwinger, a crucible we had borrowed from a goldsmith, and some ordinary sulphur we bought on the way. Setonius did not touch any of these things. He asked for a fire to be lit, ordered the lead and sulphur to be put into a crucible over the fire, the mass to be stirred, and the lid to be put on. Meanwhile he chatted with us. At the end of a quarter of an hour he said: "Throw this bit of paper into the molten lead, but make sure that it goes right into the middle and none falls into the fire." In the paper was a heavy sort of lemon-yellow powder —but you needed good eyesight to see it. Although we were as doubting as St. Thomas himself, we did everything he told us. After the mass had been heated for another quarter of an hour, and stirred continuously with little iron rods, the goldsmith was told to extinguish the fire by pouring water over it. We found not a vestige of the lead remaining, only the finest gold, which in the opinion of the goldsmith, was a quality better even than the excellent Hungarian and Arabian gold. It weighed exactly the same as the lead we had put in originally.

We were dumbstruck. Suetonius teased us. "Now, he said, "what of your cynicism? You have seen the truth of the matter, and that is mightier than all—even than your subtleties!" Then he had a piece of the gold cut off and gave it to Zwinger as a memento. I too was given a piece weighing about 4 ducats, and I have kept it in remembrance of that day.

Seton, according to one of the myriad tales about his mysterious appearances and disappearances, performed another such transmutation in the shop of a Strasbourg goldsmith in 1603. He left the smith a small amount of red powder in thanks for the use of his laboratory. Gustenhover, the smith, turned a pound of lead to a pound of gold before his assembled friends and foolishly assumed he had become an adept. His fame increased and came to the attention of Rudolf II at Prague. The Emperor sent his secret police to kidnap the self-styled adept, planning to make use of his services in the preparation of cheap bullion.

Gustenhover had to admit he had no knowledge but had simply been given the red powder. The King refused to believe him and turning deaf ears to the foolish goldsmith's protests had him clapped in the dungeon to think things over. A brief period of reflection led him to turn over the remaining powder to the Emperor, who was delighted to see that it did indeed turn lead to gold. He demanded that a new supply be prepared at once. The hapless German was, of course, unable to produce any. He fled, but the long arm of the imperial police intercepted him and he spent the rest of his life imprisoned in Prague's White Tower.

Seton himself came to a bad end. A letter dated Warsaw, June 12, 1651, written to Pierre Borel, a seventeeth-century French historian, by the secretary to Princess Marie of Gonzaga the Queen of Poland tells of his fate. His abilities came to the attention of the Elector of Saxony, Christian II, who had him arrested and brought to the Catholic court. Seton refused the duke's commands to mass-produce gold, vowing he would rather undergo the tortures of hell than reveal his secrets to a heretic. The duke proceeded to have him horribly tortured but he kept his silence.

As he lay dying of injuries in prison Michael Sendivogius bribed the jailers to let the broken alchemist out. Sendivogius,

77. Ottoman iron helmet inlaid with gold floral patterns and inscription in gold sulus script. Sixteenth century. Topkapi Palace Museum, Istanbul.

78. Antique Roman agate vase with elaborate enameled gold mounts added during Renaissance perhaps by Cellini. British Museum.

79. The Rospigliosi Cup, long attributed to Cellini, now thought to be the work of Jacopo Bilivert, a Delft goldsmith working in Florence at the Medici court in 1573. Gold and enamel. Metropolitan Museum of Art, New York.

80. Sixteenth century Parisian goldsmith's workshop engraved by the famed goldsmith Étienne Delaulne.

81. Medieval print depicting washing gold from an alluvial deposit. Bancroft Library, University of California.

82. St. Nicholas, a gold-embellished illumination from the fifteenth century. Many illuminators were also goldsmiths.

83. Cathedral treasure, Seville.

84. Sixteenth-century Spanish ecclesiastical gold.

85. Sixteenth-century ship pendant with enameled rigging and crystal hull. Probably from Barcelona. Metropolitan Museum of Art, New York.

86. Japanese oban from the Tempo period (1836–60). The first of these large oval pieces were cast in the late sixteenth century. One gold oban was equivalent in value to almost a ton of the commonly used small copper coins. Originally reserved for ceremonial presentations or exchanged between members of the feudal aristocracy, they came to be used as payment for European imports brought by Dutch trading ships to Nagasaki.

87. A George II silver-gilt rococo sideboard ewer made in 1746 by Paul de Lamerie, famous French Huguenot goldsmith working in England.

88. Aztec goldwork. Most surviving examples come from the Oaxaca area. Many pieces have movable parts. National Museum, Mexico.

89. Aztec goldsmith drawn by an Indian for Sahagún's *Codex Florentino*.

90. Two gold disks with sun face, pre-Columbian. Colombia. University Museum, Philadelphia.

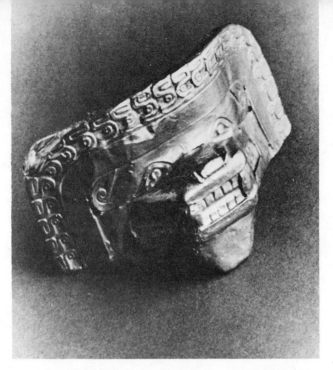

91. Pre-Columbian gold found in Lake Guatavita. Museo del Oro, Bogotá.

92. Gold raft from Colombia such as used in the ceremony on Lake Guatavita which gave rise to the El Dorado legend. Museo del Oro, Bogotá.

93. Gold figurine. Quimbaya, Colombia. University Museum, Philadelphia.

94. Lake Guaravita in Colombia, site of the ceremony which gave rise to the El Dorado legend.

95. Gold mask from mummy bundle, Chimu, Peru. Ca. A.D. 1400. University Museum, Philadelphia.

the moribund Seton, and Seton's wife escaped to Poland. Seton died soon after bequeathing an ounce of the powder to Sendivogius. In hopes of getting more the Moravian married the Scot's widow. But she proved ignorant of alchemical lore, so he was left to trial and error in an attempt to make more of the miraculous powder. He never did discover the secret but continued to deplete his inherited stock in demonstrations of his power. Emperor Rudolf summoned him to court. Sendivogius was clever enough to forestall the possible imprisonment that befell alchemists. He showed the Emperor how to perform the transmutation himself with Seton's powder and was given a post at court by the delighted sovereign.

As his supply dwindled he resorted to selling nostrums made of a few grains of the magic powder in spirits of wine and gained a following of grateful patients who claimed miraculous cures. He seems to have finally run out of Seton's powder and luck. He then resorted to blatant charlatanry making a bare living on counterfeiting coins and performing phony transmutations and then selling the "gold" to the gullible.

One of medieval Europe's most fascinating savants was the Catalan monk Raymond Lully born to a noble family at Palma on the island of Majorca about 1233. As a young man he dedicated himself to a life of fleshly pleasure but at thirty underwent a conversion only slightly less dramatic than that of Saul on the road to Damascus. Lully was a married man but pursued ardently and openly a virtuous matron of Palma, much to her distress. One day as she worshiped at mass he entered the cathedral on horseback and dropped at her feet a rhapsodic love poem. He was surprised but overjoyed when almost immediately after the cathedral scene she summoned him to her apartments for an intimate interview. Lully was sure his desires were to be fulfilled and could barely restrain his impatience. Doña Ambrosia reportedly unfastened her bodice and looked calmly at Lully as he recoiled in horror at the sight of her cancer-gnawed breast. "This is the breast you have worshiped in verse and thought," she said. "How tragic that you should devote yourself to corruptible mortal flesh rather than the pure and eternal Christ."

After recovering from shock, Lully vowed to consecrate his life to spreading the Gospel among the heathen. To prepare for missionary work he went first to the Sorbonne, where he heard the famous Englishman Duns Scotus lecture. He debated Scotus so brilliantly that he was made a lecturer himself, although he had no scholastic credentials.

Lully went on to Monpellier and became a disciple of the foremost alchemist of the time, Arnold of Villanova, a charismatic practictioner of medicine and alchemy who invoked the wrath of the Church. Arnold was condemned posthumously by the Inquisition, and almost all of his writings were burned at an auto-da-fé. In the course of experimentation he had discovered the acids later named muriatic, sulphuric, and nitric.

After Lully's studies were completed he launched his missionary travels which took him through eastern Europe, Asia Minor, and to North Africa, where he barely escaped being stoned by a mob in Tunis. He returned to Europe, where he worked with Arnold once again and gained a reputation as a great philosopher and adept.

Many extraordinary stories about Lully circulated during his lifetime. Among them is a tale, well invented, if not true, that he produced a great deal of gold for the King of England. There are a number of versions of this alchemical event, all of which illustrate the constant need of monarchs for gold and the eternal hope of getting it easily. In one account Lully transmutes tons of copper and brass to solid gold for Edward III in the Tower of London with the help of an "Abbot Cremer" of Westminster. However, since Edward came to the throne in 1327 and Lully died in 1315, that version is patently an invention. In another, Lully escaped trial by the Inquisition for sorcery by counterfeiting 6 million gold coins for Edward I. The gold was to be used to finance a crusade to the Holy Land. In a third version found in a book, *De Transmutione Animae Metallorum,* attributed to the monk, he went to England at the express invitation of the monarch and enriched the state treasury by tons of gold.

Recent evidence gleaned from historical documents indicates that Lully may indeed have gone to England about 1312 and was responsible for enriching the King. His means were not alchemical, however. It seems he used his renowned wisdom to advise the monarch to impose a new tax on the fine English wool exported to Flanders.

Lully is reputed to have turned fifty pounds of lead and mercury to gold, but like most philosophical alchemists he was a modest, retiring man, little interested in worldly gain. He returned to missionary work in North Africa and was stoned to death by a mob of unreceptive infidels at Bougie when he was eighty. After Lully's death the Lullists, a cult group, steeped in occult practices, gained prominence. The cult, precursors of the Rosicrucians, was especially powerful in Germany. Cult members made the most of Lully's reputation claiming that his soul appeared at their nocturnal meetings, which were often held in wild mountain areas near iron or copper mines. Lully supposedly revealed to them during these mysterious séances the secrets of heaven and taught them the divine art of transmuting common metals into gold.

One of these fascinating chaps was a sixteenth-century Englishman named Edward Kelley, who was associated with the eminent and respected Elizabethan mathematician, astrologer, and alchemist John Dee, who was alternately in and out of favor with Queen Elizabeth. Kelley, whose real name was Talbot, trained for the law, turned his ability to decipher old manuscripts to illicit use. He made a handsome living forging ancient land deeds until he was caught, tried, and sentenced. In punishment his ears were cropped and he was banished from Worcester.

He embarked on his alchemical career quite by accident. Wearing a cap to cover his mutilated ears, Kelley was traveling through Wales when he stopped at a lonely inn. The innkeeper learned that Kelley was an expert at reading Old Gaelic. The hostler reverently brought out a yellowed parchment he had been unable to decipher. Kelley was riveted as he puzzled out an archaic message having to do with the transmutation of metals into gold. After a number of drinks the innkeeper told Kelley, who professed to be only mildly interested, how he came to be in possession of such an unusual manuscript. It seemed there had been a very rich Catholic bishop in the area. When he died the innkeeper, who was a Protestant, had no qualms about digging up his coffin. He was vexed to find nothing in it but the manuscript with two small white balls, one containing a white powder, the other red powder. He had kept the balls and document as curiosities and was delighted when Kelley offered him a modest sum for them. Kelley was elated—sure he had managed to garner some of the legendary philosophers' stone extract, but since he had no knowledge of alchemy he contacted John Dee, already widely known as a powerful magician.

Dee examined the text and the powders and then attempted a transmutation which much to his surprise immediately turned a pound of lead into a pound of gold. Dee and Kelley joined forces. Their fame spread thanks to a number of similar demonstrations, and soon Count Laski, a Polish nobleman who was visiting Elizabeth's court, approached them. Laski was vastly wealthy, but his extravagant tastes threatened to outrun his revenues and he hoped that he might profit from the works of the Englishmen. Kelley's less than sterling character prevailed upon the essentially honest Dee not to let such a golden opportunity slip through their fingers.

The two clairvoyants were known for their séances at which Dee was the medium and Kelley received astral messages. Dee, before meeting Kelley, claimed to have had a visitation from the angel Uriel who left him with a convex black stone with a mirrorlike surface. This mirror of Mexican obsidian is today in the British Museum. Dee claimed that by concentrating on the stone he could converse with beings on other astral planes. This was the tack they took with the Pole. During a séance which they permitted him to attend the count received a "message" that he would one day be the King of Poland and would live forever. He was delighted at such good news and invited the puffers to Poland.

In 1583 Dee, Kelley, their wives and children moved lock, stock, and magic mirror to Laski's castle, where he set them up in a laboratory urging them to manufacture gold. They toiled away at one expensive alchemical experiment after another but managed to make the gullible Laski no gold. When his estate was close to exhaustion, he recognized he had been conned and sent the two puffers off to Prague, where he said they might expect a warm welcome from the mystic Emperor Rudolf. The Emperor was devoted to supporting alchemical research—often at the expense of his other duties. In Prague there is even today a street of narrow little houses in the vicinity of the royal castle called the Street of the Alchemists, and the Polish Government has preserved a number of the sixteenth-century laboratories as museum exhibits.

Kelley had saved a bit of transmutatory powder from the Welsh bishop's tomb for just such a time. The shrewd and learned Holy Roman Emperor was not likely to be as patient as Laski. Kelley, who by this time was in complete control of the weaker Dee, claimed that the angel Uriel had requested that Kelley and Dee exchange wives. Dee acquiesced and turned his lovely young wife over in return for the impudent Kelley's plainer spouse.

In Prague Kelley used his powder to astound the public in a series of transmutatory demonstrations. He made a historically recorded operation at the home of the imperial physician, Dr. Hayek, at which he used one grain of powder to turn a pound of mercury into a pound of gold. Kelley was lionized by society and quite forgot the cautions of Dee that he was not really an adept and could not replace the powder once it was gone. He went to the court of Maximilian II of Germany, where he greatly impressed the King, who rewarded him with the office of Marshal of Bohemia. Kelley's meteoric rise and arrogance embittered the Bohemian nobility, who numbered less successful alchemists among them. At their uging the King finally insisted that he immediately manufacture at least a kilo of the divine powder. Kelly was imprisoned when he refused but soon wangled his release and was sent to work in a guarded Prague laboratory with Dee. Try as they would, they were unable to manufacture any of the red powder. The volatile Kelley, chafing at the unmitigated failures, struck and killed one of the guards and was sent back to prison. Dee was allowed to go back to England, where he petitioned the Queen to intercede for his friend. There is some evidence that to please the old mathematician and occultist, Elizabeth did try unsuccessfully to have Kelley released. Kelley died of injuries sustained as he let himself out of the prison window on a rope made of bed linens in 1597. Dee died a poverty-stricken and dejected old man in 1608. His spirit had been broken when an angry mob who considered him a necromancer in league with the devil burned his library of four thousand volumes and razed his beloved laboratory.

With the specialization of various branches of science the ranks of the alchemists thinned but the lure of magical gold lingered. During the Romantic movement in literature of the nineteenth century, books were filled with stories of alchemists and their achievements. Readers thrilled at the tales but didn't take them too seriously. After World War I there was a flurry of alchemical experimentation. In 1931 the German professor Hans Methe, a twentieth-century alchemist, was positive he had transmuted base metal into gold until analysis showed that the gold came from his eyeglass frame, which had been affected by the mercury fumes.

During the Depression years normally rational men were particularly vulnerable to get-rich-quick schemes. A sharp German named Franz Tausend took advantage of the times and the current interest in popular science to perpetrate a highly profitable swindle. He appeared at various European cities giving spectacular demonstrations to carefully selected private audiences. During his performances he glibly talked of atoms, molecules, metallic composition, and the catalytic power of heat to break down the structure of substances and reassemble them in different form. He looked and sounded eminently respectable and prepared in his field. The prosperous members of the audience were given gratis bits of the gold he produced. When they found that it held up under an assayer's scrutiny, they were most impressed.

Tausend bided his time and then delivered his master stroke. The plumber turned alchemist contacted the wealthy businessmen he had bestowed bits of his Hermetic gold upon. He suggested to each of thirty men that he join the select "164 Society" and invest in his gold-making project on a large scale. Each man was assured he would be greatly enriched by the fruits of Tausend's "vibrational theory of atomic and molecular structure." These normally astute businessmen invested heavily with Tausend, supporting an elaborate laboratory. They received irregular dividends and occasionally were shown a lump of gold made in his laboratory. Tausend was a master at keeping their appetites whetted and suspicions allayed. He assured them that very soon when his procedure was in full operation, the gold they had invested with him would return five thousand pounds sterling in gold every month. Later, he promised there would be gold by the hundreds of pounds, even by the ton. Members of the exclusive society became suspicious when they learned that the former plumber had bought an extensive country estate near his laboratory and was living in an opulent manner. After an investigation the police arrested Tausend but not before his gold-greedy backers had lost half a million dollars.

The ancient alchemists' theories were vindicated in a sense in the twentieth-century nuclear physics laboratory when scientists discovered the philosophers' stone that could indeed transmute metals into gold. In 1936 by bombarding iridium and platinum with a stream of neutrons with energies ranging from 18 million to 38 million volts scientists at the University of California were able to make gold. However, the gold that was produced immediately began to decay giving off streams of electrons and X rays until, within a few hours, it had changed into other less valuable elements. Scientists at Columbia University in New York demonstrated another method of manufacturing gold. Their method entailed placing platinum for some hours near a long glass tube containing a small amount of radium. The radium emitted atomic particles that, by bombardment, changed the platinum, with an atomic weight of 195.25, into gold, with an atomic weight of 197.2 The radioactive gold in turn emitted particles which made possible the detection of the transmutation.

This twentieth-century alchemical gold, helpful for the treatment of cancerous tumors and arthritis, would please the Hermetic scientists of old who sought prolongation of life.

CHAPTER TWELVE *Renaissance Gold*

The Hanseatic merchants in 1532 commissioned their fellow German Hans Holbein the Younger of Augsburg to paint two frescoes in the Guildhall of the Hanse Steelyard in London. Holbein, who was court painter and designer of jewelry for Henry VIII, was asked to depict the Triumphs of Riches and Poverty illustrating the motto of the mighty league: "Gold is the Father of Joy and the Son of Care; He who lacks it is sad, He who has it is uneasy."

In Renaissance Europe gold figured in history as never before. The expansion of commerce and industry led to the rise of a class of prosperous bourgeoisie who supported the production of goldworks which ran the gamut from jewelry and plate to textiles and gold-enriched paintings. Increased gold production in central Europe, Christian control over Iberian gold which came with the expulsion of the Moors, and the outpourings of raw gold from the New World in the sixteenth century made gold widely available.

No longer was the use of gold confined to the nobility and priesthood. Self-confident capitalists using gold to get more gold made those countries which had developed prosperity based on such activities as banking and manufacturing the focus of Renaissance excitement. The Crusades did much to quicken the changes in European life which led up to the Renaissance.

Simple faith motivated many of the thousands of Crusaders, who took up the cross and streamed eastward for two centuries of bloody, sordid wars. Many more were impelled by greed masked as piety. The Roman Church saw in the Crusades the means to extend its dominions and might to the East; the kings and nobles of feudal Europe were aroused at the prospect of riches and territorial acquisition and the Italian cities saw great commercial promise.

The cities of Apulia, Sicily, Pisa, Genoa, and especially Venice, which was already established in the Levantine trade, heaped up profit. In 1101, for example, when Caesarea was sacked, 15 per cent of the great spoil of gold and treasure was earmarked for Genoa's sea captains and officers and the rest split among the eight thousand Genoese soldiers and sailors who each took home forty-eight gold dinars and two pounds of peppercorns. The ambitious Venetians at the beginning of the First Crusade enjoyed exclusive commercial privileges in Constantinople and were in control of the Byzantine Empire's maritime trade. But they did not scruple in 1202 to lead the scandalous Fourth Crusade, which had nothing to do with its avowed objective of liberating Jerusalem but was aimed at sacking Christian Constantinople. The wily Doge, Enrico Dandolo, coerced the host of departing French and Flemish Crusaders into seizing the rival port city of Zara on the Dalmatian coast from the Hungarians on their way to the Holy Land. Zara's population was Christian, and Pope Innocent III threatened all participants with excommunication but the lure of gold was too strong. The Crusaders' fleets took Zara, stripping it of all gold, which was split fifty-fifty. Seeking to preserve a vestige of morality, the Crusaders petitioned the Pope for absolution. He gave it on condition they return Zara's treasures. The Crusaders took the absolution, kept the gold, and then set sail for the conquest and sacking of Constantinople, the Christian capital of Byzantium.

Churches, shops, palaces, homes, were sacked by the gold-crazed Men of the Cross. The Venetians, who knew the city well, left random looting to the others and chose, with discrimination, the most precious goldworks, antiquities, manuscripts, and textiles. The great altar of St. Sophia was stripped and ripped to pieces and the gold, silver, and jewels in every church were rifled in an orgy of looting that not even the Turks matched when they conquered the city in 1453. The gold and bejeweled masterpieces and the four great bronze horses which adorn St. Mark's Basilica in Venice came from that rape.

The epoch of the Crusades made a deep impression on those

who came into contact with the wonders of the East. Countless thousands whose lives in feudal Europe had been bleak and circumscribed brought back an appreciation of eastern culture, a taste for independent action and for the gold that made it possible. Spices, foodstuffs, textiles, medicines, carpets, and crossbows came home with the returning pilgrims and soldiers, changing European life. Words of Arabic origin introduced into European languages during that era such as "mattress," "sofa," "cotton," and "lute" indicate the refinements in living which a small newly born middle class aspired to share with princes of the blood.

The contact between East and West opened up new markets for European goods after the Crusades. Venice, Queen of the Adriatic, was in the most favored position to reap a rich harvest from trade with the East because of her years of close connection with the Eastern Empire during which she had virtually no rival in Mediterranean trade. Venice was known as Venetia Aurea, "Venice, the Golden." No city in Europe boasted such verve, such richness of life, or such devotion to profit. A contemporary Greek wrote, "The Venetians are born of the sea. They are rogues like the Phoenicians but of great cunning." With no hinterland to expand into and no mineral resources, Venice rose out of the mist-shrouded salt marshes settled in the mid-fifth century A.D., to rule the seas and dazzle the world with her naval prowess and consummate commercial genius. Each year after 998 on Ascension Day the Doge was rowed to sea in a magnificent golden galley. As the leading figures of the republic and foreign ambassadors looked on, he acknowledged Venice's debt to the sea, throwing a consecrated gold ring into the Adriatic and symbolically taking dominion over her as a husband over a wife.

The currents of East and West, North and South, met at Venice. Merchandise arrived, changed hands, and departed or was absorbed by her luxury-loving inhabitants. Every transaction brought gold to Venice and made the dynamic city the envy of all. But rivers of gold ducats poured out, draining east as Roman gold had earlier. The market for Asian and African goods was greater than the capacity of those areas to absorb European products. In the fourteenth and fifteenth centuries each year 300,000 gold ducats went from Venice to Alexandria alone, an indication of the unbalanced trade which led to a severe drain on Europe's gold reserves eased only in the sixteenth century by the massive transfusions of American treasure.

The prosperity of much of Europe north of the Alps was due to the activities of the Hanse, a medieval league of free towns in northern Germany and adjoining countries which formed for mutual security and to establish trading monopolies. German capital and German traders had penetrated Scandinavia, Russia, and the Baltic long before the Renaissance. As early as 1000 German merchants were operating in London, and in 1282 they established their own guildhall and steelyard there and enjoyed great privileges until the Elizabethan era.

Foreign merchants with gold to spend were drawn to pre-Renaissance France by the great trade fairs in the industrial towns of Flanders, Champagne, and Normandy. Paris was the bustling capital of a country where relative plentifulness of gold and money favored commerce and during the Renaissance site of a royal court which often led the way in inventing new and marvelous ways of working gold.

Florence, whose wool trade and magnificent florin had made her the financial center of the world with scores of banking houses, was one of a number of Italian cities with a solid bourgeoisie which began to be less concerned with the life hereafter and more attuned to the attractions of the classical past.

European communities, then, were ready to respond, some earlier, some later, to the glorious burst of creative energy that was centered on Florence but flowed throughout the pulsating urban centers of Europe. The Renaissance with its rediscovery of reason and the power of logic over superstition was born in Florence by the Medici rulers who led the rich middle class in nurturing the most brilliant development of artistic and intellectual achievement since Periclean Athens. The humanistic emphasis on worldly pleasure rather than heavenly hope, the patronage of many wealthy clients, and the availability of raw materials gave birth to the great goldsmithing of the Renaissance.

The medieval taste for rich color and lavish use of stones continued into the early Renaissance. Jewelers retained the taste for reducing the ethereal arches and spires of Gothic architecture to a miniature scale, creating miracles of exquisite sculpture in gold and gems. In the workshops of Florence, Rome, and Milan Italian goldsmiths observed the details of surviving Greco-Roman architecture and sought out classical sculptures and antiquities which were being dug up daily from under their feet. Throughout the medieval period classical cameos and intaglios which had miraculously avoided the disfigurement of gold jewelry had been incorporated in such important pieces as royal crowns and scepters. These were the only link with the jeweler's art of the classical world available to the Renaissance goldsmith. The imagery of Renaissance jewelry and ornament was largely inspired by classical and mythological themes. In the early Renaissance before table cutting of stones was perfected, Italian jewelers created masterpieces of sculptural virtuosity out of gold and enamel. They also developed superior white and red enamels which were used to emphasize the design modeled in gold.

The medieval tradition of wearing a badge of rank or devotion on one's cap was popular with men of distinction in the Renaissance as well. Renaissance hat medallions were enameled, set with jewels, and often worked with figures in the round. They were among the most beautiful of Renaissance pieces and the most highly prized. Popes and kings often gave them as gifts. As so much goldsmithing was, they were greatly inspired by miniature paintings. One hat medallion which survived is a sculptural bas-relief from the mid-sixteenth century which depicts a battle scene with twelve minuscule, beautifully delineated gold-suited warriors and eight white horses which stand out against a green enameled background. An earlier hat jewel depicts St. John in the Wilderness in enameled gold in a setting of pearls and diamonds. Cellini, the best known of all Renaissance goldsmiths, described several hat ensigns he executed for clients including one of Hercules and the Nemean lion, one of Leda and the Swan, and another of Atlas bearing a crystal globe, engraved with the signs of the zodiac.

The list of Renaissance artists who had early training in working gold is impressive. Apprenticeship in a goldsmith's bottega was considered excellent preparation for all artistic pursuits. Lorenzo Ghiberti, who boasted that his talents outranked his contemporaries', was trained as an "orefice," as were the sculptor

Donatello; Filippo Brunelleschi, whose architecture derives its beauty from the purity of its proportions; Luca della Robbia; the famed clockmaker Gólpaia; the painter and sculptor Andrea del Verrocchio, in whose bottega Leonardo da Vinci was apprenticed; the multitalented Antonio Pollaiulo; the painters Ghirlandaio, Michelozzo, Caradosso, Andrea Mantegna, Sandro Botticelli; and many more.

Albrecht Dürer, leader of German Renaissance painting, was the son of a goldsmith and apprenticed to his father, one of many artists who owed their exquisite clarity of style to such training. The Elizabethan miniaturist Nicholas Hilliard, who was trained by his goldsmith father, worked in gold throughout his life. He was especially celebrated for his graceful miniature paintings circled by delicate golden frames.

Renaissance imagery north of the Alps spread slowly. The guild system required that every apprentice goldsmith spend time traveling abroad. In 1469 there were 112 master smiths working in London—such international circulation tended to blur national styles and spread the characteristics of the leaders in goldwork. In some northern areas the Gothic style lingered on until printed books of designs for jewelry and plate of classical derivation were widely available. Sophisticated rulers summoned to their courts the goldsmith best suited to the commissions at hand, regardless of nationality.

In the sixteenth century the centers of goldworking were widespread—France, England, Germany, Flanders, and Hungary. Work of note was done in gold-rich Spain, where Toledo carried on a much earlier tradition indulging in a taste for the lavish, exuberant, and often grandiose. Spain's golden textiles were universally prized. Hispano-Saracenic silks enriched with gold threads in geometric patterns were the precursors of later silk stuffs in which gold weft threads formed the figures or in which "Cyprian gold," beaten gold on vellum, was wrapped around a silk or linen core and incorporated into the fabric. These brilliant textiles influenced the elaborate stuffs produced in Sicily, Florence, Lucca, Genoa, and Venice. The weaving centers were also exposed to magnificent examples of brocades and cloth of gold coming from the East. The Chinese exported textiles woven of narrow strips of gilt leather to the Moslem world in the thirteenth and fourteenth centuries. Superb Ming dynasty embroidered badges and roundels worked in gold and silk threads and peacock feather filaments made for enjoyment of highly placed Chinese occasionally reached the West, where they were much admired.

The embroiderers who had used gold threads to illuminate ecclesiastical trappings in the Middle Ages turned to secular themes in the Renaissance. Flemish embroidery was particularly lavish with gold, silk, jewels, and pearls as the paintings of Hans Memling and the Van Ecyks show. French craftsmen in Burgundy evolved a remarkable technique of using gold and dyed silk threads on a ground of couched gold so that the gold shines through the silk making the work resemble the translucent enamels of the period.

French religious embroidery evolved into the most sumptuous Renaissance work which gave maximum splendor to the costumes and palaces of the nobility. An overwhelming richness of effect was achieved by piling gold on gold. Spangles, tinsel, and gold tissue were sometimes sewn onto fabrics already embroidered in gold. In the early seventeenth century women's stomachers were often solidly encrusted with gold and precious stones and men went to battle in gold and gem strewn doublets, provoking Louis XIII to issue a sumptuary decree prohibiting embroidery.

In the first half of the sixteenth century Francis I gave free reign to a galaxy of international talents he assembled at the Parisian court. "*Osez!*" he challenged the most dashing of goldsmiths, "Dare!" Benvenuto Cellini was released from a Roman prison at the request of the cultured French King, who promised "I will choke you with gold." He responded by creating the famous saltcellar now in the Museum in Vienna and the only one of his jewels extant.

Cellini was a mercurial genius, a goldsmith, jeweler, mintmaster, sculptor, and designer whose turbulent life and work were marred by murders, lawsuits, imprisonments, and scrapes of every kind. His unusually frank autobiography details his amours, brawls, and creativity. It gives an intimate account of his experiences in the Rome of Pope Clement VII, whose jeweler and mintmaster he was, of the elegant court of Francis I, and the Florence of Cosimo de' Medici, where he was mintmaster when the first Florentine portrait coins were issued.

The only authenticated piece of his today is the virtuoso Venus and Neptune salt. Critics suggest his fame as a goldsmith is unmerited and cavil at his mannerist tendencies yet tastes have changed and a letter of Michelangelo's to Cellini which has survived reads in part, "I have known you all these years as the greatest goldsmith of whom the world has ever heard." Certainly he embodied the spirit of the age, and his lively immodest "Vita" or the treatise on goldsmithing written to instruct "all those many youths always springing up and eager to learn the beautiful art of the goldsmith" give singular insight into the character of Renaissance talent.

Embossed and richly gilded armor, very little of which has survived, was made throughout the sixteenth century in the French royal workshops. The Louvre school, so called, reached its apogee in mid-century under Henry II crafting such marvels as a parade helmet, now in the Metropolitan Museum in New York, which is completely covered with elaborate patterns and features a swirling scene of the battle between the Lapiths and the centaurs. The goldsmith worked with the blacksmith and armorer to create the magnificent weapons, glittering body armor, and horse trappings which were essential to the knightly culture in tournament and battle.

Golden spurs often bearing his armorial device were a knight's badge of rank and were bestowed upon a novice in the solemn knighting ceremony. Gold, pure, shining, and eternal, was the embodiment of a Christian knight's professed dedication to the ideal. A knight's armor was his prize possession, on which goldsmiths lavished their greatest skill. They covered the entire surface of the pieces of body armor with decoration symbolic of a knight's ideals using a variety of techniques: niello, damascene, filigree, chasing, cloisonné, and casting. A masterpiece of such jewelry is the armor, also in the Metropolitan, from Henry VIII's Royal English Armory at Greenwich made in 1527 for presentation to the Grand Master of the Artillery of France, Galiot de Genouilhac. The gleaming set comprised a full field armor with accessory pieces to be worn in tournament, an armored saddle, and matching horse armor. The entire golden surface was chased with a most elaborate decoration including the Labors of Hercules. It is thought that the armor was designed by Holbein, who was then in England.

Holbein was not himself a goldsmith but a designer of goldworks. From 1537 until his death seven years later he served Henry—painting, decorating and designing jewelry, garments, weapons, tableware, seals, bookbindings, and royal buttons and buckles. Most of Holbein's designs were executed by his goldsmith friend Hans of Antwerp, another foreigner who found the climate of Renaissance England congenial.

Toward the mid-sixteenth century Renaissance goldwork became less static and heavy. Jewelry and even plate became more complex and showy than before as goldsmiths soared on flights of fancy, creating eccentric virtuosities designed to amaze even the most jaded sophisticates. Pendants were exceedingly popular. The vogue for large colorful baroque pearls led to their incorporation into pendants where they formed parts of dragons, mermaids, griffins, lizards, sea horses, or heroes surrounded by the most intricate goldwork, enamel, and inlaid gems.

Two excellent examples of these fanciful jewels are in the Metropolitan. One is attributed to Netherlandish goldsmiths working for Spanish overlords during the occupation of the Low Countries. Two gold chains with gem-set links hang from a gold fleur-de-lis enameled in red, green, white, and black. The chains support an openwork gold-enameled basket hung with three baroque pearls, the chief element of the pendant, which is slightly more than eight inches long. Atop the basket, Zeus in the form of an enameled and jeweled bull gallops away with Europa gracefully reclining on his broad back, her red mantle billowing in the wind. The other pendant is the late-sixteenth-century product of a German workshop and depicts a high-stepping camel, enameled white and garnished with faceted rubies and diamonds in golden frames. A youth in Roman dress is mounted on the exotic beast from each of whose hoofs a large pearl dangles. The head and neck are linked to chains of gold and rubies which terminate in an enameled piece of worked gold set with a diamond.

The epitome of the Renaissance fashion for pendants is the famous ship's jewels. The sixteenth-century emphasis on maritime exploration inspired the creation of ships of gold, stones, and pearls. Some were votive offerings to saints in thanks for a safe return; others were exhanged as tokens of friendship or love. The ship's jewel in the hands of a master Renaissance goldsmith was a tour de force of the jeweler's art with rigging, sails, figurehead, even seamen executed with finesse and regard for detail. One in the Metropolitan in New York is a three-master with a crystal hull and enameled gold keel, decks, and rigging. Among the heirlooms in England's Berkeley Castle is a magnificent ship alleged to have been presented to Queen Elizabeth by Sir Francis Drake. The masts and rigging of pearl-studded, enameled gold rise from a hull of ebony, set with a diamond. On deck Cupid crowns an enameled Victory, and a miniature dinghy dangles below.

The profusion of gold jewelery and golden textiles in Renaissance paintings furnishes a good idea not only of the design of individual pieces but of how they were combined for effect in an era when personal attire reached a peak of magnificence. Bodices and sleeves, stomachers and doublets, were festooned with gold embroidery, pearls, jewels in gold mounts. Gold cords or gold networks were held together with pearls. Golden embroidered flowers were adorned with jewels. Velvet coats and silk farthingales were covered with patterns in gold which glowed true even as long use and infrequent cleaning dimmed the beauty of the fabric. An important element in sixteenth-century dress was the ruff, which Catherine de' Medici brought to France in 1533. It quickly became popular in England and was described in 1583 by a certain Philip Stubbes, who wrote that they were "pleated and crested ful curiously, God wot. Then last of all they are either clogged with golde, silver or silk lace of stately price, wrought all over with needle woork, speckled and sparkled here and there with the sonne, the moone, the stares, and many other antiquities straunge to beholde."

Holbein's many portraits of Henry VIII, who epitomized the High Renaissance love of ostentatious display, show him weighted down with gold. The extravagant Henry was perpetually short of money, having run through his great inheritance in short order. He not only debased the currency but confiscated the accumulated gold and treasures of the monasteries to finance his wars and furnish his jewelry. From the Shrine of St. Thomas à Becket alone he got two enormous storage chests, so filled with jewels and gold that it took eight men to lift them. Henry kept his goldsmiths busy creating the most splendid personal ornaments. His attire on one occasion is described by the Venetian ambassador in a letter home. "He wore a cap of crimson velvet in the French fashion, and the brim was looped up all around with gold enamelled tags . . . very close around his neck he wore a gold collar, from which there hung a rough cut diamond, the size of the largest walnut I ever saw, and from this was suspended a most beautiful and large round pearl . . . over his mantle was a very handsome gold collar with a pendant of St. George entirely of diamonds . . . and his fingers were one mass of jewelled rings."

Gold chains were very much in fashion in the sixteenth century. In most countries they were part of male attire, although in Flanders and Germany women wore them and almost every portrait by Lucas Cranach the Elder after 1506 shows ladies with numbers of such chains. The English chronicler Edward Hall distinguishes a man's rank and wealth by his gold chains. At a court fete he noted that "every garment was full of poysees, made of letters of fine gold in bullion as thicke as they might be, and every person had his name in like letters of massy gold." Henry VIII had a chain of massive links which weighed ninety-eight ounces, and Sir Percival Hart is shown in a portrait with a tremendous chain with links like fetters. In Tudor times such "masseye gold cheynes" were given as presents to ambassadors and gentlemen who performed a service for the sovereign.

Perhaps because there were a considerable number of powerful women who reigned during the Renaissance, goldsmiths devised elaborate little accessories for women to hang about them. These included pomanders, delicate spheres of gold openwork, some in the form of pomegranates to hold perfumes or ambergris which a lady lifted to her nose to dispel unpleasant odors. A variety of other trinkets might hang from a lady's girdle including small enameled and jeweled devotional book covers, scissors, whistles for calling the servants, magnifying glasses in gold frames, and gold-covered pages for the household accounts.

A majority of the Renaissance jewels extant probably come

from the workshops of two northern cities—Augsburg and Nuremberg—which shone above all others until the Thirty Years' War ended Germany's eminence in goldwork. Augsburg was the home of the great Fugger banking dynasty and of the comparably wealthy Welser banking family. Augsburg, in Bavaria, was where the trade routes between northern Europe and Italy crossed. The "Golden Counting House" of the Fuggers lent money to kings, the Church, states, and cities. The Fuggers were richer than any private family had ever been. In 1519 Jakob Fugger was so incredibly wealthy he had enough liquid capital to lend Charles V 544,000 gold florins out of a total of 852,000 he needed. In return for the loan the Emperor handed over the lease of the revenues of the Spanish mines. The Fuggers also held the lease on the papal mint for almost twenty years during which time Cellini was employed as mintmaster and engraved a number of magnificent papal dies.

The founder of the line was a fourteenth-century weaver whose sons entered the textiles trade. The family rose to almost frightening power through the profits of an intensive banking and commercial network which had agents in every important center from Seville to London and Antwerp to Venice. The famous Fugger newsletters, which kept the family at Augsburg abreast of international happenings, dealt with such matters as delayed shipments of Spanish gold from America, a report that the government of Venice had a well-known alchemist named Bragadini producing vast amounts of gold coins for them, and who was wearing what jewelry at a reception at the French court.

The Fuggers controlled much of the lucrative cloth trade and multiplied their golden fortunes with monopolistic interests in gold, silver, copper, and iron mines in the Tyrol, Hungary, and Carinthia and in the mercury mines of Spain. They were devout Catholics and lovers of art—perfect patrons for the goldsmiths and jewelers who were drawn to Augsburg.

Nuremberg was, if possible, an even richer city, for it lay at a juncture of the trade between the Mediterranean and the north and served for a time as the intermediary between Italy and the Orient. Both the great Bavarian cities were destined to decline because of the discovery of the Americas and the new sea route to India. So, in fact, were many of the other centers grown rich through trade in eastern luxuries which were eclipsed by Portugal and Spain whose mariners discovered new worlds.

Venice stands out as an example of a city adversely affected by the Age of Discovery. Yet in the thirteenth-century Venetians had been among Europe's boldest travelers. The republic had been in the fortunate position of being the conduit through which the gold and silver of Europe were channeled into the markets of Africa, India, and Asia. She profited from the processing, coining, transporting, and exchanging of the precious metals. Venetian law stipulated that bullion had to be refined before export. Goldsmiths staffed the mint where the gold of the Balkans, Hungary, and Germany was struck as ducats. Other smiths crafted the magnificent plate and jewelry favored by the merchant aristocracy.

To keep ahead of mounting competition from the other Italian merchant republics, the Venetian trading network had been extended to southern Russia and the Black Sea, where several important caravan routes from central Asia terminated and merchandise from the Persian Gulf ports was brought for trade. The clever merchant princes of Venice were always alert to profitable opportunities and were among the first Europeans to travel in the East.

Two brothers, Niccolò and Matteo Polo, father and uncle of the more famous Marco, were typical of the adventurous, self-confident capitalists who established connections in the East during the late Middle Ages. Others had preceded the Polo brothers.

The best known of these early travelers was a portly aged Franciscan, John of Pian de Carpini, who wrote in detail about the Mongol Khan's court, his "Golden Orda," a huge brocade tent supported by golden columns. For Guyuk Khan's thirteenth-century enthronement, which he witnessed, the Golden Orda was set up on a river plain in view of lofty mountains. A great feast was held of mare's milk, mead, and boiled meat in salted broth. Afterward the King ascended the throne "which was of gold, ivory and set with pearls and precious stones." The Khan received the papal emissary but paid him and his European companion scant honor. They received barely enough food to keep alive, Carpini noted, and couldn't even buy any because the market was too far away. "If the Lord had not sent us a certain Russian, by the name Cosmas, a goldsmith and a favorite of the Emperor, who supported us to some extent, we would, I believe, have died."

In 1253 St. Louis sent William of Rubruck, a Fleming, to the court of the Khan, and then two years later the Polo brothers traveled to central Asia. They were jewelers who had a trading station in Constantinople and branches in the Crimea where agents purchased gems from the Far Eastern caravans. They spent three years in Bukhara and were received at the court of the Kublai Khan, where they lingered several years. They left with letters to the Pope and a golden tablet which served as their safe conduct through the vast Mongol domains to Acre, the Crusader port in modern Israel, which they reached in 1269. Those early journeys were leisurely affairs; the traders had been away for thirteen years and returned to find Niccolò's wife dead and his son, Marco, a lad of fifteen.

Two years later the brothers, accompanied by Niccolo's son Marco, set out for the Kublai Khan's court, via Baghdad, Pamir, and thence across the Gobi Desert. The two older men were medieval merchants who limited their observations to commercial affairs. But Marco Polo, as his book reveals, foreshadowed the Renaissance with his intellectual curiosity, and delight in experience for its own sake. The Kublai Khan, whose grandfather had led his horsemen out of Mongolia to take China, ruled over an area which united most of Asia, the Near East, and eastern Europe. He took a liking to the bright young Venetian, and for fifteen years Marco Polo served him traveling through much of China, Cochin China, Burma, and India and then returning to Italy by sea by way of Sumatra, India, and Persia.

Marco Polo observed, absorbed, and recorded with sympathy and verve what he saw and heard during those twenty-four years. His famous *Book of Various Experiences* was dictated while he was a prisoner in Genoa in 1297. It immediately became popular and, more than any other account, colored the geographic outlook of the succeeding two hundred years. Although he was not the first European in Asia, he created it for the western mind. It was the handbook of every gold seeker. Columbus, took it with him in 1492 when he set out to find the gold-roofed palaces of Cipango (Japan) which Polo had described second-hand. His book is filled with gold and provided the impetus for many of the ocean voyages at the dawn of the age of exploration.

Thirteenth-century China was a highly civilized and prosperous state with many bustling industrial towns and ports thronged with ships laden with the precious spices, gold, silver, cotton, and textiles of India, Ceylon, and the Indonesian archipelago. Revenue poured into the customs houses and tribute in gold, silver, precious gems, horses, tigers, and weapons poured into the gilded Mongol capital from vassal states.

Marco Polo described the elaborate rituals of the court at Peking. The Khan thirteen times a year bestowed rich robes of cloth of gold adorned with pearls and stones to his twelve thousand barons and knights. Polo reckons the value of some of the robes at ten thousand gold bezants. The palace was of amazing size and loveliness. "The inside walls of the halls and rooms are all covered with gold and silver and on them are painted beautiful pictures of ladies and knights and dragons and beasts. . . . The ceiling is also made in such a way that no one sees anything else on it but pictures and gold. The great hall is so large that quite six thousands men could banquet there."

Polo noted that the Khan, a handsome well-made man who habitually dressed in robes of gold, had four legitimate wives who were greatly honored and in addition countless concubines, who were selected in a rather unusual manner. Every second year he sent agents to the Tartar province of Ungrat, renowned for its beauties. The recruiters appraised the charms of the Tartar maidens feature by feature, as if they were examining gold. Some damsels, Polo explained, "were appraised at 16 carats, others at 17, 18, 20 or more or less, according as they are more or less beautiful. And if the Great Khan has ordered that those to be brought to him should be of 20 or 21 carats, the required number of that value are taken to him."

The gold accumulated by the Khan paid for the luxuries of his court, which was opulent but not decadent, for the Mongol ruler was a man of scholarly interests and moderate tastes. He established an excellent system of provincial administration with a fine network of roads and grain and clothing for the urban poor. He accepted no substitute for gold as payment of taxes, yet the money issued from his mint was the famous "flying money" which rulers in China had developed in the third century B.C.

The first flying money was made from foot-square pieces of skin from an albino stag slain by Emperor Shih Huang Ti. Kublai Khan had money made of the underbark of the mulberry tree. "It is so arranged," wrote Polo, "that one may well say the Great Khan is an alchemist!"

In the course of his duties Polo traveled over much of the empire, even in areas so remote that the Khan's paper money was unknown. In Tibet, where abundant gold was found in several streams rising in the eastern zone and women made marvelous gold cloths, he found coral used as a medium of exchange. In Yunnan another product of the distant sea circulated as money—cowrie shells from Bengal, which may have reached China via the trade fairs organized on the Indian and Burmese borders of the empire where foreign merchants, not allowed to enter China, came to conduct trade. Chinese traders penetrated the inhospitable mountains beyond the frontier to trade silver for gold, exchanging it at a rate of 5 to 1 with tribespeople who were heavily tattooed and covered their teeth with gold plates.

Polo noted that many of the rivers of Yunnan contained gold dust and in the province of Karazan gold was found as dust, in nuggets, and in veins in the mountains. In the western part of the empire in Kain-Du Province the money of larger denominations was gold formed into small rods which were cut in certain lengths and circulated with no markings. Money of less value was in the form of salt cakes bearing the Khan's stamp. Eighty salt cakes were worth "a saggio of gold" (the saggio of Venice was a sixth of an ounce). Polo mentioned that in the remotest mountain areas the uncivilized people who collected gold were so avid for salt that they eagerly traded a saggio of gold for as few as forty or fifty salt cakes. The Venetian noted more than a dozen major sources of gold in his book, including several like Japan and Borneo he had not visited himself but had heard much of.

The island of Japan lay tantalizingly beyond the Khan's grasp. The Chinese believed that the people of Cipango, as it was known, lived in golden palaces whose brilliant spires pierced the sky. Polo repeats the words of a Chinese visitor to the Japanese royal palace who described walls and floors covered with gold, golden furniture, and windows with golden ornaments. These were the visions which danced before Columbus as he vainly sought a sign of golden spires amid the rude thatched huts of the Antilles.

In 1542 Japan was inadvertently discovered by two Portuguese castaways who wrecked on the shore. Three years later Mendes Pinto, a Portuguese pirate, visisted Japan briefly. His glowing reports of the magnificence of the court and great amounts of gold spurred the Portuguese to initiate trade with the reluctant xenophobic Japanese. It seems that in the early fifteenth century the Japanese had discovered a number of rich gold sources which allowed the introduction of a gold currency. Gold dust was packed in bamboo tubes or encased in brocade pouches and valued by weight. Trade in feudal Japan was considered demeaning and money unclean. So the little bags or tubes were not opened from one generation to the next, merely weighed when they changed hands. Gold was also formed into ingots or plates and pieces cut off to the value of each transaction.

In the late sixteenth century raw gold was cast into "oban," which were five-inch-long oval gold planchets of fixed weight. They bore the government crest of four flowers and were inscribed in India ink with the name of the mint supervisor and the value. The beautiful oban had a very limited circulation. They were primarily reserved for ceremonial presentations or transactions among the nobility. One oban was worth almost a ton of the copper coins used in everyday transactions. Later they were employed to pay for European imports brought to Japan by the Dutch from Batavia (Jakarta) in the East Indies who had exclusive trading privileges with the Japanese from 1624 to 1853.

Portuguese trade stimulated the organization of Japanese gold mining, and by the mid-sixteenth century the relatively modest annual production from alluvial washings had burgeoned into a yield of about ten thousand pounds. A great deal of the gold came from Sado, which the Portuguese called "a treasure island made of nothing but gold and silver." Missionaries led by St. Francis Xavier Christianized a number of the noble families and it was from them that they got most of the gold. The nobles and priests enslaved segments of the population to work in the mines. In 1638 the Portuguese traders were expelled and Japan was closed off from the outside world save for contact through a few Chinese traders and the Dutch, who were subjected to many indignities but tolerated because of the extraordinarily high returns on the Japanese trade.

In the early 1700s the Japanese restricted the number of Dutch vessels calling at Japan to two a year and fixed artificially high prices on their merchandise and on gold, making trade unprofitable for the Dutch. The government was moved to such action in part by a desire to reduce foreign contamination. Another motive was offered in a petition presented to the Shogun in 1706 by a finance minister. "A thousand years ago," he wrote, in a vein reminiscent of Greek race memories of a Golden Age, "gold, silver and copper [the mainstay of the Dutch trade] were unknown in Japan, yet there was no lack of what men needed. The earth was fertile and produced the best sort of wealth. Gangin was the first prince who caused the mines to be worked diligently and during his reign so great a quantity of gold and silver was extracted from them as no one could have any conception of, and since these metals resemble the bones of the human body, inasmuch as what is once extracted from the earth is not reproduced, if the mines continue to be thus worked in less than a thousand years they will be exhausted.

"Since these metals were discovered the heart of man has become more and more depraved. With the exception of medicines we can dispense with everything that is brought to us from abroad. The stuffs and other articles are of no real benefit to us. If we squander our treasure in exchange for them what shall we subsist on? Let the successors of Gangin reflect on this matter, and the wealth of Japan will last as long as the heavens and the earth."

The Chinese have a much longer tradition in goldwork than the Japanese, although gold does not appear to have been abundant in ancient times. There was little gold coinage, and the copious Chinese chronicles make scant mention of mining or gold gathering. Tombs have been, as in so many parts of the world, the prime source of information about early goldworking. Goldsmiths of the rich Bronze Age culture of the Shang dynasty (circa

1400) knew how to fire-gild bronze axes. During the Chou dynasty (1000–256 B.C.) international trade in copper, silk, salt, fish, and then iron brought material wealth to Chinese who commissioned gold and jade ornaments.

Chou goldsmiths excelled at inlaying gold, sometimes in combination with green malachite or turquoise, in bronze. The inlay was made either by fashioning a mosaic of minute gold wires side by side to fill the desired space or by cutting gold plate into a desired shape and fitting it into the apposite depression cut in the bronze. Gold plaques, perhaps made for attachment to lacquered wood coffins, were made in the form of beasts with birdlike beaks. The surfaces were worked in repoussé with striations, rope patterns, scales, and various flourishes. Chariot and horse trappings and gold vessels have also been found decorated with hammered areas giving smooth contoured relief. Within the contoured zones the Chou smiths chased intricate patterns. They were also skilled at casting. Gold grave goods excavated from Chou tombs include a belt hook, almost five inches long, cast in the form of a dragon whose swirling tail scallops around a smooth piece of jade and a gold hilt from a small dagger in the shape of a pair of animal heads grasping an oval ring of light green jade.

Han China rivaled the Roman Empire in splendor, wealth, and might. The goldsmiths of the Han dynasty (202 B.C.–A.D. 222) were admirably skilled. Sumptuous examples of their work has been found in numerous tombs in China and Korea, confirming the splendor of the period. In 1968 Chinese soldiers stumbled on cave tombs hewn out of cliffs in Hopei Province near Peking. The archaeological world was amazed and delighted at the wealth of objects found in the precisely dated (113 B.C.) tomb. Among the items found were the now famous jade funerary suits. Archaeologists were familiar with literary accounts of the elaborate burial customs of Han feudal lords of two thousand years ago, but the discovery of the tombs of Liu Sheng, Prince Ching, and his consort, the princess Tou Wan, provided the first complete funerary suits.

The two multichambered tombs contained 2,800 Han artifacts, including a number of bronze vessels inlaid with gold, cast-gold animal head finials, two beautiful and intricately decorated gilded bronze containers, tubes with gold rings, dozens of gold repoussé ornaments and silks, a number of exquisite small gold and silver *t'ao-t'ieh* masks, and the remarkable Poshan incense burner inlaid with gold in an elaborate pattern. Its lid is shaped like a mountain with undulating peaks over which hunters give chase to wild beasts.

The most stunning of the artifacts were the shrouds fashioned of jade plaques held together with flexible gold wire. Each funerary suit took an estimated ten years to make. Such funerary armor was bestowed upon high-ranking nobility by the Emperor. Jade was believed to guard the wearer through eternity and preserve the body forever. But when the princess' tomb was opened a pinch of dust was all that remained of her. The suit of 2,156 handcrafted jade plaques was still held together by twenty-four ounces of gold wire, some of it twelve fine strands wound together. The prince's body had been encased in a similar suit of 2,690 plaques. They covered the entire bodies—a helmet, a face mask, a trunk-encasing part with the arms and fingers separately sheathed, trousers, and shoes for the feet.

The T'ang dynasty was China's Golden Age, and a variety of T'ang goldworks from tombs, including those of an emperor, an empress, and several princes, attest to the full flowering of the goldsmith's art during the period from A.D. 618 to 907. In one burial a carved stone outer coffin held three nested gold and silver caskets each inlaid with precious and semiprecious stones.

In 1970 near modern Sian workers found two pottery jars which held 1,023 pieces of gold, silver, gems, gold jewelry, jade objects, Chinese and foreign coins, and medicinal minerals such as amethyst, stalactites, and cinnabar—a marvelous hoard. Among the objects were a Byzantine gold coin of Heraclius (A.D. 610–641), a Sassanian silver coin of Chosroes II (A.D. 590–627), and five Japanese coins of the early eighth century.

The T'ang goldsmiths worked with supreme confidence, favoring naturalistic forms and rich surface decoration over the geometric and animal designs of archaic goldsmiths. Supernatural beasts gave way to rich foliate designs or patterns depicting people and familiar creatures. Two octagonal gold cups from the Sian hoard are enlivened with musicians and dancers depicted in high relief on each facet. A cup is shaped like a lotus, a dish like a peach. Foxes, lions, horses, parrots, ducks, and tortoise sport among leaves and flowers on a variety of gilded silver vessels. No technique was too difficult for the accomplished T'ang goldsmith. He excelled at the most delicate openwork filigree, the finest granulation, casting, tracing, repoussé, inlay, and soldering. Often the repoussé pictorial element of silver pieces was gilded and the background ring-matted for emphasis. Ring-matting was done with a ring-outline tracer which, when hammered, made a pattern of fine circles.

In the following centuries the goldsmiths of the Sung, Yuan, and Ming dynasties continued to produce goldworks of high technical and artistic level, often combining gold and silver for a magnificent effect. Gold bowls, boxes, combs, earrings, and hairpins have been found, some inlaid with precious stones and almost all richly decorated with a profusion of graceful, refined designs. Chinese goldsmiths produced enameled gold objects which displayed the subtlety of coloring so well known from Chinese ceramics. Gold was also widely used in lacquering and in textiles.

The peoples of ancient Southeast Asia also had a long history of goldworking. The tribes living by the Gulf of Thailand in the first century A.D., for example, united to form the dynamic kingdom of Funan, which produced lovely, sensitive gold jewelry. They were open to the cultural currents brought from India by traders who established trading posts among them. An excavation at Oc Ēo brought to light sophisticated treasures in gold and gems including a gold ring surmounted by a sitting bull, a gold and sapphire ring, necklaces of variously shaped gold beads, an elaborate dagger pommel with soldered floral decoration, gold bells, buckles, and pins, and also an interesting Roman gold medal dated A.D. 152, portraying the Emperor Antoninus Pius.

About 1300 A.D. Chou Ta-kuan returned from a trip to the Khmer kingdom of Cambodia. The Chinese chronicler wrote of the all powerful deva-raja, the god-king, and his court and of eight great golden statues of the Buddha. He described a tower of gold which stood at the very center of the kingdom. More than twenty stone towers and hundreds of stone cells surrounded it. A second large tower was made of copper. In a third, covered with gold, were the King's apartments. Outside a gold-covered bridge was flanked by lions of gold. The interior of the palace was said to be filled with gold and other treasures, but the Chinese visitor was forbidden entrance.

He did view, however, a public appearance of the King. He headed a parade of five hundred palace maidens who carried lighted torches in spite of the daylight. The gold and silver paraphernalia of the court including gold table plate was displayed by a troop of richly costumed girls who marched in the procession. They were followed by a unit of girls bearing arms who were the King's private guard. Then came carriages, all decorated with gold, as were the trappings of the goats and horses which pulled them. The ministers and princes of the Cambodian court shaded by scarlet parasols paraded on elephants. The King's four wives and four hundred concubines filed by in a panoply of gold parasols, elephants, palanquins, and carriages. The deva-raja appeared standing on a huge elephant, whose tusks were wrapped with gold. His escorts carried twenty gold-decorated parasols of white silk with golden handles.

"It is all these wonders," writes the Khan's emissary, "which we think have inspired merchants to speak glowingly of 'rich and noble Cambodia' since they first came here."

Despite the gems of geographical and ethnographic knowledge amassed by Polo and presented to the European world, cartographers persisted in clinging to their traditional misconceptions. The medieval period was rich in geographical romances, which mingled strong elements of mineral and spiritual gold. Maps of the early Middle Ages showed Jerusalem at the center of the world with the Garden of Eden slightly north of it and Paradise at varying sites in the East. The ancient legend of the gold of Ophir was closely linked to Paradise. Explorers sought the source of Solomon's gold and other golden lands, even more will-o'-the-wisp, well into the modern era.

The greatest golden myth of all was that of Prester John. The mysterious Christian priest-king spawned myriad works of pious fiction which were a synthesis of implausible marvels from many sources. As early as A.D. 1120 reports of "Presbyter Johannes" circulated in Europe following the arrival at the papal court of a mysterious character who styled himself "John, Patriarch of the

Indians." He stayed in Rome for two years amazing the Lateran with tales of his country through which flowed the paradisical river Physon "whose clear waters cast forth the most precious gold and gems." He described the golden shrine of the Apostle Thomas which housed the saint's perfectly preserved body in a great silver shell which opened so the saint might miraculously offer consecrated wafers at mass "so carefully that one would take him to be not dead but living."

Actual exploits of various eastern figures such as Genghis Khan were attributed to the composite figure of Prester John. Marco Polo sparked a hunt for a "Golden King" in central Asia by describing his opulent court in his book. The nomadic Moslems of central Asia had been defeated by a Chinese-educated Buddhist, the ruler of Black Cathay in the early twelfth century. By the time report of the bloody battle had traveled over two thousand miles to Syria with traders, the Buddhist had become a Christian priest-king John, who ruled over a vast area "beyond Persia and Armenia." Bishop Hugh of Syria sent an intelligence report to the Pope in Rome saying this King, descendant of the Magi, wished to come to the aid of the beleaguered Christians in Jerusalem but couldn't breach the Tigris. With time the search for John's golden kingdom focused on Ethiopia.

Crusading Europe was desperately eager to believe in the existence of a devout and mighty Christian potentate somewhere in the East who would come to their aid in the fight against the Infidel. Vague reports of garbled fact and medieval fancy prepared the West for the mysterious arrival at Constantinople in 1165 of a letter addressed to Emperor Manuel I, who was, despite the decline of the Byzantine Empire, the world's most powerful monarch. The document written in Latin and signed by "Presbyter Johannes" electrified Europe. It came to be known as "The Letter" and was the greatest literary hoax of the Middle Ages. It sparked a centuries' long gold rush which propelled men into unexplored zones of Asia and Africa.

The Byzantine Emperor forwarded the long letter describing the golden realms and great deeds of Prester John to Barbarossa and to Pope Alexander III. The Letter was immediately copied; one hundred manuscript copies of the Latin version alone have survived. Countless versions of it made the rounds. With each copying the text was shamelessly embellished with elements ransacked from Greek and Roman sources, Sinbad's adventures, the accounts of early European and Arab travelers to Asia and Africa, and medieval bestiaries. In the fourteenth century the French version by the famous traveler and physician Sir John Mandeville became a best seller, popular as late as the eighteenth century.

The original letter really needed no enlivening. It was filled with page after page of marvels and was most likely written by a western monk or learned Crusader who had been in the East and was familiar with both eastern and Byzantine legends. The author may have concocted the document to amuse, but it is more plausible that his aim was to rally the sagging spirits of the Crusaders with the promise of an ally powerful and wealthy beyond compare.

Whatever his intentions were, the net result was that goldseekers, traders, and missionaries were drawn to Ethiopia and the opulent court of Prester John who had described a magnificent fairyland palace where he slept on a bed of sapphire in a chamber of gold and gems, a river filled with precious stones and gold, and two burning mountains flanking a mountain of gold. The treasure seekers were not put off by the "many monsters there, such as griffins that guard the golden mountains."

It was well known that Ethiopia was ruled by a Christian monarch and was very rich in gold. In the sixth century A.D. Cosmas Indicopleustes visited the Axumite kingdom in northern Ethiopia and southwestern Arabia writing of the great trading caravans which twice yearly pushed into the interior to trade salt, iron, and cattle for gold. The Byzantine Emperor Justinian had sent an ambassador to Axum in the sixth century who returned with tales of the King's gold throne, costume, and shield and his gold chariot pulled by four elephants. Until the Moslems occupied the Ethiopian coast and isolated Axum, cultivated ambassadors from the golden Christian kingdom had graced the courts of Byzantium, India, and Persia.

In the thirteenth century Ethiopia had regained some of her former splendor, and European travelers returning in the early fourteenth century from Egypt reported the Sultan of Egypt paid annual tribute to "Prester John" in the form of a solid gold ball topped with a cross. The incident upon which these reports were based was the threat made by the Ethiopian King 'Amda-Seyon, who vowed to turn Egypt into a desert by cutting off the flow of Ethiopian waters which feed the Nile if the Sultan didn't halt persecution of Egypt's Coptic Christians.

Egypt and Ethiopia thus established relations, and for the first time in almost eight hundred years there was contact between one of the world's most ancient sources of gold and the Mediterranean as the caravan routes to Alexandria were reopened. The gold of Africa—West Africa, Ethiopia, Nubia, and southeastern Africa—played an important part in the dawn of the modern age. The legends of Prester John, the golden Empire of Monomotapa, Ophir, and the River of Gold beckoned enticingly to the Renaissance adventurer, luring many men to dusty deaths and watery graves as they expanded the known world. Portuguese explorers, under Prince Henry the Navigator, the greatest patron of discovery, led the way in tracking the illusory myths to golden conclusions

Without the lure of gold it is unlikely the epoch-making voyages would have been undertaken. Portugal until the fifteenth century was little more than a strife-torn appendage of Spain, a poor agricultural state insulated from the more advanced parts of Europe. When João of Avis, Prince Henry's father, came to the throne, post-Crusade Europe was facing an acute shortage of gold. The demand for imported luxuries was insatiable. Gold flowed through Venetian and Genoese hands into the pockets of Arab and Indian merchants. The Moslems were doubly enriched because the major source of European gold was that of sub-Saharan Africa controlled by the Moslem Tuareg and desert Arabs. Gold for Europe also came from the southeastern African area, also in Moslem control. The European mines no longer produced sufficient gold and silver to make up for the outflow of bullion.

Money was short, currencies debased, and inflation rocking every state. The collapse of the Byzantine Empire, the Hundred Years' War, and upheavals in eastern Europe greatly increased the drain on Europe's gold. It was imperative that new sources be found. The Arabs were understandably secretive about their gold supplies. It would be a stunning victory if Portugal could find a way to gain control of the West African gold trade and eliminate the Arab middlemen.

The Portuguese were not alone in eying the African gold. In 1450 the powerful mercantile banking house of Centurione in Genoa sent a prospector-banker named Malfante to find out precisely where the renowned gold of Wangara came from and how to procure it directly. He traveled as far south as the Saharan oasis of Tuat, where he learned there was no gold in the desert as Europeans had thought but that it came by Arab caravan from very much farther south. "I have asked often enough where the gold is found and collected," he wrote to a friend. "My protector answered me, 'I spent 14 years among the Negroes and always kept my ears open but I never found anyone who could state from certain knowledge, "I have seen it thus, or it is found and collected so." ' "

Queen Philippa, João's English-born Queen, had dreamed of cutting into the Arab gold trade and the Italian monopolies of the spice markets. The determined Queen urged her husband to obtain a stronghold on the North African coast and seek an overland route east to the Red Sea ports where Arab dhows sailing from the Malabar coast of India brought the spices, cosmetics, gums, perfumes, dyes, medicines, and incense that all fell into the broad category of "spices." She and others postulated that somewhere in the heart of the great continent was the friendly kingdom of Prester John, who could support the Portuguese efforts.

Philippa's dreams didn't materialize quite as she had foreseen. There were hostile Moors and shifting desert sands with no oasis of Christianity. However, her celibate and pious son Henry pursued the vision of forming a mighty Christian alliance to outflank the Moslems and at the same time find a sea route which would lead to the gold of Africa as well as to Ethiopia and thence to India. In 1415 the Portuguese had taken Ceuta from the Moors and Henry was made governor of the strategic "key to the Mediterranean." Ceuta, overlooking the Strait of Gibraltar, was a terminus of the caravans bringing Guinea, (African) gold across the Sahara. The palaces and warehouses of the Arab city yielded an impressive amount of golden treasure to the Portuguese victors. Arab informants told young Henry of the River of Gold which emptied into the sea somewhere below the bulge of Cape Bojador, on the West African coast, and of the rich trading center of Cantor on the Gambia River. A Tuareg described the fabulous golden city of Timbuktu and of camel trains of three hundred beasts laden with gold. Henry also heard of the Senegal River, long thought to be a western branch of the Nile which would lead across Africa to Prester John's realms.

Henry established a school of navigation at Lagos and a great center at Sagres, a rocky promontory on Portugal's southwest coast, which was the nerve center for Portuguese exploration. The prince himself never traveled farther than Ceuta, but for forty years he presided over his informal center which attracted scores of captains, navigators, geographers, and historians. He enlisted Jewish astronomers and Moslem cartographers in his grand enterprise and signed up Spaniards, Italians, Germans, and Danes to sail for him.

From 1418 onward, little by little the systematic voyages of discovery probed farther down the forbidding westerly bulge of Africa, through what the Arabs called the "Green Sea of Darkness." The Atlantic voyagers of antiquity, the accounts in Herodotus and Pliny, had been forgotten. Sailors trembled at the thought of piercing the unknown southern waters teeming with frightful monsters and clogged with vast zones of slime too thick to sail through. Cape Bojador's powerful currents and thunderous waves crashing on offshore reefs intimidated the most seasoned mariners who had inherited the Arab belief that the world ended in boiling water just south of the cape.

In 1433 the first ship managed to round Cape Bojador without any of the anticipated nightmares. From then on expansion was rapid as gold and slaves, "Black Gold," began to flow into Portugal. In 1455 Alvise da Ca Da Mosto, a Venetian in the service of Prince Henry, explored the Senegal and Gambia rivers and discovered the Cape Verde Islands. His objective was to pinpoint the elusive Wangara region in the swampy area of the middle Niger. In his search for gold Ca Da Mosto's keen eye noted every detail of African life. He recorded his impressions, delighting in natural beauty, the tropical flora and fauna, and the curious customs of the local chieftains who often received him with a great show of hospitality. He failed to find the gold fields but brought back a great deal of information on the gold trade, which was carried on as the silent barter of the Phoenicians had been.

The Tuareg brought great salt blocks across the desert to Timbuktu, a journey of some forty days. From there they traveled another thirty days to southeastern Mali, where they exchanged the salt slabs for gold with local traders. The salt was broken into smaller pieces by the African traders and carried into the tangled interior on the heads of porters. Somewhere in the marshes of the middle Niger in a traditional clearing the small salt blocks were set in rows by each merchant. They withdrew, coming back the next day to find a pile of gold beside each piece of salt. If the exchange was considered fair, the gold was removed; if not, the trader retired again and waited. It was said no one ever saw the people of the thick forests, although some men alleged they had the heads and tails of dogs.

Today the ancient caravan routes are still traversed by camel trains carrying salt slabs from the Sahara to the Niger, where they are taken upriver to market in Mali. But they are no longer exchanged for gold, and Timbuktu, the sophisticated "City of Gold," famed as far as Venice and Genoa for its libraries and mosques, is now a drab and drowsy provincial town with no hint of its former glory.

The people of West Africa have retained their ancestors' love of gold. The Malinke, descendants of the ancient gold kings, are prohibited by the Mali Government from mining gold and encouraged to grow tobacco, but they still revere the tribal treasures handed down generation after generation. The Fulani and the Peul, nomads of the Niger Delta, display their wealth in gold ornaments. Women wear giant lunate earrings of gold, sometimes so heavy that a head strap must be worn to support them. As a family's fortunes grow, through marriage or an increase in cattle, gold is added to the earrings. In addition, women wear gold finger and nose rings, bracelets, and neck ornaments decorated with patterns in filigree and repoussé work.

The rich past of the Akan coastal tribes is evoked in twentieth-century ceremonies which feature ancestral treasures as well as newer objects fashioned by goldsmiths who carry on the artistic traditions of West Africa. The gold-filled ceremonies of the Twi-speaking Ashanti region of Ghana are especially colorful. The 2 million Ashanti are descended from trading and agricultural peoples united in the 1670s under the sign of the Golden Stool. The early Ashanti culture was centered on the gold trade. Gold and later slaves were exchanged for firearms, used to gain control of the trade routes from the coast to the northern Sudan.

Gold was a royal monopoly which had religious overtones. The gleaming metal symbolized the sun and was used by the King to reinforce his link with the life-giving orb. Ashanti goldsmiths worked almost exclusively for the court. Kings honored their own goldsmiths and even enticed foreign craftsmen to their compounds where they worked under close scrutiny to prevent any mismanagement of the royal gold as it was being fashioned into ceremonial objects or personal ornaments.

In 1874 the Ashanti lost a war with England and for the first time came under European domination. However, they were able to maintain their unity and heritage. When the present King of the Ashanti, a London-educated barrister, was enthroned, the most cherished Ashanti possession, the seventeenth-century Golden Stool played an important part in the ceremony. According to tradition it came down from heaven and embodies the soul of the Ashanti people.

When the King holds tribal councils or visits outlying villages, the gleaming regalia is displayed. Rectangular gold tablets, their surfaces completely covered with intricate repoussé patterns, are worn on the heads of high court officials. Ceremonial swords, staves, knives, rifles, and pouches of the royal body guard are covered with decorated sheet gold. The linguists who speak for the chiefs carry gold-covered staffs of ebony topped with cast-gold figures of men and animals. The King and chiefs are a splendid sight in brilliantly colored hand-woven togas. Their arms and fingers are covered with gorgeous gold jewelry of elaborate workmanship, some of it inherited and some of contemporary workmanship.

A chief of the Baule, an Akan tribe of the Ivory Coast wears an ancient gold headdress covered with three-dimensional symbols and a number of cast-gold rings in whimsical forms such as scorpions and lions. He also has a massive gold watch made for him in 1965 by an Ashanti goldsmith. The chief had the smith work in his house, as his forefathers had done, and closely supervised the project. It is one of his greatest treasures—even though it has no movement inside.

Among the heirlooms treasured by the Akan peoples, particularly the Ashanti, are the small beam scales with circular pans, weights, spoons, and boxes used in the measuring, weighing, and storing of the gold dust and nuggets which were the basis of Ashanti wealth and power.

Until the turn of the century Akan boys on the threshold of manhood were given a small amount of gold dust by their fathers. They were also presented with a small scale and miniature brass- or bronze-cast weights and spoons so they might learn how to handle commercial transactions which were generally carried out in gold dust, even down to the smallest value.

The Ashanti weights were marvels of imagination and often reflect a highly developed sense of humor. They were cast by the goldsmiths to the chiefs in countless forms reflecting Ashanti life. These miniature sculptures might be in the shape of a hammer, a crocodile, bird, or insect or portray people involved in various familiar activities such as making love, preparing medicine, harvesting, or sacrificing. They were highly valued and passed down the generations along the matrilinear descent group.

European products began to infiltrate the Gold Coast after the English conquest. Sir Richard Burton noted that in the 1880s European pomade pots were being used by the Akans for storage of alluvial gold dust. Bogus gold dust was manufactured in Birmingham, England, for sale to Africans who tricked Europeans and each other with it. Today European influence is pervasive on the Gold Coast, but a man generally still cherishes a *suman* or *bosun*, a fetish that he believes keeps him in communication with the powerful spirits. The fetish may be made or natural, but to be effective it must be kept with a bit of gold. The most powerful fetish of all is one made of gold. And when a man dies he is often buried, as his ancestors were, with a tiny bundle of river gold dust tied to his loincloth.

The secret of the Akan peoples' gold source evaded the sixteenth-century Portuguese in spite of the intensity of their search. They were never able to eliminate the Arab middlemen, although they managed to siphon off much of the gold that used to travel north by camel. It was the gold of Guinea that drew little Portugal out of the lingering medieval shadows. The Treaty of Tordesillas in 1494 assigned West Africa, Guinea, and the islands of the ocean to Portugal. Henry was granted sole right by his brother, the King, to license traders and explorers to those areas. One fifth of all the products and profits were due him. Portugal began to grow rich trading in gold, slaves, pepper, and ivory. Huge fortress trading posts were erected along the miasmic coast to serve as collecting points and keep pirates and intruders away. The feitoria at Arguim built in 1448 was the first European trading post overseas. Until about 1530 Portugal was able to keep interlopers out of the golden Guinea trade.

Henry died in 1460, twenty years before Africa fulfilled her golden promise. After his death exploratory activity slackened for a time, and in 1469 King Alfonso V sold a five-year monopoly on the Guinea trade to Fernão Gomes, a Lisbon merchant who agreed to explore a further one hundred leagues of coast a year starting south from Sierra Leone. One of Gomes' expeditions landed in the area of Cape Three Points which came to be known as the Gold Coast. So much gold was found there that Gomes became a tremendously rich and powerful man, although his lease was not renewed but given to the heir apparent, João II, who was entitled "King of the Algarve and Lord of Guinea."

In 1482 the great fortress of São Jorge da Mina (Elmina) was established in the center of the Gold Coast, about sixty miles west of modern Accra. Elmina dominated the coast from Sierra Leone to Benin and sealed off the gold-producing interior from foreign penetration.

The fifty years following the fort's construction were golden ones indeed for Portugal, which managed to stave off repeated attacks by the French, Spanish, and English. One of the first visitors to the fortress was the young Genoese Christopher Columbus, who, like many of the daring breed who were to explore the New World, cut his teeth on the tropical waters of the African coast.

Elmina (the mine) was built of stones shipped out from Portugal. It was situated on a headland site approved of by the local chief Caramansa, who was consulted by the Portuguese in charge of the project. The meeting was a masterpiece of fifteenth-century diplomacy. Don Diogo, resplendent in full court dress, sparkling with gold and jewels, received the solemn African chief who headed a long procession and was bedecked with gold in the form of bracelets, necklaces, and little gold bells tinkling from his hair, wrists, and ankles. The chief and his people converted to Christianity and remained loyal allies until 1637, when the Dutch captured Elmina.

In addition to the gold dust collected along the 150-mile stretch of the Gold Coast, the Portuguese obtained a somewhat smaller amount, which came from an unspecified location in the interior, through barter at Cape Verde and Senegambia. This trade was conducted by exceptionally hardy Portuguese, often exiles or criminals, who roamed the rivers and creeks of the area. Frequently these men joined African communities, adopting tribal ways. They and their mulatto descendants, called Tangomaos or Lançados, were responsible for the diffusion of Portuguese as the lingua franca along the stretch south of Cape Verde to the Gold Coast.

After Vasco da Gama had discovered the sea route to India and Álvares Cabral sailed to Brazil and India returning with spices, Lisbon became the chief distributing center in Europe for Oriental goods from as far away as Indonesia, Siam, and China.

At the beginning of the sixteenth century while Spain was harvesting the gold of the Aztecs and Incas, Portugal monopolized West African and Japanese gold production. The tantalizing gold of East Africa, however, proved difficult to control or even to collect. Vasco da Gama rounding the tip of southern Africa in 1497 found the coast south of Ethiopia in the hands of Arabs, who protected their gold trade with a string of prosperous Arab-Swahili coastal settlements peopled by Africanized Arabs. The Swahili traders had been established for hundreds of years as a thirteenth-century Chinese work, the *Record of Foreign Peoples*, reveals. The Cantonese author lists a country whose "inhabitants are of Ta-shi [Arab stock] and follow the Arab religion; they wrap themselves in blue cotton stuffs and wear red leather shoes. This country of Tsang-bat [a transliteration of the Arabic for "Coast of the Zanj," as East Africa was called] reaches to a great mountain [Kilimanjaro?]." The book, published in

1226, lists the products of Zanj as native gold, elephant tusks, ambergris, and sandalwood and notes that every year ships from the Indian kingdom of Gujarat and from Arab coastal towns go there to barter giving beads, white and red cloth, copper, and porcelain.

Da Gama 270 years later looked enviously upon gold-rich Sofala and Kilwa, the most important trading port south of Mombasa. He threatened to burn Kilwa to the ground if an annual tribute in gold dust were not paid to the King of Portugal. Within a decade of Da Gama's voyage the Portuguese had established an Indian Ocean maritime empire by means of ruthless savagery and terror.

Portuguese oppression and cruelty alienated the people. The gold of the east coast, which had seemed to be in their grasp, vanished as the Swahili traders fled inland. At the same time the flow of gold to the coast slowed with the weakening of the Makalanga Tribal Confederacy which the Portuguese indentified with the golden Empire of Monomotapa. Deadly tropical fevers, tribal warfare, and continued hostility from the many Swahili traders who roamed the interior kept the gold-hungry Europeans from penetrating the bush. Expectations of filling the national treasury with the gold of Ophir fell sadly short, although a fair amount of gold was obtained. A magnificent jeweled monstrance on display in the cathedral at Belém was crafted by the goldsmith-poet Gil Vicente from the first gold shipped from East Africa in 1506.

A fort was built at Sofala as a first step in gaining control of the ancient gold sources. The crown received very little gold and complained that Sofala "contributes nothing but expenses." Some Portuguese, particularly officials, made fortunes dealing in contraband gold. There were others too, like a convict ship's carpenter named Antonio Fernandes, who took to the jungle trading gold and ivory with the natives. Like the Tangomaos on the Gold Coast these men were often fugitives or outcasts who abandoned European mores in favor of African ways.

João Fernandes is the best known of these gold seekers because he was regarded as a quasi-divine figure by the Africans. Fernandes was a remarkable explorer. In 1514 he made two scouting trips for the crown deep into the interior from Sofala. He managed to penetrate four hundred miles into the hinterland and came back with glowing tales of gold fields two hundred miles upcountry from Sofala and of the Monomotapa (corrupted to Benemetapa by Portuguese writers) and his Kingdom of Gold. Historians subsequently identified the Monomotapa as a ruler and priest in southern Rhodesia who had his citadel at Zimbabwe. Fernandes' report set off yet another flurry of unsuccessful and frequently fatal attempts to find the Kingdom of the Monomotapa which many, ever hopeful, took to be either the kingdom of Prester John or the biblical Ophir.

The Iberians had a monopoly on gold and discovery. But the moment came in the mid-sixteenth century when England launched a series of maritime explorations which ultimately overshadowed, in commercial importance, those of Portugal and Spain. In 1553 an expedition under the command of Thomas Wyndham traded and plundered along the Gold Coast. Avoiding Elmina the English fleet sailed up the Niger to the Benin court, where tropical fevers felled all but forty of the men. The survivors made it back to London with 150 pounds of gold dust and encouraging reports of the gold they had seen at the African court.

From that time on the English made annual voyages to the Gold Coast which the Portuguese were unable to halt either through diplomatic channels, by fortifying more positions along the coast, or even by dispatching armed convoys to patrol the area. English mercantile tycoons financed the highly profitable voyages which took place during the bearable months between May and September, known as the Guinea Season—whence came the name of the English gold coin, the guinea. The Dutch captured Elmina and by the end of the seventeenth century Dutch, British, and Danish trading posts were located on the Gold Coast, and Portugal had lost her permanent bases although she continued with the French to sail the coast.

In the seventeenth century the Dutch and English attained global commercial supremacy through the activities of joint stock companies such as the English East India Company, the Levant Company, and the Dutch East India Company. Profits poured into the countinghouses beyond the Alps, and the northern ports became the focus of enterprise, signaling a shift in power from the old Mediterranean ports of Italy, Portugal, Spain, and southern France. In the first flush of enthusiasm England concentrated on voyages south such as Wyndham's to the coast of Guinea and northwest in search of a sea route to Cathay and India which would be of obvious advantage to the English.

In 1576 Martin Frobisher, veteran privateer who had once been captured and imprisoned by the Portuguese in Guinea, set out to find the northwest passage to China. Such a route was fervently believed to exist by many including John Dee, the Elizabethan mathematician and alchemist. At Dee's urging and inspired too by an enthusiastic book on such a route to riches written by a half brother of Sir Walter Raleigh, the wealthy Lok family, which had made its money in the West African gold trade, underwrote Frobisher's venture.

Frobisher sailed for the southern tip of Greenland with three small vessels. Only one, the *Gabriel,* made it as far as Baffin Land, where Eskimos captured five of the crew. The remaining thirteen men made it back to England with a curious cargo. Among their souvenirs were an Eskimo and his kayak which Frobisher, possessed of incredible strength, had singlehandedly lifted out of the water and onto the deck of the English ship as the hapless fellow paddled by.

It was not the exotic Eskimo which cast a spell over the English imagination, however, but samples of some "black earth" from Newfoundland, which rumor spreading like wildfire held to be gold ore. The Queen herself was sufficiently excited by this report to subscribe a thousand pounds and the loan of the Royal Navy vessel *Aid* for a much larger return expedition the following year.

The Cathay Company was formed by Michael Lok, and Frobisher was named High Admiral of all lands and waters he might discover. In 1577 three vessels and 120 men, including a number of professional miners, sailed north. The plan was for one ship to load the gold ore at Baffin Bay and the other two to proceed to the Pacific and China through the strait Frobisher mistakenly thought he had discovered on his previous voyage.

Frobisher was too consumed by gold fever to sail on. He loaded all three ships with the ore, two hundred tons of the stuff, and beat back to England. The ore was deposited under guard in the

Tower of London and subjected to a series of analyses. It was not widely known that the goldsmiths' efforts to smelt the ore were not proceeding well. One smith complained he couldn't get a furnace hot enough to extract the gold.

In 1578, amid some rumblings of skepticism, a third expedition of fifteen ships was organized which made no pretense at exploration. It sailed with Queen Elizabeth's blessing to establish a mining colony and to bring back more ore. The whole affair was a disaster. Stormy weather and broken ice sank the ship carrying most of the mining equipment, and the one hundred men who were to have remained as guards at the mine flatly refused to stay. Less than four months after setting out Frobisher's fleet returned to England and a chilly reception. They found that further assay had shown the ore which alchemical assayers had said was gold to be nothing more than iron pyrite—fool's gold. The Cathay Company was in bankruptcy, Lok was in debtor's prison. Frobisher found himself accused by irate investors of having intentionally raised false hopes of gold to gain support for his voyages. Thus ended the short-lived northern gold rush.

CHAPTER THIRTEEN *Explorers' Gold*

At no time in history was gold more of a critical factor in shaping the destinies of men and nations than in the period following the Spanish Conquest of the New World when gold in unprecedented volume poured into Europe through Spain. The prevailing European mood in 1492 at the dawn of the Conquest, was one of disillusionment and pessimism. Most of the continent lay exhausted from years of internecene strife. The specter of Islam haunted a disunited Christendom, which had failed to regain the Holy Sepulcher of Jerusalem. The Church had lost it moral leadership and the papacy was in the corrupt hands of a Borgia. The hostile Turks occupied most of Greece, Albania, and Serbia, pressing ever closer to the European heartland. They blocked the logical routes of expansion east and south to the spices of the Indies and the fabled gold of Cathay and Japan, which Marco Polo's narrative had brought to the attention of men and nations perennially hungry for the precious metal. Gold was the object of virtually every voyage of discovery and every exploratory effort.

Portugal, alone among the nations of Europe, had access to Guinea gold and the spices of the Indies which were brought back to Lisbon by carracks plying the southern route to the East. So it was to the King of Portugal that the Genoese navigator and cartographer Christopher Columbus logically applied for backing to discover a new quicker route to the Indies. But he was turned down. Finally, after years of petitioning at one court after another, Columbus, whose theories were supported by the eminent Florentine geographer Toscanelli, was received by the King and Queen of Castile. Fifteenth-century Spain was essentially still a medieval country. It had been greatly impoverished when the Jews and Moors were expelled, taking their gold with them. Ferdinand and Isabella were nearly bankrupt and keenly interested in Columbus' proposal. The negotiations which ensued dealt in large part with gold, which was in short supply in Europe. Columbus proposed sailing due west to reach the golden palaces of Japan and the golden wealth of the cities of India. The contract agreed upon specifically mentioned gold. Columbus was to retain a tenth of all revenues and precious metals derived from all islands and mainlands he might discover. In addition he was ennobled, created Great Admiral of the Ocean Seas, and made perpetual viceroy and governor of the lands he claimed for the Spanish crown.

Queen Isabella donated her golden jewelry to launch the expedition. The rich Pinzon brothers, merchants of Palos, underwrote an eighth of the venture in return for a percentage of the profits. Columbus set sail with a heavily annotated copy of Polo's travels, a letter addressed to the Grand Khan of China by Ferdinand and Isabella, and visions of palaces all roofed and paved with gold. His first landfall in the Bahamas was disappointing. The natives went about naked and there were no glittering palaces. But he did note that they wore simple gold trinkets and gold nose ornaments. "I was attentive and took trouble to ascertain if there was gold," he wrote in his journal of October 13, 1492, the day after landing in the Bahamas. This voyage and the three that followed were, in effect, gold prospecting expeditions on which exploration and discovery were of secondary importance. Columbus was sure that he had reached the Indies, despite the absence of gilded pleasure domes and silk-brocaded potentates. The sanguine navigator wrote a glowing letter to Pope Alexander VI, "The Island of Hispaniola is Tarshish, Ophir and Cipango. In my second voyage I have discovered 140 islands and 333 miles of the continent of Asia."

On his third voyage Columbus planned to sail south near the equator where ancient tradition asserted all precious things were to be found. He subscribed to the views of the Renaissance lapidary Teener that a sure sign of the presence of gold in an area would be the dark color of the inhabitants. "From the great heat which I suffer," he wrote in his journal while sailing along the coast of Cuba, "the country must be rich in gold."

The hunger for gold that drove Columbus across the great uncharted Ocean Sea to discover the New World touched off the first gold rush in modern history. The greatest geographical discovery was the fruit of a monumental geographical error which at first paid off handsomely for Spain, impoverished from the long struggle against the Moors. In the first years small amounts of gold brought from the Antilles whetted the appetite of Europe, attracting increasing numbers of rough and ready men, many of them veterans of the Moorish wars or campaigns in Italy, who had little to lose by embarking on the perilous voyage to the Indies.

Columbus returned to the Spanish court with samples of the gold fishhooks, nuggets, and ornaments he had collected from the gentle and hospitable Caribbean Indians whose good will was rewarded with merciless exploitation, enslavement, and extermination in the relentless Spanish pursuit of ever more gold. With the conquest of the two great civilizations of America—the Aztecs and then Peru—the floodgates opened. A deluge of gold flowed into Europe which had reached a peak of domestic production in the fourteenth and fifteenth centuries and was again starved for precious metal. For the next 250 years the New World was the world's major source of gold. By 1550 the stocks of European gold and silver had increased by half as much again as had existed when Columbus set sail in 1492. By the mid-sixteenth century Spain had laid claim to all of Central and South America with the exceptions of Brazil and Guiana, which fell to the Portuguese by virtue of the Treaty of Tordesillas.

Post-Conquest Europe erupted in a sunburst of golden splendor. Much of the American gold found its way into the hands of merchant bankers who gradually gained control of the vast gold supplies once in royal hands. American treasure financed gold currencies in almost every nation. England became the most important gold center where in 1717 the modern world's first real gold standard was established by Sir Isaac Newton. A new wave of commercial expansion and prosperity followed the Conquest, and the eternal metal figured more dazzlingly than ever in the pomp and ceremony of courts and churches. Dress and jewelry surfeited the eye with gold worked in every conceivable manner. Burghers, merchants, even the small man could aspire to accessories, snuff boxes, and watches crafted from American gold.

The effects of such colossal amounts of gold, supplemented by production from Japan, the central European mines, and later the mines of Brazil, were felt on many levels. The Renaissance was nourished by American gold. It was not only the goldsmith with his increased supplies of the malleable, gleaming metal who enjoyed the fruits of the mines. Painters, poets, all men of talent, were amply rewarded in gold by patrons moved by the Renaissance spirit. The rivers of newly mined gold infused into the European economy particularly aided the rise to power of manufacturing states, such as England, Germany, and the Low Countries.

Ironically the nation that reaped bitter fruit from the golden harvest was Spain itself. In 1608 an Englishman noted that "whence it seems not without reason, the Spaniards say in discourse, that it [the New World treasure] worketh the same effect upon them that a shower of rain doth upon the tops and covering of houses which falling thereupon, doth all at last descend below to the ground leaving no benefit to those that first received it."

When Ferdinand died in 1516 too little gold from the Antilles had been found to alleviate the state's financial embarrassment. "Ferdinand the Catholic," wrote a chronicler a few days after the King's death, "was so impoverished that it was difficult to procure money to furnish decent clothing for the servants at his funeral."

A few years later the golden deluge began. Spanish adventurers made colossal fortunes, and the Spanish crown was gratifyingly enriched in the early period following the Conquest. But after the great silver mines of Potosí were opened in 1545 little of the gold and silver that sailed up the Guadalquivir River to Seville remained in Spain. Most of it went immediately to pay the crushing debts owed the great banking houses like the Fuggers and the Welsers. American gold caused such an increase in gold supplies that the metal depreciated, sparking horrendous inflation felt not only in nonindustrial Spain but all over Europe. New World gold flowed into Spain and right out again to pay for the import of manufactured goods. Gold sapped Spain's strength. The lure of treasure emptied Iberia of much of her able-bodied male population. What gold and silver did accrue in Spain allowed her rulers to disastrously embroil themselves in European problems. Precious metal financed the costly Catholic-Protestant wars and fostered extravagance and decadence. Had it been wisely used to develop domestic manufacturing and a viable economy, Spain would not be one of Europe's least prosperous states today.

Columbus found no Cathay, no Japan, but like gold seekers throughout history his hopes never dimmed for long. His objective was to find inexhaustible gold mines. But at first he contented himself with the worked gold of the Indians, who gladly traded it for fishhooks, red cloth, beads, and tinkling bells. When the Spaniards asked where the gold came from, the Indians invariably pointed, indicating it lay just beyond. Some accurately waved in the direction of Hispaniola, the island now divided into Haiti and the Dominican Republic. Others maintained that much gold was found on an island called Babeque, where it was gathered in moonlight and hammered into little ingots.

On Cuba, which Columbus had initially decided was Japan, they found no gold at all. The embassy he sent inland had returned from their mission chagrined. They had been led not to the anticipated golden city and its Emperor "el Gran Kan," but to a palm-thatched village where they were warmly received but found no court of Oriental splendor. On the trip back to the ships the men encountered what was to prove in the long run more valuable than gold—tobacco in the form of a cigar shared by Indians walking along.

Columbus sailed on to Hispaniola. He was sure his golden dreams had been fulfilled when gold-embellished Indians gathered on the shore. He invited a young chief bedecked with solid-gold ornaments onto his ship. After entertaining the Indian, he had him courteously piped ashore with all honors and then noted in his journal with the callousness that marked so much of the Age of Discovery that the natives were ripe for exploitation. To the King he wrote repeatedly of how sweet the natives were, how freely they gave their gold and offered gifts of live parrots, fruits, and vegetables. Of the people he had no scruples of enslaving he wrote, "They are a loving, uncovetous people, so docile in all things, I assure your Highness, I believe in all the world there is not a better people or better country; they love their neighbors as themselves and they have the sweetest way of speaking in all the world and always with a smile."

96. Inca gold.

97. Spanish soldiers sacking an Inca temple. Real Eight Museum of Sunken Treasure, Cape Canaveral, Florida.

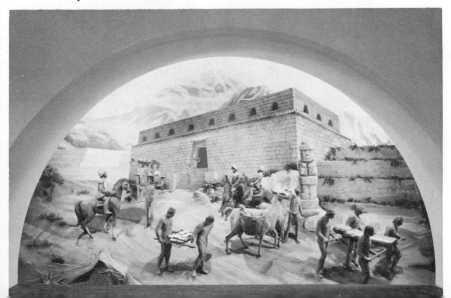

98. Gold and emerald pendant, Coclé, Panama. Ca. A.D. 1000. University Museum, Philadelphia.

99. Gold alligator pendant almost six inches long. Chiriquí, Panama. American Museum of Natural History, New York.

100. Highly stylized anthropomorphic pectoral, Darién style. Formed by soldering separately cast bits to a polished gold sheet. Museo del Oro, Bogotá.

101. Spanish New World mint. Diorama at Real Eight Museum of Sunken Treasure, Port Canaveral, Florida.

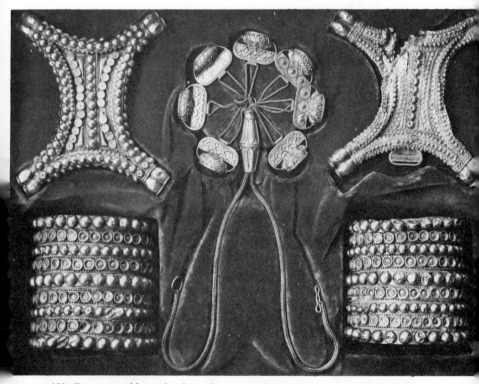

102. Tartessan gold jewelry from the Carambolo Treasure. Museo Arqueológico Hispalense, Seville.

103. Spanish four real found on a shipwreck in the Florida Keys. 1732, Mexico mint. This coin brought $17,500 at a 1976 auction.

104. Obverse of four real piece with bust of Philip V.

105. Gold and emerald cross with pearls from late-sixteenth-century Spanish shipwreck in Bermuda waters.

106. Treasure including gold and emerald cross from Spanish wreck sunk off Bermuda in 1595.

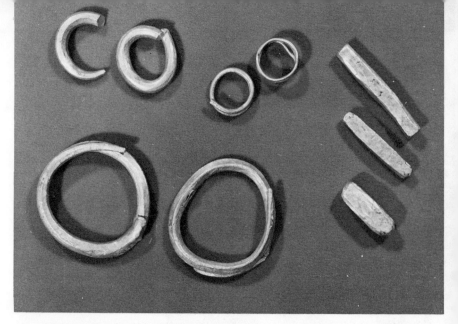

107. Contraband gold found on sunken sixteenth-century Portuguese ship off Bermuda.

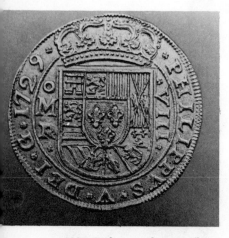

108. Eight escudos struck at Mexico City mint in 1729 during reign of Philip V (1700–46). Obverse.

109. Eight escudos reverse.

110. Imperial Crown of Rudolph II, sixteenth century. It has two unusual chased and repoussé decorated panels depicting the Emperor, who was a patron of goldsmithing, as conqueror and in coronation processions. The panels are bordered by bands enameled with fruit, flowers, insects, and birds. The cross on top is surmounted by an enormous sapphire.

111. German silver-gilt tankard. Ca. 1600.

112. Gold watch in painted enamel case. Made by Blaise Foucher of Blois. Ca. 1645. British Museum.

114. Basket of yellow gold with lilies of the valley by Fabergé, presented to Czarina Alexandra in 1896 by the management of the Siberian Iron Works. Yellow gold, green gold, nephrite, pearls, and rose diamonds.

113. Nineteenth-century gold kris handle from Bali. Set with semiprecious stones. Collection of the author.

115. Appalachian Indians gathering alluvial gold with hollow reeds in sixteenth century. From Théodore de Bry's *Americae*. New York Public Library, Rare Book Division.

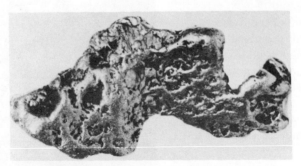

116. Large gold nugget found near Greenville, California. 82 ounces. Smithsonian Institution, Washington, D.C.

Columbus sent shiploads of these gentle people to be sold as slaves in Spain. In 1500 Queen Isabella prohibited the enslavement of the Indians; however, there were so many exceptions to this law that the Conquistadors found ample reasons for the continual enslavement of the Indians needed to work the New World gold deposits. Before long the gentle people had been wiped out as a result of the barbarous treatment they received at the hands of the Spaniards and exposure to European diseases.

Native informants spoke of Cibao, or central Hispaniola, where there were great quantities of gold. Columbus wrote, "Our Lord in his goodness guide me that I may find this gold, I mean their mines. . . ." He fully expected to find rich mines, unaware that all of the gold had been collected from placer deposits. But before he could set off in search of the mines, disaster struck and the *Santa María* was wrecked on a reef. The cacique, Guacanagari, offered condolence to the Spaniards, offering them everything of value he possessed. The villagers traded nuggets for lance points and Guacanagari gave Columbus four pieces of gold as big as his palm assuring him that he could give him a great deal more. Columbus was greatly encouraged. He decided to construct a fort ashore and sail for Spain with the glad tidings. He left a few men behind at Fort Navidad, expecting them to accumulate great amounts of gold before his return, not taking into account the fact that the gold he had been shown was the accumulation of generations of fairly casual production.

In bankrupt Spain Columbus was received with great celebration. His tales of rich gold mines, of rivers shining with the stuff, and his display of a suite of captive Indians wearing little but gold ornaments made him an overnight celebrity and riveted attention on the faraway Indies. He had barely been able to sign up enough men to sail out of port the first time. But when the Admiral of the Ocean Seas embarked again in September of 1493 he had seventeen ships instead of three and fifteen hundred crewmen in addition to almost a hundred stowaways—all anticipating piles of gold at Fort Navidad. Instead they found that the forty volunteers who had eagerly stayed behind to seek the gold mines of Cibao were dead and the fort destroyed. The ruffians had roamed the island demanding gold and raping women until an enraged cacique put a stop to their depredations.

The Spaniards erected a new fort and went into the interior in search of the mines. What they found in the foothills were rivers that flowed over sands spangled with gold dust. Small grains of gold flecked the earth and they found some nuggets but no rich mines. Columbus was still loathe to relinquish his illusion of having found the fabled Indies. He was so cheered at what his men found that he let his imagination dominate good sense. In one place, concave depressions in the ground led him to conjecture that this was the very Ophir where King Solomon's fleet had found gold to build the celebrated temple.

Columbus reasoned that the rich veins which had given birth to the small grains of gold in the rivers must be high in the mountains. He sent an armed military party with trumpeters and waving banners up into the mountains to seek out the mother-lode. The reconaissance party received packets of food and gifts of gold dust from friendly Indians whose villages they passed through and they also found some gold on their own but no mines. "On that trip," wrote Cuneo, a member of the party, "we spent twenty-nine days with terrible weather, bad food and worse drink; nevertheless out of covetousness for that gold, we all kept strong and lusty." One river, the Yaqui, still yields gold to women who work placer deposits and collect the gold dust in turkey quills. It was especially promising. Columbus reported gold grains the size of lentils adhered to the barrel hoops when water casks were filled.

The Spaniards watched the Indians working the placer deposits of the mountain streams of Cibao. Their method was most unsophisticated, involving no more than sorting a handful of sand for flecks of gold. The Indians gladly traded the gold for trinkets, and the party eventually returned to the main camp with about two hundred ounces of gold dust and some nuggets—one weighing twenty ounces. Indians told them of another area in the mountains where nuggets weighing over 25 pounds were frequently found. But like so many treasure tales they were never able to find the spot and verify the tantalizing story. A few years later a huge nugget weighing in excess of 330 pounds was discovered in that area but unfortunately went down on a ship which sank during a hurricane on its way to Spain.

The modest amount of gold brought back by the first reconnaissance party was a disappointment to the rough band of gold hunters who had come out to the Indies. Living conditions in the base camp left a great deal to be desired. Food was scarce because no one wanted to cultivate or hunt. There was little water and an abundance of malarial mosquitoes. The men were angry at being required to work on the construction of the settlement, to cut coral blocks for a church and to hack down trees for huts. When they refused to perform manual labor, Columbus withheld their rations. "All of us made merry," wrote one colonist, "not caring any more about spicery but only for this blessed gold."

Columbus sent samples to his royal patrons including a reported thirty thousand ducats' worth of gold, cotton, parrots, and twenty-six Indians from different islands. Among his requests for aid from the Castillian monarchs was a contingent of skilled miners to be recruited from Estremadura—Spain's chief mining center—so sure was he of the promise of Cibao.

It soon became apparent that the gold of Cibao could only be gathered by slave labor. A poll tax in gold dust was levied on the natives of Hispaniola. Almost immediately the inheritance of generations was exhausted. The poor Indians couldn't begin to meet the quotas no matter how feverishly they washed the rivers. Failure to render the full amount was punishable by death. Every Indian over the age of fourteen had to render four hawk's bills full of gold dust annually, and the caciques were committed to paying much more on a monthly basis.

Bartolomé de Las Casas, advocate and friend of the Indians, wrote the remarkable *Historia de las Indias* in which he narrates the effect of the gold dust on the Castillians and their slaves. He indicted the abominable and irrational tribute system. Labor as they might, the Indians were unable to produce sufficient gold by sluicing streams or felling trees to clear the land which they then flooded and washed. Even after the quotas had been halved they could not be met. Armed Spaniards rode into the hills with their dogs hunting down and slaughtering those who tried to escape the gold workings. Great numbers died at the hands of their torturers; others starved to death in the mountains or took cassava poison.

By 1508 a census listed only 60,000 remaining natives of an estimated 1492 population of 300,000. In 1519 only 2,000 of the defenseless Indians remained. Slaves were already being imported from Africa to work the mines. By 1548 Fernández de Oviedo reckoned no more than 500 were still alive.

In 1496 the intolerable tribute system was transformed into a new form of exploitation. Under the encomienda or repartimiento system an individual was granted lordship over a certain number of Indians. He was, in theory, to protect them (one wonders from what) and instruct them in Christianity. In return they would gratefully labor for their master. It was in practice a much abused system of vassalage derived from the feudal estates of Spain.

Columbus, an Italian, had enemies at the Spanish court as well as among the disenchanted gold seekers who accompanied him. Detractors claimed that he had found very little gold on Hispaniola and had salted his meager supply with Guinea gold to bait the hook for investors. Some said that he had "made" the gold. A Seville goldsmith who had been with Columbus told the court he had assayed the gold from the Indies and none of it was genuine. The motive for some of these stories seems to have been to excuse clandestine gold that disaffected Spaniards had illegally wrung from the Indians and kept, without rendering Columbus his due tenth and the crown its royal fifth.

Columbus' grandiose plans for Hispaniola envisioned a permanent settlement of 2,000 inhabitants barred to foreigners, Jews, infidels, and heretics where a closed season on gold hunting would ensure the cultivation of crops. The colonists would be granted a gold-gathering license in return for manual labor. He recognized that it would be difficult to get the Indians to come to the Europeans. Each Spaniard would go to the interior to trade for gold or get it however he might and then return to the town at stated intervals to hand over his gold for smelting and removal of percentage for the crown, for Columbus, and for the Church.

In 1495 master miner Pedro Belvio was sent to Hispaniola by the crown. With him went supplies of mercury from Almadén and Estremadurans trained at using it to separate gold from ore in the amalgamation process. "Get Gold," ordered King Ferdinand, "humanely if possible, but at all costs get gold." Spain sent out more colonists to erect a mint on Hispaniola, the first in the New World. Spain's empty coffers began to fill, the faltering nation to revive.

But Columbus, a proud and sensitive man and a foreigner, saw his star fall. His many enemies prevailed, and reports of mismanagement prompted the royal couple to order him arrested and brought home in chains. When the Admiral of the Ocean Seas arrived in Spain, he was unfettered and the charges against him dismissed. However, he passed the remaining few years of his life an embittered man. He was stripped of titles, honors, and pecuniary rights. Broken in health and spirit, Columbus made vain and humiliating appeals to Isabella, who was on her deathbed, and then to Ferdinand.

The man who once had written "Gold is most excellent. With gold the possessor of it does all that he desires in the world and arrives at sending souls into paradises [by the paying of masses]" bitterly watched the heavy laden ships unloading great chests of gold from the Indies "and none for me." It was to beckon to countless thousands in the following centuries. The admiral's "Indies" yielded more gold than mankind had ever accumulated in history. Ironically, those who craved it were rewarded with sorrow far more often than joy.

Columbus' New World ventures left him bitter but not poor. He had acquired a great number of gold ornaments in Veragua (Panama) on his fourth and last voyage and had some of the revenue due him from the diggings on Hispaniola. He had been given a chest of gold coins by Ovando, who replaced him as governor on Hispaniola, and was permitted by Genoese bankers in Seville to draw on 60,000 pesos d'oro he claimed to have left on the island. But he felt that this was far less than his rightful share and made persistent attempts to get more, so the gold he gained brought him very little pleasure.

Columbus had been replaced by Nicolás de Ovando as governor of Hispaniola in 1502. He arrived at the island with 2,500 men. The handful of men they found in the camp said that a native woman had recently found a huge nugget and everyone had gone to find more. Fired by such exciting news, the inexperienced Spaniards disappeared into the jungle interior where more than a thousand soon perished from disease and starvation. Those who survived often found that when the official melting came every eight months they had no gold left by the time the King's fifth was taken and they had paid back the amount advanced over the season for provisions. As in the nineteenth-century gold rushes it was the shipowner and shrewd merchant who grew fat while the miner, pursuing the golden will-o'-the-wisp, remained poor.

Columbus had found a promise of gold on the South American mainland. On his third voyage he touched on the lush coast of Venezuela. Naked Indians adorned by large polished disks of gold around their necks welcomed the Spanish expedition. They were delighted to barter their gold preferring objects of copper, whose odor they sniffed with pleasure. They deemed copper, which came to them only through trade with Central America, far more valuable than gold. The Venezuelans were far more advanced in metallurgy than the inhabitants of the Caribbean Islands. They made objects of guanin, called today tumbaga, which is an alloy of gold, silver, and copper in which the gold content ranged from 9 to 80 per cent and the copper from 11 to 74 per cent. Their sophisticated goldsmiths had discovered that when the copper content of a gold alloy was between 14 and 40 per cent the melting point was reduced from the 1,073° Fahrenheit of pure gold to a much lower temperature, making the metal more easily workable.

In the great age of discovery the most stunning achievements and the most incredible barbarities were the products of the determined search for gold that let nothing stand in its way. The chimera of gold lured Magellan to his death in the Philippines, Balboa to the Pacific, Cortés from Mexico to Lower California, De Soto from Nicaragua to Peru. Gold lust compelled countless others to explore the most forbidding zones of the Western Hemisphere. By 1520 most of the large islands of the West Indies had been explored and a few settled. Cuba served as the base from which expeditions fanned out hunting for the precious metal. There was as yet little effort to establish settled colonies with an agricultural base. The adventurers who came out of Spain were the restless, reckless, and greedy men who have always flocked to gold fields. At the rumor of a new strike they would drop everything. Heedless of what hardship lay ahead, they plunged into labyrinthine jungles and trackless deserts.

Arrogant and contemptuous of danger, the conquistadores were drawn to America by the promise of easy riches, glory, and honor. They came from a poor land, from poor families or impoverished noble families. They had been raised on the chivalrous Christian romances of the Middle Ages. They knew the way was hard and death faced them at every step; however, if they survived they could return to Castille as rich men.

In 1513 a gold hunter named Vasco Núñez de Balboa went prospecting on the mainland with a small group of Spaniards. He crossed the Isthmus of Darien and became the first European to see the Pacific. At the time it seemed far more significant that he had found an abundance of gold. His men pillaged every Indian settlement they came upon nestled in the verdant defiles of the Isthmus, torturing Indians and throwing captive chiefs to the dogs. One of the adventurers in the band was stirred by the tales he heard of a land to the south where gold was so plentiful it could be caught by fishing with nets. He was Francisco Pizarro, who later found that southern land—Peru—and made the most stupendous gold haul in history.

The Spanish King, excited by Balboa's discovery of auriferous gravels, sent a large expedition of fifteen hundred men to Panama. Among them were priests, a governor, and a veedor—an official overseer who accompanied every expedition to assure that the King got his royal cut. The priests were responsible for the absurd *requerimiento*—a notification the invaders were required to read to the Indians before making war on them. It was inevitably "read to the trees" and assembled Spaniards, who approvingly listened to the terms which claimed all the lands, gold, and Indians as vassals and property of the Pope and King.

Gradually the Spanish conquistadores ranged farther south and inland from both coasts, finding even richer sources of gold. Following streams inland up to the mountains, the prospectors often found the "purse" or rich mother lode from which *pepitas,* little nuggets, were torn and tumbled in streams and rivers. Colombia was by far the richest area for placer deposits. Gold was almost everywhere. By the middle of the eighteenth century this vast area became Spain's main source of gold. In the mid-nineteenth century there was still enough to keep 15,000 persons employed in the workings.

The gold the conquistadores found in South America would have dazzled Columbus. Panama, Venezuela, and Guiana, although not as rich as Mexico, Peru, or Colombia, had ample supplies of gold. Chile, Ecuador, and Bolivia on the Pacific coast were exploited for tremendous amounts of gold eroded from the rocks of the towering Andes, source of all the Inca gold as well. From 1492 until 1600 it has been roughly figured that Spain's New World workings yielded 800,000 pounds of gold. The figure is undoubtedly higher. A great deal of gold was never submitted to officials for assay and taxation. Some of it stayed in the colonies, some was clandestinely traded to foreign merchants whose ships violated Spanish prohibitions to trade with the colonists, and a lot, as recent discoveries of sunken ships of the period have shown, was smuggled back to Spain and other countries in Europe. Spanish shipwrecks have been excavated which yielded twice and even three times the gold that was listed on the official manifest.

In the sixteenth century the greatest mother lode of them all was the Andes chain. The great mountain system, which stretches 4,500 miles from Panama to Tierra del Fuejo, is still a major producer of gold, platinum, silver, copper, tin, lead, and other minerals. After Balboa's sighting of the Pacific the Spaniards established themselves in Panama and began the penetration down the west coast of South America into Ecuador, Bolivia, Peru, and Chile. The abundance and purity of the easily collected placer and alluvial gold deposits they found astounded even seasoned prospectors. For hundreds of years after the great mass of Inca treasure had been seized, the volcanic mountains continued to fulfill their early promise.

The treasures of the Aztecs and Incas exceeded any visions ever stimulated by Marco Polo or the story of Solomon. The speed with which the conquistadores took the two great centers of high American civilization was astonishing. Their numbers were small, their horses few, the climate and terrain hostile; yet Cortés in Mexico and Pizarro in Peru felled the two great empires with almost lightning rapidity.

Mexico had been discovered by Juan de Grijalva less than ten years after Columbus first set foot on the continent. In 1519 the governor of Cuba sent out an expedition to conquer Mexico. At the head of the force of about six hundred men and sixteen horses and equipped with only a few small cannons was a brilliant, shrewd adventurer named Hernán Cortés. Cortés, a dapper man who habitually wore a diamond ring and a massive gold chain, had Cuban encomienda of Indian vassals. "How many of whom died in extracting this gold for him, God will have kept a better record than I," commented Las Casas.

Cortés left Cuba despite a last-minute order from the governor, who feared his ambition, barring his departure. After first making a brief stop on the island of Cozumel, Cortés landed near Vera Cruz, dismantling his ships to keep his men from deserting, and founded a town in an attempt to legalize his independent command. The Spaniards headed through the steamy, jungle-covered mountains toward the Aztec capital accompanied by one thousand cannibal Cempoalan Indians who were eager to fight their Aztec adversaries. The Spaniards were aided in their conquest, both in Mexico and in Peru, by exploiting the lack of unity between various native groups. In addition they were able to make use of local legends and weaken enemy resistance by playing on superstition.

In Yucatán hospitable Mayan chiefs had given Cortés gifts of gold, food, and women. Among the women was an Aztec princess who became his mistress and interpreter. Doña Marina, as she was called, had been given as a child to a Mayan chieftain. She proved invaluable to the Spaniards when they reached the Aztec capital.

Messengers from Montezuma, the Aztec Emperor, begged "the white gods" to stay in the east and proceed no farther. This embassy brought food and rich gifts of intricate cast-gold jewelry. Once the Spaniards had seen the glint of gold there was no question of turning back as Montezuma asked.

The Aztecs were a mighty people with an all-powerful bloodthirsty religion. In the twelfth century they had achieved political ascendancy over the Toltecs in the fertile area of central Mexico. By the fourteenth century they had founded the capital city of Tenochtitlán, a New World Venice on a small island in Lake Texcoco. Gradually the warlike Aztecs subjected the people of the surrounding areas. By the time of the Conquest they had established a large empire with a complex military, religious, and civil bureaucracy. Vassal states rendered them tribute in gold and provided sacrificial victims essential to their formidable religion. The sun-god, who died every evening, required copious offerings of human blood, the precious liquid of life, to assure his rebirth at dawn.

According to one legend, the Aztecs had conquered the Itza, whose great god was a tall bearded white man. He was known as Quetzalcoatl to the Itza and Kulkulcan to the Maya. The Aztecs included him in their pantheon of gods. To prevent his retribution they erected the highest temple pyramids in his honor and lavished gold and human blood on his altars, for they knew that the god had sailed away to the rising sun, promising the Itza he would return one day and avenge their enemies.

Montezuma was uncertain and puzzled by the arrival of the Spaniards. Perhaps the bearded strangers were the fulfillment of the prophecy: Certainly, they must be divine beings. He accordingly sent offerings worthy of the gods. Aztec informants later reported to the chronicler Bernardino de Sahagún, "They gave the 'gods' golden necklaces and ensigns of gold and quetzal feathers. And when they were given these presents, the Spaniards burst into smiles; their eyes shone with pleasure; they were delighted with them. They picked up the gold and fingered it like monkeys; they seemed to be transported by joy, as if their hearts were illumined and made new. The truth is that they longed and lusted for gold. Their bodies swelled with greed, and their hunger was ravenous; they hungered like pigs for the gold. They snatched at the golden ensigns, waved them from side to side and examined every inch of them."

Montezuma's bewilderment was turned to Spanish advantage. Cortés sent him presents and a message that he had come from the mightiest King on earth who desired to establish trade relations with him. The conquistador sent a Spanish helmet back to the capital asking that it be brought back filled with grains of gold so he might see what their gold looked like. "Let him send it to me," said Cortés, "for we Spanish have a disease of the heart which can only be cured by gold."

The helmet was returned brimming with gold dust, "just as they got it from the mines." The Emperor sent other gifts; the most splendid was a huge sun disk. As big as a cart wheel, it weighed almost two hundred pounds and was made of fine gold inscribed with the signs of the Aztec calendar. There was an even larger wheel of silver, many cast-gold ducks, a large number of charming animal figures in gold, jewels, and exquisite featherwork. With these Montezuma sent yet another request that the strangers proceed no further.

But now the gold fever burned too hot. Cortés marched and fought for three months through searing heat and numbing cold, across mountains, rivers, and jungles. Montezuma sent frequent embassies with gifts and pleas to the white gods to turn back, but they pushed relentlessly on toward the setting sun. Then, one day they looked down through the crystalline air to the gleaming canal-laced city of 300,000 which lay 7,500 feet below in the Valley of Mexico. As they descended to the great causeway that led to the capital, Montezuma came out to meet them. He was no half-clad savage but a golden-crowned monarch, borne on a shining gilded litter and clad in superbly colored garments of cotton, embellished with gold and jewels, and a mantle of iridescent feathers. The very soles of his sandals were of gold.

Bowing to the inevitable, the Emperor welcomed the bearded gods. They were lodged in the palace that had belonged to his father, and given rich robes, women, and slaves who served them from gold platters. The rough Spaniards were stunned at such magnificence and hospitality. The Aztec leader further inflamed their cupidity with many splendid gifts. But in spite of all this, the men realized they were in effect prisoners in a gilded cage. Exit from the city was controlled by drawbridges and the Spaniards were greatly outnumbered. The frequent agonized screams of sacrificial victims from a nearby temple increased the Spaniards' anxiety.

While exploring the large palace, some of the men had discovered a secret treasure room where the wealth accumulated by Montezuma's father was stored. The sight of great slabs of refined gold, masses of finely wrought gold jewelry, plate, and ornaments along with treasures of gems and silver intoxicated the men. They were no longer content to stay confined as honored guests in the palace. With a boldness born of desperation Cortés seized the Emperor and kept him chained as the Aztec tribute collectors brought mounting piles of gold to the

Spaniards. The men were unbelieving at what they saw; some wondered whether they might not be dreaming it all. The Aztec Emperor was pressured to assign men to lead Cortés' soldiers to the mines in Cuzula, Tamazulapa, Malinaltepic, Teniz, and Muchitepeque. The soldiers returned with glowing reports of resources rivaling those of Solomon.

Mexico was exceedingly rich in gold, but the Valley of Mexico had no native gold so the Aztecs had organized several methods of acquiring great amounts of it. Some they got in trade but most came in tribute from subject towns. This system interested the exploitive Spaniards. Cortés queried Montezuma at length on the subject and was pleased to learn that nearly two tons of gold a year reached the capital in various forms. The Tlapanec's tribute, for example, consisted of twenty chocolate jugs full of gold dust and ten gold plates each four fingers wide, two feet long, and the thickness of parchment. From the rich Mixtec region, which still produces some 200,000 fine ounces of gold annually, came worked gold including crescentic collars, pendants, bells, head-dresses, and labrets (lip plugs) of coral and rock crystal mounted on gold.

Throughout the winter and spring of 1520 the pile of gold mounted in Tenochtitlán. As rapidly as it came the barely literate Cortés and his men melted it down. An estimated two thousand pounds of Aztec goldwork went into specially constructed furnaces to be cast into small stamped bars. Some of the soldiers had their shares fashioned into great gold chains many yards in length. These were easily transported and, like all gold jewelry, were not subjected to tax if worn upon debarkation in Spain.

Cortés had left Cuba against the orders of the governor, who feared with ample justification that he would try and carve out a personal empire. When the governor learned that Cortés had sent a shipment of the royal fifth to King Charles V by which he hoped to legitimize his enterprise, the governor took action. He sent a force of one thousand men to Mexico, led by Pánfilo de Narváez, who was empowered to deprive him of his command. Cortés, leaving a garrison of eighty Spaniards in Tenochtitlán, surprised the force near the coast, made Narváez his prisoner, and easily enlisted the men on his side with the promise of gold. The treasure ship Cortés had dispatched to the King never did arrive in Spain. It was captured by French pirates, and Francis I, Cellini's patron, kept the stolen gold.

When Cortés returned to Tenochtitlán he found the garrison besieged by Aztec forces. Montezuma was stoned to death by his own contemptuous people when he appealed to them to cease their attacks. The Spaniards were overwhelmed by seemingly endless waves of Indians. Escape from the city under cover of darkness was planned. A portable bridge to breach the gaps in the causeway was secretly constructed. The treasure was divided up, and on the dark rainy night of June 30, 1520, remembered as "La Noche Triste," the Spaniards fled. They were attacked by swarms of Aztecs on foot and in canoes. The King's fifth of the treasure, laden on wounded horses, sank quickly beneath the lake. Many men flung their treasure into the water and scrambled over the piled bodies of their slain comrades which spanned one of the causeway gaps. Others, reluctant to part with their gold, sank with it or were captured and later sacrificed. Most of Montezuma's treasure was lost in the bloodied lake.

A battered remnant of a few hundred men, including Cortés and his prisoner Narváez, retreated for six days. On July 7 they won an almost miraculous victory against an Aztec pursuit force at the battle of Otumba. Cortés and his hungry, poorly equipped men fought with desperate courage routing a force reckoned at 200,000 Indians led by a prince resplendent in gold war dress. Cortés Tlaxcalan allies helped the Spaniards consolidate their control of Mexico. But it wasn't until a year later that they captured Tenochtitlán, marking the fall of the Aztec Empire.

The Aztec Empire was dead and Charles V gained one of Spain's richest possessions. Cortés was named Governor and Captain General of New Spain by the grateful King. He established a large plantation and devoted himself to mining, but enemies continued to thwart him and he died frustrated and bitter, like so many other gold-hungry conquistadores whose ambitions were destined to outrun their fortunes.

One treasure-laden ship bearing Montezuma's gifts to King Charles V managed to reach Spain. Renaissance Europe was thrilled with the fabulous Aztec treasures which were displayed with great ceremony at Seville, Valladolid, and finally at the court at Brussels. The most sophisticated observers were amazed at the forms the New World goldsmiths had coaxed out of the yellow metal they called *teocuitlatl* or "the excrement of the gods." Sadly, little remains of the state gifts but the impressions recorded by some of those who saw them.

Peter Martyr, the respected Hapsburg historian and a member of the powerful Council of the Indies, wrote: "But surely if ever the wits and inventions of men deserved honor or commendation in such arts, these seem most worthy to be held in admiration. I do not marvel at gold and precious stones. But I am astonished to see workmanship excell the substance. For I have with wondering eyes beheld a thousand forms and similitures, of which I am not able to write. I never saw anything that might so allure the eye of man."

Among the marvels were gold miters, animals, birds, and fishes splendidly crafted to resemble the living creatures, shields of gold and mother-of-pearl, bracelets and neck pieces set with jade and gems, gold bells, a gold scepter studded with pearls and a costume with a mask of topaz alleged to have been worn by Quetzalcoatl, a jaguar skin coat set with jewels, anklets of gold, labrets, pendants, and a necklace with 183 emeralds. Most dazzling was the great "sun all of gold" nearly seven feet in diameter mentioned by Albrecht Dürer. Trained as a goldsmith, Dürer was agog at the Aztec gifts. He noted, "Also did I see the things which had been brought to the king from the new golden land. . . . And I have seen nothing in all my livelong days which so filled my heart with joy as these things. . . . I was astounded at the subtle genius of the people in foreign lands."

By the time the Spaniards arrived Mexican goldsmiths were masters at making exquisite miniature articulated gold figurines, working with fine gold wire as opposed to true filigree, cire-perdue casting, and gilding on copper as well as the simpler techniques of repoussé and hammering sheet gold. No one has ever equaled their skill at crafting miniature pieces of a very complex and intricate nature.

The Mexican goldsmiths, above all the southern Mixtecs, were superior to those of Spain according to a Franciscan who accompanied the conquistadores. He wrote that "they could cast a bird with a moveable tongue, head and wings; and cast a mon-

key or other beasts with moveable head, tongue, feet and hands
and in the hand put a toy so that it appeared to dance with it;
and even more they cast a piece, one half gold and one half silver, and cast a fish with all its scales, one scale of silver, one of
gold, at which the Spanish goldsmiths would much marvel." The
most famous of Renaissance goldsmiths, the Florentine Benvenuto Cellini, is said to have spent weeks vainly trying to dupli-
cate such a flexible polychromed fish after he had seen the Aztec
treasure which fell into the hands of Francis I.

The history of goldworking in Mexico began rather late and is
puzzling inasmuch as there is little evidence of an archaic or
technologically primitive period preceding the flowering of a full
range of techniques. Gold was held to be of divine origin. Prized
accordingly for its spiritual associations and impervious beauty,
it was never employed as a medium of exchange. Indigenous
goldwork didn't appear until the tenth century A.D., when, rather
rapidly, goldsmiths reached a high level of technical skill in casting. The Mexican smiths, whose work finds its highest expression
in the intricate Mixtec cast gold, eschewed ostentatious displays
of large expanses of shining metal. In this, they were certainly
influenced by the fact that there was far less gold in Mexico than
Peru, where goldwork at times relied on the dramatic impact of
masses of highly burnished metal at the expense of fine workmanship and balance.

Knowledge of pre-Columbian goldwork in Mexico is chiefly
derived from the remarkable illustrated encyclopedia of Indian
life compiled by a precursor of the modern anthropologist, the
Spanish friar Bernardino de Sahagún. His key work is commonly
known as the Florentine Codex because the Medici Library in
Florence contains the original manuscript. It was compiled in
the years after the conquest by Sahagún, who trained the sons of
the Aztec nobility to interview informants and transcribe their
answers in Nahuatl written with Latin characters. His work details the operations of the goldbeaters, who limited their activities to thinning gold on a stone and polishing it, and of the
master goldsmiths or finishers. It features many illustrations
showing the processes of cire-perdue casting involving clay,
charcoal, beeswax, and alum.

The Aztecs took captive Mixtec smiths from Oaxaca to work in the capital. But Aztec goldsmiths, unlike those of the Inca who were employed by the state and closely supervised, were generally independent craftsmen. They bartered their goods at a gold market held every fifth day in the capital where there were separate stalls for the purveyors of gold objects and those dealing in dust and nuggets. A small town on the shores of the lake was the home of many goldsmiths. Other artisans lived in a special quarter of Tenochtitlán where they were protected by the divinity Xipe-totec, Our Lord of the Flayed One. At an annual festival those who had been caught stealing gold the preceding year were sacrificed and skinned before his idol.

Systematic grave robbing has been carried out in all areas of the New World where gold was found. It began early. Bernal Díaz, the chronicler who accompanied Cortés, mentions a soldier who extracted some fifty pounds of gold and a great many jewels from the tombs of chiefs in the first recorded instance of American grave robbing. The rapacious Spaniards were so intent on turning the wrought gold of the subjugated peoples into crude, anonymous bullion that virtually nothing that was not buried escaped them. What exists today is chiefly the result of grave robbing in the last sixty years.

Until not too long ago the *guaceros,* who take their name from the *guacas,* or gold artifacts they extract from tombs, sold their finds by weight to men who melted them down and sold them for dental gold, to jewelers and hoarders. The governor of the Bank of England reported in the late 1850s that each year the bank received pre-Columbian gold artifacts worth several thousand pounds in bullion to be melted down. Between 1859 and 1861 in the Chiriquí province of Panama gold artifacts worth at least several hundred thousand dollars were stolen from ancient tombs. One grave yielded 701 gold sun disks. Today, fortunately even the simplest *guacero* realizes the enhanced value of such pieces if they are sold as is. Because gold artifacts were sometimes concealed in the noses of stone statues in Colombia, many treasure hunters, while not destroying worked gold, have smashed countless idols. In most countries pre-Columbian artifacts are claimed by the government as part of the national patrimony. In practice, many are illegally smuggled to private collections in Latin America and auction houses, galleries, collections, and museums in the United States and Europe.

Examples of indigenous goldwork have been found in many parts of the New World. However, there are three areas where the art of the goldsmith reached peerless heights of technical skill and artistic expression. One, of course, is Mexico. The other two are much broader in area. The earliest metalwork appears in a region centered in Peru and touching Ecuador and Bolivia. The Chimu of the north coast of Peru who worked marvels in gold between A.D. 1200 and 1450 were the greatest goldsmiths of the area. The other is the vast expanse centered in the rich auriferous valleys of Colombia, where the virtuoso Quimbaya smiths worked. It stretches west through Panama and Costa Rica and east to Venezuela's Lake Maracaibo, where superb objects were made by smiths working with stone hammers and crude winddraft casting furnaces.

In this last region many different cultures developed, each with distinctive characteristics but sharing a wide range of imagery. The predominant motifs are carefully studied natural forms abstracted into symbolic stylizations of human figures and the creatures of air, land, and sea. Whether Tairona, Sinú, Darién, Calima, Quimbaya, Chibcha, or Coclé, the pre-Columbian goldsmiths, while varying in particulars, were all expert practitioners of a wide range of goldworking techniques. Their cast pieces, the subjects of which were the familiar inhabitants of the natural world around them, are masterpieces of restrained vitality, infused with magic. They reflect a pantheistic oneness with nature; every image contains the essence of the thing it represents.

In some areas the goldsmiths practiced several highly developed techniques working in platinum and in tumbaga. Through a process called mise-en-couleur the surface copper in tumbaga pieces of gold and copper was removed by immersing the object in acid baths. Some specialists conjecture that this highly complex process as well as the techniques of granulation and filigree casting may have been introduced from Southeast Asia. There is persuasive speculation, backed by mounting evidence, from the noted Austrian archaeologist Robert Heine-Geldern that metallurgy was introduced into pre-Hispanic America through con-

tact with coastal China after the eighth century B.C. Dr. Heine-
Geldern, an Austrian archaeologist, suggests that transpacific
voyages from the Dongson area of Indochina influenced goldworking from Costa Rica to northwestern Argentina. The archaeologist theorizes that it might have been knowledge of gold deposits in Peru and Ecuador which stimulated repeated Chinese
voyages and even fostered permanent settlements. It appears
that complex Asiatic metallurgical techniques spread from the
Pacific Coast to the gold-rich areas of Panama and Colombia but
never reached the Caribbean islands where the level of goldworking remained primitive.

Among the cultures which made use of tumbaga with its low
melting point were the Quimbaya of Colombia. Quimbaya cast-
gold sculptures, figurines, and ceremonial vessels with their elegant, restrained, and senuous countours rank with the world's
finest goldsmithing. The artisans of Darién, in present-day
Panama, fashioned spectacular anthropomorphic gold pendants in
which the human figure has been highly abstracted. These pieces
were evidently widely appreciated and traded to other cultures.
One such pendant was excavated from the sacred Mayan cenote
of Chichén Itzá in northern Yucatán.

The exceptional goldsmiths along the Sinú River, which flows
into the Caribbean across Colombia's Western Cordillera, perfected filigree casting. They specialized at producing extremely
tricky hollow cast sculptured figurines in the form of animals and
birds as well as large, intricate lacelike earrings.

The only Colombian culture which the Spanish documented in
any detail was that of the Muisca, sometimes referred to as the
Chibcha, who inhabited the highland basin around Bogotá. In
1537 the Spaniards conquered the Chibcha and their gold. At the
end of the first day's looting so much gold had been amassed that
one mounted conquistador couldn't see another over the heaped
treasure. The Muisca civilization was not very advanced; their
historical memory went back a mere sixty years. They lived in
crude huts and their goldwork was relatively primitive. But they
had a great deal of precious metal, and the Spaniards, whose
concern was for quantity rather than quality, were much
impressed with the golden displays in the simple villages. The
temples and chief's dwellings, made of saplings and straw, were

hung, inside out, with thin gold plates and golden wind chimes. The chiefs were borne on gold-covered litters and adorned with shining ornaments.

All their gold was imported from neighboring areas. The Muiscas traded salt, emeralds, and cotton for gold. They made offerings of small cast-gold effigies in the form of humans, real and mythical animals, and miniature atlatls, or throwing sticks. One of their gods, Chibchachun, was the patron of both merchants and goldsmiths. Recently the sites of ancient goldsmiths' workshops have been found and excavated. Among the fragmentary evidence they furnished were strips of gold, gold dust, stone molds for casting, crucibles of refractory clay, and chisels and tools of tumbaga.

In the middle of the last century an amazing discovery was made in a Colombian lake. Fishermen pulled up a gold raft with five figures representing a chief and nobles on it. This marvelous gleaming object fanned the flames of the famous El Dorado legend. For centuries, the quest for El Dorado, or the land of the Golden One, lured adventurers of many nations to their fate. As early as 1530 the Spaniards' curiosity had been piqued by tales heard in the lowlands of a Golden Land and its fabulous Golden King. The stories the Indians told had their origins in a religious ritual performed by a Muisca chief on the sacred Lake Guatavita in the area of Bogotá.

The chief, regarded as divine descendant of the sun, made a solemn sacrifice at an annual festival. At dawn of the appointed day he covered his resin-anointed body with gold dust, donned golden regalia, and was rowed on a ceremonial raft into the lake while his people watched from shore. As the sun broke over the horizon, the resplendent chief cast gold and emeralds into the waters beneath which the sun-god lived and then dove in himself. The actual ceremony ceased about 1480 when the tribe was subjugated by a more powerful one, but the legend of El Dorado, the gilded one, persisted. No one doubted that a continent that had yielded so much gold contained a golden kingdom. The intrepid Europeans who persisted in the search of El Dorado from Quesada to the Elizabethan Raleigh explored much of northern South America in the process, the way North America was deflowered by men searching for the Seven Cities of Cibola and Golden Quivira. Just as the hazy location of Prestor John's golden kingdom shifted during the Middle Ages from Asia to Africa, so El Dorado, originally sought in the forbidding ten-thousand-foot-high volcanic lake of Guatavita, was moved to the mysterious regions of the Venezuela-Guiana frontier.

Gold-hungry explorers launched searches from Ecuador, Peru, Colombia, Venezuela, Guiana, and Trinidad Island. In Ecuador one of Pizarro's lieutenants, Sebastián Mojano de Belalcázar, who conquered Nicaragua and later betrayed Pizarro, put together a band of two hundred gold seekers, including criminals and scoundrels of every stripe. They made an incredible trek from Quito covering a thousand miles of hellish terrain. Belalcázar reached the great plain in 1538 to find Spaniards already there. In the spring of 1536 another expedition, headed by the cultivated lawyer Jiménez de Quesada, had left for El Dorado from Santa Marta on Colombia's Caribbean coast. Quesada's ragged force reduced to 167 emaciated men and 59 fever-ridden horses was the first to reach the reported site of El Dorado in January of 1537 and managed to subdue a large number of Chibchas. They got a great deal of the Muisca gold mentioned above, but Spanish accounts tell of great treasures hidden from all of them, including a life-sized idol toppled into the lake by the Indians. By strange coincidence a third expedition converged on the almost inaccessible plain at about the same time. Such was the attraction of gold that three expeditions starting from widely divergent points, penetrating hostile unexplored country, managed to reach a remote spot despite indescribable suffering along the way.

The third expedition was unusual because it was organized by Germans. In return for a desperately needed loan, Charles V had been persuaded to grant the great banking house of the Welsers a patent for conquering and settling Venezuela. The Augsburg merchant princes sent out an explorer named Nikolaus Federmann, one of the few German explorers in the Age of Discovery. For three years he wandered with the remnant of a force of five hundred through the harrowing Orinoco swamps and over tenthousand-foot-high mountain passes in search of El Dorado. He emerged on the plain of Bogotá with his starving men where he met Quesada, who had arrived six months before and was soon joined by Belalcázar, whose forces like those of the other two had been decimated by poisoned arrows, tropical fevers, skin ulcers, serpents, alligators, jaguars, and hunger.

In 1541 Pizarro's younger brother sought El Dorado. Gonzalo Pizarro crossed the Andes with a party of two-hundred Spaniards, four thousand Indians, five thousand pigs, one thousand llamas, and a pack of bloodhounds. Half the men perished and his supplies were exhausted, but Pizarro, clinging doggedly to the vision of El Dorado, reached the plateau of Bogotá and disenchantment. El Dorado was clearly not the village of beehive-shaped huts. Indians indicated it lay beyond the mountains toward the impenetrable wilderness of Venezuela. Not much later, Quesada's brother became the first man to go beyond the mountains. He returned to Bogotá after a two-year quest for El Dorado in Venezuela with only twenty-five men left of the three hundred Spaniards and fifteen hundred Indian porters who had set out so hopefully with visions of a dazzling city and its fabled King drawing them on.

The Welsers sent another German agent into Venezuela. After slaughtering large numbers of Indians he was himself slain. Two years later a Welser gold hunter named George Von Speier looking for El Dorado explored almost to the equator in upper Brazil. The last German expedition of the Renaissance ended when a knight was slain in a village in the Orinoco jungles rumored to be filled with gold statues. By the time that the tale of El Dorado had migrated to the Venezuelan jungles it had been greatly embellished. The village on Lake Guatavia had become the fabulous city of Manoa where the streets were paved with precious metal. Over the years, scores of men were seduced by the enchanting tale of the Land of Gold.

One man who had succumbed to the lure of El Dorado was Sir Walter Raleigh, who lost his head, figuratively and then literally. His 1596 book *The Discoverie of the Large and Bewtiful Empire of Guiana*, was widely read and fired English dreams of a golden land to rival Spain's. Raleigh was a conquistador after his time; a man obsessed with gold who overvalued its importance to a nation developing a stable economy based on trade and cloth manufacturing. "Where there is a store of gold it is in effect needless to remember other commodities for trade," he asserted. His dream was of "discovering a better Indies for her Majesty than the King of Spain hath any." "It is his Indian gold," Raleigh wrote, "that endangereth and disturbeth all the nations of Europe." A courageous but improvident man, he sunk his entire fortune and that of his wife into the quest for El Dorado. Raleigh believed abundant gold would give Protestant England financial superiority over Catholic Spain and quickly wither the Spanish sinews of war.

Poor Raleigh, already out of favor with the Queen, returned from his first expedition with pathetic samples of gold ore he had carved from a piece of quartz. His detractors claimed that he had never even crossed the Atlantic but had hidden in Devon or sailed to the Barbary Coast and traded for the gold. The ore brought back was assayed and pronounced worthless. The quixotic adventurer, with a tenacity that matched Columbus' hopes for Hispaniola and Cuba, persisted in believing in the limitless wealth of Guiana. Confident that "the Prince that possesses that land shall be lord of more gold than that gained in Peru, Colombia or Mexico," he continued to pursue El Dorado, which had become a fever raging in his brain. He explored further, still convinced the land was full of gold mines, rivers, and tombs, but came back empty-handed. In 1616 Raleigh was released from his long imprisonment in the Tower to bring back gold from Guiana on one last try. Again he failed. His son was killed on the disastrous expedition, and his chief lieutenant committed suicide. Two years later Raleigh, a sick and broken man, was beheaded on Tower Hill.

The myth of El Dorado lived on, appearing frequently in European literature. Voltaire's Candide traveled there and described children at play with golden quoits. On seventeenth-century maps of all nations it was vaguely marked and labeled "the largest citie in the entyre world." In 1637 two Franciscans combed the east slope of the Andes for a "Temple of the Golden Sun." Although a number of geographers had openly begun to doubt the existence of El Dorado, the Portuguese mounted an expedition from Brazil exploring north for the fabled land, and in 1714 the Dutch West India Company sent an exploratory force to find El Dorado, or Manoa, a nonexistent city on a nonexistent lake in Venezuela.

At the end of the eighteenth century the great Prussian scientist Alexander von Humboldt made a thorough study of the El Dorado myth. He followed earlier dream seekers, tracing a route through swampland, jungle, mountains, along the Orinoco until he reached Colombia's Lake Guatavita. The German naturalist reasoned that if Quesada had found gold worth 4,000 pesos de oro when he had the lake partially drained in the sixteenth century, there must be much more treasure there. Humboldt came up with an estimated figure of 500,000 gold pieces, which was printed in papers around the world inspiring dozens of lake drainage schemes.

In 1912 Contractors, Ltd., of London made an ambitious recovery effort, shipping $150,000 worth of equipment to Bogotá and then draining Lake Guatavita, which was already very low as the result of long drought. Indian gold worth $10,000 was recovered by the group, but they failed to make a profit, since expenses ran over $160,000.

North America had its share of legendary gold. The Seven Golden Cities of Cibola, the kingdom of Quivira, California, a golden land of Amazons, and other fables circulated widely during the Age of Discovery. The image of shining cities with golden buildings four and five stories high kept Hernando de Soto and his men slogging ahead on a relentless four-year march that covered over 350,000 square miles of unexplored North America. De Soto died on the shores of the Mississippi without finding any gold. At the same time Coronado searched the Southwest for the golden cities of Cibola. He discovered that the towering golden buildings men spoke of were the Indian pueblos of Arizona and New Mexico whose pale adobe walls gleamed golden under the setting sun. Coronado then turned north, pursuing another golden realm called Quivira. He never found it but Spanish chain-mail armor has been excavated from the remains of the Quiviran Indian villages on the Kansas prairies. By 1543 other expeditions looking for the Cities of Gold had explored along the Gulf of California and reached up to Oregon.

Men believed in golden cities because one had been found which surpassed their wildest dreams. Cuzco, the Inca capital, which fell to the illiterate conquistador Francisco Pizarro and two hundred soldiers in 1531, was the seat of the Inca Empire. It was the richest city in the hemisphere at the time, containing vast amounts of gold accumulated over two millennia. Its inhabitants were still producing prodigious amounts of the precious metal under highly organized state control. During his sojourn with Balboa in Panama, Pizarro had heard of the great southern country where there was an endless supply of gold. He had made two earlier landings on the coast of Peru and received small offerings of Inca goldwork which whetted his appetite. However, he was totally unprepared for the colossal amount of Inca gold he found in Cuzco.

The highland Incas reigned over an empire of 6 million inhabitants extending from the southern border of Colombia halfway down the coast of Chile—a distance of 3,000 miles. The empire was united by the official Quechua language, sun worship, and a remarkable network of roads with relay stations over which runners made as much as 150 miles a day carrying messages and even live fish from the Pacific. The traditional list of twelve Inca rulers begins around A.D. 1250, but the empire had reached its zenith only one hundred years before the Conquest. The Incas' treasures held vast amounts of tribal gold. Tribute was paid by every man; the poorest paid in lice to demonstrate all owed something to the Great Inca.

The trustworthy chronicler Cieza de León wrote that in the final years of the empire the amount of gold extracted annually amounted to more than 381,000 pounds—over 190 tons. The Incas regarded gold as "the sweat of the divine sun"; gold nuggets were the sun's "tears." Every aspect of its production and crafting was carefully controlled by the state. Raw metal was doled out to the *kori-camayoc,* or "he who is in charge of gold." Goldsmiths fashioned splendid, dramatic, and highly sophisticated pieces. Commoners were forbidden to keep or use raw gold or ornaments. The collecting of metals was an obligation of the great mass of commoners who labored for the Great Inca and his nobles. The Peruvians regarded the mines as living spirits. They worshiped the hills and gold-bearing rivers and held special religious ceremonies in their honor.

All Inca gold was alluvial. It was carried as dust, spangles, grains, and nuggets in the high rushing streams of the altiplano and came especially from deposits in the Valley of Curimayo, northwest of Cajamarca. But above alluvial gold there is always the vein system from which it has been torn away. Eventually the Spanish found such lodes in the formidable crags of the Andes and organized mining operations.

As early as 800 B.C. coastal Indians panned placer deposits of gold in Peru. The Chavíns, Peru's earliest goldworkers, made many objects of both decorative and utilitarian nature. More than a thousand years before Pizarro they had discovered that soft gold nuggets hammered into sheets eventually became brittle and broke under the repeated blows but could be made malleable again by heating the metal. Chavín artisans manufactured repoussé pectorals, ear spoons, flutes, plaques to be attached to garments, crowns, and even tweezers of gold. They made a great advance when they learned to solder individual pieces of gold together to form large flexible pieces and figurines.

Goldsmiths made use of large sheets of polished gold for dramatic effect and crafted sculptural pieces of great beauty characterized by the play of flowing lines. Mochica smiths combined shell, turquoise, and other materials with gold in elegant mosaic motifs. In Ecuador goldsmiths learned the secrets of cire-perdue casting and of fusion gilding of copper—alloying gold with silver and then copper. In Ecuador goldsmiths worked with platinum many centuries before Europeans knew how. In a technique called sintering, later forgotten until the nineteenth century, fine grains of platinum, which has a melting point of 1,773° centigrade compared to 1,063° centigrade for gold, were mixed with gold dust. The combined metals were alternately hammered and heated with a blowpipe on charcoal until they fused. The Spaniards had discovered platinum in the northwest section of South America but thought it inferior to gold, going as far as to make gilded platinum counterfeit coins.

The Incas believed in resurrection after death, so each dead Inca leader was provided with an imperial palace which was maintained by a complete staff and furnished with precious appointments made of the sun's metal. The mummified body of the Great Inca was kept with his predecessors in the great Temple of the Sun. A life-sized golden effigy called his *pucarina* was cared for as if it were the deceased ruler himself. Spanish chronicles tell how the retinue of one *pucarina* bore him in a golden litter to the palace of another dead ruler for "visits." During his lifetime each Great Inca prepared for death by constructing his palace, covering its walls with great plates of gold and silver, and filling it with treasure. In the palace of Huayana Capac, the Great Inca whose sons, Atahualpa and Huascar, were contesting the crown at the time Pizarro arrived in Peru, the invaders found great piles of golden furnishings and ornaments in addition to 100,000 pounds of gold ingots, each weighing about five pounds.

The swift Spanish conquest of the Inca Empire benefited from internicene strife. The empire had been torn by the struggle between Huascar and his half-brother Atahualpa. Huascar was an iconoclast who wanted to strip the dead of their gold. Shortly before Pizarro arrived, Atahualpa had captured Huascar. The conquistadores exploited the prediction made by Huayana Capac before his death that white men, sons of the great creator god Viracocha, who had long ago disappeared into the sea, would return and conquer the Incas. Pizarro ambushed Atahualpa and his five thousand followers at Cajamarca; two thousand Incas fell, their white cotton tunics stained crimson. The Spaniards kept Atahualpa prisoner, dined with him, allowed him his harem, and waited as his promise of gold for the white gods was fulfilled.

Atahualpa, noting the gold lust of the invaders, had conceived of a plan for his release. He promised to fill a chamber twenty-two by twenty-seven feet with gold as high as he could reach. Pizarro agreed and gave him two months. From Cajamarca runners went out to every corner of the kingdom requesting ransom. Immediately porters thronged the roads bearing gold to Cajamarca—great hammered plaques, animal figurines, vases, pots, dishes, masks, every conceivable object wrought in the precious metal. Not less than 13,000 pounds of gold artifacts, the fruit of centuries of craftsmanship, piled up, the greatest ransom ever accumulated. One contemporary chronicler reported that no fewer than 100,000 *cargas* (litters), borne by four men each reached the town. Pizarro considered Atahualpa's throne and litter the single most precious item in the ransom. It was made of 190 pounds of sixteen-carat gold paved with clusters of emeralds and other gems and required twenty-five men to carry it.

Large figurines of gold and silver were plentiful in sixteenth-century Peru where they represented ancestors. These venerated *guacas*, or totems, were among the objects most pleasing to the Spaniards, not for their artistic qualities, but for their intrinsic value in gold. Each ruler also had his own guardian deities called *huauqui*. One of these, made of solid gold, was part of the ransom; a figure so large that it had to be broken up for transport to Cajamarca. Indian goldsmiths were forced to melt down all of the treasures in specially built clay furnaces and cast them into easily divisible ingots. There was so much ransom it took them a full month, ten times as long as the melting down of Montezuma's treasure in Mexico. In thanks, Atahualpa was strangled to death and given a fine Christian funeral at which the priest who had urged his execution intoned a solemn mass for the dead.

While Atahualpa's ransom was piling up, some of Pizarro's men were already raping the country for whatever treasure they could find, terrorizing and killing the people. As soon as the Inca was dead the flow of treasure ceased. Runners on the highways, on their way to Cajamarca, got the word and disappeared. What happened to the gold they were carrying? Many believe the treasures lie hidden in mountain caves and bottomless lakes. According to one, there was a businessman in Quito in the late sixteenth century named Suárez who had been kind to one of his servants, an Indian named Cantuña. When Suárez found himself in dire financial straits, Cantuña told him to construct a hidden smelting furnace and then disappeared. He returned a few nights later with 100,000 gold pesos' worth of gold plate and ornaments; more deliveries followed. The Spaniard died leaving all his wealth to Cantuña, who, when questioned by suspicious authorities, swore he had sold his soul to the devil in exchange for an endless supply of gold. He died without revealing the source of the treasure.

Something else the Spaniards never got in the ransom was the famous Chain of Huascar which had been commissioned by Huayana Capac to celebrate the birth of his heir, Huascar. Indian informants told the Spaniards that it took two hundred dancers to carry the seven-hundred-foot "great woolen chain of many colors, garnished with plates of gold, and two red fringes at the end." The chain, life-sized statues, animals in gold, gold bars, plate, and ornaments, all described by the Indians but never found by the conquistadores, are sought today by modern treasure hunters in the Andean wilderness.

The Inca capital was the richest prize of all; nowhere else in the New World was such astounding wealth found. Pizarro and his men marched on Cuzco, making golden horseshoes for their horses as the iron ones wore out. A contingent of soldiers had gone ahead to the Andean city and reported the most dazzling sight yet seen. The Great Temple of the Sun in Prescott's words was "literally covered with plates of gold. The number of plates they tore from the temple was seven hundred; and though of no great thickness, probably they are compared in size to the lid of a chest 10 or 12 inches wide. A cornice of pure gold encircled the edifice, but so strongly set in stone that it fortunately defied the efforts of the spoilers." The soldiers sent back the embossed gold as part of the ransom, supervising its removal by captive Indians.

Inside the sanctuary the golden-clad mummies of the Great Incas were enthroned with golden masks and crowns. At one end of the lofty chamber was the figure of the sun, a great disk with flaming rays made of a double thickness of gold. Outside the temple was one of the incredible Inca gardens whose like has never been seen in any part of the world where grazed 20 gold llamas. The splendid flock was guarded by shepherds of the same precious metal. Nearby was a gold-plated fountain where sacred corn drink was kept.

Pizarro entered the imperial city a year to the day after he had taken Cajamarca. The temple had already been stripped of its other treasures; however, the city yielded far more than Atahualpa's ransom. Sent back to Spain, the fantastic amount of gold—easily as much as $200 million—had a sharp and immediate effect on prices in Spain, sending them soaring. Pizarro, although not sensitive himself to artistic genius, had sent the King some examples of Inca goldwork. Not one of the ten full-sized statues of women, four life-sized llamas, a "cistern" of thirty-eight vases—all of solid gold—is known to have survived the melting pot. The crown desperately needed every ounce of bullion and could ill afford collecting art.

The walled city of Cuzco was a blend of the sophisticated and the simple. Low, windowless, shock-resistant buildings, thatched with straw, were laid out on streets at right angles. In the dim light of the interior, gold and silver wires were interwoven in the thatch and gold and silver plates sheathed the walls. The mansions of the rulers were built of stone so carefully fitted together no mortar was used, although sometimes molten lead, silver, or even gold was used to fill the cracks, which explains why the Spaniards tore down so many walls.

Garcilaso de la Vega, son of a pre-Conquest Inca princess and Spanish captain, was the most widely known writer on Peru. His *Royal Commentaries of the Incas* describes the sacred buildings and royal chambers which were lined with gold:

> In preparing the stone they left niches and empty spaces in which to put all sorts of human or animal figures . . . all of which were of gold or silver. Imitation of nature was so thorough that they even reproduced the leaves and little plants that grow on walls; they also scattered here and there, gold or silver lizards, butterflies, mice and snakes which were so well made and so cunningly placed that one had the impression of seeing them run about in all directions. . . . All the tableware in the house whether for the kitchen or the dining hall was of solid gold, and all of the royal mansions in the empire were abundantly furnished in tableware, so the king need take nothing with him when he travelled or went to war. . . .

He goes on to describe the fairy-tale gardens whose marvels were melted down with the rest of the new world's treasures.

> In all the royal mansions there were gardens and orchards, given over to the Great Inca's moments of relaxation. Here were planted the finest trees and the most beautiful flowers and sweet-smelling herbs in the kingdom, while quantities of others were reproduced in gold and silver, at every stage of their growth. . . . They made fields of maize, with their leaves, cobs, canes, roots and flowers all exactly imitated. . . . They

did the same with other plants making the flowers, or any part that became yellow of gold, and the rest of silver. In addition to this there were all kinds of gold and silver animals in these gardens, such as rabbits, mice, lizards, snakes, butterflies, foxes and wildcats, there being no domestic cats. There were birds set in trees, as though they were about to sing, and others bent over the flowers, breathing in their nectar. There were roe deer, lions, and tigers, all the animals of creation, in fact, each placed just where it should be. Each one of these mansions had its bathing suite, with large gold and silver basins into which the water flowed through pipes made of the same metals.

The disastrous effect the gold of the gods ultimately had on Spain might be considered ample revenge for their sixteenth-century desecrations and the annihilation of whole civilizations. Following the discovery of the New World with its promise of endless bounty, no one would have guessed that so much gold and silver could bring anything but wealth, power, and national prosperity. It seemed inconceivable that the American treasure would spark an inflationary spiral that would turn Spain into one of the continent's poorest countries and have harmful effects which still persist today.

For a number of years following the conquest of Mexico and Peru the gold and silver greatly enriched Spain. A current of energy was felt in almost every sector, particularly in literature and the arts which enjoyed a tardy renaissance. The genius of Lope de Vega, Cervantes, El Greco, and Velázquez was acclaimed throughout Europe and distracted attention from the adverse effects of the American treasure. With time the aura of prosperity fostered a debilitating decadence. The rise in domestic prices generated by the treasure was successfully coped with at first, but before long a disturbing volume of gold and silver was going to pay other nations for their goods. Spain found herself in the trying position of maintaining an impossibly large empire, battling both Protestant and Moor and losing most of the gold and silver for which she so dangerously strained her resources. Overall in the centuries of Spanish rule, only about 10 per cent of

America's vast gold production actually came to the crown. The import of such huge amounts of treasure produced by slave labor appeared to be the greatest blessing and made Spain the envy of all Europe. Only a very few contemporary economists, among them a group at the University of Salamanca, had the insight to warn of the repercussions of such a massive influx of bullion into an economy which made no parallel effort to develop industry. During the sixteenth century commodity prices in the country soared, rising with each new shipment of American treasure.

The Spanish crown was perennially in debt to the great banking houses of Germany, the Low Countries, and Italy. On a number of occasions banking firms were ruined when the King suspended payments. In the latter part of the seventeenth century the country had almost no exports to attract foreign capital. Some years fully two thirds of the New World treasure production was mortgaged in advance to foreign creditors and never entered the country. The loss of so much bullion combined with the expenses of maintaining the colonies drained the nation of economic vitality and worsened inflation. The royal preference shown to the merchants of Seville and the loss of so many young men to the colonies weakened the country further. Each monarch added to the mounting debt and passed it on to his successor. The currency was repeatedly debased with the result that prices went up even more. The crown defaulted seven times between 1557 and the 1680s when a chain of royal bankruptcies flared into widespread rioting.

New World treasure inspired Counter Reformation ambitions in the Catholic sovereigns of Spain. The Hapsburgs made their country the center of Catholic military operations but failed to stem the forces of Protestantism. Despite every attempt on the part of the crown to maintain their official monopoly on trade in the colonies, the economy of the two began to separate. England and Holland found increasing commercial profit in clandestine dealings with the colonists who were delighted at the lower prices of their goods. Pirates and privateers grew bolder, preying upon Spanish shipping and making incursions into Spanish coastal settlements to strip them of all treasure. All of these factors contributed to the ruin of the Spanish Empire.

Alonso Morgada, in his history of Seville published in 1587, wrote: "the bullion from the New World which has come into Seville, is enough to pave the streets of Seville with blocks of gold and silver." Peter Martyr writing in 1516 stated that the annual production of gold in Hispaniola exceeded 400,000 ducats. Modern-day historians and economists differ greatly in calculating the total amounts of precious metals extracted from the New World. Some estimate that between 1492 and 1550—by which time the Indian hoards were exhausted and extensive mining had been organized—no less than 500,000 pounds of gold reached Spain. Another claims that less than a quarter of this amount reached Spain for the same period. It is possible that as much as 2½ million pounds of gold were sent to Spain between the discovery of America and the outbreak of the Mexican Revolution during the first decade of the nineteenth century. Spanish historians after the conquest of Peru estimated that in the years immediately following the Conquest as much as 381,000 pounds of gold was being produced annually in South America. Some experts believe that as much as 5 million pounds of gold came to Europe from the mines of the New World through the eighteenth century. As late as 1804 the mines of Spanish America were still producing close to 30,000 pounds of gold annually.

The great discrepancy between the high figures given for New World gold production and the rather low figures which appear on the cargo manifests of the galleons carrying the treasure back to Spain can be accounted for in part by the fact that so much gold was smuggled into Europe. Anyone who wished to convert his wealth, even if it was in silver, and avoid heavy taxation made arrangements to smuggle contraband gold in the form of bullion, coins, and jewelry—such as the enormous gold chains which have been found on a number of Spanish shipwrecks in the Caribbean. An example of the magnitude of smuggling was revealed in 1551 when a returning treasure ship wrecked on the southern shore of Spain. Salvors recovered over ten times the amount of gold listed on the ship's manifest.

The volume of silver reaching Spain was probably about five to ten times as great as gold and there were in addition precious gems and pearls. Whatever the exact figures were for the gold mined and carried to Spain, the net result was that the mineral wealth pumped into the country altered the political balance of Europe, gradually weakening and impoverishing nonindustrial Spain and boosting the economies of manufacturing countries such as England and Holland.

As the chief supplier of European gold, until Brazilian gold was discovered in great abundance by the Portuguese in the late seventeenth century, the Spanish crown rigidly controlled the production of New World gold to the detriment of her own colonists. Licenses were necessary for emigration to America and concessions sold for mining rights and collecting gold under the encomienda system. All gold, by law, had to be delivered at regular intervals to the royal assayers, where it was refined, scrupulously weighed, stamped, and the King's portion removed. Although silver coins were being struck in Mexico City as early as 1536, the first gold coins were not struck until 1621 in Bogotá. Later gold coins were also minted in Lima, Cuzco, Mexico City, and Guatemala. Royal officials were entrusted with the frustrating task of preventing contraband gold from being smuggled aboard the homeward-bound ships. All treasure cargoes were restricted to landing at Seville. Treasure was immediately transferred to the House of Trade, seat of the organization that had total authority over all intercourse between the mother country and the New World colonies. Generally after the treasure was cross-checked with the ships' manifests, most of it sailed off again to pay Spain's numerous creditors.

Seville was also the main commercial center of Spain and the base for the wholesalers who supplied the goods needed by the colonists, who were forbidden to produce whatever the mother country could supply such as wine, olive oil, figs, cloth, iron, hardware, paper, books, tools, and weapons. The Seville merchants charged outrageous prices since they had no competition, at least not until Europeans defied the Spanish monopoly and sold to the colonies at much lower prices. Besides treasure the returning galleons brought back other commodities such as spices, dye woods, indigo, cochineal, sugar, tobacco, and hides. They also carried Eastern luxuries transhipped from the Manila galleons which landed at Acapulco. The Asian treasures included gold and silver jewelry, gem stones, ivory, silks, spices, porcelains, and some tea.

During the first half of the sixteenth century small vessels were used to carry the precious cargoes between the New and Old Worlds. By the middle of the century, after freebooters had managed to capture a number of valuable treasure-laden ships, the crown introduced the famous galleons and passed laws stipulating that all returning ships had to sail in convoys, known as flotas. By the end of the century there were three flotas sailing to and from the New World each year, and the traffic increased from an average of 50 ships in 1550 to more than 150 by 1600. The flotas made scheduled stops at such ports as Nombre de Dios and Portobello in Panama, Cartagena on the Caribbean coast of Colombia, and at Vera Cruz, Mexico. They regrouped at Havana and sailed together back to Spain. Although many attempts were made to intercept and capture the rich galleons, only the Dutch admiral, Peit Heyn, was successful in capturing a complete flota, a feat he accomplished in 1628 off Matanzas, Cuba.

Far more crippling to Spanish shipping than pirates or privateers was the loss of ships due to storms and faulty navigational practices. Over the centuries hundreds of the lumbering treasure galleons wrecked on the treacherous reefs of the Caribbean and many more were sunk in hurricanes. When the ships went down in shallow water, Negro and Indian slave divers were employed to salvage the precious cargoes. Often, however, by the time salvors reached the area of a wreck, shifting sands had covered it over. Many of these wrecks have been discovered in recent years by scuba divers. Appreciable amounts of treasure and many beautiful artifacts have been recovered from them.

Foreigners were also active in trying to salvage the treasures of the Spanish galleons. Wracking, as the profession was called, was one of the main occupations of places like Port Royal, Jamaica, and Nassau in the Bahamas. On occasion foreign interlopers were fortunate to find Spanish gold without any effort. In 1724 sailors on a British merchant ship sailing between Florida and the Bahamas spied what appeared to be an unmanned longboat. Upon closer inspection it proved to contain the desiccated bodies of four Spaniards whose ship must have sunk. Aboard the boat the Englishmen discovered a sack of gold dust weighing eighty-three pounds, a chest containing 4,700 gold doubloons, another filled with silver plate, and a small bag of pearls. In 1678 a Dutch vessel investigated the scattered remains of a ship on a deserted cay near the Caicos Islands. Ashore they found the bleached skeletons of more than two hundred Spaniards who had survived a shipwreck only to perish of hunger and thirst. Evidently a part of their cargo had been salvaged, for the Dutch found more than three tons of gold in specie and bars, forty-three tons of silver bars, and 340,000 silver pieces of eight on the cay. The lone survivor couldn't explain the tragedy. He was a small dog who was taken back to Holland by the sailors who all became rich men. An expedition was sent out by the Dutch to relocate the wreck and see if it contained any more treasure, but, as often happened, it could not be found.

Everyone rejoiced when the flotas reached home. The arrival of ships that sailed up the Guadalquivir to Seville was scrutinized by ambassadors and economic spies of governments and of the great merchant-banking houses of Europe. On many occasions their arrival saved the Spanish monarchs from imminent bankruptcy and disaster.

In a Fugger newsletter written in 1583 we read: "there came word that the fleet from the Spanish India, praise be to God, arrived without misfortune. It carries a consignment of 15,000,000 in gold and silver and people say that they unloaded and left a million in Havana because the ships were too heavily laden. It is a pretty sum and will give new life to commerce." The Venetian ambassador in Madrid wrote to the Doge nine years later when another flota reached Seville: "After the arrival of the Indies fleet His Majesty has ordered a revision of the account for the West Indies and especially for Mexico, with the result that he finds he hath been robbed of upwards of five million ducats in gold." No doubt many heads were lopped off when the royal investigation was completed.

Pirates, privateers, and adventurers of many nations were attracted to the lure of the New World treasures from the outset. The ship carrying Aztec gold to Charles V had been captured by the Florentine pirate Giovanni da Verrazano, who was sailing under patent from the French King, Francis I. Besides the great amount of gold, the pirates also nabbed 608 pounds of pearls and a large amount of emeralds—one reported to be as large as a palm. The French King refused to give back the spectacular haul. He scorned the Treaty of Tordesillas which divided the world between the Spanish and Portuguese, declaring "the Sun shines for me as well as for the others. . . . I should very much like to see the clause in Adam's will that excludes me from a share of the world."

The French, English, and Dutch of the Reformation all considered Spanish shipping fair game and they followed in the wake of Verrazano plundering large numbers of Spanish ships over the centuries. Piracy was a national policy employed by many of Spain's enemies in the interimperialistic struggles which had religious, political, and commercial motives. Because Spain financed Catholic Europe's Counter Reformation activities it was a matter of vital Protestant policy to sap her strength, and the best way to do so was to keep her New World treasure from reaching Spain.

Although the French were the first on the scene, their feats were surpassed by the cunning Elizabethan privateers whose Queen endorsed their profitable ventures and excursions in the New World. Elizabeth was badly in need of bullion and faced with mounting inflation. Although she encouraged their depredations, the privateers knew that if they were caught the Queen had no choice but to disavow all association with them. One of the most successful was Captain Christopher Newport, dubbed "One Hand," having had the other "strooken off" during an attempt to capture a treasure galleon off the coast of Cuba. Newport's third wife was a Glanville of the leading goldsmith family of London. He had tested his mettle on one of the first English privateering expeditions to the Brazilian coast. He sailed with Sir Francis Drake for a time. After many years spent harassing Spanish shipping and raiding towns in the Caribbean he amassed a considerable fortune and became admiral of the Virginia Company.

The Glanvilles financed many privateering expeditions and bought choice items from the privateers. They got their start in the illicit business through dealing in bullion and gems. They had ships and capital and were set up for evaluating and marketing prize goods. They also had the clout to obtain credit when necessary.

The man who was the greatest Elizabethan seaman and personification of the Elizabethan spirit was Sir Francis Drake. He was a cousin of John Hawkins, who was one of the first Englishmen to undertake illegal trade with the Spaniards in the New World. Drake had established his reputation as a privateer with a daring raid on a mule train bearing Peruvian treasure across the Isthmus of Panama to the Caribbean port of Nombre de Dios. His small band of men intercepted the treasure caravan and managed to get their booty back to their waiting ships and home to England, much to the delight of his Queen. When he first landed in Panama he told his men: "I have brought you here to the Treasure House of the World. Blame nobody but yourselves if you go away empty."

To the governor of Nombre de Dios he declared that he had come "to reap some of your harvest which you get out of the earth and send into Spain to trouble all the earth."

Drake's next mission took place between 1577 and 1580 and was the first English circumnavigation of the world. Sailing in the *Golden Hind* and with four smaller vessels, Drake and his men first sacked settlements and took a number of vessels along the coasts of Chile and Peru before capturing the famous treasure galleon *Cacafuego* (*Spitfire*). The amount of treasure taken from the *Spitfire* was so great that Drake had to be content with keeping some twenty to thirty tons of gold and chests of gems and jewelry, jettisoning all the rest. Some two hundred tons of silver lie off the Isla de Plata off the coast of Ecuador. Although they already had a king's ransom in gold, the English privateers made a stop along the northern coast of California where his men scratched about finding "a reasonable quantitie of gold and silver" almost three hundred years before gold was discovered at Sutter's Mill.

The ostensible object of the circumnavigation had been to establish trading relations with the leaders of the treasure and spice states of the Far East. Drake did load six tons of precious cloves in the Moluccas, but almost all of it was lost when one of his ships ran aground on a reef. In spite of this, he returned to England with such colossal amounts of Spanish gold and treasures that he became a very rich man and returned a dividend of 4,700 per cent to the shareholders who had financed the expedition. The Queen rewarded him with knighthood and he went on to officially attack other Spanish possessions in the Caribbean: first sacking Santo Domingo where the Venetian ambassador in Madrid wrote to the Doge that he had captured "1,500,000 in gold booty," then capturing and sacking Cartagena and St. Augustine in Florida.

In April of 1586 the ambassador wrote another letter to the Doge stating, "News from Lisbon and Seville brings identical news on Drake, that he had landed troops and seized Santo Domingo, Puerto Rico and Havana; this latter a real disaster as the Duke of Medina Sidonia told me that they had two millions in gold there." Four months later he wrote again saying, "We just learned that Drake has returned to England with thirty-eight ships laden with much booty." This correspondence gives an indication of how closely Drake's exploits were followed. This great haul paid for the defenses which were later to repeal the Invincible Armada in 1588, and much of England's court plate and jewelry was made from this stolen gold.

In an effort to prevent Peruvian treasure from reaching Spain, Drake was sent in 1595 by Queen Elizabeth to capture Nombre de Dios and Panama City and hold them for ransom. Although Nombre de Dios was captured, along with a considerable amount of treasure, Drake fell victim to a fatal bout of dysentery and was buried at sea in a lead coffin off Portobello. The man whose name struck fear in every Spanish American heart had opened the door of the New World to future colonization by English and other European nations.

The Italian navigator Amerigo Vespucci, while searching for an eastern passage to the East Indies in 1501, had sailed along the Brazilian littoral, stopping at each cape and harbor, claiming them for the Portuguese monarch. He encountered various groups of Indians who seemed to prize feathers above all and when offered a gift of a gold cross usually preferred to take a wooden comb or a mirror. The natives told him "wonderous things about the gold and other metal," but the overly cautious Vespucci remarked, "I am of those like St. Thomas who are slow to believe." Neither he nor the government was sanguine about the area's potential, and almost two centuries went by before the Portuguese began to tap the great gold wealth of Brazil.

Portugal claimed Brazil under the terms of the Treaty of Tordesillas but considered the vast land of little value and made scant effort to colonize it. In the early 1500s a small group of converted Jews fled the Inquisition to Brazil, where they exported brazilwood, which was highly valued in Europe as a dyewood. By the beginning of the seventeenth century there were large settlements along the coast exporting sugar, tobacco, salt, and other products. Little by little the interior in the south was penetrated by the Paulistas and the vaqueros, or cowboys. The Paulistas, inhabitants of the highland plateau of São Paulo, were poor farmers of mixed Amerindian blood. Unable to purchase Negro slaves as wealthier men did, they took to the bush of Minas Gerais to capture Indians. During one of these sorties in the 1690s they discovered large deposits of gold and the rush was on.

Throughout the sixteenth and seventeenth centuries the Brazilian settlers had found scattered deposits of gold, and some gold had come into Portuguese hands through clandestine trade with Peru. Men who found gold in the Spanish colony sometimes smuggled it into Brazil, where they could sell it without having to pay the onerous Spanish taxes. But such gold activity was desultory and gave no warning of the real rush precipitated by the discovery of the Minas Gerais (General Mines). New discoveries were made almost daily. It seemed as if every rivulet and stream sparkled with gold. For many years all gold from Brazil was in the form of dust and nuggets washed down from the placer deposits where it had accumulated undisturbed for hundreds of thousands of years.

The Minas Gerais rush, foreshadowing those of the nineteenth century, drew young and old, rich nobles and illiterate mendicants. They set out with no more than a pack on their back for the new El Dorado. Vast numbers of adventurous gold hunters converged on the large auriferous area on three trails: from Bahia, Rio de Janiero, and São Paulo. Many died of starvation, disease, or in frequent skirmishes with one another. The Governor General labeled them "Vagabond and disorderly people, for the most part base and immoral."

The discoverers, the Paulistas, felt cheated by the arrival of such large numbers of men. The interlopers came not only from

Brazil with their Negro slaves but from Portugal as well. In 1709 the "War of the Emboabas," as the newcomers were called, flared up, and after several years of escalating hostilities the pioneer paulistas were chased away. The Portuguese King, Dom João V, sent a governor to rule Minas Gerais. He was to establish a mint there and collect the royal tenth on all gold found. Colonial officials, aware of the damage that American gold had done to Spain's economy, were both exhilarated and apprehensive. They feared that Brazilian gold might flow into Lisbon and right back out again to pay for imports from other European nations. Their fears were well founded, for between half and three fourths of the gold that reached the mother country was indeed funneled to northern Europe.

The Paulistas, who had been evicted by the Emboabas, pushed westward through hostile country where they were rewarded by the discovery of the gold fields of Cuiabá, Goiás, and Mato Grosso. The word of their finds spread like the wind, attracting hordes of gold-crazed prospectors. According to one source the "good gold," that of twenty-three carats, "made clefts in the nuggets as if it were bursting out on all sides, while from within it gave off reflections that looked like rays of sunlight."

In 1719 a royal decree ordered the establishment of processing plants in all areas where gold was found and forbid the circulation of gold dust as currency. At the mints where the gold was converted into bars and coins, one fifth was removed. Part went to the crown and part to cover "pin money for the queen" and processing costs. When diamonds were discovered the following year in the Minas Gerais district, the entire area was made into a sealed-off crown reserve which could only be entered by presenting an official permit.

By the middle of the eighteenth century the output of gold from the mines and rivers of Brazil matched that of Spanish America. The chief beneficiary of the Brazilian gold as in the case of the Spanish gold was not the country that controlled it but the most economically developed nations of Europe. England attracted most of the Portuguese colony's treasure with her manufactured goods. A country with virtually no domestic production, she became one of the foremost gold markets of Europe. So many Spanish and Portuguese coins circulated in England that merchants and bankers carried scales designed to equate the foreign pieces with English currency.

Brazil has been credited with a total production in the eighteenth century of over 1¾ million pounds. Production rose from some 33,000 pounds in the last decade of the seventeenth century to about 375,000 pounds between 1720 and 1740. The peak of production, the twenty years following 1740, yielded a total of more than 625,000 pounds of gold. The official figures never reflected the large amounts smuggled past the eyes of the royal officials. The Brazilian gold was carried back to Lisbon in fleets of warships, and their arrival was carefully observed throughout Europe. In London in December 1736 a report was published declaring that "the Brazil fleet, consisting of 14 ships, arrived this month at Lisbon with a rich cargo of 2130 octaves of diamonds and six and a half million in gold cruzadoes, of which four and a half belong to the king and the other two to private merchants." And in September of 1748 twenty-one ships brought back "21,740 pounds of gold, 439,980 cruzadoes in silver and many chests of gem stones."

The discovery of gold and diamonds in Brazil had a number of effects on the country. Men suddenly abandoned their work on sugar and tobacco plantations or in the coastal towns and flocked to the mines. In addition, prices rose sharply because of labor shortages, and there was a great increase in the slave trade with Africa. The governor of Rio de Janiero reported to the crown in 1726 that "there is not a white miner who can live without at least one Negress from Dahomey for they say that only with them do they have any luck."

Brazil remained the focus of treasure hunters and pseudo-scientific investigations long after the gold boom days were over. The mysterious tangled heart of the vast land was made to order for persons with visions of finding lost mines and ancient cities blazing with gold. The German Krupp family was much taken with seductive tales of such a city in the Mato Grosso region. In the early 1900s they mounted a huge expedition to find it. They outfitted themselves with the best of everything. The expedition had such a vast amount of supplies and equipment that masses of pack animals were required to carry it all. Once in the trackless jungle the animals starved for lack of fodder and the project ended in a shambles, another statistic in the history of gold's power to enchant men with myth.

A French gold prospector, Apollinaire Frot, spent many years in the 1920s and 1930s exploring the Brazilian wilds. When he emerged from time to time, he alluded to amazing discoveries, so startling he feared to publish them. Frot claimed to have found a number of ancient petroglyphs in the province of Amazonas which proved that ancestors of the Egyptians had once mined gold in Brazil. One set of hieroglyphs carved on stone supposedly led him to one such mine. In 1932 a German-sponsored expedition claimed to have found a large city of stone buildings plated with gold and a monumental pyramid filled with gold. They reported they found not only gold but a number of white-bearded dwarfs, but were unable to produce any convincing evidence. Even today treasure hunters still plunge recklessly into the heart of the continent to seek the elusive gold.

Some of the gold that reached Spain from the New World came via her Pacific territory, the Philippine Islands through the Manila galleon trade. Gold in the form of bullion and jewelry from the Orient was carried east on the Manila galleons to Acapulco, despite Spain's ban on importation of gold manufactures. A contraband gold cargo intercepted in 1767 at Acapulco included Chinese and Philippine objects which included votive images, a large bird, alligator teeth capped with gold, dishes and platters of solid gold, hundreds of gem-set rings, and all kinds of jewelry, much of which was studded with diamonds and emeralds.

In the early years of the transpacific sailings to Mexico, most of the gold came in the form of bartered gold tribute rendered by the natives of the Philippines. Antonio Pigafetta, the chronicler who accompanied Magellan on his voyage of discovery to the archipelago, wrote of alluvial deposits worked by natives in the streams of Visayas. The auriferous sands yielded "pieces of gold, of the size of walnuts and eggs." Miguel López de Legaspi, the conqueror of the islands, wrote to Philip II that the people wore many gold ornaments and that gold was to be found in varying quantities in almost all of the islands. The natives, he feared, were too little interested in hard work to make working the gold deposits profitable to the crown. The Spaniards organized very little mining. They contented themselves with the considerable amounts of gold they could wring from the natives.

The initial payment in gold by two provinces of Luzon alone amounted to more than 110,000 ounces. Thereafter the amounts which went into the Spanish treasury declined. The Spanish governor in 1583 reported that 60,000 to 70,000 pesos in gold were shipped to Mexico in some years. But production was much higher. An increasing amount of gold was siphoned off into illicit trade between the natives and other Europeans who trade with them, such as the Dutch and English. Francisco Martínez de la Costa reckoned that as late as 1783 2 million pesos' worth of gold was mined in the country and traded to foreigners. His figure, however, may be regarded with some suspicion since he also makes the exaggerated claim that Thomas Cavendish, the English privateer, got a prize of 658,000 pounds of Philippine gold when he captured the Manila Galleon *Santa Ana*. In any case, the Spanish never recognized the great wealth of gold that lay in the mountains and rivers of her Pacific colony. In the eighteenth and nineteenth centuries Chinese entrepreneurs organized some gold mining. In the twentieth century the United States began large-scale exploitation of rich deposits, particularly on the island of Luzon, which yielded as much as $23 million a year in the 1930s (based on gold at $35 an ounce) and made gold one of the country's leading exports, although production sharply declined in the last several decades.

During the course of the seventeenth century it became increasingly clear that the beneficiaries of the great golden wealth of the New World mines were neither the Iberians who claimed it, the indigenous Americans whose cultures and very existence were sacrificed to it, nor the masses of West Africans who were enslaved for it. The richest harvest was gathered instead by those northern manufacturing countries which had little gold of their own.

The tons of bullion that sailed up the Guadalquivir to Seville passed into the pockets of the northern entrepreneurs, stimulating their developing industries and enriching their mode of living. As they prospered, they joined the nobles and ecclesiastics in patronizing the goldsmith. In the sixteenth century artisans in such commercial centers as Nuremberg and Augsburg lavished infinite care and detail on an expanding variety of gold and silver-gilt objects. Germany was the northern leader in goldwork until it was ravaged by the Thirty Years' War in mid-seventeenth century. Distinctive national characteristics developed in the plate and jewelry of Germany, Holland, Flanders, and England where merchant princes, princelings, and the powerful guild organizations flourished. Goldsmiths added novelties from the New World to their stock of images: Pineapples, coconuts, potatoes, vines, shells, and "noble savages" appeared on jewelry and the elaborate sculptured cups then in vogue. In the late sixteenth century the Age of Discovery inspired the gold globe cups which incorporated a modeled figure of Atlas, muscles bulging as he supported a terrestrial or celestial globe, or sometimes one above the other. In the hands of a master craftsman, with the northern commitment to perfection, these were magnificent pieces of sculpture.

In the seventeenth century the richness and florid splendor of the sixteenth-century Renaissance jewelry with its colorful enamels and baroque pearls gave way to the age of the diamond. Italy no longer set the fashion. France became the arbiter of elegance, grace, and refinement. Lapidaries, particularly those of the Low Countries, made great advances in the faceting of gems. The rose-cut diamond replaced the earlier table cut, revealing the stone's true brilliance for the first time. The diamond became the queen of gems and the emphasis in jewelry shifted from the soft glow of precious metal to the brilliant dazzle of the stones, although enameling remained very popular. The Italian Renaissance motifs of great swags of fruit, masks, and mythological creatures were replaced by French-inspired floral and vegetable themes, delicate bowls, and scrolls. The French used gold to great effect on wallpapers, architectural elements, and particularly the ornate gilded furniture of the period.

Less jewelry from the war-torn seventeenth century survives than from centuries preceding or following it. This is in part because Renaissance jewelry relied heavily on enameling and had few stones. It could be broken into smaller components without destroying its beauty. However, with the new vogue there was less reliance on the intrinsic beauty of gold and more on gems, which could easily be removed from their settings and remounted in a more fashionable setting. Faceted stones could even be recut. Until the seventeenth century a goldsmith had been both jeweler and worker in precious metals, using his own designs and cutting his own cabochon stones. With the new emphasis on faceted stones, the crafts separated. The goldsmith chiefly worked on ceremonial and domestic plate. The jeweler, using his own designs or copying from others which were circulated internationally in book form, created jewelry and accessories of gold set with gems, which he purchased from an independent lapidary who cut and polished them. Even enameling became a distinct craft.

In seventeenth-century England forced plate sales ordered by the crown accounted for the destruction of a great deal of jewelry and plate. In 1627 King Charles I levied a loan of 120,000 pounds sterling on the City of London to finance the war effort. This was a huge sum and the Worshipful Company of Goldsmiths, which had a large collection of precious jewelry and goldwork, was forced to relinquish many pieces then and more later. By the beginning of the eighteenth century they had little left. In 1641 the King ordered all plate melted down at the Royal Mint. Not only the prosperous guilds but the nobility, the goldsmith's traditional patrons, were forced to hand over their personal possessions for the King and Parliament party.

In the eighteenth century European goldsmiths following trends set in Paris gave free rein to their imagination in the execution of small personal accessories such as snuff boxes, watches, fobs, and the chatelaines they hung from. The baroque heaviness of the Renaissance was replaced with jewelry of airy lightness—elegant and delicate.

In the eighteenth century gold came into its own as a commodity and more of it was coined in Europe. Up until this time there had not been enough gold in Britain to institute a gold standard. But as Spain and Portugal pressed slaves to extract precious metals in distant lands, vainly counting on the American treasure to resolve increasingly intricate economic and political problems, the English had embarked on a road that was to lead to the Industrial Revolution. The pound sterling had served as the basis of the English monetary system since Saxon times, but increased trade with the Orient was draining much silver East where its value was appreciably higher. At the same time there was a tremendous increase in the amount of gold in Britain. It came not only from Brazil but after 1750 also from Russia.

In 1717 Sir Isaac Newton was Master of the Mint. As a mathematician he made a careful study of trade factors, gold production, and international price levels. He slightly lowered the mint price for gold, establishing a fixed price of 84 shillings and 11½ pence per troy ounce ($10.20 at 1968 exchange rate). In 1816 the country formally went on the gold standard which had been in effect for almost a century and amazingly Newton's price held stable more than two centuries until 1931.

In the early eighteenth century the China trade provided England with a small but interesting source of gold. The merchant ships which returned from the Orient with precious cargoes of tea, silks, porcelains, and drugs such as ginseng root and rhubarb often brought back gold which had been profitably exchanged for silver. Silver was in great demand in China, where it formed the basic medium of exchange. Gold was widely used in the Chinese decorative arts—in laquerwork, gilding of furniture and ornaments, and for the gold threads in sumptuous brocades—but it played no monetary role. In Europe the value of gold to silver was ten to one and even higher in England. English traders made a profit of more than 60 per cent on the deal. Ship's officers shared in the trade. They were generally permitted to leave England with a limited amount of silver to exchange for Chinese gold.

The nineteenth century was the true age of gold. It began with the continued working of the Czar's Ural mines and ended with the discovery of the world's greatest gold deposits in South Africa. The Russian gold was mined by serfs who were in effect slaves of feudal landlords and the Emperor. Extracting the South African gold, buried deep in ancient quartz reefs, requires massive organization of capital by giant corporations and depends on modern technology. In between came the halcyon years of the individual prospector who worked for himself and kept what he found. In California, Australia, New Zealand, Nevada, Colorado, Idaho, South Dakota, and finally the incredible Klondike the golden dreams of many men were fulfilled and the lives of many others broken.

Until 1848 it was Russia that led nineteenth-century gold production. The rich pockets of alluvial gold in rivers and steams on the ancient trade routes to the Black Sea and the Mediterranean had been worked since prehistory. They furnished much of the gold that shone so splendidly in the Persian, Greek, and Byzantine eras. In modern times the great era of mining was set off by the discovery in 1744 of a quartz outcrop near Ekaterinburg on the eastern slopes of the Urals. Under Catherine the Great serfs panned 84,000 ounces of high-purity gold from the rich alluvial beds in the first four decades of systematic production. The Czars sent out prospecting expeditions in the early nineteenth century, and in the remote Altai mountain valleys west of Lake Baikal they found many new deposits of auriferous sands. This forbidding region of Siberia, haunt of the fabled gold-guarding griffins of Herodotus, yielded more than 175,000 pounds of gold between 1814 and 1839, and during the 1840s as much as 17,000 pounds was being produced each year. Russia was then furnishing the world with over 60 per cent of her newly mined production.

Conditions in the gold fields were unspeakably harsh. The forced labor of the peasant serf recalled the past sufferings of slave miners from Egypt to Mexico and foreshadowed Stalin's twentieth-century slave gold miners. Working for a small number of feudal lords who had crown licenses or for the crown directly, the serfs toiled on the frozen tundra in a curtain of fog or snow six days a week from 5 A.M. to 8 P.M. They had no rights and existed joylessly on meager rations. European travelers reported that the landlords lived opulently, priding themselves on being able to offer guests the oranges of Sicily, the wines of France, and Havana cigars. They escorted visitors to their diggings and consumed champagne and caviar while casually observing the serfs at their labors.

The surge in Russian gold production was reflected in the splendor of the Imperial Court, which set the tone for the lavish displays affected by the Russian nobility. The Siberian gold made possible a proliferation of precious regalia which reflected a passion for diamonds. Empress Catherine wore a crown of gold in which 2,075 diamonds of 1,400 karats completely hid the gold. The best known of all Russian jewelers was Peter Carl Fabergé, a virtuoso of French Huguenot descent, whose workshop turned out unique objets d'art for the czars and their families at the end of the nineteenth-century. Fabergé designed fantasies of comsummate workmanship, combining gold, enamel (he could produce 144 different shades), and a variety of precious and semi-precious stones to produce exquisite objects with subtle rainbow nuances of color.

In the nineteenth-century the wilderness of the New World once again beckoned to the gold seeker. Myth and reality, mingled since the dawn of history, had propelled the conquistadores and their successors through the vast uncharted territories on the quest for treasure. Gradually the hazy outlines and features of the new lands came into focus. The Spanish had

117. 1796 quarter eagle from the Philadelphia mint. Early American gold coins were not marked with a denomination but valued according to their weight and purity in relationship to the fluctuating market price of gold.

118. Reverse of 1796 quarter eagle.

119. Late-eighteenth-century French gold coin.

120. Reverse of eighteenth-century French coin.

121. 1855 French napoleon.

123. A Forty-niner operating a rocker or cradle. *Harper's New Monthly Magazine.*

122. Obverse of French napoleon.

124. Mining scene in California ca. 1849. Honeyman Collection, Bancroft Library.

125. Prospectors panning for gold from John Sherer's *Adventures of a Gold Digger.*

126. A pocket-size gold weighing set. Wells Fargo Bank History Room.

127. The famed Holtermann Nugget, Australia. Australian Information Service.

128. Government inspector checking gold mining license, Australia. Australian Information Service.

129. Restored nineteenth-century works at Ballarat. Australian Information Service.

130. Prospectors crossing the 3,500-foot-high Chilkoot Pass to the Klondike in 1895 or 1896.

131. Working the beaches of Nome for gold. Photo by E.A. Hegg.

132. Men in protective shoes prepare gold bars for weighing in the subterranean vaults of New York's Federal Reserve Bank. NYFRB.

133. U.S. gold bar and foreign bar. Caption on reverse. NYFRB.

130. Prospectors crossing the 3,500-foot-high Chilkoot Pass to the Klondike in 1895 or 1896.

131. Working the beaches of Nome for gold. Photo by E.A. Hegg.

132. Men in protective shoes prepare gold bars for weighing in the subterranean vaults of New York's Federal Reserve Bank. NYFRB.

133. U.S. gold bar and foreign bar. Caption on reverse. NYFRB.

134. Gold bars. NYFRB.

135. Molten gold. Kloof Mine, South Africa. Dr. Harold Edgerton.

found a storehouse of gold beyond all expectations, but the ancient dream of the golden land just beyond the next mountain or lying deep in the trackless jungle remained strong.

The English settlers at Jamestown in 1607, bowdlerized textbooks notwithstanding, were just as much interested in gold as anyone else. One man complained that "There was no talk, no hope, no work but to dig gold, wash gold, refine gold, load gold." In 1608 Captain John Smith sent samples of what appeared to be rich ore back to London for assay. It turned out to be worthless. Other prospectors fared no better and gradually high hopes of finding gold in North America faded. In 1790 Benjamin Franklin attested that "gold and silver are not the produce of North America, which has no mines."

Nine years later a boy playing with a bow and arrow near the Rocky River of central North Carolina discovered a 2½-pound lump of gold where an arrow landed. He took the lump home and his father, a man named Reed, suggested that they use it as a door stop. After a couple of years a friend suggested he trade it for money. He did and then started mining in the river, collecting some 115 pounds of gold in the next ten years. Other prospectors made strikes in the same area and some large nuggets were found including one weighing 28 pounds, "of the shape and size of a domestic smoothing iron." In 1821 a mass of almost 50 pounds of gold was found in a rock crevice. A letter to Thomas Jefferson from the director of the U. S. Mint in Philadelphia in 1805 noted that "very considerable" quantities of gold were being produced in the North Carolina gold fields. Gold seekers began to flock to the area in a minuscule gold rush. They came from as far away as Europe, where the find was front-page news.

Until 1828 all of the $138,000 of domestic gold coined by the U. S. Mint came from North Carolina. Quite a bit of the local ore remained in the state, where it circulated in the form of dust and nuggets until a shrewd local businessman decided to open a private mint. Christopher Bechtler, a metalsmith from Germany, had come with his family to Rutherford, North Carolina, in 1830 where he opened a shop making jewelry out of Appalachian gold. His family mint operated until 1852 when many miners went West to try their luck on the richer diggings. But Bechtler coins continued to circulate for a number of years. Because they were a local southern product they enjoyed greater confidence than "Yankee" gold. It was not unusual for Confederate States of America contracts to specify payment in Bechtler gold rather than Confederate paper.

Small amounts of gold were washed from the streams of Virginia, South Carolina, Tennessee, and Alabama, but the second mini-strike of the century was in northeastern Georgia where gold was found on Ward's Creek. Local lore has it that the first big nugget was kicked up by a deer in 1829. This was within the Cherokee Nation: the area which had been guaranteed in 1785 to the Cherokee for "as long as the grass shall grow and the river shall run." Within a year of the strike it was reported that "4,000 persons are engaged in gathering gold at the Yahoola mines, in Cherokee country and their daily products are worth $10,000." With characteristic disregard for honoring treaties with the native Americans, Andrew Jackson promptly rescinded the federal government's agreement and the hapless Cherokees were driven along the "Trail of Tears" to settle in dusty Oklahoma. The miners moved in to work the Appalachian gold fields, the "golden land of the Yupaha" which had eluded De Soto three centuries earlier.

During 1539 and 1540 as De Soto explored the Southeast, one of his lieutenants was told by Indians in northern Florida of a province called Cale where gold was abundant and of another land where men wore gold helmets. De Soto led his men to Cale and there learned of a much richer land called Apalache, seven days farther west. They went there and found no gold. But a captive boy from a distant land called Yupaha which lay "toward the sunrise," told them of his golden land. A woman ruled and the town where she lived was of wonderful size. She collected tribute from many of the neighboring chiefs, some of whom gave her clothing and others gold in abundance. The Yupaha boy told how it was taken from the mines, melted, and refined, "just as if he had seen it done," wrote De Soto's chronicler. But the expedition never found Yupaha.

The U. S. Government established mints at Charlotte, North Carolina, and Dahlonega, Georgia, in 1838. Dahlonega, from an Indian word meaning "yellow metal," attracted throngs of get-rich-quick characters. Most of them remained poor and anonymous. However, a number of prominent southern families made fortunes from gold mines which produced an estimated 50,000 pounds by 1850. One of the best known was the statesman and orator John C. Calhoun, whose family mine near Dahlonega yielded over $4 million in pre-Civil War gold. Calhoun had a vital personal interest in the perpetuation of slavery, for his mines were worked by slaves. When the Civil War ended, the Calhoun Mine, already close to exhaustion, was forced to close down. In all, the Appalachian gold deposits yielded less than $20 million in bullion, not more than an average $300,000 a year. The majority of the alluvial deposits were worked out by 1847, and by 1866 the remaining quartz mines had also been exhausted.

The little boom in the southeastern United States was a prelude to the great gold rushes of the second half of the century when waves of eager men and women swept restlessly back and forth across the world from California to Australia to Alaska seeking gold at the end of the rainbow. The frenetic half century before the initiation of gold mining on an industrial scale in South Africa was the era of the free-lance miner. The prizes went to the strong, the persistent, and the lucky. The miner's independent spirit and perennial optimism were the hallmarks of the most stupendous gold rush in history. The saga of the prospectors is filled with stories of sudden riches, heartbreaking failures, fortitude, and undiminished hope. Most men were to learn that for every ounce of gold wrested from the earth they paid a high price in sweat, suffering, and loneliness. After fifty years little remained but ghost towns rotting in the sun and the spirited, often poignant tales told by yellowing photographs, journals, and survivors.

The dramatic discovery of gold at Sutter's Mill on January 24, 1848, sparked the California gold rush, one of the greatest mass movements of population in history. The discovery of gold in the wild, largely unexplored and unpopulated territory came less than ten days before the United States acquired California from Mexico by the peace treaty of Guadalupe Hidalgo on February 2, 1848.

It was not the first find of precious metal in California. Scattered strikes had been made by Indians, Spaniards, and others in the centuries before Mexico gained independence from Spain in 1820. Cortés had explored Baja California for the gold that was linked in the Spanish imagination with the island of "California." One of the manifold legends of mystic golden lands, this was the concoction of medieval romancers, an island "lying on the right hand of the Indies," peopled by magnificent Black Amazons who rode domesticated wild beasts adorned with gold. Montalvo, the Spanish fantasist, wrote of their bare-breasted Queen Calafía in whose land there was no metal save gold.

Cortés found no California, and one by one, through centuries of fruitless search, the shimmering myths so deeply rooted in the Spanish mentality lost their luster: the will-o'-the-wisps of California, El Dorado, Quivira, Yupaha, and the Seven Shining Cities of Cibola. No treasures to match those of Montezuma and the Incas were to be found again in the New World. Of all the dream seekers' goals only one fulfilled its golden promise. California turned out to be no island realm of hostile women, but it was a land exceedingly rich in the precious metals. In the last half of the nineteenth-century California and the West produced more gold and silver than any area before in the history of mankind.

In 1769 Spain occupied Alta California, and the padres founded the first of the California missions. Bartering Indians brought alluvial gold gathered in willow baskets to the priests who apparently were more interested in saving souls than getting rich. They accepted the gold but made little effort to find its source. Europe was dimly aware that there was gold in California; an 1816 English book on metallurgy noted in detail the gold found in the mountains there. The pioneer trapper Jedediah Smith panned alluvial gold in the Sierras a decade later and in 1840 Richard Henry Dana wrote of California gold in *Two Years Before the Mast*. In 1842 a third-generation Californian, Don Francisco López, dug up some wild onions for his wife while he was out hunting in the hills above Los Angeles. Tiny flakes which he recognized as gold clung to the roots. For a number of years his family quietly and successfully collected gold in the hills. In 1843 a prosperous Los Angeles merchant shipped a packet of gold to the U. S. Mint in Philadelphia where it was coined into the first California gold coins. But it aroused little interest because California belonged to Mexico.

James Marshall's celebrated discovery of gold at Johann Sutter's millrace on the American River came at a fortuitous time for the adolescent United States which was making the painful transition from an agrarian age to an industrial age. The country in the 1840s was in a tumult. Politics were corrupt, banking and investment precarious, and slavery becoming an emotional issue. Mass immigration, averaging around 100,000 a year, reached 296,000 in 1848, the year of the Irish potato famine, and dangerously strained the national economy which was already reeling after the Mexican War. Gold was in short supply. When word leaked out of gold in the California find, the nation was thrown into a frenzy. The dream of American gold was reborn. One journalist commented, "The farmers have thrown aside their plows, the lawyers their briefs, the doctors their pills, the priests their prayer books, and all are now digging gold." He was not exaggerating. Tens of thousands of Americans and immigrants converged on the Pacific wilderness to seek their fortunes. In the process they gave a tremendous boost to the country's economy and morale, supplying an average of 175,000 pounds of gold annually by 1851.

The fateful gold nugget gave no clue to the magnitude of what was to come, for it was no bigger than a pea. James Marshall, who started it all, was an itinerant Jack-of-all-trades, hired to construct a sawmill for the landowner Johann Sutter. Marshall was a moody and ineffectual man, born under an unlucky star. "My finding gold," he said, "was to deprive me of my rights of a settler and an American citizen." His homestead was overrun by swarms of prospectors. He abandoned it and took up a pan and shovel himself, but through years of prospecting, gold such as had caught his eye that fateful January morning eluded him. His last years were spent in drink and abject poverty. He repeatedly petitioned the California legislature for a pension. Finally it was granted but then cruelly withdrawn when he showed up drunk at a legislative session. Only after he died did the state erect a statue in his honor.

Johann Augustus Sutter suffered an even more precipitous de-

cline and fall. A German-born Swiss who had come to the
United States via Hawaii, with a record of bankruptcies and for-
geries behind him, Sutter got a land grant from the Mexican
Government for 230 square miles of lush land in the central valley of California. He ruled benevolently over an agrarian empire
of some 142,000 acres, issuing his own coins and trading produce
as far away as the Pacific Islands and South America. He ought
to have been a Croesus from his trading alone not to mention the
gold found on his land. But he was a generous, genial fellow, not
much of a businessman and perennially in debt. The discovery of
gold, far from enriching him, destroyed his empire and his life.

When Marshall came to him with the yellow flakes and grains
from the millrace, Sutter begged him to keep the find secret at
least for six weeks. But as a Spanish proverb says, "Gold and
love affairs are hard to hide," and before long the word was out.
At first men were skeptical. One of San Francisco's two fledgling
papers, the *California Star*, reported that it was all a "sham; a
supurb takein as was ever got up to guzzle the gullible." But Sutter's mill hands quit and devoted themselves to working with a
rocker, or cradle as it was sometimes called, getting gold worth
up to fifty dollars a day from the river, and the news inevitably spread. His thousands of employees abandoned work. More
men made their way to the Sutter land but Sutter was unable to
hire any of them to harvest the crops which rotted in the fields,
to tend his livestock, milk his cows, or finish his mill.

Like creatures possessed, men took baskets, even kitchen
sieves, to gather the gold with. The fortunate made as much as
$800 a day in some places, and by the end of the year an es-
timated $6 million worth had been found. Ruffians camped out
anywhere, helping themselves to the stock from Sutter's store, his
crops and animals. Sutter, long a drinker, immersed himself ever
deeper in an alcoholic daze. Eventually he prosecuted 17,221
squatters and demanded $25 million in compensation from the
state of California which had become part of the Union in 1850.
On May 15, 1855, the highest judge in the state ruled in his
favor declaring that the huge territory was indeed his. Jubilation
was brief, followed by havoc. A mob of more than ten thousand,
angered by the decision, burned the court, seized the state ar-

chives, tried to lynch the judge, and plundered Sutter's property and buildings leaving them in flames. His eldest son shot himself, the second son was murdered, and the third drowned on his way to Europe. The broken Sutter never recovered. For the following twenty-five years a deranged, stumbling old man in general's uniform haunted the Congress pleading his case with one legislator after another. The story goes that one afternooon as he sat on the Capitol steps, a group of mischievous boys hailed him with cries of "You've won, you've won! Congress has settled it!" Hearing this, the old man rose to his full height for the first time in many years and then keeled over dead, his suffering ended.

There were many treasure hunters deluded at the end of the rainbow. But never in history had so many men actually found the tantalizing pot of gold and been free to keep it or squander it. In 1845 there had only been some 700 United States citizens in California. In 1848 California's population stood at 14,000 (excluding Indians, who weren't counted in those days), of whom 6,500 were "foreigners." But by the end of 1849 no fewer than 100,000 Argonauts, as the gold seekers were called, had descended on the territory. They came from everywhere. The average American prospector in the early rush days was not a grizzled old sourdough but a man in his twenties, educated and reasonably well off. A large number were new immigrants—poor and often illiterate.

For many, California's gold offered the only way to a better life. A poignant extract from a miner's letter to his wife in 1852 expresses the sentiments of many lonely prospectors:

> Jane I left you and them boys for no other reason than this to come here to procure a little property by the sweat of my brow so that we could have a place of our own that I mite not be a dog for other people any longer. . . . there are murders commited about every day on the account of licker and gambling but I have not bought a glass of licker since I left home. . . . I never knew what it was to leave home til I left a wife and children. . . . I know you feel lonsom when night appears but let us think that it is for the best so to be

and do the best we can for two years or so and I hope
Jane that we shall be reworded for so doing and meet
in a famely sircal once more. that is my prayer.

In the great migration thousands of every culture, class and
calling flowed to the gold fields. Mormons heedless of patriarch
Brigham Young's command to stay home rallied to the cry of
"California! To California! To the Gold of Ophir!" Men came
from Hawaii (the Sandwich Islands), from Europe and Latin
America. They came from Great Britain and the colonies. Men
like the famed African explorer Henry Morton Stanley mingled
with jailbirds from the convict colony of Australia. The clannish
French who came in large numbers were referred to as "Kesky-
dees," because their inevitable reply to a question in English was
a puzzled *"Qu'est-ce qu'il dit?"* So many Chinese came that by
1852 there were 25,000 in the state who were the object of discrimination and often restricted to sifting another man's leavings
for minute bits of overlooked gold. There were 120,000 miners
digging in the California foothills at the peak of the gold rush.
Twenty years later there were only 30,000—half of them the persistent Chinese gleaning worked-over gravels.

More Chinese came to the gold fields than any other foreign
group. Not all who set out for the Golden Land made it. Some
fell victim to unscrupulous countrymen who lured them from
their villages to Chinese ports, bilked them, and disappeared.
One group of 800 Chinese who sailed for California in the mid-
nineteenth-century ended up as slaves digging guano on the
scorching, Godforsaken Chincha Islands off the coast of Peru. An
1853 article in the New York *Times* described the nightmare life
of the poor creatures who worked, nearly naked, feeding like
dogs and sleeping in caves. They were kept at their work by
whip-wielding black overseers. An American visitor testified to
the welted bodies of the emaciated coolies who wore thick bandages over their faces in an effort to filter out the acrid, choking
fumes from the guano, which could eventually cause blindness.
Their only release was death. Many flung themselves over the
precipices into the sea in the belief that their spirits would
awaken once again in their homeland.

Not many women went to the gold fields. Those that did faced a rough life in the raw tumult of the mining camps. The California census of 1850 lists less than 8 per cent of the population as female. Some of the women who followed their men were hard workers like Mrs. R., who, according to an admiring miner, was a "magnificent woman! . . . earnt her old man $900 in nine weeks taking in washing." The gold fields attracted a handful of earnest and unsuccessful temperance lecturers like a Miss Farnham who conceived of a scheme to end the pervasive lawlessness of the frontier by the importation of "5,000 virtuous New England women."

Women were indeed imported from the East; not all of them were virtuous. An industrious prostitute could easily make a fortune. One young woman retired after a year's activity which netted her $50,000. On the other hand unsuspecting working girls back East who were hired to be "domestics" sometimes found themselves in bordellos and gambling halls. More of them than Miss Farnham would have admitted made the best of it taking advantage of a market in which an attractive girl could name her price. Men fresh from the rigors of the camps were starved for entertainment. They showered bags of gold dust on actresses and dancers. In the remote camps a woman's satin slipper, well worn, could bring fifty dollars.

In the early days, gold dust circulated as currency along with coins of every nation and coins and stamped ingots issued by various private mints. Men carried a leather poke to hold their gold and a miniature balance scale to weigh it. A pinch was worth about twenty-five cents. An ounce of gold was valued at sixteen dollars but often brought less. It was not uncommon for adulterated gold dust or bogus "retort nuggets" alloyed with base metals to be fobbed off on the unwary. A determined prostitute from Hong Kong once took a client to court in San Francisco because he had paid her in watered gold dust—and won.

Ladies of "virtue" were very much in demand. One woman, of this scarce breed buried her husband on one day and married the chief mourner the next. Funerals were a common sight. The Forty-niners were a profane lot but highly superstitious and they never failed to say a few words over a fallen comrade. One cloudy day a group of men bowed their heads around a freshly dug grave as a preacher intoned a prayer. Suddenly, the sun came out lighting up flecks of gold, spangling the newly turned earth at their feet. Every mourner, including the preacher, whooped and immediately fell to his knees scrabbling at the pay dirt, the deceased already forgotten.

In the universal rush for riches it was a foregone conclusion that although the prospectors might not hit pay dirt, the merchants, whores, shipowners, and wagon train outfitters would. The way to the gold fields was long and dangerous whether one went by land or by sea. Profiteers operating at both ends of the journey congratulated themselves on heady profits.

Eager neophytes who had elected the overland route, which covered some of the most hostile terrain in North America, gathered at the chaotic staging points along the Missouri River. They bought "guides" full of misinformation which marked trails where there were none, showed fodder and water where there was burning desert, and lopped two to three hundred miles off the route with a stroke of the pen. They invested their precious grubstake in "gold extractors" and other worthless equipment peddled by unscrupulous knaves. They set out with flaming hopes, but the brutal trails across the West were littered with broken wagons, abandoned equipment, and the carcasses and skeletons of mules, horses, and cattle. The way led across dusty plains, hellish deserts, and freezing mountains, some so steep horses and prairie schooners had to be lowered over cliffs with slings. Rude crosses marked the lonely graves of the more than five thousand souls who never made it to the Promised Land.

The other, equally harrowing route to the gold fields was by sea. One could go around Cape Horn, an eighteen-hundred-mile voyage through treacherous seas in foul, overcrowded ships, which took six to eight months until the advent of the swift clipper ships reduced the time to a little over three months. The alternative route was quicker taking as little as thirty-four days, and accordingly more expensive, but it was certainly no more pleasant. It involved sailing from an East Coast port south to Chagres or Aspinwall on the Atlantic coast of the Isthmus of Panama. Once there men who had paid an extortionate $380 for a first-class passage from New York to San Francisco, the great port of the gold rush, had to cough up an additional fee to be guided up the fever-infested Chagres River and then overland by mule through teeming jungle mud to Panama City on the Pacific. Men who chose this route because it was the fastest often found themselves waiting up to eight weeks in the pest hole of Panama City for a berth to San Francisco. One New York man who had sailed with $475 arrived in California with his grubstake reduced by the frustrating six-week wait to a mere $6.

The overlanders who survived the punishment of the elements, Indian attack, hunger, thirst, and illness arrived totally exhausted, resources drained. Those who had made the ocean voyage were no better off. Huddled fire-prone shanty towns of lean-tos or tents took them in. Swift-springing settlements appeared along the gold fields: towns with names like Bedbug, Timbuctoo, Rough and Ready, Second Garrote, Ophir, and Hoodoo Bar. Many names mirror their founding fathers: Spanish Flat, Dutch Flat, Chinese Camp (where the great Tong War took place), Cherokee, and Hornitos, so-called after the oven-shaped tombs of Mexican settlers who had been forced out of nearby Quartzburg by a "Law and Order Committee." They staked claims on the Mother Lode—a belt of gold-bearing quartz ranging from a few hundred feet to two miles wide and more than one hundred miles long—and set to work.

There were no laws to either hinder or protect them. Such a mixture of cultures, class, and character inevitably made a volatile brew. Murder and robbery were punished swiftly with lynch mob justice. A Mexican dance hall girl who killed an American in self-defense was hanged before an enthusiastic crowd despite the fact that she was pregnant. A Yankee shopkeeper who remembered the event wrote in a letter: "I always think of the Spanish girl standing on a plank of the bridge, tossing her hat to a friend and putting the rope around her neck, folding her hands and facing death with bravery that shamed us men. And girls," he added wistfully, "were so scarce in those days too."

San Francisco, the warehouse of the gold rush, was founded as Yerba Buena by a Spanish explorer in 1776. It was no more than a dusty village on the bay in 1848. By the end of 1849 more than 40,000 men had passed through and there were 25,000 inhabitants living in ramshackle huts and canvas houses scattered on the hills and shore. The bay was crowded with hundreds of rotting deserted ships, many with cargoes never unloaded. In the ten years following Marshall's discovery California had produced $55 million in gold and most of it passed through San Francisco. The archetypal boomtown, San Francisco, in the 1850s averaged thirty new houses, two murders, and one fire daily. It lured gold-laden pleasure seekers with a thousand gambling dens and more than five hundred saloons. The fledgling metropolis was razed by fire six times in a year and a half.

Con men profited handsomely from the gold rush without hefting a shovel. Mark Twain is credited with the observation that "a gold or silver mine is nothing more than a hole in the ground with a liar on top." Exaggerated tales were as common as fleas in the gold camps and gambling halls of the old West. Most of them were simply prospectors' braggadocio. But for every simple boaster there was a flimflam man who found the starry-eyed greenhorn easy prey.

A man who had depleted an alluvial claim and wanted to unload it and move on would sometimes chew gold dust with his tobacco and spit into the water where he was panning. This introduced "color" to impress any prospective purchaser who might be within range.

The bunco artists had countless ploys to exercise on gold-struck suckers who believed the precious stuff was everywhere. Some were as crude as throwing a few ounces of gold dust at the bottom of a sterile open digging to clinch a sale. There were many other forms of "salting." A shotgun loaded with bits of dust could be fired at a gravel or rock face so that bits would stick as though they had been there for aeons. A prospective buyer would be taken to the claim and encouraged to take a sample for assay. Claims that had once been famous bonanza strikes were especially easy to salt and sell to the unsophisticated prospector who failed to consider they might have become exhausted.

Less ingenuous investors insisted on enlisting the advice of geologists, engineers, and assayers before laying out large sums. But even these experts could be hornswoggled. To evaluate a vein, mining engineers and their crews made random shallow grooves along the vein in question, spreading canvas to collect the chips and then placing the samples in canvas bags which were fastened with a lead seal and identified by groove location. Clever swindlers would paint the surface of the area to be sampled with a solution of gold chloride or inject a little gold dust into crevices.

Or a lead-sealed sack of virgin ore could be tampered with. Ingenious salters made counterfeit seals from wax impressions so they could open the sacks while they were in storage, introduce a little gold dust, and then reseal them. Sometimes a bit of "color" might be sprinkled onto the rough surface of the canvas bags before they were used. Another method of salting was as straightforward as gaining solitary access to the sealed bags, opening a seam, and after "salt" had been put in, sewing the seams up. There were cases of gold chloride solution squirted into sealed bags by hypodermic needles and gold dust blown in through goose quills. Occasionally a wary potential sucker unmasked a swindler by placing bags of ore already tested and known to be sterile in a place where the salter had access to them. The jig was up if they miraculously contained gold when re-examined.

In San Francisco and the other supply centers, inflation devoured a miner's gold. Building lots in San Francisco went almost overnight from $12 to $10,000; bricks cost as much as $1, shovels $10, and eggs $1 apiece. In the more remote camps along the Sierras a sack of flour could cost $100, a barrel of the same $800, an egg $3, and a potato and slice of bread $1 each. Miners purchasing the indispensable picks, shovels, and pans in remote areas paid as much as one hundred dollars for each. Some even paid as much as ten ounces of gold for each of these tools.

Men with quick wits could make a killing. A ship captain brought a cargo of stray cats to rat-plagued San Francisco, where they sold quickly for $10 a head. A young wheelbarrow maker named John Studebaker and a butcher named Armour launched their empires in the gold rush towns. Almost every conceivable item sold well even at twenty times its purchase price. One merchant, however, who found himself with an oversupply of tin pans priced at ten cents each, found a way to move them. At night he sprinkled an ounce of gold dust in the streets around his store. Next day, with a great show he swept up a panful of dirt and professed great amazement when gold glittered among the dust. Within minutes he had sold all his ten-cent wash pans for two dollars.

In the palmy first couple of years many prospectors averaged $30 to $50 a day, but it meant backbreaking work with one's legs in icy, muddy water, toiling under blistering sun or bone-chilling rain. There were men who made great strikes but few were lucky or disciplined enough to keep their finds and retire wealthy. A few prospectors found spectacular nuggets, but most of the gold was dust which showed as "color" in a stream, flakes, grains, or small nuggets. The famous nugget found at Sutter's Mill weighed less than a quarter of an ounce. The largest piece of native gold found at Carson Hill in 1854 was a mass weighing 195 pounds. The largest true nugget weighed a magnificent 54 pounds troy and was found at Magalia in 1859. Until a few years ago a celebration was held annually in its honor. Finding a large nugget sometimes had a peculiar effect: a Frenchman found a beauty worth over $5,000 one day, became insane the next, and was shut up in an asylum, although his family in France received the income from the sale of the nugget.

For the first time in civilized history men were free to take treasure from the wilderness; free gold for whoever found it. In the first delirious days, the soaring dreams of a real "strike," came true for many amateurs. A man hunting rabbits near Angel's Camp stuck a stick in the ground by a manzanita bush exposing a piece of gold-bearing quartz. He used a knife to dig $700 worth of gold out of it that day. He returned the next with better tools and gouged out an additional $2,000 more, and $7,000 the third day. Three German prospectors exploring on a high tributary of the Feather River used spoons to dig $36,000 of gold flakes out of cracks in the rock. The news of the strike leaked out and men dropped everything to rush to the area, aptly named "Rich Bar." It was so lucrative claims were limited to ten square feet; one pan of dirt easily yielded $1,500 to $2,000 and the record was said to have been a pan worth $2,900. But such phenomenal strikes were characteristic only of the early days when prospectors were working virgin ground. By 1852 the zenith had been reached; the heyday of the man with a dream and a shovel was over.

In the first few years the yield varied widely from one area to another. More than 40 per cent of California's gold was washed from placer deposits of the western Sierra Nevada. At Sutter's Mill men generally made $25 to $30 a day working a rocker. However, in the gravel bars of the North Fork of the American, the Yuba, Trinity, Feather, and Stanislaus rivers it was not uncommon for men to find gold worth $500 to $5,000 in a single day. Gold production increased annually to 2½ million ounces in 1851 and peaked at 3 million in 1853. In 1852 the known alluvial deposits began giving out, although the following year the fabulous placers at Colombia, California, yielded the first real colossal amounts of gold, which was not depleted until the early 1860s.

In 1852 miners, realizing that much gold lay trapped in quartz deep beneath the earth, began sinking shafts in the first extensive underground mining of ancient buried river channels. Stamping mills for processing the mined ore were built. Underground tunnels were carved through solid rock. To get at the subterranean gravels, miners sunk "coyote holes," deep shafts to lower levels near bedrock with horizontal tunnels or "drifts" radiating out. It was difficult, dangerous, and expensive. Cave-ins frequently resulted from weak framing and many lives were lost. At Grass Valley the workings of the Empire Star Mine plunged a mile deep to a honeycomb of over two hundred miles of galleries. Such mining changed the complexion of California gold production, for it required significant capital and sophisticated organization. George Hearst, father of the famous news baron, and Leland Stanford were among the men who made colossal fortunes from hard-rock mine holdings.

In the first flush of discovery the forty-niners had been content to skim the cream, the easily collected gold from the streams and adjacent banks of the western Sierra Nevada. The average gold seeker had no knowledge of mining or metallurgy. All he needed was an eye for "color," a strong back, a pan, a shovel, and perhaps a cradle. Pan washing requires no more than a shallow iron dish, patience, and a deft hand. Some of the gold-bearing sand, mixed with water, is scooped up. With a practiced move of the wrist the sand or mud swirls to the edge of the pan and is washed away, while the heavy yellow grains collect in the center.

A slightly more specialized piece of equipment is the cradle or rocker used by the Forty-niners and later in Australia and elsewhere. It is a wooden trough about six feet long, fitted on wooden rockers in a sloping position. The bottom is fitted with transverse wooden slats or riffles. The auriferous sand is shoveled in through a screen at one end, and as the cradle is rocked a stream of water is flushed through to carry the sand away leaving the gold particles trapped in the riffles.

With time the more ingenious miners devised new methods or revived old techniques to increase their production. They used such ancient and rudimentary techniques as winnowing the ore in baskets as was done in Ancient Egypt or trapping gold particles in rough woolen blankets reminiscent of the Black Sea area fleeces. Mercury was used in the amalgamation process. They built sluice boxes including one called the "long tom" which was almost exactly like a device described in Agricola's medieval treatise. It was a long wooden trough shaped like an inverted funnel through which a continuous stream of water ran. While one or two men continually shoveled dirt another removed stones and debris which impeded the flow through. The heavy gold particles were trapped on a slatted bottom as the waterborne detritus washed away. With such a system a much greater volume of earth could be processed.

The long tom and its more elaborate variations required running water. When an immediate source wasn't handy a system of flumes and ditches was dug to carry water, sometimes from several miles away, to the gold-bearing earth. After 1850, millions of tons of gravel were washed in almost 5,000 miles of channels which veined the landscape. Joint-stock companies were formed to supply the co-operative labor, equipment, and capital such an effort required. The individual miner who had neither the inclination nor the means to join in such undertakings often set out by himself. Restless and determined, he prospected through the tangled mountain wilderness, tracing the source of every creek and stream in a search for the Mother Lode, the chief vein from which downstream bits had been eroded.

In 1850 miners, impatient with having to dig into gold-laden hillsides and gorges with pick and shovel, developed a new technique called ground sluicing to handle low-grade gravels near the surface. They dug a narrow gully down the hillside they intended to wash. A flume was directed to the top of the channel and water channeled to rush down it as the men shoveled dirt into the artificial stream. A good deal of gold that passed through it was lost, but fair quantities caught on the rocks and other natural obstructions. Every few weeks the debris that had settled in the natural riffles would be washed through a long tom to separate the gold.

By 1852 this had led to a revival of hydraulic mining such as the Romans used in Spain. Water was piped under pressure up to thirty thousand gallons a minute through hoses directed on gold-bearing slopes, hills, even mountains. It was a cheap, efficient, and profitable way to get at the gold but horribly destructive. The California landscape is dotted with massive jumbles of barren rock and sheared mountains, time-softened to an eerie beauty. They are scars of the raw wounds which defaced the mining districts where hydraulicking washed away forests, hills, whole mountains. Farm lands were flooded and rivers clogged. Even San Francisco Bay was discolored by hydraulic detritus. This was the chief method of gold production from 1864 until 1884, when the practice was outlawed. Hydraulic mining was controlled by highly capitalized gravel mining companies. The free-lance miner was able to find some gold by hand processing the tailings from hydraulic operations (they were sometimes quite rich), but it was investors in New York, San Francisco, and London who made the real profits.

Gold seekers who had made the trek to the rolling foothills of the Sierra Nevada too late to find loose surface gold, who had combed the overgrown ravines, panned hundreds of streams, and dug through bedrock without finding a bonanza, were understandably bitter. One recalled that "sudden disappointment on reaching the mines did not only sink the heart but sometimes the minds of the gold seekers." One man wrote that he did find gold but had to dig through bedrock to get it. He could dig only a dozen pans a day from which he gleaned an ounce of gold. "Out of this," he wrote, "it required about $10 per day to supply my food which was usually beef or pickled pork, hard bread and coffee. By extra economy, I sometimes managed to subsist on $8 per day. Since an ounce of gold was officially priced at $16, he like most prospectors was eking out a marginal living.

Dreams of gold didn't wither easily in spite of disillusion. Many men, having been bitten by the gold bug, moved on to seek El Dorado elsewhere. Some prospected throughout the coastal and Rocky Mountain regions with modest success.

In 1858 a cry of "Gold, Gold" went up on British Columbia's Fraser River, and during the short-lived boom six out of every hundred persons in California shouldered pick and shovel and trekked north to Canada to join the trappers, traders, and Indians who swarmed into the territory, swelling the total to 25,000. The sourdoughs in British Columbia found that the British crown had organized admirably to avoid the lawlessness and confusion of the California camps. The digging was government-controlled and licenses were issued for payment of a monthly fee. Miners were supervised and permission to prospect was revoked if there was rowdiness. The Canadian officials, environmentalists before their time, withdrew permission from miners who polluted streams or needlessly destroyed trees. The amount of British Columbian gold turned out to be grossly exaggerated. More than thirty other unjustified "rushes" occurred during the fifties. At the merest whisper of gold, fevered prospectors zeroed in on remote parts of California, Washington, Oregon, and even South America.

In 1858 veterans from California's depleted gold fields found rich, shallow deposits of placer gold in Arizona. The landscape of the Southwest was already pocked with sites sporadically worked by Spaniards and Indians in the two and a half centuries before New Mexico and Arizona became states. The new mining excitement was ephemeral. In the first rosy flush the merchants, traders, gamblers, and saloon keepers, who always found more gold was to be had from working the miners than the mines, were drawn to the area as by a magnet. Overnight Gila City sprang up to accommodate the boom. Then, almost as suddenly, the auriferous earth of the canyons and gulches gave out. Within a week the city was all but deserted.

The slightest hint of a strike drew the peripatetic treasure hunters like flies. They swarmed to Utah, New Mexico, Colorado, Idaho, Nevada, and South Dakota. Almost everywhere they encountered disappointment and often recalcitrant Indians. Gold was deposited in some of the earth's least agreeable regions, and the mining frontier of the Southwest was particularly hostile. The vast distances across arid, rough land made transportation and communication extremely difficult. Geography and geology made mining hard labor, indeed, but men who had the fever met all challenges.

In 1859 in a dry, sagebrush-covered gully of Washoe County near Carson City, Nevada, two poor Irish prospectors saw a ground squirrel's burrow in front of which was a pile of peculiarly colored black dirt. Mixed in with it was the "damned blue stuff" prospectors had been throwing away for years. The Irishmen had a sample tested. The black earth proved to contain a large amount of electrum; the blue earth was rich in silver. The men, who had been averaging a dollar a day, staked a claim. They called it Ophir and it lived up to its name. It was part of the fabulous Comstock Lode. The famous lode, four miles long, is best known today for its silver, but it was so packed with gold that in twenty years following its discovery it was the country's chief gold producer. The Comstock made a score of men magnates for life and was responsible for the "flash in the pan" wealth of many others.

George Hearst, the California mine speculator and developer, got wind of the Ophir find where gold, albeit pale and worth less per ounce because of the silver content, was being taken out by the pound. He sold his California gold mine, borrowed some money, and bought an interest along with several other opportunist entrepreneurs. As for the discoverers, McLaughlin sold his share for $3,500 and ultimately had a pauper's funeral. O'Riley held on for a while and then sold for $40,000—far less than the claim was worth. He lost his money on the stock market and died in an insane asylum. The shrewd Hearst, antithesis of the starry-eyed prospectors, parlayed his interest in the Ophir into a fortune, which he then used to involve himself in almost all the major lode-mining operations of the West.

In the Comstock mines Hearst's engineers were faced with age-old problems endemic to deep mining. The techniques they developed to cope with ventilation and ground support problems are still employed today. First they tried methods Agricola had described such as carving out rock supports to shore up the stopes, or rooms; but these collapsed because the ore body was too soft. Subsequently timber-stope mining was introduced in which square-set timbers were used to brace the walls and roofs of a stope as the ore was removed. The wooden cages could be piled on top of each other, the roof of one serving as the floor of another as the miners worked their way upward. Waste rock was emptied below to fill the area already worked.

The independent Argonaut found little scope for his dream in the new mines where he was only a wage laborer. His pans and cradle were of no use at three thousand feet below where muckers toiled on fifteen-minute shifts, always fearful of being scalded by steaming subterranean water at 170° Fahrenheit. By 1880 Nevada's Washoe Boom was over. The capitalists who had made their fortunes withdrew to their San Francisco mansions. The miners—greenhorns and veterans of earlier strikes—moved on, leaving Virginia City as a monument to the nineteenth-century boom-and-bust phenomenon. "The miners were like quicksilver," wrote H. H. Bancroft in his history of the Northwest. "A mass of them dropped in any locality and broke off into individual globules, and ran off after any atom of gold in their vicinity. They stayed nowhere longer than the gold attracted them."

In 1859 the infamous "Pike's Peak" rush got under way as 100,000 sanguine prospectors streamed across the vast stretches of the Great Plains to the Rocky Mountains gold fields. Fewer than half stuck it out and reached the Rockies. The rush was set off by the rumor of a solid mass of gold weighing tens of millions of tons deep in the bowels of the mountains, pieces of which had been exposed by aeons of erosion, broken off and washed into the streams of the eastern slopes. Such ridiculous claims were solemnly printed in midwestern and eastern newspapers and fervently believed by the masses who set out in ox-drawn prairie schooners with the cry "Pike's Peak or bust!" ringing in the air.

Pike's Peak was a superb example of promotion. There was some gold at the end of the trail; but not much, certainly not enough to support the overblown expectations of the thousands who had read highly colored newspaper accounts and deliberately misleading guidebooks. The rumor was fed by the string of towns along the Missouri River down to St. Louis. The financial panic of 1857—one of the nation's most severe depressions—had left them in dire straits. A gold rush would boost the economy nicely, and so the actual discovery of a gold pocket on Cherry Creek near the present site of Denver, by a veteran of both the Georgia and California gold fields, was inflated out of all proportion.

The outfitters in the towns of the Kansas and Missouri frontiers rubbed their hands as the newspapers manufactured banner headlines proclaiming "The New Golconda." Callous promoters published dozens of guides like those which earlier misled the Forty-niners. They promised gold in every shovelful of dirt and twisted the truth, inventing bridges where there were none, inventing roads as smooth as silk, and ample water and grass for the oxen all along the route. They shortened the journey by hundreds of miles and took poetic license to turn brutal arid desert into lush grassland. In actuality the trail was long and arduous, stretches of it were largely unexplored, water holes were dry, and at times great walls of fire swept over the parched prairies. Hunger, thirst, and exhaustion were the companions of many who made it to Pike's Peak only to find that they had been flimflammed. Many others fell by the wayside as provisions ran out, and there were several recorded instances of cannibalism.

Within a year the bubble burst and the bitterly disappointed miners, who had been badly fleeced, threatened "burning down all the towns on the Missouri." Most of the disillusioned returned home but some stayed on, with Denver as their supply center, to find gold in such places as Gregory Gulch—the richest of the mini-strikes—Idaho Springs, and Gold Hill. Enough gold was produced so that by 1866 Denver merited a United States mint.

In 1892 the richest gold mining area in the Rockies was discovered at Cripple Creek just southwest of Pike's Peak. A treasure-hunting carpenter who had been prospecting on weekends for twenty years tested a rock called sylvanite—so common it was used in construction—and found it was a telluride of gold and silver. He followed the trail of sylvanite to its source at the mouth of an extinct volcano, staked a claim, sold it for $20 million, and retired. Within months a town with a 125-room hotel appeared at Cripple Creek attracting crowds of treasure hunters and scoundrels. "Crime in our fair city," wrote the marshal of Colorado Springs, "is at an all time low. All the criminals have moved to Cripple Creek." One mine after another was sunk, and by the end of 1896 nearly $22 million worth of gold had been produced. In 1900 the district population burgeoned to fifty thousand and production accounted for almost a quarter of the country's gold supply. It continued to pour out gold until the 1960s, employing upward of six thousand men during peak periods.

Just as during the conquistadores' gold rushes, it was the native population that suffered most. "You are already taking our country from us fast enough," an Arizona Indian told J. Ross Browne, "we will soon have no place of safety left. If we show you where these yellow stones are, you will come there in thousands and drive us away and kill us." And that is what happened. The gold seekers were the first into the native American's ancestral lands. They blazed the trail followed by the stockman and farmer and gradually the Indian lost his land and holy places. Despite his encroachment on tribal lands the treasure hunter was at first tolerated by the Indian. The lone prospector roaming the hills made little difference in the wide-open spaces of the West. But towns were born and grew into permanent settlements attracting increasing numbers of men, women, traders, farmers, and ranchers and then the railroad cut across the country. The native found his land was being devoured by the spreading white man's world and his hunting grounds closed to him. The Indians protested in the only way that seemed to be listened to. They attacked the Argonauts' wagon trains and mining camps.

The response of the United States Government was sharp and shameful as one late example amply shows. The massive forest-carpeted Black Hills of South Dakota were the Holy Wilderness of the Sioux, their sacred hunting grounds. There were rumors among the white men that the home of the thunder god was filled with gold. The Sioux had found gold but tried to keep it secret, aware of how the white men lusted after it.

In 1874 General George A. Custer with the 7th Cavalry and a force of geologists, prospectors, assayers, and reporters entered the sacred Black Hills for the purpose of "exploration." This act violated the Sioux-United States treaty forbidding prospecting or settlement by the white men in the territory of the Dakota Nation. The men of Custer's ridiculously large expedition found ample evidence of gold in the rushing streams and cataracts of the primeval hills.

When Custer returned from what had effectively been a pleasant three-month vacation spent panning for gold, collecting butterflies, hunting elk, and pressing flowers at government expense, he reported that gold had been found but that "the hasty examination [although three months would seem to be time for more than a cursory investigation] we were forced to make did not enable us to determine in any satisfactory degree the richness or extent of the gold deposits in that region." Despite his moderate assessment, the nation received word of the gold in Dakota with eagerness.

For a while the government forbade entrance into the Dakota Nation. But even as the army attempted to turn them back companies of miners, organized in eastern and midwestern cities, managed to get past. The national economy had been crippled by the panic of 1873, which came after two years of wild railroad speculation, and the government was under great pressure to somehow make the gold of the Black Hills available to "Americans." In 1875 a group of Sioux chiefs were brought to Washington in an effort to have them sell the Black Hills. They refused, so the government organized a tribal council of twenty thousand Sioux requesting them to relinquish their sacred lands. Of course the council refused.

They were ordered back to their reservations on pain of being treated as hostile enemies. Only a few went home. The government launched an offensive against the rest, the Sioux and Cheyenne who were led by the great strategist Chief Sitting Bull. The Indians defeated the United States forces at the Battle of the Rosebud and then wiped out General Custer and his famous 7th Cavalry at the Battle of Little Big Horn. But they were hollow victories, for as the harsh winter approached and the Indians looked forward to returning to the reservations, the government announced that it would refuse to feed them unless they signed over the Black Hills. They did so on September 26, 1876.

The Manuel brothers, Moses and Fred, late of the gold fields of six other states and Alaska, were among the thousands who swarmed into the narrow defiles and canyons of the new bonanza area. They located a lucrative placer deposit which they worked through the snowy winter. In the spring, with the thaws, they traced it to its source or lead and found a quartz outcrop laden with gold. They took out $5,000 in gold and then sold the claim in 1878 for $70,000 to the Homestake Mining Company, which George Hearst had formed with two partners in California the year before. The Homestake Company bought up claim after claim as the easy placer gold dwindled, parlaying the company into the largest gold mining firm in the Western Hemisphere. By the mid 1880s the starry-eyed prospectors and their cradles had departed with the last of the alluvial wealth and were replaced by cadres of hard-rock miners working for the Homestake Company. By 1924 the Homestake accounted for about 90 per cent of the total of more than $230 million in gold extracted from the Black Hills since 1876. The two hundred miles of workings on thirty-four levels still yields an average of 400,000 ounces annually.

The United States ranks fourth in world production of newly mined gold today. The Homestake is the nation's largest producer, processing a ton of ore, brought up from mile-deep galleries, to produce a lump of refined gold about the size of a gumdrop weighing three tenths of an ounce. The ghostly shades of the lone prospectors who made the American gold rush one of mankind's most exciting epics pale in the roar of the giant machinery at the great industrialized mines. But in the streams, rivers, canyons, and hills of the Southwest the ghosts of the nineteenth-century gold seekers have recently been joined by legions of men, women, and children who have turned weekend prospecting into a pleasureful and sometimes profitable pastime.

One of the Australians who prospected in California, Edward Hammond Hargraves, wrote home that the land on which the gold was found looked much like the countryside of New South Wales. In 1850 he returned home with no fortune but a great deal of experience. He confidently predicted that he would find gold within a week of setting out on a prospecting expedition. True to his word he found gold on Australia's Macquarie River near Bathurst in New South Wales in February of 1851.

The rush was on. The seventy-mile-long stretch of gold-bearing ore he found was on government land. The crown colony was apprehensive about the impact the strike would have on the 45,000 convicts who made up the bulk of the population. However, it was impossible to ignore such a find so Hargraves was named Commissioner for Lands, awarded ten thousand pounds and a life pension. The Bathurst *Free Press* reported, "A complete metal madness appears to have seized almost every member of the community. There has been a universal rush to the diggings."

Men flocked to the Macquarie from as far away as California. The "fossickers," so called from the word meaning to dig a ditch, spread out discovering bonanzas in the neighboring state of Victoria. In 1852 a flood of 370,000 assorted immigrant gold seekers joined the small sparsely populated colony. They extracted 45,000 pounds of gold that year. By 1855 there were more than 1¼ million newcomers in Australia. News of the strike reached England, and hordes of men applied for ship space, wanting to chance their luck in the faraway colony. The clipper ships, which had first been built in Baltimore in 1833, were put to good use. Capable of achieving the exceptional speed of eighteen knots, they left all other ships standing. The clippers went from New York to San Francisco in as little as 90 days. The slower sailing ships took 160. During the first four years of the Australian gold rush more than 150 clipper ships were built to accommodate the mobs wanting to reach Australia.

The government made every effort to avoid the violence and vice that had marked the early California discoveries. No one was permitted to prospect unless he purchased a license for thirty shippings a month. Like their brethren in California, the "fossickers" were an independent lot and chafed under the close supervision of the diggings. Resentment of the "digger hunters" who came to collect the monthly fee sometimes flared into pitched battles.

The discovery of gold in Australia was instrumental in making London the center of the world gold market. A great deal of the gold from California and Australia accrued to industrial England, the universal creditor. The gold reserve of the Bank of England soared from 12.8 million pounds in 1848 to 20 million in 1852. Eighty per cent of the Australian production was channeled through the London market. Until the first decade of this century when production declined sharply, an average annual yield of almost 230,000 pounds of gold was taken from Australia.

Australia was a gold hunter's dream strewn with nuggets, shining chunks of yellow stuff weighing up to 200 pounds. In 1869 the famous "Welcome Stranger" nugget, the biggest in history, a 2,280-ounce mass of almost pure gold, was found near Ballarat in Victoria. Two partners trying to move a provision-laden wagon out of a muddy rut saw something gleam in the mire and uncovered the two-foot-long chunk of gold. Leery of being seen by others, the men waited until dark and then moved it to their cabin and concealed it in the fireplace until they managed to get it to Melbourne. The "Holterman Reef," an even bigger mass of gold with quartz mixed in, was found in New South Wales in 1872. Its gold content accounted for 7,560 ounces of its total weight of 10,080 ounces. A 93-pound true nugget was found by a prospector picking wild flowers for his lady. He pulled up a bloom which came up with roots spangled with gold flakes. He dug down and uncovered the golden prize. As late as 1975 two lucky Australian prospectors made $25,000 in one day when they found a nugget weighing 182 ounces, the biggest in the twentieth century, in Victoria province.

From Victoria, which produced 1¾ million pounds of gold in the ten years following Hargraves' discovery, prospectors fanned out to follow a puffed-up rumor of gold in Queensland in 1858. In the early 1860s New Zealand attracted fossickers in a minirush. The climax of the Pacific rushes came with the discovery of gold at Kalgoorlie in the ancient seabed which makes up Western Australia. Paddy Hannan's horse in 1893 picked up a gold nugget in his hoof starting a stampede. In the arid desert where there was not enough water to wash gold, the fossickers adapted a method of separating the precious metal from sand called dry blowing which had been used by Mexican miners in the New World. The miner slowly emptied a panful of auriferous sand held above his head onto a pan on the ground letting the wind winnow the gold from the lighter sand particles. Soon, a variation of the cradle called the shaker was introduced, and in the twenty-three years after 1892 more than 14 million ounces of gold was separated from the sandy chaff of the desert. Mining still continues around Kalgoorlie; in the first nine months of 1974 a total of 432,000 ounces of fine gold was mined.

One of the men drawn to the bleak, treeless Australian plain was Herbert Hoover, who arrived in 1896 as a twenty-two-year-old mining engineer employed by a London firm. He traveled over the desert by horse and buggy to inspect the mines. For a while he was superintendent of the Sons of Gwalia mine. In 1898 he left for similar work in China, Africa, Central and South America, and ultimately the presidency of the United States.

The site of the next great treasure find was Africa, the vast continent which had produced such a wealth of gold for the Egyptians, Phoenicians, Romans, Byzantines, Arabs, and of course the tribal Africans. The treasure, however, was not gold but diamonds, discovered in large numbers at Kimberley along South Africa's Vaal River in 1867. The diamond fields drew thousands of starry-eyed men who easily transferred their passion from glowing gold to sparkling diamonds. Six tons were mined in the two decades following the opening of the Kimberley fields.

While some men searched for diamonds others spread out exploring for gold, finding some alluvial deposits in the Transvaal, which were worked in a random manner. But these discoveries attracted little attention in the excitement of the fabulous diamond pits. Then in 1886 came the crucial discovery, one that was to lead to the world's greatest source of gold, a stratum of gold ore deposited aeons ago when the sea lapped at the long ridge of the White Waters, Witwatersrand in central South Africa.

When the world was young, roaring rivers tumbled to the sea bearing auriferous pebbles torn from the surrounding mountains. During the geologic cataclysms of successive ages silt layered over the pebbles and grains of gold, slowly compressing into shales. The shales were periodically covered with hundreds of feet of volcanic lava. Then, once again, gold would wash down the mighty rivers and settle. Violent twisting earthquake activity periodically thrust some areas of the gold-bearing layer up as much as 350 feet, dropping others as much as 500. The salt waters receded and millions of years later a small colony of Boer farmers settled the grassy rolling veldt around today's Johannesburg. They had no idea of the three-hundred-mile-long golden crescent that lay beneath the fertile prairie's gentle slopes.

The actual discovery was far from spectacular. In February of 1886 an Australian fossicker and itinerant laborer named George Harrison had been hired by the widow Oosthuizen to build a stone house on Langlaagte Farm, a few miles south of where Johannesburg now stands. One Sunday he and a prospector friend, George Walker, were digging stones for the foundation out of a rock outcrop of the south slope of the Witwatersrand when they came across some gray pebble conglomerates which looked as if they might contain gold. The men took one home, crushed it, and used a frying pan to swirl the ore around in. It was rich in gold. They staked claims and then Harrison informed the government of the Transvaal Republic in Pretoria of his find, writing, "I have a long experience as an Australian gold digger and I think it a payable gold field."

Gold seekers poured into the Transvaal following the perennial dream of a bonanza which had swept some of them back and forth across oceans and continents since 1849. The early acts of the South African drama followed a now familiar course—discovery, influx of prospectors, overnight mushrooming shanty town (this time supervised from the outset by government army officers), and then the withdrawal of the protagonists with scant reward. Walker got fifteen hundred dollars for his claim and died in poverty in 1924. According to one account, Harrison sold his claim for about fifty dollars and then wandered off into the wilderness and was eaten by a lion.

From that point on the script was radically different. The hordes of treasure hunters who descended on the area with no more than a pick and a pan were scarcely better rewarded than the discoverers. This gold rush was to be unlike any other. There was no place for the lone miner. The nature of the reef, which curves in a wide arc three hundred miles east and southeast of Johannesburg, required gold to get gold. There were few outcrops of easily accessible gold ore; most of it lies in bands varying in thickness from one tenth of an inch to one hundred feet, averaging no more than a foot, all deeply buried beneath thousands of feet of rock. To trace and extract the deeply imprisoned gold, which was present as tiny, sometimes invisible, specks of gold mixed in a quartz conglomerate, required engineering, metallurgical, and geological expertise in addition to capital. It cost, even then, more than $8 million to open a mine. Almost at once men appeared on the scene who had the money to invest. They were the diamond barons who had made a killing at Kimberley. Among the financiers who quickly gained control of the gold fields were Cecil Rhodes and his partner, C. D. Rudd, who bought $100,000 worth of mining properties. They formed the Gold Fields Company with an eye to purchasing more gold mines. Sale of their stock on the London market attracted British capital and interest. By 1888 four of the present seven mining finance houses had been founded, all established by magnates who made their fortunes in diamonds, and the Transvaal was soon supplying almost 5 per cent of the world's gold.

Massive capital was needed to process the rich ore brought up from veins which inclined steeply into the bowels of the earth. At first the crushed ore, treated with mercury, yielded only about 75 per cent of the gold it contained. It was discovered that ore brought up from more than 150 feet below the surface was refractory. The gold was enclosed in "sulpherets," metallic sulphides which prevented mercury from releasing all of the gold from its matrix. No matter how finely it was milled a great deal of gold was lost, making the mining effort unprofitable, since a ton of crushed ore yielded only one-third ounce of gold and sometimes less. The huge volume of tailings was sold to make gold-filled cement for the growing city of Johannesburg located at the center of the Rand, as Witwatersrand was called.

From the outset Rhodes had entertained second thoughts about his heavy investment in the Rand. He was dining in London with Lord Rothschild and an American mining engineer, when news of the appearance of pyrites in the ore arrived from South Africa. "What do you do," he queried the engineer, "when you strike sulphide ores?" The American replied, "Then we say, Oh God!" The next day Rhodes unloaded his shares and the value of the Rand mines plummeted by three quarters, forcing some two hundred companies with interest in the reef out of business. In 1890 it seemed as if the South African gold boom, like others before it, had bottomed out.

South Africa's gold industry was saved by three scientists in Glasgow, Scotland, who developed the cyanide process of extracting gold from crush conglomerate. In 1887 John S. MacAr-

thur and Robert and William Forrest patented the revolutionary
process which when applied in the Rand Mines provided a
cheap and efficient way of extracting more than 95 per cent of
the gold out of the refractory crushed ore. The process, still used
today, takes advantage of gold's affinity for cyanide. The ore is
ground to a fine powder called slime and circulated through
tanks of a weak solution of sodium or potassium cyanide. The
gold in the slime, in a complex series of chemical reactions, com-
bines with the cyanide forming a cyanide of gold, which dis-
solves in the solution. The sterile rock dust is filtered off and then
zinc dust is added to the solution to separate the gold from the
cyanide. The gold in the form of an impure black powder is
melted with fluxes such as borax. As the mixture cools the fluxes
combine with impurities and float as slag. The gold cools in the
bottom of a conical mold and emerges 90 per cent pure and 10
per cent silver. Further refining yields a 99.6 per cent pure product.

In 1890 the first cyanide treatment plants were set up in the
Rand. Deeper mine shafts were sunk, and by 1892 South Africa
was supplying over 1 million ounces of newly mined gold a year;
more than 15 per cent of the world's production. In 1898, the
year before the growing conflict between the farming Boers and
the mine-oriented Uitlanders, outsiders, erupted in the bitter
Boer War, South Africa outproduced the United States for the
first time. The Rand mines that year yielded a total of 4 million
ounces, more than 25 per cent of the world's gold production.

The Boer War interrupted mining for three years. The British
victory in 1902 led to equalization of the British-Afrikaaner population and the formation of the Union of South Africa in 1910.
Mining was resumed on a massive scale largely controlled, as it
is today, by the seven major mining houses which make up the
Chamber of Mines of South Africa. Since 1884 the mines of the
Witwatersrand basin have contributed an average of more than
49 per cent of the free world's annual newly mined gold. The
highest production was 78.2 per cent in 1971. The fifty mines of
the Rand produce about 900 metric tons of gold a year. In 1972
the richest mine, West Driefontein, yielded 2,418,398 fine ounces
of gold, or 75.2 metric tons, which was more than twice the annual production of the United States. South Africa is currently

producing about three quarters of the free world's gold, more than fourteen times the second largest producer, Canada. Overall, South Africa has accounted for about 40 per cent of all the gold produced in history.

Today partially refined 1,000-ounce bullion bars are delivered to the Rand refinery owned by the Chamber of Mines where they are melted, assayed (so the parent mine receives credit for the actual amount of gold in the bullion), and recast into 400-ounce bars. In the final process the gold is melted in batches of about 500 kilograms (1,100 pounds) in clay-lined crucibles of graphite and then mixed with borax. Chloride gas is then passed through it. Silver and other base metals are converted to chlorides by the gas and rise to the surface and are skimmed off. The liquid gold is then poured into the form of 400-ounce bars. The process is so efficient that only .01 per cent of the gold is lost. At periodic intervals the furnace debris, crucibles, and floor sweepings are burned to recover gold lost in the form of gas during the refining procedure.

The South African Reserve Bank in Pretoria is responsible for the sale, transport, and safekeeping of the Rand gold. The bulk of the South African gold is destined for the London gold market where it is sold at the prevailing price, which changes from day to day. In London the Bank of England functions as the South African Reserve Bank's selling agent, just as in the United States the Federal Reserve Bank does.

Modern gold mining is a very expensive, highly technical business. It cost $150 million to establish the Western Deep Mine. It requires tremendous outlays to dig shafts as deep as 12,000 feet and to ventilate and condition the humid air, which reaches a searing 130° Fahrenheit at that depth. To produce one ounce of fine gold requires crushing and treating an average three tons of ore (compared with less than two and a half in 1967), thirty-eight man-hours, 1,400 gallons of water, electricity to run a large house for ten days, 282 to 565 cubic feet of air under straining pressure, and quantities of chemicals including cyanide, acids, lead, borax, and lime.

What makes the huge profits of the mines (approximately $3.5 billion in 1974) possible is the supply of cheap labor. In the half century before 1971 the low wages of the black mine laborers remained static, making possible great profits and also shoring up the gold-based monetary systems of the Western world. In the past few years wages have risen threefold. But like the working and housing conditions they are far from adequate. In the early 1970s as many as 80 per cent of the Bantu workers were from outside the country. The proportion of foreign laborers has declined sharply, however, since the governments of Mozambique and the other traditional labor pools refuse to supply men on such demeaning terms, even though the men may make more than in their homeland. Increasing labor unrest at the mines points up the fact that South Africa can no longer count on the docile underpaid laborers to keep profits up. The industry is aware of the need to offer better wages, better working and living conditions. An effort is being made to train more Africans for skilled jobs.

Today the seven major gold fields employ 370,000 black Africans and 44,000 whites. The racist policies of the government restrict the kind of work blacks can do. Whites occupy the aboveground and managerial positions. The blacks from more than fifty different tribes are recruited on contracts. Labeled Bantu by the government, they make an average of $100 a month plus food and lodging. They live in sterile compounds resembling modern penal institutions from which their women and families are excluded. The average white miner receives about $1,000 a month. By contrast, a senior white official, in the words of a South African government publication, "lives in an eight room house with a large garden—and pays little rent. His golf, tennis and club facilities are subsidized. A mining man enjoys benefits of provident and pension funds, sick leave and five or more weeks of holiday a year." The gold mines set the tone for inequality in South African industry. By law whites are not permitted to work more than forty-eight hours a week amid the intense heat and humidity underground. In contrast blacks work sixty hours underground on twelve-hour shifts, although it seems certain the government will very soon be forced to make drastic improvements in conditions and opportunities for black mine laborers.

Bantu recruits undergo rigorous training. They are subjected to a regimen simulating the intense heat, pressure, and humidity encountered two to three miles underground. To build up stamina and heat tolerance a recruit spends four hours daily in a stiflingly hot room endlessly stepping on and off a block. He begins at twelve steps a minute on and off the block and at the end of eight days, if he has successfully completed the trial, is racing at double speed. Each man takes an aptitude test and is then trained in an aboveground mock-up for such unskilled tasks as shoveling ore, fitting support timbers, drilling, and blasting.

One of the first things a man learns is the five hundred or so crucial words of the miners' lingua franca, Fanakalo. It is a pidgin combination of Afrikaans, English, Zulu, and other African dialects with a vocabulary of about two thousand words. Mastering the most important terms is vital to a man's safety in the mines where he must crawl through forty-inch-high stopes to blast, drill, shovel, and load ore. There is the possibility of an accident at any moment. Among the dangers are cave-ins, accidental blasts, runaway cages (each of the huge elevators carries 120 men down, plummeting three thousand feet a minute, and can lift twenty tons of ore a load), rocks exploding under pressure, scalding water which can jet from fissures in the rock face, and asphyxiation. Gold mines, for all the technical advances of the modern era, remain what they were for the ancient slave miners of the Egyptians, Greeks, and Romans—an environment hostile to men who work in constant discomfort, haunted by the ever-present threat of disfigurement or death.

The Klondike gave the gold seekers one final rainbow to follow. There was treasure at the end of it but also more suffering and sorrow than the eternally optimistic Argonauts had ever encountered before. The last of the nineteenth-century gold rushes, the epic Klondike Stampede, was set off by a thumb-sized nugget found on the Klondike tributary of the Yukon River, as close to the North Pole as northern Siberia. It is a saga of endurance and heartbreak unparalleled in freemen's pursuit of gold.

> "Klondike or bust!" rang the slogan, "Every man for his own.
> Oh, how we flogged the horses, staggering skin and bone!
> Oh, how we cursed their weakness, auguish they could not tell,
> Breaking their hearts in our passion, lashing them till they fell!
> Never will I forget it, there on the mountain face,

Antlike, men with their burdens, clinging in the icy space;
Dogged, determined and dauntless, cruel and callous and cold,
Cursing, blaspheming, reviling, and ever the battle-cry 'Gold'!"

Robert Service

Few men ventured into that remote wilderness area of moose pasture, mountains, and rivers which were frozen from September to May; even fewer lived there. But an American, George Washington Carmack, son of a failed Forty-niner and born in a covered wagon crossing the Great Plain, had come north in 1855 to prospect. He stayed on to marry a Tagish Indian chief's daughter. "Siwash George," the "squaw man," as he was derisively called by the few sourdoughs who prospected the area, was more interested in salmon fishing and moose hunting than gold. He was considered a strange man, a lover of Indian life who read *Scientific American*, had an organ in his cabin, and composed sentimental couplets.

One night George had a visionary dream in which a huge king salmon shooting up the rapids stood on its tail before him. The fish's scales were golden and its eyes were twenty-dollar gold pieces. The next morning he went fishing for salmon on the Trondiuck River—an Indian name meaning "abundant fish"— which became the Klondike. On the way Siwash George and his two brothers-in-law, Tagish Charley and Skookum Jim, encountered Robert Henderson, a grizzled old sourdough from Nova Scotia who had spent his life seeking gold first in Australia and New Zealand, then trying his luck across the world in the Rocky Mountain states, and had finally been borne along with the north-flowing tide to Alaska.

He told Carmack of a likely area he had just found but not yet explored. It was a creek that drained off the Dome, the highest mountain thereabouts. Carmack was welcome to stake a claim there, "but I don't want any Siwashes staking on that creek," he added. His anti-Indian remark cost him a fortune, for a few days later the squaw man and his brothers-in-law went up to Rabbit Creek and found the nugget that started the Klondike Odyssey on August 17, 1896. They staked claims. The accounts are not clear but probably because of Henderson's remark the three men didn't keep a verbal agreement to bring him in for a share if they found anything. On the way home they passed Henderson without mentioning their find but told everybody else they met.

The word flashed up and down the Yukon Valley. Men turned the town of Fortymile into a ghost town overnight. The scattered gold camps along the wilderness streams emptied as the old-timers once again responded to the cry of gold. Where moose had pastured a camp sprung up called Dawson City. Men straggled in every day eager to stake a claim. The area along Rabbit Creek, renamed Bonanza, was quickly taken up, and latecomers, cheechakos, probed other streams flowing off the Dome. Five lucky men staked claims on one of these rivulets. Spurned by the more experienced miners as the Bonanza "pups," they eventually produced a million dollars in gold. One of the men who was drawn to the gold strike was a barber from Circle City whose claim yielded $50,000 a year for five years. Those first months, before word had spread across the sparsely settled northern wilderness, many men reaped rich rewards; the average take at first, by one estimate, was about $850 a day. But they paid a high price in suffering and deprivation.

The following summer, after the thaw, two ships reached Seattle and San Francisco bringing three tons of ore and a number of frostbitten sourdoughs who had made enough to retire rich. In Seattle the sight of men minus noses, fingers, and ears didn't dampen the enthusiasm of a crowd of five thousand that watched the men debark escorted by Wells Fargo guards with their gold in moose hide pokes. Three hours after the *Portland* had docked at Seattle the waterfront was teeming with men shoving and jostling in an effort to book passage north: pimps, teamsters, bankers, ministers, merchants, lawyers, and even a number of enterprising "box-house" girls—everyone wanted to go.

"Gold! Gold!" trumpeted headlines across the country. Within ten days fifteen hundred people sailed from Seattle paying one thousand dollars for tickets and the stampede was on. Two routes led to the Klondike. The easier, more expensive way into Alaska's interior and the forbidding Yukon wilderness was the all-water voyage up the Pacific to the Bering Sea and thence 2,300 miles up the Yukon by steam-wheeler to Dawson. However, the Bering Sea at St. Michael is frozen from late September to late June. The trip, depending on whether a ship got caught in the ice, could last from forty days to eight months and thus was either the quickest or the slowest way to the gold fields.

Many more men bought passage on dangerously overcrowded vessels as far as Juneau, Skagway, or Dyea and then trekked 600 miles over Chilkoot or White Pass. Sled dogs were snapped up at $250 and more a piece and soon gone. Horses, glue-factory material brought from the States by profiteers, fell on the trail and rotted. Of the three thousand horses which set out from Skagway to cross White Pass in 1897 no more than a dozen survived. Major J. M. Walsh, sent as Commissioner of the Yukon, wrote, "such a scene of havoc and destruction . . . can scarcely be imagined. Thousands of pack animals lie dead along the way, sometimes in bunches under cliffs, with pack saddles and packs where they have fallen from the rock above. . . . The inhumanity which this trail has been witness to, the heartbreak and suffering which so many have undergone, cannot be imagined."

Jack London also chronicled the ghastly scene:

> The horses died like mosquitos in the first frost and from Skagway to Bennett they rotted in heaps. They died at the rocks, they were poisoned at the summit, and they starved at the lakes; they fell off the trail, what there was of it and they went through it; in the river they drowned under their loads or were smashed to pieces against the boulders; they snapped their legs in the crevices and broke their backs falling backwards with their packs; in the sloughs they sank from fright or smothered in the slime; they were disemboweled in the bogs where the corduroy logs turned end up in the mud; men shot them and worked them to death and when they were gone went back to the beach and bought more. Some did not bother to shoot them, stripping the saddles off and the shoes and leaving them where they fell. Their hearts turned to stone—those which did not break—and they became beasts, the men on the Dead Horse Trail.

Men fared a little better, although of the 100,000 who set out for Dawson only 30,000 to 40,000 made it and, according to

Pierre Berton in his excellent book *Klondike* (London: W. H. Allen, 1960) only half of those who reached the "Paris of Alaska" bothered to prospect for gold. Perhaps four or five thousand found some but only a few hundred realized their golden dreams, becoming really rich.

The brutal passes were hellish at any time of the year, and yet in the winter of '97 more than 30,000 Argonauts hopelessly in thrall to the age-old desire for shining gold made it over the sheer walls of ice, forcing themselves ahead step by slogging step in a line that had no end. It was an appalling spectacle, recalling the forced marches of slave armies to the Egyptian desert mines so many thousand years before. It seemed incredible that these nineteenth-century men would willingly undertake such a journey no matter how much they lusted for gold.

On their backs they packed everything they would need. They were forced to their hands and knees by the shifting snow on the high passes where the temperature was forty below. A relentless wind flung splinters of shattered ice to lacerate any exposed flesh; sweat froze, binding clothing to the skin with one step and ripping the frozen skin away with the next. Blizzards blinded and glacier ice toppled. Men without a year's supply of food were turned back by the Canadian North-West Mounted Police in scarlet jackets and white helmets who were posted atop the passes in an effort to prevent disaster. Once over the summits the men pushed on to Lake Bennett. They built crude rafts from green lumber as members of the police circulated among them warning of the dangerous rapids, reefs, and narrows that lay ahead for five hundred miles, advising the weary men to build their craft long and strong. When the Yukon thawed, the police counted 7,124 boats ready to depart. Most made it; crosses on the banks below White Horse Rapids testify to those who didn't.

There was an even crueler route to Dawson, the sinister Ashcroft trail which wound through the dripping wilds of British Columbia to Dawson. At least fifteen hundred gold seekers and three thousand pack animals attempted the journey. They found a desolate land bare of fodder, a terrain of bottomless bogs where they suffered unremitting torture from mosquitoes and flies. In rainy fir forests, dark in daylight, putrid carcasses of animals marked the trail. Men drowned, were murdered, died of hunger and fever, or blew their own brains out.

The embryo town, four thousand miles from civilization, was crushed beneath the 30,000 sourdoughs who crowded in by spring of '98. If a man lost sight of his partner, he might not find him again for days. Exhausted but sanguine gold seekers arrived daily. Dawson had just come through nine frozen months of starvation, scurvy, and typhoid. During that time the police would take no one in the town's jail unless he had his own beans and provisions. Food was shared and rationed. Women sold themselves to the highest bidder for enough to eat and men lay muffled in blankets most of the long gray days.

In the spring after the thaw fresh supplies arrived along with throngs of cheechakos and sourdoughs. Dawson suddenly became a bazaar by day and a frenzied carnival at night. Among the tents and plank shacks were two banks, two newspapers, five churches, and dozens of saloons, dancing halls, and gaming houses. The currency of every country competed with gold dust and even Confederate notes to buy champagne, fresh grapes, oysters, ostrich feathers, and opera glasses. Within two years there was a telegraph, steam heat, electricity, and the railroad. Thanks to the calm authority of the Mounties reasonable order was maintained. The police commander ordered the San Francisco dancing girls to change their bloomers for more modest skirts and was obeyed. The closest things Dawson City saw to a murder in 1898 was an altercation between Coatless Curly Munro and his wife. In the heat of the fight they each went for revolvers they kept under the bed pillows but fled the room by separate doors before firing.

In 1899 the sourdoughs wrested some 5,000 pounds of bright gold from the frozen ground. By 1900 a peak of 45,000 pounds was reached and the stampede was over, although commercial mining continued to be profitable until 1966.

Gold! We leapt from our benches. Gold! We sprung from our stools.
Gold! We wheeled in the furrow, fired with the faith of fools.
Fearless, unfound, unfitted, far from the night and the cold,
Heard we the clarion summons, followed the master-lure—Gold!

Robert Service, poet laureate of the Klondike, wrote eloquently of the trail of '98, of the "big shiny nuggets like plums"

that danced before the eyes, and of the men on the tortured trail
to Dawson City. Little wonder that so many of those who survived didn't even bother to look for the shiny stuff once they
reached there. Despite the fact that Siwash George and others of
the sourdoughs first on the scene had washed abundant gold
from the streams and rivers, the Klondike was not nugget
country.

It quickly became apparent there was only one way to get the
most out of a claim—by digging, which was slow, agonizing
work. The gold lay in a gravel matrix, in benches and shelves,
buried five to thirty feet beneath heavy, boggy tundra. During
the long, dark winters, when the temperature hovered around
60° below, a shroud of smoke hung over the diggings as men
used fire to soften the ground, doggedly hacking through the
permafrost. To get wood for the fires they logged the streams or
struggled to bring felled trees from the forested mountain sides.
They lit the fires at night and dug by day. A foot a day was the
average rate of descent to bedrock. The cold was bitter and in-
sistent. Men spread a thick layer of bacon grease mixed with
ashes on their faces to protect them from frostbite. At 42° below
zero the mercury froze and at 80° below an ax blade shattered.
Even their Hudson Bay rum froze and the sourdoughs huddled
in their tiny cabins. In a desperate bid to warm their bones they
fed the fire with chairs, sluice boxes, anything to keep it alive.
Occasionally a man fell prey to "cabin fever" and wandered off
to a crazed death in the frozen expanses of snow and ice.

When the streams thawed in the spring there was water for
sluicing the great piles of dirty gravel that had mounted up over
the winter. Water was diverted to the sluices and pay dirt was
washed under the eerie midnight sun.

Some men found that frostbite, gangrene, loneliness, and
hardship had paid off handsomely. A relative few became overnight millionaires. Within a few years most of these had been
parted from their gold. Drink, gambling, and women accounted
for the loss of a lot of the hard-won gold. The story of Charley
Anderson is the story of many. Anderson, the "Lucky Swede"
who had bought a million-dollar claim for $800, ultimately lost
his dance-hall wife and his fortune which had been heavily
invested in earthquake-prone San Francisco real estate. He died

in 1939 pushing a wheelbarrow in a British Columbia sawmill. But until the day he died he wholeheartedly believed that some-day soon he would strike it rich again.

Prospectors were notoriously poor businessmen. The Croesus' of the Klondike went on to lose their gold in dubious mining in-vestments elsewhere or went bankrupt investing in real estate, railroads, and banks. It was not surprising in the light of the ex-traordinary circumstances surrounding the last nineteenth-cen-tury gold rush that there was a fair share of madness and suicide among the winners as well as the losers of the Klondike.

However, contrary to precedent, the man who started it all ended his days well off. Carmack made and kept a fortune and even wrote an account of the whole saga. His Indian wife fared less well. He had abandoned her in 1900 and she died on a reser-vation in 1917 wearing a cheap cotton dress and the only thing she had to show from the Klondike, a necklace of nuggets taken out of Bonanza Creek. Carmack married again. His second wife had run a "cigar store," a bawdy house in Dawson where busi-ness was so good she had been able to glean about thirty dollars in gold dust from the sawdust on the bar floor every morning. Robert Henderson, the inveterate and embittered prospector, who felt that he had been cheated by Carmack, was recognized as the cofounder of the Klondike and awarded a Canadian gov-ernment pension of two hundred dollars a month. He never ceased looking for gold and died of cancer in 1933 still talking of the bonanza he was going to find over the next hill.

Veterans of the Klondike included men of character and enter-prise who made their fortunes later. Among them were Augustus Mack, inventor of the Mack automobile; Sid Grauman, who built Hollywood's Chinese Theater; Key Pittman, Nevada senator and chairman of the Foreign Relations Committee; and the three Mizner brothers.

No one who took part in the amazing saga of the Klondike came through unchanged. As Pierre Berton noted, that singular era produced men and women of every conceivable background who were joined by a common bond. Many of them were indi-viduals of unusual mettle, wise beyond their years, who had been tried and proven. They were survivors, achievers whose lives and characters were shaped by the Klondike experience.

Within three years of Carmack's discovery the stampede was over. Dawson, like most other mining camps, emptied as word of fortunes to be made on Nome's beaches reached town. In one week in August eight thousand persons left Dawson. Men moved on to other new strikes which followed at Nome, Fairbanks, Keno Hill, and Atlin. But the day of the Forty-niner, the fossicker, the sourdough, was over.

At Nome, on the Bering Sea just across from Siberia, men panned over a million dollars of fine gold dust (at sixteen dollars an ounce) from the rich, blue beach sands in the first two months following the strike in 1899. When the gold gave out on the shore, thousands of men moved inland to the hills and gulleys with their pans, rockers, and wheelbarrows. Today the beaches are littered with rusted machinery left by the sourdoughs. One group of seven men took out $750,000 in the first season. But again, as in the Yukon, most of the gold lay in subterranean gravel and soon mining syndicates, financed out of San Francisco, London, and New York, gained control. They worked the gold fields with huge hydraulic machines and dredges which in one day equalled the labor of a thousand sourdoughs. By 1907 the tide turned and Alaska retreated into oblivion.

Gold in the nineteenth century was the great population builder, the opener of new country. Gold built railroads, cities, states, and territories as well as of fortunes and character. Out of the gold rushes came inventions and improvements in mining technology and engineering and countless fascinating stories of unusual men and women.

Economically the future of gold production in the western United States is dim. Almost all of the gold and silver mined today is a by-product of base minerals. To make a profit gold mining concerns in Nevada, for example, have to process seven tons of ore in which the gold particles are so minute they can only be seen with an electron microscope, just to recover one ounce of gold. In the 130 years since the 1849 gold rush all the gold and silver mined in the West, excluding Alaska, probably totals not more than $30 billion. That figure, which sounds like a great deal, is actually less than three years of the area's annual agricultural product. But it was not so much the actual worth of the treasure which made it significant as the profound and far-reaching effects it had. The era began as a free-for-all for every man and ended as a corporate take-over. Too many quested after too little gold in the explosive decades as hypnotized prospectors darted from one rumored strike to another with swindlers, profiteers, developers, and stock manipulators in their wake.

During the Depression when there was little but hope and dreams, ten to fifteen thousand people returned to the Sierra Nevada streams and foothills, abandoned for almost seventy-five years, to search for gold. Today tourists explore the crumbling ghost towns, mountainous piles of tailings, and rusted hulks of machinery trying to recapture the feeling of the nineteenth century where men were made and unmade by inert shining metal. Weekend scuba divers comb the streams and rivers of the Sierra Nevada. Families pan for gold and countless treasure hunters eagerly track lost mines and buried treasure. The dream dies hard. Human nature has not changed.

CHAPTER FIFTEEN *The Twentieth Century*

The gold discoveries of the nineteenth century were made by men in thrall to compelling instinct. The lure of gold is as old as man; from time immemorial gold, precious and rare, has been regarded as the universal panacea. Soft, warm, and lustrous, the yellow metal has been linked with myth, religion, the economics of political power, personal prestige, and artistic expression. Gold has moved through human history unchanging and seductive, evoking awe by its beauty and power. Focusing on any one substance in history tends to exaggerate its importance. But it is safe to say that no single substance has stimulated such an impressive variety of response or so strongly influenced the course of history as gold.

Even now, in spite of the hard cold statistical data regarding the role of gold in the twentieth century and the complexity of large-scale production and marketing, an aura of romance still clings to the yellow metal. In a shrunken world of instant communications and computerized technology there is little place for the dreaming Argonaut. However, men are still lured by gossamer tales, still covet the yellow metal. Gold—buried, sunken, emtombed—calls to those who seek lost lands and legendary treasures in every corner of the world. Dogged men follow the footsteps of long-vanished explorers searching for elusive gold mines and ancient golden cities. In the Andes they hunt for the gold of the Incas; in Italy they probe for Etruscan treasures. In Asia Minor their objective is gold buried during the migratory waves, such as the sixth century B.C.; Lydian hoard smuggled from a dig in Anatolian Turkey and bought by the Metropolitan Museum of Art in New York. Men probe lakes and oceans for

sunken ships laden with gold, sacrifical treasure. They still seek
the mystical golden spires of Atlantis.

The high price of gold has spurred exploration for new gold in
areas which once supplied significant amounts. In oil-rich Saudi
Arabia geologists are searching the rock plateau called the
Arabian Shield along the Red Sea. In the northern section of this
scorched 300,000-square-mile area geologists are probing an ancient mine at Mahd Adh Dhahab which produced colossal
amounts of gold three thousand years ago during the time of
King Solomon.

The Arabs, like the other OPEC nations, have little interest in
increasing their minimal national gold reserves, although individually they love the reassuring shimmer of gold in jewelry, fountain pens, and watches. The OPEC members have official oil
reserves equaling some forty years of oil output at today's rates,
while the major Western nations have gold stocks equaling more
than thirty years of gold production. The oil producing nations
see no reason to switch from a reserve they control to one they
do not.

In spite of this official stance, many wealthy individuals in the
oil producing nations hold gold among their other investments.
The poor in most parts of the world have traditionally viewed
gold as the safest hedge against uncertain times. Interestingly
enough, one of the greatest private gold hoards of all time was
accumulated in 1948–49 by a United States firm, ARAMCO, for
the late ibn-Saud, who had stipulated that his oil royalties be
paid in gold. If dollars were substituted, the royalty went up by
almost a third. ARAMCO finally found in the Central Bank of
Argentina a big enough holding of gold sovereigns and paid off
the Arabian monarch with $32 million worth of the English gold
coins. Subsequent contracts called for easier-to-get dollars and
sterling.

The French are the West's greatest hoarders. Gold's great
champion Charles de Gaulle in 1965 expressed the sentiments of
his countrymen and others whose states have a history of invasions, frequent devaluations (France has suffered thirteen devaluations of the franc since 1928), hyperinflation, and allied political and economic shocks. He stated, "There can be no other
criterion, no other standard than gold. Yes, gold which never

changes, which can be shaped into ingots, bars, coins, which has no nationality and which is externally and universally accepted as the unalterable fiduciary value par excellence."

It was De Gaulle who restored sufficient confidence in government to Frenchmen so that the French unearthed much of their hoarded gold by 1960. In spite of this, an estimated five thousand tons of gold is stashed away in safe-deposit boxes and mattresses, under floorboards, and in gardens. When he was Finance Minister, Valéry Giscard d'Estaing explained that "the Frenchman's feeling for gold is, if you will, a penchant for unpleasant memories, an expression of distrust." The Gallic fondness for gold was demonstrated at a 1975 press luncheon held by Giscard at the Élysée Palace. Although four waiters and a headwaiter were assigned to each of the tables at the luncheon, thirteen pieces of heavy gold cutlery were missing at the end of the meal.

Today gold still has its passionate advocates and equally vehement adversaries who seek to strip the metal of its powerful mystique and reduce it to the level of a trading commodity. But gold resists being ranked with soybeans and pork bellies. Although it has been dethroned from international monetary supremacy, it remains the ultimate acceptable form of payment between individuals and nations whatever their philosophies.

Lately, gold has played a part in the ransom demands of international terrorist groups and hijackers. The French ambassador of Somalia was kidnaped in Mogadishio, the Somali capital, by members of the Front for Liberation of the Somali Coast. Five days later, in Yemen, he was exchanged for some forty-seven pounds of gold bullion. To millions of twentieth-century people gold is still the only safe way of holding on to one's wealth in a world buffeted by global inflation and political and social upheaval.

South Africa still ranks as the world's largest supplier of gold. In 1974 South African production was 852.3 metric tons, accounting for 74.6 per cent of the free world's production. For each ton of gold 100,000 tons of ore were mined and processed at a cost of $80 an ounce, which serves as an effective floor to skidding gold prices.

The second largest producer is the Soviet Union, where gold is a state monopoly; ownership is forbidden to citizens and production figures are a closely guarded secret. However, the estimated production for 1974 was 370 metric tons. Although most of the world's economists have moved toward agreement with Lenin's 1921 contention that gold is best suited "for the purpose of building lavatories," the Kremlin favors a policy of maintaining a key monetary role for gold. A feature article in *Pravda* in November of 1974 echoed an earlier statement by a Soviet trade official that "world trade must rest on a more solid foundation and that foundation can only be gold." The Russians used part of their gold reserves, which are estimated at from 2,000 tons to almost 3,000 tons, to raise some $750 million for grain purchases from the United States. As much as 100 to 130 tons of gold were reported to have been placed on world markets by August 1, 1975.

The world's third largest producer of gold is Canada, whose mines yielded 60 metric tons in 1973. The other leading producers in order of importance are the United States, Central and South America, Ghana, Papua New Guinea, Australia, Philippines, and Rhodesia. The European countries together account for an average output of 14 metric tons.

World-wide gold production has fallen in the past several years. It declined to 48.2 million ounces in 1973, and 47.7 million ounces in 1974, from the yearly average of 50.8 million ounces during the 1968–72 period. The higher free market prices made it profitable to mine lower grade ores in the free world, but with rising costs mining companies are hard pressed to keep their profits up. The decline also resulted from South Africa's labor unrest and a government policy requiring the transfer of men and equipment to poorer-quality veins in the Rand Mines in an attempt to conserve high-grade ore and extend the life of the mines.

The superb beauty of gold which enhanced its special, often magic, appeal in past ages is seldom apparent today. Churches, afraid of theft, daren't display their golden offerings, gold currency no longer circulates, and jewelry is mass-produced. Most of the world's gold is in bullion. It is a pity to think of all the shimmering bars stacked in subterranean vaults where almost no one ever looks at them.

Global stocks held by central banks and the amount of gold in private hands roughly totals 3.7 billion ounces. Central banks alone hold more than twenty-five years annual production. About 57 per cent of the monetary gold owned by central banks and international organizations is stored in the United States. The United States owns the largest share, some 23 per cent of central bank holdings or about 8,600 metric tons. West Germany comes next with reserves of approximately 3,700 metric tons, followed by France, the Soviet Union, Switzerland, Italy, the Netherlands, Belgium, the Middle East, and finally Canada, United Kingdom, Japan, and South Africa. The rest of the world holds some 2,900 metric tons. The big Western producers, South Africa and Canada, hold very little gold, less than 700 metric tons each.

Today the largest portion of newly mined gold goes into the fabrication of jewelry, watches, spectacles, dental fillings, medals, and other industrial uses including space, defense, and electronics. However, this share of annual consumption fell sharply in 1974 as the price of gold soared. Jewelers offered consumers articles of lower grade, ten-karat gold and increased production of pieces in vermeil, a plating of gold at least 100 millionths of an inch thick, over sterling in an attempt to cope with the upsetting price rise. Between 1973 and 1974 the United States, which is the largest industrial consumer of gold, reduced its imports of bullion by more than one-third and world-wide net purchases of gold by industrial users fell to the lowest point in ten years.

In 1974 almost 34 per cent of free world gold output went into speculation and investment, 3.1. per cent went into hoards in such countries as France and India, and a negligible 3.5 per cent went into monetary reserves. That same year industrial use accounted for some 54 per cent of the approximate 40 million fine ounces of newly mined gold that moved onto the world market. Of this, the largest amount—38.5 per cent—went to fabricate coins, and the medals and medallions which have become increasingly popular with consumers. They are struck by private mints and commemorate everything from Motherhood to Mohammed Ali.

About 34 per cent of the industrial gold went into jewelry. Italy is the main producer of gold jewelry, the giant firm of Gori and Zucchi in Arezzo operates the world's largest plant and consumes up to a staggering 5 per cent of the West's gold output each year. Each year the Italian company uses a third more gold than the total United States annual production, turning it into more than six thousand different products from wedding rings to toothpicks to trophies.

The United States is the second largest manufacturer of gold jewelry but the largest consumer not only of gold jewelry but of all gold. Class rings, engagement and wedding rings, which spew out of automated machines by the thousands, account for about half the gold used in jewelry. While Italian jewelry tends to be high-quality 18-carat gold, American jewelry is usually lower. Class rings are generally 9.5 carats, although marked as 10, a practice which is legal in the United States.

Gold as money has passed through a number of phases. For some two thousand years, until the late seventeenth century, rulers intermittently allowed citizens to take gold, when it was available, to licensed moneyers who minted it, keeping a small bit for themselves and removing another portion for the potentate or city whose dies gave the coins their face value. Varieties of coins proliferated with private issues; for example, in fifteenth-century Germany six hundred or more mints issued coins. A relative few coins gained international acceptance such as the daric, bezant, florin, and ducat. But there were long stretches when no gold was available to coin.

The second phase in gold currency was the era of the gold standard made possible by the dramatic nineteenth-century increases in gold supplies from western United States, Australia, Alaska, and especially South Africa. The half century following the discovery of gold in California saw the production of more than 20 per cent of all gold extracted since the sixteenth century and greatly stimulated global production. After 1900 production increased even further, yet the demand still outran the supply. After 1850 the enormous amplification of gold stocks fueled the great bimetallism dispute which led most of Europe onto a single gold standard by the 1870s following England's official lead in 1816. At the turn of the century the United States and India belatedly abandoned the bimetallic system of silver and gold in favor of the gold standard.

On a domestic level the gold standard meant a fixed price for gold, with gold coins circulating alone or with paper currency which was totally redeemable in gold. From 1834 to 1934 the U. S. Treasury fixed the price of gold at $20.67 per fine ounce troy. At an international level the gold standard meant freedom to import or export gold without restriction and all balance-of-payment deficits payable in gold. Theoretically this meant that the supply of gold held in reserve controlled the economy of a country. When nations on the full gold standard were dealing with each other, exchange fluctuation was minimal. There was no speculation in currency exchange, and international capital investments could be made with confidence. Gold flowed out of a nation which ran a balance-of-payments deficit, bringing prices down, making exports more competitive, and leading to an improved balance of payments. By the same token, a country enjoying a favorable balance of payments attracted gold which expanded the economy.

In the closing decades of the nineteenth century, and the years before World War I economies expanded as never before, and for much of that period prices fell. However, the outbreak of war effectively crippled the gold standard in Great Britain and elsewhere as nations earmarked gold stocks for munitions and war supplies. The gold standard was dead, although it wasn't until 1919 in Britain and 1933 in the United States that it was officially declared at an end. Politicians dependent on pleasing voters applauded its demise; they disliked the gold standard which prevented spending beyond a nation's resources since the amount of circulating currency was controlled by the nation's gold stocks.

In 1925 Britain, at the insistence of Winston Churchill, then Chancellor of the Exchequer, and Montagu Norman, governor of the Bank of England, embarked on an ill-fated return to gold in the form of the gold bullion standard. Under the bullion standard gold coins did not circulate internally and were not exchanged for other coins, although notes were redeemable upon demand for 400-ounce bullion bars worth $8,000.

The gold exchange standard of the 1930s ushered in yet another era in the history of fiscal gold. The exchange standard, which held until it was abolished in 1972, provided that central banks used certain key currencies (primarily dollars) which could be redeemed for gold to supplement their own gold reserves which could not possibly keep pace with demand. In 1944 more than one thousand international delegates assembled at Bretton Woods, New Hampshire, to chart a new course for the world's monetary affairs. A system was worked out in which a currency was no longer convertible to gold for private citizens but only for the settlement of net payment deficits between governments. The Bretton Woods system functioned effectively for a quarter of a century during which the United States dollar, "as good as gold," was the cornerstone of the era of fixed exchange.

Perhaps the most significant achievement of the conference was the creation of the International Monetary Fund, dedicated to the preservation of international monetary stability. The IMF was established in an effort to retain the advantages of the gold standard while eliminating some of its rigidity. The Bretton Woods conference agreed to use the IMF, which is essentially an agency acting as an international bank, to foster monetary cooperation among member nations, stabilizing their various currencies through the coupled use of the dollar and gold under a gold-exchange standard.

Under the system the United States stood ready to exchange gold at $35 an ounce from its vast reserves for official holders of dollars. In 1949 the United States gold hoard, the world's largest by far, peaked at $24.7 billion and so did her might. From the outset there was doubt about the long-range viability of such a system, which could last only as long as the United States had enough gold to back all of the dollars held abroad. In 1945 federal law required a minimal 40 per cent gold backing for the U.S. dollar. Later this was reduced to 25 per cent, meaning four dollars could be printed for every dollar held in gold. In 1965 gold backing for Federal Reserve deposits was discontinued. Today about $295 billion circulates in the United States. Paper bills account for about $65 billion, coins for about $8 billion, and checking accounts for a whopping $221 billion—about 75 per cent of the total money supply.

In the late 1940s and the 1950s the U. S. Army, U.S. foreign aid, foreign investments, flocks of free-spending U.S. tourists, and a proliferation of imports all contributed to far more American money being spent abroad than was coming in. By 1958 it was apparent the American balance-of-payments deficit had greatly increased and that the gold standard, in the words of France's General de Gaulle, "no longer corresponds to present realities."

In March of 1968 international monetary authorities dissolved the gold pool and established a two-tier market in gold in which monetary gold would maintain a fixed price of $35 an ounce and the price of gold on the free market would be allowed to fluctuate with supply and demand. This followed four months after the British pound, regarded as the world's second strongest currency, was devalued by 14.3 per cent. The pound devaluation triggered a huge surge of gold buying all over the world by people who feared further drops. The London gold market, which had previously traded sixteen to eighteen tons of gold a week, was suddenly besieged with orders that totaled that much in one day. The United States and the gold exchange standard were in trouble. U.S. gold reserves couldn't begin to meet the demand if all holders of dollars abroad presented their "good as gold" dollars for exchange.

By mid-1971 imports into the United States were running above exports for the first time since 1893. The annual deficit was a staggering $23.2 billion and U.S. gold reserves had sunk to $10 billion. Foreign claims outstanding against the dollar amounted to more than $48 billion by the middle of August when President Nixon severed the link between the ailing U.S. dollar and gold, bringing the era of Bretton Woods to an end. In December the dollar was devalued by 8 per cent, the first devaluation since 1934, and the official price of gold was raised from $35 to $38 an ounce.

After Nixon's moves the nations which had kept faith with the United States and held on to their dollars when they might have exchanged them for gold were left with paper of eroding value. Those countries which had questioned the integrity of the U.S. dollar and redeemed surplus dollars for gold had made huge profits. The French had opted for gold. The bullion De Gaulle had purchased for $2 billion in 1964 was worth $10 billion ten years later. The free market price of gold continued to climb in relation to the dollar, and in February 1973 the dollar was devalued a further 10 per cent and gold officially, and more realistically, set at a par value of $42.22 an ounce.

During the years of heated international debate among economists, bankers, statesmen, and politicians about what role gold should play in monetary affairs, members of the IMF considered several methods of ensuring the continuation of a system of fixed exchange rates which depended upon an expanding reserve base to underpin the world's economic growth. Some experts argued early for a raise in the official price of gold so as to increase the value of gold reserves. Others argued with increasing success for an abandonment of gold as the basic reserve. In 1969 the governors of the IMF created the SDR, the Special Drawing Right, a computerized accounting unit distributed to IMF members in accordance with a country's reserves, to serve as the medium of payment in settling international accounts. The value is determined daily in terms of sixteen world currencies. Dubbed "paper gold," SDRs are gaining prominence as a key financial medium in the international market place, pushing aside the world's major trading currencies. The SDRs are strictly an exchange medium between governments designed to create an internationally acceptable paper substitute for mankind's traditional numeraise, the unit against which the values of all currencies are measured.

Advocates of the electronic currency point out that SDRs cost less to produce than gold, they pay interest, and they provide a means for internationally controlling the growth of world liquidity. Their use in commercial transactions between governments is spreading rapidly. Looking forward to the time when the SDR might function in the private sector, some countries have begun to express their exchange rates in SDRs. The OPEC countries are considering an SDR pricing system for oil; tolls on the Suez Canal are now quoted in SDRs, and world-wide airline passenger fares, cargo rates, and other transportation transactions are quoted in "paper gold."

A number of experts are dubious about the efficacy of this system which is aimed at replacing gold in the fiscal realm. The role of gold in world finances has steadily diminished and no one seriously contemplates a return to the pure gold standard. Yet there are economists, particularly in Europe, who feel that without guarantees that credit or paper money can be exchanged for something of intrinsic value, people may lose confidence in the system, particularly in times of major wars or international financial panic. Specialists continue to debate, weighing economic, political, and psychological factors in an effort to hammer out a new monetary system "as good as gold" which would insure the benefits of continued world trade while minimizing the possibility of international monetary crises.

In January of 1976 the powerful interim committee of the IMF met in Kingston, Jamaica, to set the structure of such a system. Twenty finance ministers confirmed the right of the United States to maintain the floating value of the dollar which helped bring about a record trade surplus of more than $10 billion in 1975. The IMF plans to auction off 25 million ounces or one sixth of the fund's gold stock of its collectively held gold over a four-year period in a controlled manner designed not to upset the world market. The aim of the sixteen auctions (begun in June of 1976) is to further reduce gold's status as a monetary asset and ostensibly to aid developing countries by raising a trust fund of some $7 billion.

The IMF expects gold to average approximately $125 an ounce over the four years. Critics say the auctions will benefit the poor nations very little and merely help rich member nations such as France which might buy auctioned gold to boost their holdings through an interim arrangement with the Swiss-based Bank for International Settlements at Basel and later directly through central banks. (It is currently illegal for central banks of the IMF's 128 members to buy gold at more than the official $42.22 an ounce even though the recent market price has been nearer $170 an ounce.)

In 1974 President Ford, signing his first bill after assuming office, lifted the long ban on U.S. private ownership of gold bullion: a strong indication of the government's commitment to the demonetization of gold and its relegation to commodity status. Banner headlines proclaimed "The New Gold Rush"; magazine covers blazed with stacks of gold ingots as the United States Government prepared to end the forty-one-year ban on the private ownership of gold by citizens. "Not since the great rush west of 1849 has the American psyche been so passionately infected by gold fever," *Newsweek* proclaimed two weeks before the free market on gold bullion was established on December 31, 1974. The "Gold Frenzy" mounted as European speculators bought heavily in anticipation of profitable resales to avid Americans at the first of the year. The price on the London market rose sharply; gold stocks, gold futures, and the sale of coins soared. Goldbugs predicted a shining future for mankind's traditional insurance in times of uncertainty. Gold, they crowed, would surge upward to $300, perhaps $400 an ounce. Certainly the conditions were favorable. Historically gold investment has been encouraged by widespread recession coupled by high inflation. In light of the double-digit inflation, the political turmoil prevailing in much of the world, the decline of the dollar after 1971, and the sickening fall in the world's stock markets, the goldbugs thought it inevitable that Americans would rush to invest their eroding savings in gold, the oldest form of refuge, the tested store of value, the currency hedge, and money of last resort par excellence.

"Experts" predicted Americans would buy between 5 and 15 million ounces of gold in 1975 at prices between $150 and $250 an ounce. Conferences of economists, bankers, and seers were organized to prepare the public. Articles, books, and pamphlets issued warnings and instructions on the coming event. Banks and department stores made elaborate preparations to sell gold in the form of wafers, ingots, coins, and medals. Jewelers stocked up on wildly overpriced miniature ingots to be hung around one's neck. The fertile minds of promoters spawned myriad schemes for making a killing. Dial soap's "Free Gold Giveaway" featured a grand prize of "a shining 14-carat gold electroplated bar of Dial Soap" plus $10,000 in cash. Gold fever was, for a short time at least, rampant.

For almost forty years the price of gold remained amazingly stable. Gold in the fall of 1970 brought around $36 or $37 an ounce on the major markets of London and Zurich. Then it began the upward climb. As recently as the beginning of 1973 an ounce fetched $65. By the end of the year gold had climbed to $112, and near the close of 1974 it reached as high as $200 an ounce versus the official price of $42.22.

Then came the fateful day legalizing American ownership of gold. But where were the frenzied hordes clamoring to exchange depreciating dollars for eternally shining gold? The anticipated Rush was barely a trickle; Americans, with relatively little expe-

rience with the chaos of war and invasion, simply were not psy-
chologically conditioned to be interested in draining their savings accounts for small, heavy bars of soft yellow metal. Those
who purchased ingots or wafers numbered only in the thousands.
Nine out of ten gold buyers in 1975 bought favorite bullion-type
coins such as the South African krugerrand, the Austrian one-
hundred corona, and the Mexican fifty-peso piece. The American
public held on to its money despite the shrinking of the dollar
which in 1975 bought only one quarter of what it had in 1939,
even though since 1971 it has had no tangible backing save the
borrowing power of the federal government and the confidence
that money, taken in payment for goods and services, will be accepted by others in like manner.

The U. S. Treasury held an auction in January of 1975 at
which two million ounces of the country's gold reserves or somewhat over 276 million ounces were offered for sale. It was touted
as the Auction of the Century, but only one third of the gold
offered was purchased in lackluster bidding at an average price
of $165.67 an ounce. Another auction in June met with much the
same disinterest. In all, the government disposed of $208 million
of gold at the two sales. Dealers who had imported a record
4.2 million ounces of gold bullion and 3.1 million ounces of gold
coins in anticipation of the stampede of '75 actually shipped
back 168,000 ounces to foreign dealers in the first six months of
the year. This helped make the United States a net exporter of
gold for the first time in four decades.

The novelty wore off quickly in a nation where there is no tradition of gold hoarding. These developments were not entirely
unexpected by the government, which was delighted at the progress of its efforts to dislodge the king of metals from its traditional role in monetary affairs. The government is committed to
the demonetization of gold and its relegation to the status of a
commodity metal like copper or silver. For weeks preceding the
official sales the government had cautioned citizens on the pit-
falls of gold speculation. Millions, who had toyed with the idea,
heeded the warnings and chose not to invest in gold in any way.

Speculation sent the world market price of gold soaring to
nearly $200 a troy ounce in late 1974. But when few Americans
turned out to be gold bugs, gold began a tailspin. In August of

1976 an ounce fetched only $103.50. In 1977, however, it edged back up past the $160 level. Anxious about inflation and the weakness of the dollar in international currency markets, more Americans than ever before are investing in gold. Sales of the krugerrand, a one-ounce South African coin promoted on U.S. television, topped $100 million in the first ten months of 1977.

In recent years Japan, Iran, the Philippines, and several other countries have joined those nations which do not impose restrictions on private ownership of gold. At the same time private holdings in the countries such as India, France, and Pakistan where gold has traditionally been hoarded have been shrinking since 1972. This is because the poor who used to invest in gold can no longer afford the escalating prices and because of government efforts to draw gold out of hiding and put it to work in the national economies. Countries like Lebanon, Laos, Cambodia, and Vietnam which once absorbed great amounts of smuggled gold are currently outside the arena of gold action.

Dealing in gold had long been important in Europe where central banks currently hold some 36,000 tons of the metal and transactions on the Zurich and London markets run to six or seven tons a day. The London gold pool controls the world's largest wholesale gold market, dealing in standard "good delivery" bars of minimum quality of 995 parts per 1,000 fine gold which range in weight from 360 fine ounces to a maximum of 430 fine ounces. Following a tradition established in 1919 the free market price of gold has been fixed daily at the London headquarters of N. M. Rothschild & Sons, Ltd. The London price is generally followed, with some fluctuations, by other trading centers including New York, Zurich, Paris, Frankfort, Milan, Hong Kong, Bombay, and Beirut.

Robert Guy, a Rothschild executive, serves as chairman of a committee representing the five bullion investment firms of the London Gold Market. The men from Rothschild, Mocatta and Goldsmid, Samuel Montagu & Co., Sharps, Pixley & Co., and Johnson, Matthey (Bankers), Ltd. meet for the ritual in a small room in the Rothschild offices at 10:30 A.M. and 3:30 P.M. every weekday. Each man has an open telephone line to his firm. A miniature British Union Jack lies on its side before him. Orders on hand at the various firms determine how supply is to be balanced with price. When a dealer wishes to halt trading or to phone his firm for any other reason, he calls "Flag" and waves his Union Jack or places it on its stand. When all flags are down the five men resume the fixing, taking into account the spread each firm is quoting for gold, offers, bids, and unusual movements of gold such as the dumping of gold by a government, a large gold purchase elsewhere, or such occurrences as a gold mine disaster or outbreak of war.

After the two-tier gold market was established in March of 1968 with the monetary price of gold fixed at $42.22 an ounce and the free market price allowed to float, London had to compete with the gold market formed in Zurich, which now claims a large part of the business of merchandising the annual production of newly mined gold. The Swiss gold pool was formed by three banks—Swiss Bank Corporation, Swiss Credit Bank, and Union Bank of Switzerland—each of which has at least one subsidiary refinery. For years, a number of Americans invested illegally in gold through Switzerland, taking advantage of the anonymity of Swiss accounts, and the absence of taxes on bullion gold.

American citizens have had less direct experience with gold than the people of many other nations. The first official gold coinage in the United States was issued in 1795 in the form of $10 eagles and $5 half eagles. The last gold coins were struck in 1934: the famous $20 double eagles and $10 eagles. Total gold coinage amounted to $4,526,477,500. The total of all gold denominations turned in and melted under the Gold Reserve Act, from fiscal 1933 through fiscal 1954, when the mint tabulation was discontinued, amounted to $1,603,134,046.

The United States gold ban was a child of the Depression. In the dark days of 1933 the newly elected President, Franklin Delano Roosevelt, imposed the ban as long lines of anxious depositors waited to withdraw their savings from troubled banks all over the country. The nation's economic structure trembled as banks failed and "runs" on financial institutions mounted. People turned to gold as a haven for their life savings. The years of World War I brought U.S. reserves to over 11 billion in gold; by 1933 they had dwindled to 3.5 billion. From day to day demand mounted until more than $200 million in gold was vanishing from the Treasury's stockpile each week. The day before Roosevelt's inauguration, $109 million in gold was withdrawn. "So great" was the pull, Roosevelt noted, in his first "fireside chat," that the soundest of banks could not get enough currency [gold coins and convertible gold notes] to meet the demand."

To stimulate economic recovery Roosevelt and his New Deal economists sought to force idle gold out of hiding in exchange for paper currency. His inaugural address gave warning that he was going to chase the money-changers from the Temple; two days later, on March 6, 1933, he declared the Bank Holiday. When the banks reopened, the President announced the country was moving to "a managed currency." All gold and gold coins held by individuals and corporations were to be turned over to the Federal Reserve Banks by May 1, 1933. Only $100 worth could be kept legally, as well as gold coins having a rare numismatic value. Natural nuggets, jewelry, and art works were all excepted. Failure to surrender gold was punishable by a fine of not more than $10,000, imprisonment for not more than ten years, and confiscation of the gold.

Even before the deadline millions of dollars in gold was flowing into the Philadelphia mint to be melted down. Women in fur coats brought in pocketfuls of double eagles, scruffy men lugged in battered cardboard suitcases crammed with gold fortunes. The gold came in as old eyeglass frames, trophies, tea sets, and coins of every nation—an estimated 77 million troy ounces which swelled the government's reserve to $2.5 billion at the official government exchange rate of $20.67 an ounce. This price, established in 1834, had more or less been in effect since the Napoleonic Wars of the early 1800s.

For several months the price of gold fluctuated on the new government market Roosevelt established in October of 1933. The daily price was determined in the President's bedroom each morning as he breakfasted with his advisers, who were strongly influenced by the economic doctrines of John M. Keynes. This peculiar situation ended in January of 1934 when the gold price was fixed at $35 an ounce. After the United States boosted its price, some of the French gold moving onto the market to take advantage of the increase was still in the original wrappings from Jefferson's administration when it was sent to Napoleon to pay for Louisiana.

With the rise in the price of gold the value of the dollar fell by 40 per cent. This sparked an inflow of gold from the European nations into the United States Treasury as foreign markets paid for American exports. The revaluation of gold also stimulated mining production throughout the world. In 1929 total annual output was 19,673,000 fine ounces and by 1935 it had increased to 35,254,000 fine ounces. American critics grumbled at Roosevelt's "rubber dollar," but by October of 1939 the United States had gathered in its vaults over half the world's stock of gold, more than $17 billion at $35 an ounce. The gold was stored in the various Federal Reserve Banks and in the vaults of the mints. A new bullion depository was constructed at Fort Knox, Kentucky, near Louisville, to house part of the nation's shining treasure.

During World War II American gold mines were closed by government order and global production was paralyzed. Nations in jeopardy sent gold to the United States for safekeeping and great amounts of gold flowed into the U.S. vaults in payment for war supplies. At the end of the war the United States held 75 per cent of the world's gold worth $24 billion.

Throughout most of history gold served as a "war chest" in times of conflict. In the twentieth century this has been less true. Britain, for example, financed less than 5 per cent of its imports during World War II by sales of gold and fought on credit as did Russia, although Germany financed much of her war effort in the time-honored way. However, gold in wartime still assumes an increased importance and has figured in countless episodes involving seizure, escape, smuggling, counterfeiting, and hoarding. In tumultuous times gold's qualities of universal acceptance, divisibility, and imperishability are without peer. Commandos, pilots, and spies are still furnished with gold coins or ingots as part of their survival kit.

The belief in gold as fuel for the war machine led Mussolini to confiscate the golden wedding bands of the Italians to finance the war in Abyssinia. However, in the 1960s the traditional hoarders of India resisted the government's plea to turn in their gold to aid the war against Pakistan.

A great deal of gold is shuffled about during wartime and much of it is lost. A couple of years ago an Englishman, currently in prison for smuggling illegal immigrants into Britain, found a World War I German U-boat, sunk in the North Sea. He and two fellow divers found the wreck in eighty feet of water about fifty miles off the Dutch coast and claimed it was "brim full of gold bars." He claimed that they had been salvaging the bars for two years, selling them through a French syndicate on the black market. They received only about a third of the bars' current value of $25,000, putting the money in numbered accounts in the Bahamas and Liechtenstein.

Gold plays a part in the cold war as a recent incident illustrates. Fan Yuan-yen, a Chinese pilot, defected to Taiwan with his MIG-19 jet fighter in 1977. In line with a standing offer Taiwan has made to defecting air force officers from China, Fan was commissioned a lieutenant colonel in the Nationalist Chinese Air Force. The former squadron leader in the Communist air force also received a promised 5,000 ounces of gold. Fan turned the gold, in the form of ten bars, over to the Central Bank of China to keep for him. Gold trading is outlawed on Taiwan and Fan will have to sell his reward to the government for between $600,000 and $800,000, depending on the exchange rate.

In the aftermath of the Russian Revolution, the Red Government's paper currency depreciated in the face of continuing conflict with the White Armies of anticommunists. Lenin, in spite of his derision of gold, had seized about 164 million ounces of it from the Russian State Bank and planned to use it to purchase ammunition and supplies. The Reds loaded the gold onto a train to take it to safety at Kazan, east of Moscow on the Volga. However, the entire train was taken in August of 1918 by Admiral Aleksandr Kolchak's White Army. But Red loss turned to gain when Kolchak made the decision to hang on to the gold at any price. The massive load severely restricted the White Army's mobility. Cavalry could go freely over the vast and trackless steppes; heavily laden trucks could not. So Kolchak clung to the railroad line which ran toward frozen Siberia into enemy territory. The free-wheeling Reds preyed on the dogged Whites who rode and marched along the railroad track, guarding their precious gold until they were fatally weakened. Kolchak was captured and executed and the Reds took possession once again of the imperial gold.

During the Spanish Civil War the Spanish Republican Government shipped 11,428,570 troy ounces of bullion to the Soviet Union for "safekeeping." Forty years later it is still there. Spain would like the gold hoard back; it was valued at $400 million when it was shipped and is worth more than three and a half times as much today. Thus far the Soviets have refused to return the treasure. Such a gesture, however, would not be without precedence. In 1954 eleven tons of gold which had been seized by Soviet forces in Tabrīz were returned to Iran.

One unsolved mystery is the fate of the 6 million marks in gold sent as a gift from Hitler to Mussolini in 1938. The gold was aboard a Lufthansa plane bound from Berlin to Milan. The pilot radioed a routine message from over the Engadine region of the Swiss Alps and was never heard from again. In 1954 a frontier guard spotted metal fragments on the Gemelli Glacier. A search party explored the icy site and found several perfectly preserved bodies and some evidence that they had been on the ill-starred gold flight—but there was no gold.

Though Mussolini never got Hitler's gift, he nevertheless accumulated a vast amount of gold. In April of 1945 he was trying to smuggle it out of northern Italy when he and Claretta Petacci were discovered hiding beneath a load of sacking in a truck. They were killed and hung upside down, and the treasure somehow vanished at Dongo, a small town on the west bank of Lake Como.

A reputed 800 kilograms of Fascist Italian gold lies under the floor of the Cathedral of Asmara in northern Ethiopia, buried when Eritrea was an Italian possession. It was the product of the Ethiopian mines and hidden with the bishop's permission as the English advanced in March of 1941. For vague reasons it allegedly was never retrieved.

Since 1941 a gold hoard valued at $2.5 million has lain in the remote Greek mountains north of Thessalonica. That April the British in Greece were routed by the invading Nazis. As they fled before the advance of fifteen Nazi divisions and nine hundred aircraft, the 1st British Armoured Brigade was entrusted with five cases of gold sovereigns, constituting the British Army's payroll and bullion which had been given to the army by Greek banks of Thessalonica which wanted it evacuated. The truck with three British Army soldiers bearing the treasure left the main column of retreating troops in an attempt to reach the coast where Allied warships were standing by. But the three became trapped in the mountains and buried the treasure in a cave near Mount Siniatsikon. The two officers drew a map of the location before collapsing the roof of the cave with explosives. Eventually they escaped to North Africa. They were subsequently killed in the war, and the lone survivor, who somehow had the treasure map, died recently in England. In classic style the old soldier made a deathbed declaration revealing the long-held secret of the buried treasure to a friend to whom he gave the map.

In 1975 an American treasure hunter, notorious for illegal smuggling of gold artifacts in Central and South America, got wind of the map. He made a deal with the owner, went to Greece, and found the gully where the cave was. But before he could unearth the gold, local villagers suspecting he was an American CIA agent called in the Greek police. He is currently negotiating with the Greek Government for a share of the treasure if and when he finds it. Meanwhile dozens of others lured by the tale of buried gold pore over the records in London's Imperial War Museum of the battered 1st British Armoured Brigade's retreat.

In 1974 a silt dredger for the Bombay Port Authority sucked up a 26-pound gold bar, reviving memories of the great 1944 Bombay Harbor explosion when the British lost an undisclosed amount of gold on the American cargo ship *Fort Stikine*. The gold was to bolster the British colonial government's war efforts. The ship was also carrying 1,400 tons of explosives and ammunition. As she steamed up to the Bombay docks a mysterious fire broke out, followed by a cataclysmic explosion which shook the whole city and was recorded as a miniature earthquake on a seismograph more than one thousand miles away. Minor explosions went on until the next day keeping the fire brigades from approaching the site. Ten ships berthed nearby were wrecked, windowpanes shattered within a three-mile radius, and a number of people hit with flying chunks of gold.

During World War II Germany bought huge amounts of essential war supplies from the neutral nations such as Sweden, Switzerland, Turkey, and Spain which demanded payment in gold. Gold confiscated from Germany's victims swelled the gold holdings of those nations.

The Allied nations looked to the United States and Canada as a secure place to store their gold reserves during the war. Britain sent gold to New York in the fall of 1939 and more to Canada the following summer after France had fallen to the Nazis and it appeared that England would be invaded next. British gold reserves in the form of ingots and at least fifty thousand sacks of gold coins including hundreds of thousands of French "Napoleons" and Louis d'or sovereigns, half sovereigns, rare Elizabethan crowns, coins from the reign of George III, gold thalers from Germany, and the coins of the Netherlands, Scandinavia, and other countries were ferried to Halifax and then transshipped for deposit in the Bank of Canada vault in Ottawa. More than 130 Allied ships were sunk in the U-boat-infested waters of the North Atlantic during the three months of the convoys, but miraculously all of the gold shipments arrived safely.

In mid-1940 the greatest mass movement of gold in history brought the gold of France, Belgium, the Netherlands, Yugoslavia, Greece, Czechoslovakia, and the neutral nations into America at the rate of $100 to $250 million a day. The perigrinations of the beleaguered Norwegian national treasure illustrate the incredible difficulty of moving heavy gold in great volume. When the German fleet entered the fjord of Oslo on April 9, 1940, the Norwegians had already shipped $33 million to the United States to keep it out of German hands. However, the bulk of her $84 million gold reserve was still in Oslo. The Finance Minister immediately ordered it transported ninety miles north to newly constructed vaults at Lillehammer. The 120,000 pounds of gold were hastily packed in 1,538 crates, loaded on trucks, and rushed north.

A week later as the Germans advanced on Lillehammer the mass of gold was put aboard freight cars and moved by night to Åndalsnes, a port at the end of the railroad line where the British cruiser *Galatea* was unloading troops and munitions. The *Galatea*'s captain agreed to take the treasure to England. Some of the boxes were carried down to the wharf in the darkness, but when only 200 of the boxes had been loaded, Nazi planes swooped down to bomb the cruiser and word came that the Germans were approaching the city. The ship put to sea leaving 1,338 cumbersome crates still on the freight cars. They were transferred to a fleet of twenty-five assorted trucks which set off for the coastal town of Molde, where the Norwegian King had fled. The Nazis were aware of the gold transport and managed to bomb several of the trucks but somehow the treasure reached Molde, where it was hidden in the rubble of a bombed building. The town was in flames when a British vessel, the *Glasgow,* was sent to evacuate the King and gold.

The gold-filled boxes were once again brought to a wharf. Before more than a few had been stowed aboard the *Glasgow,* bombs exploded on the dock and the vessel had to cast off. Again the exhausted Norwegian task force was faced with keeping the gold from the menacing Germans. Hiding in the forest by day and moving at night, the small band continued its way farther north. Somewhere along the coast the treasure was put aboard five fishing boats which were pursued by the Nazis. As capture by the Nazis seemed inevitable, the courageous Norwegians effected a transfer of the gold to two larger fishing boats one night. At dawn the five smaller vessels each set off in a different direction to draw attention from the gold-laden boats. These were able, after three weeks of zigzag sailing among the myriad coastal islands, to reach Tromsø at the tip of the country. The Germans attacked Tromsø by land and air but the gold was successfully embarked on the British cruiser *Enterprise* and eventually reached the vaults of the Bank of England in London.

But the Battle of Britain had started and the gold was no longer safe in England. It was split among fifteen freighters and finally reached the Federal Reserve Bank in New York. On one vessel, the gold was loaded aboard two sailing yachts which were lashed to the deck so they could be cut loose in case of attack and slide off safely into the water. On another ship the gold was packed in barrels which were lashed to empty barrels and stowed on deck. In case of torpedo attack, the empty barrels would buoy the heavy ones, keeping them afloat. Few countries or individuals were as fortunate as Norway, which managed to protect her treasure through thirty separate loadings and unloadings. There are many tales of Jews fleeing Hitler who turned all of their assets into diamonds or gold which they, then, not always successfully, smuggled out of homelands they would never see again. A favorite gold-smuggling gambit was to have the mass of gold which sometimes represented every bit of personal wealth, cast or hand-crafted into automobile parts such as a radiator grill, headlight casing, or dashboard component which could be painted over to conceal the precious metal.

In September of 1939 Hitler invaded Warsaw with an eye on the seventy-five tons of gold in the Bank of Poland's vaults which he sorely needed to purchase supplies from the neutrals. At the last minute bank officials loaded the gold onto trucks along with women and children so that the trucks looked like all the others in the river of refugees streaming out of the besieged city. German planes bombed the convoy as it crossed into Romania but the bulk of the gold got through to the Black Sea port of Constanța, where it was put aboard a Turkish ship. The golden cargo was taken to Syria and transferred to a French ship. On October 14, 1939, about $64 million of the more than $70 million which had started out was deposited in the Bank of France.

In the spring of 1940 as the Nazi Panzers were crashing into the forests of northern France the French shipped their gold to New York. The Polish bankers asked France to send their gold to America as well. However, instead of sending the Polish gold to ports for shipment, the French, over Polish protestations, sent it inland. The treasure was then secretly transported north into dangerous territory without consulting the Polish bank officials. The day after Marshal Pétain surrendered to the Nazis the gold was embarked for Dakar in French West Africa where it was hidden somewhere in the interior. Five years passed before the Poles were able to regain control of the gold they had "in trust and confidence" given to their French allies for safekeeping.

Czechoslovakia is still waiting for twenty tons of gold, part of a prewar reserve of forty-five tons, to be returned by the United States. The gold was looted from occupied Bohemia-Moravia by retreating German troops in 1945. The cache was discovered in the Western-occupied zone by Allied forces and its return blocked when the Communists seized power in 1948. Six tons were returned before 1948 by the Tripartite Commission for the Restitution of Monetary Gold which was formed in Paris to help restore Nazi loot to its rightful owners. Some 9.4 tons of Czech gold are currently held in Great Britain and the rest at undisclosed locations in the United States. The Communists seized American-owned property; and Czech gold is being held pending compensation for $72.6 million of United State properties nationalized by Czechoslovakia. An agreement was tentatively reached to return the gold in 1974 but rejected by the U. S. Senate until all claims are paid in full. In 1975 a bill was passed containing an amendment which could open the Czech hoard to court suits. Under the amendment should the Czechs refuse to pay claimants who may file suit in U. S. District Court, the court is empowered to rule on whether the gold in the United States may be seized and sold at auction with the proceeds going to the claim holders.

Bullion is not the only form of gold in dispute. Hungary fought for years to regain the thousand-year-old crown of St. Stephen, the Hungarian national symbol. The gold crown which belonged to the first Christian King of Hungary was taken in 1945 by German forces retreating from Hungary into Germany. After the Nazi surrender, it was handed over to the U. S. Army. It remained in Fort Knox despite the fact that most of the obstacles to improve relations between the two countries have been removed and there has been a settlement of property claims by United States citizens and the exodus of Joszef Cardinal Mindszenty from the U. S. Embassy in Budapest. In 1977 President Carter arranged for its return to Warsaw.

When war broke out, Belgium split its national gold reserve in three parts and sent one third to New York, one third to London, and the remainder to the Bank of France. The last shipments were made as the Nazis shelled Brussels. The directors of the National Bank of Belgium congratulated themselves on having saved the nation's reserves, but they were wrong. Two weeks after Belgium surrendered to the Nazis the bank directors fled to Bordeaux where their gold was supposed to be stored. They requested its release and expressed a desire to supervise its loading on a waiting British cruiser. The governor of the Bank of France refused to hand over the gold or to reveal its hiding place.

The gold had been shipped, like the Polish treasure, to Dakar.

After Belgium fell the Germans appointed a majority of quislings to the Bank of Belgium's board. Following Nazi instructions these men requested the Vichy Government to return the gold to Europe. In 1941 the Bank of France began shipping tons of Belgian gold to Casablanca and Algiers. It was all delivered to Marseilles, where it was handed over to representatives of the German Reichsbank, who flew it directly to Berlin. Eventually the De Gaulle government conceded the Belgian claim against the Bank of France which had been filed in 1941 in New York State's Supreme Court. As a result workers at the New York Federal Reserve Bank shifted a lot of gold bars from the underground vault of the French to that of the Belgians.

The French themselves had taken no chances with their own reserves. About $900 million (prewar value) had been shipped to the United States. A slightly smaller amount had been transported to Dakar and then cached in various hiding places in the bush. A final portion, a bit less than $300 million, had been hastily shipped to Halifax and thence to Martinique as Marshal Pétain was signing the armistice. The Vichy Government issued repeated orders to Admiral Georges Robert in Martinique to throw the gold into the sea in an area too deep for diving in case the United Nations intervened in the islands. Robert chose to disobey and when the bloodless struggle for the French island ended in mid-1943, American and French officials found all of the gold packed in 8,766 boxes at Fort Desaix in Fort-de-France. There it remained throughout the war, under Allied guard.

The Nazis were thus deprived of some of their victims' bullion, but they piled up mountains of looted treasure. At the end of the war Allied forces found numerous caches of gold, silver, gems, art treasures, and other precious objects including the famous hoards at the Eisenach salt mine, the Merkers salt mine, and the gold treasure in the cellars of the burgomaster of Badgastein—where more than $35 million worth of British, American, and Italian gold bars and coins were found under the pavement. The cache near Eisenach came to light one night in April of 1945 when American military police stopped two women out after curfew. They claimed they were fetching the midwife for a neighbor in labor. The police released the women who gratefully pointed across a field and blurted out that hidden in a salt mine there was "all the gold of Germany." The 90th Infantry Division of the U. S. Third Army explored the mine finding miles of corridors and chambers, many of them sealed shut. In one chamber was a collection of paintings including works by Dürer, Van Dyck, Raphael, and Rembrandt. Behind a massive steel-plated door, which they blew open, lay hundreds of canvas sacks containing tons of gold bars and coins.

Such discoveries inevitably gave rise to many stories of other buried and sunken Nazi treasures. According to various documents a Junker 88 carrying gold and platinum bars was shot down by an American plane on May 5, 1945, and fell into the Attersee in Upper Austria. Another story concerns Göring, who is alleged to have concealed a treasure of gold loot. Some are certain it lies at the bottom of the Zellersee; others equally sure it is somewhere in his castle at Veldenstein. One persistent tale avers that "Hitler's Treasure" is hidden near the Lake of Kochel near Salzburg, Austria, where many of the most important Nazis found their last refuge. Numerous expeditions have searched for the alleged treasure in gold but thus far in vain.

The most sought after of all Nazi gold, real or imagined, is the treasure that Rommel accumulated during his North African campaign. In recent years various groups of treasure hunters have sought the six cases of gold, platinum, and diamonds said to have been hidden the night of September 17, 1943, in an underwater cave near Bastia on the coast of Corsica, an island famous for buried treasures dating back more than a thousand years. In the years since there have been several mysterious boat explosions and a couple of unsolved murders of divers who were after Rommel's gold.

Sunken World War II gold in gratifying amounts has been found and much more still lies beneath the Atlantic and Pacific oceans and in a number of European lakes. In 1944 a convoy of Allied ships sailed from New York for Britain. Two hundred miles south of Newfoundland in a fog, one vessel rammed the British freighter *Empire Manor,* slicing the 7,107-ton vessel in half. Royal Navy gunners sunk the bow section as a navigational hazard. They had no idea they were sending over a million pounds sterling in gold to the bottom. Twenty-nine years later, divers from the salvage vessel *Doxford,* one of the most advanced salvage vessels in the world, belonging to the Risdon,

Beazley Marine Company, located the sunken ship. The crew worked for four months on the wreck, which lay 330 feet deep beneath an incredibly stormy sea. The divers cut through the hull and moved tons of rusted machinery to inch their way into the forward hold where the bullion was stored. They found that the ingots had toppled out of the ship and lay buried under a foot of mud. Despite the disruptions of two hurricanes, the entire treasure was recovered, landed in England in conditions of tight security, and deposited in the vaults of the Bank of England.

In an even more remarkable salvage operation, a still greater fortune in gold was recovered soon after it was lost. On June 19, 1940, the Australian mail steamer *Niagara* ran into a floating enemy mine while bound for Vancouver, British Columbia. The ship went to the bottom with $12 million (prewar value) in gold bullion about thirty miles from the entrance to Whangarei Harbour, New Zealand. Within nine weeks the Australians, using newly developed echo-sounding equipment and dodging Japanese submarines, located the *Niagara* lying on its side at a seventy-degree angle in 438 feet of water in a heavily mined area. In nine months of perilous work, divers managed to blast a diagonal path to the strong room through deck after deck. Once they reached the gold it was a fairly simple job to remove it. In seven weeks all but 6 per cent was recovered; the remainder was believed to have fallen through a hole deeper into the wreck as a result of the blasting. Since the Japanese had gotten wind of the salvage operation, the Australians decided not to risk going after what seemed like chicken feed in comparison to what they had recovered. At today's prices that means some $2 million in gold bars still lies waiting to be retrieved.

Nazi gold continues to fascinate certain people such as the man who recently bid $3,500 for the gold-plated license plate used on the parade limousines of Hitler and his mistress, Eva Braun, or the persistent treasure hunters who seek Nazi gold in Alpine lakes, European caves, and Mediterranean coves.

During wartime there has always been an increase in the counterfeiting of currency. At the bottom of Lake Toplitz divers found the printing plates which Hitler planned to use to counterfeit sterling in amounts sufficient to bring about the collapse of the British monetary system.

The British gold sovereign during and after World War II be-

came the preferred currency for underground international payments in the Axis-occupied countries, the Middle East, and
North Africa. The paper money of the Axis nations was unac-
ceptable once the fortunes of the war began to turn against
them. Soon after the war, in the period of uncontrollable
inflation, the gold sovereigns were also used in illicit trade. The
number circulating seemed too great to be creditable so the
Bank of England launched an investigation. British agents
were sent to the Far and Middle East. (In the Moslem East, incidentally, where feminism has not made much headway, gold
sovereigns bearing Queen Victoria's likeness bring as much as 3
per cent less than those stamped with the head of a king.) The
agents discovered that some of the gold coins were turned out by
a factory near Tangier but that the vast majority were made in
Italy, near Milan.

When first approached, the counterfeiters declined to cease
their operation, pointing out that there was nothing illegal in
copying foreign coins. In addition, they noted that their product
was more valuable than the original, because of a lower alloy
content. The treasury agents paid a reported 5 million pounds to
counterfeiters in an effort to halt the production of a further 2
million pounds' worth of bogus sovereigns. Some dies were
handed over to the British but the undercover operation was not
totally successful and later the British Government had to approach the Italian Government in an official and public capacity
to have the counterfeiting rings smashed.

At the end of the war, when the United States held enormous
amounts of gold, the demand for the precious metal was so great
in Europe and Asia that highly organized smuggling rings, partly
to pay for the growing narcotics trade, were formed. They
bought gold earmarked for industrial use from unscrupulous
United States firms and shipped it abroad—gas tanks, hollow
books, even salamis. The U. S. Assay Office issued licenses to
jewelers, manufacturers, and suppliers of dental gold. Dealers in
contraband gold would present records showing an exaggerated
need for gold.

One such man, Sicilian by birth, who had served time in
prison for armed robbery before the war, established a legitimate
mail-order business dealing in birthstone and wedding rings. In

1946 his business accounts showed a dramatic increase in sales. Orders of a million wedding bands a month made authorities suspicious, but for years they were unable to prove anything. Then in February of 1951 a man who sailed frequently on Cunard liners delivered his Buick to a North River pier for embarkation on the *Queen Elizabeth*. Customs officials found 164 gold bars wrapped in black cloth and weighing almost 5,000 ounces concealed in the gas tank and other parts of the car. Although the identification marks on the bars had been removed, experts at the U. S. Assay Office were able to decipher the serial numbers and trace them to the mail-order magnate to whom they had been issued. As a result he and sixty-four others were convicted.

The masterminds of international gold smuggling, most of them Lebanese, Syrians, Greeks, or Levantine Jews, almost never carry gold themselves. It is all too easy to find a student, a housewife, or other respectable-looking runner to pose as a tourist on airline flights. The courier enjoys a pleasant vacation and earns a tidy sum and the ringleader, who is careful to remain anonymous, runs no risk. There are many men and women carrying diplomatic passports who abuse their privilege of avoiding inspection to smuggle both gold and drugs. Customs agents are aware of this contraband traffic but are powerless to stop it.

Smuggling is an art; the successful smuggler has a thousand ruses and earns grudging admiration from the most seasoned customs inspector. A great deal of gold is still smuggled into Great Britain, where citizens have been forbidden to hold bullion or coin since 1947; often it is molded to the contours of an automobile chassis. Couriers have smuggled gold wrought into bird cages into Pakistan. It has also been secreted in poultry, fish, or hollowed-out vegetables, in every conceivable place. So much contraband gold was smuggled across the borders of Pakistan in camel caravans that customs officials resorted to dosing both camels and drivers with an emetic at the border.

No matter how diligently the customs men work, the ingenuity of the smuggler can always come up with a new angle. Customs agents apprehended a man on his way from the Philippines to Hong Kong with miniature bits of gold stuck all over his body with bits of adhesive tape. Recently Israeli police had a morale boost when they were able to nail a man long suspected of smuggling. Customs police followed his car as he went from Jordan to his home in East Jerusalem. When he realized that he was being followed, he speeded up and the police gave chase while another police car picked up the thirty-three pounds of gold coins which had spewed from the speeding car, having come loose from their hiding place. Another eighty-three pounds were found at his home. But for every smuggler caught many more got through.

Smugglers' opportunities in the past several years have been reduced by the fluctuating price of free gold which can eliminate a profit and by beefed-up surveillance at airports and docks. However, as long as inflation rages as in Argentina or governments crumble as Allende's in Chile, smuggled gold will command a market. Many people have a psychological addiction to gold, and as long as nations restrict the ownership of mankind's oldest and most cherished metal, there will be men and women willing to supply it.

Airplane search procedures growing out of hijackings have seriously curtailed the jet-borne smuggler, but where there's a will there's a way. Gold has been found concealed in airplane toilets, in engine cowlings, and on the bodies of both crew and passengers. In the past year several gold-bar-lined smuggling jackets made of stout canvas were abandoned on planes entering India and Pakistan and fifty bars worth $50,000 were found in the waste bin of the toilet of a plane landing in Karachi. On a number of occasions gold has been dropped from planes to smugglers below only to fall in front of tipped-off police.

Gold is also smuggled on a large scale in ships, from the smallest dhows to the largest liners, concealed in air ducts, ceilings, behind bulkheads, and in mattresses and galley supplies.

The tiny desert sheikhdom of Dubai on the Persian Gulf not long ago handled one fifth of the world's annual supply of new gold. In 1968 it supplied Indian hoarders with 144 tons of smuggled gold. As late as 1971 it was the single largest buyer of gold on the London market. The government of the sweltering emirate has no laws against export of gold so no official records were kept regarding the disposition of the crates of 3.7-ounce gold bars (the preferred form of bullion in the Middle East and India) which arrived on regular jet flights from London. But everyone knew they were carried in smuggling jackets aboard swift dhows fitted with powerful deisel engines for the 1,200-mile trip across the gulf to India near Bombay, where rendezvous are made with fishing trawlers. Initially the smuggling operation was financed by organizers from London, Beirut, and Switzerland (the big three Swiss banks provided a large part of the gold). Eventually the merchants of Dubai managed by themselves, offering shares in their venture to speculators. Lately the profit margin has been drastically reduced by fluctuating gold prices and a crackdown by the Indian Government. Smugglers still carry some gold but have increasingly turned to American cigarettes, Scotch whisky, and Japanese transistor radios.

The Indian clients who break the law by receiving smuggled gold usually pay in one of three ways. Indian currency is no longer accepted in the Gulf States at the urging of the Indian Government, which was concerned about the drain on her currency to purchase the illicit gold. However, black-market dollars and traveler's checks are acceptable forms of payment. Payment can also be in silver, which is freely flown to Zurich and London for resale. But the chief source of payment for Dubai gold is in foreign exchange earned by Indians and Pakistanis working abroad.

In 1963 when the drain on Indian currency by gold smugglers was running a catastrophic $100 million annually, the Indian Finance Minister Morarji Desai anounced new government measures to clamp controls on India's vast private gold holdings and "end the age of gold." "To buy gold is treason," he said. The government hoped to pry loose some of the estimated 110 million ounces of immobilized gold for national defense and economic development. It was rather naïvely envisioned that Indians would willingly exchange their gold for 6½ per cent government bonds. The disclosure provision exempted jewelry but required that all other holdings in excess of one and a half ounces be declared. Priests bowed before ancient golden idols, begging their pardon as they inventoried their weight and worth for the government and Maharajas and Maharanis were expected to tally up gold tableware, swords, thrones, and cigarette lighters. Despite Desai's statement that gold ornamentation was not "socially justifiable," the government knew better than to include jewelry in the provision, although it made up an estimated 80 per cent of the total gold. Gold bangles and ornaments have been religiously sanctioned adornment and status symbol of Indian women for thousands of years and represent the commonest form of savings among the masses.

Indian womanhood joined the country's 450,000 goldsmiths in protesting a ruling that henceforth all jewelry should be made of not more than 14 carat purity (58.33 per cent gold) instead of the richly glowing 22 (91.66 pure) to 24 (unalloyed gold) carats traditionally used. Goldsmiths lamented that they couldn't work the harder gold into the preferred styles and one hundred of them committed suicide. Women who had patriotically offered $25 million in gold ornaments for the war effort against China refused to heed Desai's proclamation, scorning the 14-carat bangles as "tinsel" and rushed out to buy high-carat jewelry on a thriving black market. Three years later the law was repealed. As Mrs. Gandhi explained, "A measure of socioeconomic reform which is aimed at changing the centuries old tradition and customs cannot be expected to become fully effective within a few years."

India produces no more than three and a half tons of gold a year, most of it from the Kolar Mine in Mysore and the Hutti Mine; not nearly enough to satisfy the gold-hungry Indians. India is the country which has waged the hardest fight against gold smuggling and its corollary, gold hoarding, trying to end the awesome regard for gold. It has been an uphill battle. For five thousand years Hindu tradition has revered the metal as the purest and most sacred. When a child is born, its father should rub a bit of gold on it to assure an auspicious future. When a person dies, a speck of gold should be placed on his tongue to bring luck in the afterlife. Wearing gold brings good fortune and giving gold removes the donor's sins. Ayurvedic medicine, the traditional Hindu medicine, prescribes gold pills to kill infection and enhance energy. Given the belief in gold's relationship to the cosmic forces which is so deeply rooted in the Indian psyche, the government is having a difficult time persuading the masses that it is bad for the country to have so much capital stashed away in gold.

Indira Gandhi's government put new teeth in a law banning possession of more than four pounds of gold ornaments. The fifty-six-year-old Maharani of the fabled pink city of Jaipur was one of the first to feel the bite. The government initiated an investigation into her wealth after newspapers reported the theft of a sizable amount of jewelry from her New York hotel room when she visited the city in 1972. She was jailed for almost six months on charges of violating smuggling and currency laws after government agents raided the family palaces and found more than $17 million worth of gold ornaments, jewels, bullion, and coins in safes and concealed crypts.

Almost every family in India has a stockpile of gold but it is usually small. By some estimates 90 per cent of the hoarded gold is in the hands of only 3 per cent of the people. It is estimated that Indian hoarders by the end of 1972 still held over $7 billion worth of gold (at the official price of $42). The Bombay Bullion Association a few years ago figured that if there were one marriage in each of India's 120 million families every fifteen years and a minimum of one tola (180 grains) of gold changed hands for each wedding, the annual demand would be 8 million tolas, almost 100 tons of gold.

The youth of India has begun to publicly protest the ancient social evil of the dowry system, which has at its roots the economic dependency of woman, who according to Hindu tradition "never deserves freedom." The origin of the dowry dates back to the Vedic period (1500 B.C.). The *stredhana,* or bride's wealth, was in the form of voluntary gifts and confined to royal and aristocratic families. With time, however, the practice became an inseparable part of marriage. Many families have been ruined in an effort to provide a dowry and there have been instances of suicide, either by the girl, her father, or even the entire family when they could not meet the dowry demands. The Indian Government is eager to end the system because of its disastrous effects and because of the gold that it immobilizes. The Dowry Prohibition Act of 1961 was passed and then virtually ignored; but today it has the support of the segment of the population it most affects—the youth of India. Young people are taking mass vows to eschew dowries, and all government workers are now forbidden to engage in the ancient practice.

Gold smuggling was enormously profitable in the turbulent Southeast Asia peninsula during the years of the Vietnam War as a deluge of American dollars flooded Vietnam and her shaky neighbors. Saigon was the chief focus of the black-market action, absorbing all the gold that could be smuggled in. As fast as the dollars came into the hands of the people who generally make a profit in wartime—call girls (many of whom preferred to be paid in 22-carat gold jewelry), night club owners, contractors, black marketeers, or even washerwomen—they were exchanged for gold and hidden away.

Gold used to move through the Hong Kong–Macao market, but in the 1960s most gold came into Vietnam through a highly organized system which used neighboring Laos as the conduit. In fact, it was United States foreign aid and the gold trade which kept tiny Laos afloat. For years gold, legally imported into Vientiane, in the form of one-kilo bars of 999.9 purity from the big three Swiss banks was routinely transshipped, about 30 per cent going to Thailand and about 60 per cent to Vietnam. This trade brought the sleepy tropical country as much as $7 million annually in customs duties and was its largest single source of earned revenue. (In 1972, the year before the world's central bankers stopped sales of monetary gold to private buyers through the London-based pool, creating a free market for non-monetary gold and forcing the price up, Laos imported seventy-two tons of gold.) Some of the imported gold was funneled into the narcotics trade. Much of the world's raw opium is grown by mountain tribesmen in the so-called Golden Triangle where Burma, Laos, and Thailand join, and the Laotian gold was used to purchase the opium, which is the raw material for heroin.

The efficiency of the gold trade was in sharp contrast to the Laotian economy which functioned for the most part on the barter system. In Vientiane gold orders were placed by a small number of local Chinese importers with the French-owned Banque de L'Indochine. Then the bank discreetly forwarded the orders to Europe and the gold flowed into Vientiane on scheduled jet airlines. Importing agents picked up their boxes of gold at Wattay Airport and drove a short distance to the customs shed, paid an 8.5 per cent duty, and then turned over the merchandise to the Lao Chinese dealers who casually hauled away their orders in bamboo baskets and straw bags.

Gold was sold to individuals, many of them Vietnamese residents in Laos who had it turned into rather crude jewelry which was for a time exempted from restrictions banning gold imports into Vietnam by any of the scores of small goldsmith shops in the humid capital. These shops, many of them run by women, their teeth stained dark from chewing betel nuts, also manufactured gold for smugglers wishing to conceal their booty. They turned out shapes contoured to a woman's waistline, put it inside in shoe heels or cans of shaving cream. Gold leaves were slipped between the pages of books or concealed inside the covers. There were frequent orders for solid-gold "pigeon eggs" which could be secreted within the body. Smugglers operating on a larger scale took as much as five hundred kilograms of gold at a time into Saigon aboard military aircraft, having made arrangements in advance with South Vietnamese customs and military officials. It is alleged the United States Government tacitly approved the trade, since without it they would have had to shore up little Laos with still more dollar aid.

During the days before the Saigon government fell in the spring of 1975 hundreds of thousands of people in the refugee-swollen city of 3 million sold off houses, cars, and expensive appliances at huge losses to buy gold, the traditional emergency currency of Indochina. Over the years many Vietnamese hoarded gold in the form of small ingots, jewelry, and small paper-wrapped packets of sheet gold, each weighing one tael (37.5 grams) and embossed with the names of the four [former] Indochina capitals—Hanoi, Saigon, Phnom Penh, and Vientiane. But in the last frenectic days gold was hard to come by even at $257 an ounce.

Gold, the ideal way to store personal wealth in relatively small amounts, presents logistical problems for those who have managed to accumulate a great deal of it. In April of 1975 *Time* magazine reported that President Nguyen Van Thieu of South Vietnam and Lon Nol, former President of Cambodia, had approached a Swiss airline to handle the removal to Switzerland of "personal effects" which included sixteen tons of gold bullion. The request was rejected in part because of the logistical problems involving the size and weight of such a bullion shipment and because refueling stops necessary at Bangkok and the Arab emirate of Bahrain provided major security problems. The South Vietnamese Government vehemently denied the story. However, it is known that Thieu had made plans to remove more than twenty-eight tons of bullion from his country's gold reserves to the Federal Reserve Bank in New York. The United States had agreed to help and flew in a cargo plane to pick up the bullion. But in the confusion which followed the country's collapse the plane was forced to fly off without the gold.

Although the airlift of the "personal effects" of Thieu and Lon Nol was aborted, it is likely that they and other powerful men managed to feather their exile nests with plenty of smuggled gold. Those individuals who were evacuated to the crowded refugee camps in the United States, despite having left an estimated $16 million in gold back home, brought a great deal with them.

Swiss and American bullion dealers including Deak, Perera & Co. and the U. S. Silver Corporation established gold buying operations at all the refugee camps. When the refugees arrived they found not only the Red Cross and welfare workers but bullion dealers ready with precision scales, gold needles, and acid for testing the fineness of the precious metal—and boxes of U.S. currency. Vietnamese gold was primarily in the form of thin flexible wafers. Nicholas Deak, whose company got the first taste of Vietnamese gold when they bought $500,000 worth one day in Guam as the stream of refugees flowed through and $1,320,000 the next, said, "The refugees hide the sheet gold in shoes, belts, handkerchiefs, in bras—they pull it out from everywhere."

In five months more than $15 million changed hands as gold taels, ingots, bracelets, pendants, religious and ceremonial objects were exchanged by refugees for dollars or traveler's checks at an average price of about $20 under the London market. The president of the U. S. Silver Corporation said, "That is probably only about 10 per cent of what the Vietnamese brought with them. They will convert the rest of it as they buy new homes and invest in their own businesses and professions."

During the confused early weeks at Elgin Air Force Base camp one refugee told a junior State Department official that he did not need a sponsor or any further help. He showed statements reflecting millions in gold on deposit in Switzerland. By the time the junior official told a higher-up about the millionaire, he had been whisked off to France by the French consul general from New Orleans. "I don't know why we've got to help the French balance of payments," grumbled a State Department officer who was annoyed because no effort had been made to encourage the man to stay behind and invest in America.

Although there were complaints from the camp, particularly initially when only one company was authorized by the State Department to deal in gold at the camps, that gold buyers had been underpaying by from $20 to $36 an ounce, the Vietnamese received far more for their gold than they would have later in the year as the price continued a downward trend. The transplanted Vietnamese are making new lives in a country where there is none of the social or religious regard for gold still so strong in many parts of the world. They now find themselves among a people who have enjoyed far greater domestic tranquillity than they. Haunted by the destruction of their homeland in a senseless war, the refugees are adjusting to a self-confident nation whose wars have almost always been waged on far-distant shores. They find themselves in a young nation among a people optimistic by nature who trust their currency and the future and have spurned the opportunity to invest in gold as a hedge against uncertainty in spite of double-digit inflation, widespread unemployment, and other portents which historically indicate that difficult and unsure times lie ahead.

The unique allure of gold runs through the long course of human history like a shimmering thread woven in and out of every age and culture. Gold has been the stuff of magic, of creation, and of destruction. The inert metal has been one of history's most powerful catalysts. The role of gold in the future is uncertain. It has already been toppled as king in global economics. Mass production has diminished the once sacred function of the goldsmith and debased the quality of wrought gold. Mankind no longer honors gods, rulers, and the dead with gloriously worked gifts of gold. The golden legacy of lost cultures reposes behind glass in museums, accessible to relatively few people. In the modern world so much of the gold that is used cannot be seen. Women have so many other ways to enhance their beauty and men to bolster their status. Yet the noble metal retains a special place. Even as it is listed on the commodities exchange with base metals, peanuts, and pork bellies, gold continues to fascinate. It is unlikely mankind will ever cease to respond instinctively to the rare and lovely substance which has played such a rich and complex part in history.

Select Bibliography

Agricola, Georgius. *De Re Metallica*. Basel, 1556. Translated by Herbert C. Hoover and Lou H. Hoover. New York, 1950.

Aitcheson, Leslie. *A History of Metals*. 2 vols. London, 1960.

Allen, Gina. *Gold!* New York, 1964.

Alonso-Barba, Padre Alvaro. *Arte de los Metales*. Madrid, 1640; Potosí, 1967.

Bautier, Robert-Henri. *The Economic Development of Medieval Europe*. London, 1971.

Becatti, Giovanni. *Oreficerie Antiche*. Roma, 1955.

Berton, Pierre. *Klondike*. London, 1960.

Blake, J. W. *European Beginnings in West Africa 1454-1578*. London, 1937.

Blakemore, Kenneth. *The Book of Gold*. New York, 1971.

Boxer, C. R. *Four Centuries of Portuguese Expansion*. Johannesburg, 1969.

Bradford, Ernle. *Four Centuries of European Jewellery*. London, 1950.

Braudel, Fernand. *The Mediterranean*. 2 vols. New York, 1972-73.

Breasted, J. H. *A History of Egypt*. New York, 1909.

Bronsted, Johannes. *The Vikings*. Harmondsworth, 1960.

Carter, Howard. *The Tomb of Tutankhamen*. London, 1972.

Cary, M., and Warmington, E. H. *The Ancient Explorers*. London, 1929.

Casson, Lionel. *The Ancient Mariners*. New York, 1959.

Cellini, B. *The Treatises of Benvenuto Cellini on Goldsmithing and sculpture*. Translated by C. R. Ashbee. London, 1898.

———. *Vita*. Translated by J. A. Symonds. London, 1949.

Cennini, Cennino. *The Craftsman's Handbook*. Translated by D. V. Thompson, Jr. 2 vols. New Haven, 1932-33.

Ceram, C. W. *Gods, Graves, and Scholars*. New York, 1961.

Chaffers, W. *Gilda Aurifabrorum: a History of London Goldsmiths and Plateworkers and Their Marks Stamped on Plate*. London, 1878.

Cottrell, Leonard. *The Anvil of Civilization*. New York, 1959.

———. *Digs and Diggers*. New York, 1964.

Del Mar, Alexander. *A History of the Precious Metals*. London, 1880.

Díaz del Castillo, Bernal. *The Discovery and Conquest of Mexico*. Translated by A. P. Maudslay. New York, 1956.

Dunn, E. J. *Geology of Gold*. London, 1929.

Elliott, J. H. *Imperial Spain 1469–1716*. London, 1963.

Emmerich, André. *Sweat of the Sun and Tears of the Moon*. Seattle, 1965.

Evans, Joan. *A History of Jewellery*. London, 1953.

Frank, T., et al. *Economic Survey of Ancient Rome*. Baltimore, 1933–34.

Frazer, G. *The Golden Bough*. 2 vols. London, 1925–30.

Gold and World Monetary Problems. Proceedings of the National Industrial Conference Board Convocation, Tarrytown, N.Y., October 1965. Published by Macmillan, New York, 1966.

Green, Timothy. *The World of Gold Today*. New York, 1973.

Hall, H. R. *The Ancient History of the Near East*. London, 1950.

Hamilton, Earl J. *American Treasure and the Price Revolution in Spain, 1501–1650*. Cambridge, Mass., 1934.

Hobson, Burton. *Historic Gold Coins of the World*. New York, 1971.

Holmyard, E. J. *Alchemy*. Harmondsworth, 1957.

Jacobs, William. *An Historical Inquiry into the Production and Consumption of the Precious Metals*. 2 vols. London, 1831.

Jenkins, Romilly. *Byzantium*. New York, 1966.

Las Casas, Bartolomé de. *A History of the Indies*. Translated by A Collard. New York, 1971.

Lattimore, Owen, and Lattimore, Eleanor. *Silks, Spices and Empire*. New York, 1968.

Lister, Raymond. *The Craftsmen in Metal*. London, 1966.

Marx, Robert F. *The Treasure Fleets of the Spanish Main*. New York, 1968.

Melegari, Vezio. *I Tesori Nascosti*. Milano, 1972.

Metropolitan Museum of Art. *From the Lands of the Scythians*. New York, 1975.

New Archaeological Finds in China. Peking, 1974.

Pallottino, Massimo. *Etruscologia*. Milano, 1942.

Paul, Rodman W. *Mining Frontiers of the Far West*. New York, 1963.

Penrose, Boise, *Discovery and Travel in the Renaissance*. Cambridge, Mass., 1952.

Polo, Marco. *Travels of Marco Polo*, Edited by Manuel Komroff. New York, 1926.

Powell, T. G. *Prehistoric Art*. New York, 1966.

Prescott, W. H. *History of the Conquest of Mexico*. London, 1843.

———. *History of the Conquest of Peru*. London, 1847.

Prieto, Carlos. *La Minería en el Nuevo Mundo*. Madrid, 1969.

Rickard, T. A. *Man and Metals*. 2 vols. London, 1932.

Rostovtzeff, M. *Social and Economic History of the Hellenistic World*. London, 1941.

———. *Social and Economic History of the Roman Empire*. London, 1957.

Samhaber, Ernst. *Merchants Make History*. London, 1963.

Schliemann, H. *Troy and Its Remains*. London, 1880.

School of Salamanca: Readings in Spanish Monetary Theory 1544–1605. Oxford, 1952.

Seltman, Charles. *Approach to Greek Art*. New York, 1960.

Singer, C. et al. *A History of Technology*. 5 vols. Oxford, 1954–58.

Smith, Adam. *The Wealth of Nations*. New York, 1937.

Stephens, J. L. *Incidents of Travel in Central America, Chiapas, and Yucatan*. Rutgers, 1949.

Sutherland, C. H. V. *Gold: Its Beauty, Power and Allure*. London, 1969.

Tozer, H. F. *A History of Ancient Geography*. New York, 1964.

Triffin, Robert. *Gold and the Dollar Crisis*. New Haven, 1971.

Vicker, Ray. *Realms of Gold*. New York, 1975.

Watkins, T. H. *Gold and Silver in the West*. Palo Alto, 1971.

Wharton, David B. *The Alaska Gold Rush*. Bloomington, 1972.

The Times (London). *Gold*. Reprint of a special number of June 20, 1933.

Woolley, C. L. *Excavations at Ur*. London, 1926.

———. *The Sumerians*. London, 1929.

Zárate, Augustin de. *The Discovery and Conquest of Peru*. Translated by Thomas Nicholas in 1581. London, 1933.

Ancient sources referred to include:

Apollodorus, Ctesias, Diodorus, Herodotus, Homer, Livy, Lucretius, Pliny the Elder, Plutarch, Strabo, Tacitus, Thucydides.